境外资本市场重要法律文献译丛④
欧洲卷

欧盟证券监管法规汇编

（中英文对照本）

Laws Governing the Securities Exchange within the European Union

中国证券监督管理委员会　组织编译

法律出版社
LAW PRESS · CHINA

《境外资本市场重要法律文献译丛》

编委会

《欧盟证券监管法规汇编》

主　编：陈东征

副主编：宋丽萍　刘海波

编　委：付　彦　邱永红　沈　哲　麦学文
孙培贤　张　洁　陈　钟　邓子欣
赵晓闽　黎　亮　陈　彬

致　　谢

深圳证券交易所对本书的出版给予了大力支持！

译者说明

本书选取了欧盟证券监管领域9项重要法律文件进行翻译。这9项法律文件是欧洲议会与欧盟理事会根据欧盟委员会《金融服务行动计划》(Financial Services Action Plan, FSAP)和《莱姆法路西计划》(Lamfalussy Process),于2003年至2009年间针对欧盟内证券市场"招募说明书"、"内幕交易和市场操纵"、"发行人透明度"、"评级机构监管"四大问题所发布的指令及修订。这些指令是当前欧洲证券监管在相关领域的基本原则和规则,旨在协调欧盟各国的有关监管制度,推进欧洲资本市场一体化进程。总体而言,这些指令使欧盟证券市场的运行和监管达到了全新的水平。

具体而言,这9项法律文件涉及的主要内容包括:

(一)2003年12月31日,《欧洲议会与欧盟理事会第2003/71/EC号指令》(Directive 2003/71/EC of the European Parliament and of the Council)开始生效。该指令是框架原则、实施细则、合作与执法4项要素组合而成之四级立法模式中的第一级框架原则,对招募说明书的相关问题进行了原则性的规定,旨在修改和完善欧盟第2001/34/EC号指令,统一并集合成单一的规则,规范和提升招募说明书的信息披露水平,从而达到保护投资者权益的目的。该指令共有8章、4个附录:第一章为总则,第二章规定了招募说明书的编制,第三章为招募说明书的批准、公布等程序,第四章对跨境要约进行了单独的规定,第五章为语言和第三国发行人情形,第六章规定了主管部门的职责,第七章和第八章则分别规定了实施细则和过渡规定。另外,在正文后的4个附录中分别规定了招募说明书、注册文件、证券说明和摘要说明的结构以及必要信息。

(二)随着金融市场的快速发展,欧洲议会与欧盟理事会于2008年3月又通过了《欧洲议会与欧盟理事会第2008/11/EC号指令》(Directive 2008/11/EC of the European Parliament and of the Council),旨在根据第2006/512/EC号决定,对前述第2003/71/EC号指令进行技术性的修正,引入审查监管程序(regulatory procedure with scrutiny)。

(三)《欧洲议会与欧盟理事会第2003/6/EC号指令》(Directive 2003/6/EC of the European Parliament and of the Council)是旨在打击内幕交易和市场操纵的一项指令。该指令由22个条款组成,主要规定了对内幕交易和市场操纵行为的规制方式、内幕信息的通知方式、各国的行政管理部门、职业保密义务、对违反者采取行政措施或行政处罚以及他们的诉讼权利、各成员国主管部门之间的相互合作、欧洲证券委员会协助欧盟委员会开展工作的责任等内容。它确保了欧盟内相关活动在责任分配、执法和合作方面施行统一的规则框架。

（四）《欧洲议会与欧盟理事会第 2008/26/EC 号指令》（Directive 2008/26/EC of theEuropean Parliament and of the Council），根据第 2006/512/EC 号决定，对前述《欧洲议会与欧盟理事会第 2003/6/EC 号指令》中关于授予欧盟委员会的实施权力的规定进行了修订。

（五）《欧洲议会与欧盟理事会协调关于证券获准在受监管市场交易的发行人的信息透明度要求的第 2004/109/EC 号指令》（Directive 2004/109/EC of the European Parliament and of the Council）是一项旨在通过在欧盟推行同等的透明度要求，从而确保投资者信心、完善内部市场的指令。该指令共 7 章 35 条，分别是第一章“总则”、第二章“定期披露的信息”、第三章“持续披露的信息”、第四章“一般义务”、第五章“主管部门”、第六章“实施细则”以及第七章“过渡规定和最终条款”。

（六）《欧盟委员会第 2007/14/EC 号指令》（Commission Directive 2007/14/EC）为前述第 2004/109/EC 号指令中某些条款的实施制定了详细规则。该指令由 26 条组成，主要规定了半年度非合并财务报表至少应包含的内容、重大的关联方交易、主管部门针对做市商的控制机制、单独进行投资组合管理的管理公司和投资公司应符合的独立性条件和使其持有人有权单独自主购买附带表决权的股票的金融工具的类型等事项。

（七）《欧洲议会与欧盟理事会第 2008/22/EC 号指令》（Directive 2008/22/EC of the European Parliament and of the Council），根据第 2006/512/EC 号决定，对前述第2004/109/EC 号指令中关于授予欧盟委员会实施权力的规定进行了修订。

（八）《欧洲议会与欧盟理事会关于信用评级机构的第 1060/2009 号（欧共体）条例》[Regulation (EC) No. 1060/2009 of the European Parliament and of the Council]于 2009 年 9 月 16 日通过。此前，欧盟在这一领域缺乏相应立法，成员国各自为战，难以有效监管信用评级机构。在 2008 年 3 月召开的欧洲理事会上，各成员国终于达成了一致，希望从欧盟这一层面对信用评级机构进行规范。第 1060/2009 号条例旨在为欧洲内部市场发布的信用评级制定通用的框架，从而确保对消费者和投资者提供高标准的保护。该规章共有 4 编和 2 个附录：第一编为“标的事项、范围和定义”，第二编“信用评级的发布”规定了信用评级机构在评级过程中的人事、方法和披露规则，第三编“信用评级活动的监督”对信用评级的注册程序、主管部门、第三国合作等进行了规定，第四编包括了罚则、委员会程序、报告及过渡规定和最终条款。另外，2 个附录中分别就“独立性和利益冲突的避免”和“注册申请材料中需提供的信息”进行了补充规定。欧洲议会与欧盟理事会于 2009 年 11 月对该规章进行了勘误，形成了最后的文件（九）。

上述法律文件对欧洲金融市场具有深远的影响，特别是在招募说明书、内幕交易和市场操纵、发行人信息透明度以及评级机构监管方面，为各成员国监管机构确立了统一的架构，为金融服务机构提供了统一的规则。需要注意的是，欧盟的相关法律一直处于快速变动的状态,事实上,就在翻译的过程中,欧盟委员会仍在就有关文件提出修订草案,这也提醒我们不断关注、认识市场与规则的与时俱进。

他山之石,可以攻玉。希望通过对上述法律文件进行全面翻译,能为我国金融界从业人员及其他关注金融市场的人士了解欧洲金融市场监管手段提供便利;同时,我们也希望通过这种了解和学习,为我国证券市场的监管和改革提供有益的借鉴。

北京大学法学院　郭雳

总译校:

沈四宝,毕业于北京大学法律系,获硕士和学士学位。1981年赴美国哥伦比亚大学法学院深造,兼备深厚的中西方法学理论基础,尤其在国际商法领域有较高造诣。现任对外经济贸易大学法学院教授、博士研究生导师,上海大学法学院院长,担任教育部社会科学委员会法学部委员、中国国际经济法学研究会会长、中国仲裁法研究会副会长、上海大学仲裁与ADR研究院院长,最高人民法院专家咨询员。2006年获教育部颁发的"国家级教学名师奖",享受国务院政府特殊津贴。

审校人员:

郭雳,北京大学法学院院聘教授,康奈尔大学客座教授、范德比尔特大学访问学者、德国洪堡基金会学者。法学博士、经济学博士后,毕业于北京大学和哈佛大学。具中国、美国纽约州律师资格。出版《中国银行业创新与发展的法律思考》、《美国证券私募发行法律问题研究》、《信用征信法律框架研究》等中英文专著及论文,主编*Peking University Journal of Legal Studies*。

习超,香港中文大学法律学院副教授。中山大学法学学士,英国伦敦大学法学硕士、博士。兼任中国商法学法学硕士课程主任、吉林大学法学院教授。

洪艳蓉,北京大学法学院副教授。厦门大学国际法(国际经济法方向)博士,北京大学金融法博士后。中国执业律师,中国国际经济法学会理事、中国证券法学研究会理事。著有《资产证券化法律问题研究》、《房地产金融》(第2版)(合著)等书。

翻译人员:

瞿乃明,法国巴黎高等翻译学校翻译学硕士、法国巴黎第九大学国际企业管理硕士、台湾大学经济学学士,北京优笔客翻译中心总经理。主要翻译作品有《欧盟金融工具市场指令》、《中国证监会2011年年报》、《美国商品交易法》、《美国证券交易委员会自身组织与通用规章》、《欧盟另类投资基金管理人指令》、《美国多德—弗兰克华尔街改革与消费者保护法》等。

艾飞,北京大学法学院法学学士,2007年通过中国司法考试,北京优笔客翻译中心质量经理。主要翻译作品有《美国商品交易法》、《美国证券交易委员会自身组织与通用规章》和《美国多德—弗兰克华尔街改革与消费者保护法》等。

区欣,波兰什切青大学伊拉斯谟世界(Erasmus Mundus)硕士课程班学习欧盟法,中山大学西方哲学硕士,北京优笔客翻译中心专职译者。主要翻译作品有《欧盟金融监管体制改革法规汇编》和《美国多德—弗兰克华尔街改革与消费者保护法》等。

李芬芳,台湾大学外国语言与文学学士,北京优笔客翻译中心兼职译者。主要翻译作品有《公开发行证券的公司信息披露内容与格式准则第1号》(中译英)、《证券公司治理准则(试行)》(中译英)、《证券公司内部控制指引》(中译英)和《美国证券交易委员会自身组织与通用规章》等。

总　　序

中国资本市场是适应我国经济体制改革和对外开放的形势要求逐步建立发展起来的。为了有效借鉴境外成熟市场的制度经验，中国资本市场从成立伊始，就特别注重按照"立足国情，为我所用"的原则，不断学习、消化和吸收境外成熟市场的运行规则和监管制度。目前，中国资本市场现行有效的法律、法规、规章、规范性文件共521件，加上大量的交易所和协会的自律规则，基本形成了我国资本市场的法律制度规范体系。这些制度规范构建起一整套与国际通行原则基本相符的法律框架、交易规则和监管体系，有效维护了市场秩序，保证了市场功能和作用的发挥，保护了投资者的合法权益。

经过20余年的改革发展，我国资本市场进入了创新发展的新阶段。立足于服务实体经济发展的大局需要，重点解决资本市场自身结构不平衡、服务实体经济能力不足、为居民提供投资理财产品相对匮乏等突出现实问题，资本市场现有的以股票公开发行并在交易所上市交易为主的境内市场体系，将逐步发展成为一个公募与私募并重、股票与债券平衡、场内与场外协调发展的资本市场体系。与此相适应，需要进一步发展壮大财富管理行业，立足于功能监管的制度定位，统一资产管理行为规则，放松行政管制，增强创新活力。实现这样的改革目标，需要我们更加重视学习境外成熟市场的制度经验，充分借鉴境外市场有关私募发行、债权融资、资产管理、期货及衍生品等方面的法律制度，在尊重市场规律的前提下，大胆进行制度和机制创新，确保我们的各项制度适应和满足市场改革的实际需要。

坚持对外开放是中国资本市场改革和发展的一贯方针。在经济全球化深入发展的时代背景下，适应我国经济结构调整和经济方式转变和"逐步实现人民币资本项目可兑换"的金融对外开放的总体要求，中国资本市场必须以更加积极的态度参与全球经济竞争，提高在全球范围内配置资源，服务实体经济发展的能力。不论是支持境内企业到境外发行融资，鼓励境内机构和个人到境外进行证券投资，还是畅通境外企业到境内发行融资渠道，平等保护境外机构和个人到境内进行证券投资，都需要在立足国情的前提下，实现制度衔接互通，消除制度壁垒。特别重要的是，市场竞争首先是制度规则的竞争，增强我国资本市场的国际竞争力，一方面要确保我国市场通过制度规则体现法治环境吸引力，另一方面还要增强我国在涉及资本市场对外开放的国际规则的制定中的话语权，增强我国在国际监管合作和跨境执法合作中的主动权。

同时，我们也注意到，2008 年国际金融危机发生后，境外资本市场对监管体制、机制做了较为重大的调整，提出了不少新的监管要求，出台了不少新的法律文件。例如，美国制定了具有金融综合监管性质的《多德—弗兰克华尔街改革与消费者保护法》，英国则将原来集证券、银行、保险于一身的《2000 年金融服务与市场法》修改成《2010 年金融服务法》。对于境外相关法律制度的动态发展，需要及时掌握情况，借鉴有益经验，为进一步完善我国资本市场的基础性制度建设提供参考。

经过长期的努力，中国资本市场的制度借鉴和引进已经越过了概念化、碎片状的发展阶段，进入全面、系统、精细化的更高阶段。由于种种原因，对境外资本市场法律制度的介绍，无论是在法学界、法律界，还是在证券期货行业内，一直以来都存在及时性不够、系统性不足、权威性不强的情况。特别是翻译介绍的质量不高、精品不多，这在客观上影响了对境外经验的学习和借鉴。

为了适应资本市场学习借鉴境外制度经验的形势要求，中国证监会精选了境外资本市场国家和地区的重要法律文献，包括境外主要资本市场的重要法律、监管部门的监管规则、经典的司法判例、最新的资本市场立法成果以及相关法学理论权威著作等，组织翻译出版了这套《境外资本市场重要法律文献译丛》。译丛的翻译出版工作，在系统单位、部门和关心市场发展的专家学者的共同努力下，紧紧抓住保质量、出精品的关键环节，建立了“竞标择优确定翻译人员、知名专家评审保证翻译质量、适当报酬和学术声誉结合激励”的工作机制，落实“精选译题、精细翻译、精心审校、精致出版”的工作要求，是中国证监会打造国人了解国际资本市场法律制度权威平台的有益尝试。为此，愿以本文向参与丛书翻译、审校的国际金融、法律方面的专家和学者表示感谢，并与大家共勉，共同为建设起一个权利公平、机会公平、规则公平的资本市场而努力。

中国证监会

2013 年 2 月

序

当今世界，经济全球化、政治多极化、信息网络化正在深刻地影响着人类历史的进程。经济全球化，作为正在改变全球社会面貌的基础，其核心内容就是通过各国国内市场和国际市场的逐步统一来实现生产要素在世界范围内的优化配置。而这种市场的统一和生产要素的优化配置是通过市场背后法律规范的统一来实施，因此，国际经济全球化赋予各国法律人的重要任务就是促进各国法律的日益趋同化。所谓趋同化就是指各国在维护主权的前提下，尽量与更能反映经济发展规律的公约、国际惯例或更发达地区的较先进的法律逐步走向一致的过程。因此，介绍国际经济法和各发达国家的法律及其法律规范，成为了我国深度介入经济全球化过程中我们法学界必须承担的历史任务。

由我参与校对的《欧盟证券监管法规汇编》是欧盟数十年来的证券监管实践经验的总结，也是整合欧洲证券市场规范化的尝试。从一定意义上来说，它们又是欧美国家长期以来互通有无的产物。因此，无论从哪个角度讲，该书的出版对我国金融业尤其是证券业的法制建设都将产生较大的启迪作用。

欧盟通过的旨在为欧盟投资公司及证券市场的《欧盟证券监管法规汇编》在实际中的效用，只能通过实施结果来检验。但是，这一系列的法案生不逢时，它们的出台正处于华尔街次贷危机引发的金融海啸之际，出台不久，欧洲金融市场又如醉汉一样无力控制自己，金融危机在欧盟内部四处蔓延，欧盟重要国家的机构信用评级出现了普遍性的下调。看来，再好的法律规范在猛烈的经济衰退面前，也只能望洋兴叹。

我进入法学领域可以追溯到20世纪60年代中期的1965年，就在那年我考入北京大学法律系，从那之后就进入了法律圈而不能自拔。屈指一算，竟要接近半个世纪了！我一直对公司法和证券法情有独钟：早在20世纪80年代初就翻译出版了《美国标准公司法》；1984年又出版了全国第一部较全面系统介绍西方国家公司法的《西方国家公司法原理》（近30年来，上述两本书还多次再版和印刷）；在20世纪90年代初，又参与了由当时国务院体改委主持的全国股份制实践，之后又参加了我国《公司法》的起草和修订，并发挥了较重要的作用。公司法领域多年的教学科研和实践告诉我一个真理，即“法律的真谛是实践”：法律规定得再全面、再完善，如果不是来自于实践，又没经实践检验，就很可能只是一堆意义不大的资料。只有通过实践，才能使其产生社会效用！我相信，现在翻译出版的一系列法案，通过实践的检测，一定会对我国金融立法、执法和司法产生较大影响！

本书的翻译是多位学者、专家和教授共同辛苦劳动的结晶，作为终审者，我只是在已经栽培成功的一朵鲜花前停下来进行了微不足道的修饰，它的成功出版只能归功于具有前瞻性的深圳证券交易所和付出如此繁重劳动的翻译专家们。

沈四宝

2013 年 7 月

CONTENTS

目　　录

DIRECTIVE 2003/71/EC OF THE EUROPEAN PARLIAMENT AND OF THE COUNCIL

欧洲议会与欧盟理事会第 2003/71/EC 号指令

DIRECTIVE 2003/71/EC OF THE EUROPEAN PARLIAMENT AND OF THE COUNCIL

of 4 November 2003

on the prospectus to be published when securities are offered to the public or admitted to trading and amending Directive 2001/34/EC

(Text with EEA relevance)

THE EUROPEAN PARLIAMENT AND THE COUNCIL OF THE EUROPEAN UNION,

Having regard to the Treaty establishing the European Community, and in particular Articles 44 and 95 thereof,

Having regard to the proposal from the Commission [1],

Having regard to the opinion of the European Economic and Social Committee [2],

Having regard to the opinion of the European Central Bank [3],

Acting in accordance with the procedure laid down in Article 251 of the Treaty [4],

Whereas:

(1) Council Directives 80/390/EEC of 17 March 1980 coordinating the requirements for the drawing up, scrutiny and distribution of the listing particulars to be published for the admission of securities to official stock exchange listing [5] and 89/298/EEC of 17 April

1 OJ C 240 E, 28.8.2001, p. 272 and OJ C 20 E, 28.1.2003, p. 122.

2 OJ C 80, 3.4.2002, p. 52.

3 OJ C 344, 6.12.2001, p. 4.

4 Opinion of the European Parliament of 14 March 2002 (OJ C 47 E, 27.2.2003, p. 417) Council Common Position of 24 March 2003 (OJ C 125 E, 27.5.2003, p. 21) and Position of the European Parliament f 2 July 2003 (not yet published in the Official Journal). Decision of the Council of 15 July 2003.

5 OJ L 100, 17.4.1980, p. 1. Directive as last amended by Directive of he European Parliament and of the Council 94/18/EC (OJ L 135, 31.5.1994, p. 1).

欧洲议会与欧盟理事会
第2003/71/EC号指令

（本指令于2003年11月4日通过，关于向公众发行证券或证券获准交易时所应公布的招募说明书，修正第2001/34/EC号指令）
（欧洲经济区适用文本）

欧洲议会与欧盟理事会，

根据《欧洲共同体条约》（以下简称《条约》），特别是其中的第44条及第95条，

根据欧盟委员会的提议，[1]
根据欧洲经济与社会委员会的意见，[2]
根据欧洲中央银行的意见，[3]
依照《条约》第251条规定的程序，[4]
鉴于：

（1）多年前欧洲经济共同体理事会通过了《欧洲经济共同体理事会协调关于获准在官方证券交易所上市的证券所应公布的上市具体信息之编制、审查与发布要求的第80/390/EEC号指令》[5]（1980年3月17日）及《欧洲经济共同体理事会协调关于向公众

---

1 2001年8月28日《欧盟公报》C240E，第272页，以及2003年1月28日《欧盟公报》C20E，第122页。

2 2002年4月3日《欧盟公报》C80，第52页。

3 2001年12月6日《欧盟公报》C344，第4页。

4 2002年3月14日欧洲议会意见（2003年2月27日《欧盟公报》C47E，第417页）、2003年3月24日欧盟理事会共同立场（2003年5月27日《欧盟公报》C125E，第21页）以及2003年7月2日欧洲议会立场（尚未在《欧盟公报》公布）。2003年7月15日欧盟理事会决定。

5 1980年4月17日《欧盟公报》L100，第1页。该指令由欧洲议会与欧盟理事会第94/18/EC号指令（1994年5月31日《欧盟公报》L135，第1页）作出最新修正。

1989 coordinating the requirements for the drawing up, scrutiny and distribution of the prospectus to be published when transferable securities are offered to the public [1] were adopted several years ago introducing a partial and complex mutual recognition mechanism which is unable to achieve the objective of the single passport provided for by this Directive. Those directives should be upgraded, updated and grouped together into a single text.

(2) Meanwhile, Directive 80/390/EEC was integrated into Directive 2001/34/EC of the European Parliament and of the Council of 28 May 2001 on the admission of securities to official stock exchange listing and on information to be published on those securities [2], which codifies several directives in the field of listed securities.

(3) For reasons of consistency, however, it is appropriate to regroup the provisions of Directive 2001/34/EC which stem from Directive 80/390/EEC together with Directive 89/298/EEC and to amend Directive 2001/34/EC accordingly.

(4) This Directive constitutes an instrument essential to the achievement of the internal market as set out in timetable form in the Commission communications 'Risk capital action plan' and 'Implementing the framework for financial market: Action Plan' facilitating the widest possible access to investment capital on a Community-wide basis, including for small and medium-sized enterprises (SMEs) and start-ups, by granting a single passport to the issuer.

(5) On 17 July 2000, the Council set up the Committee of Wise Men on the regulation of European securities markets. In its initial report of 9 November 2000 the Committee stresses the lack of an agreed definition of public offer of securities, with the result that the same operation is regarded as a private placement in some Member States and not in others; the current system discourages firms from raising capital on a Community-wide basis and therefore from having real access to a large, liquid and integrated financial market.

(6) In its final report of 15 February 2001 the Committee of Wise Men proposed the introduction of new legislative techniques based on a four-level approach, namely framework principles, implementing measures, cooperation and enforcement. Level 1, the directive, should confine itself to broad, general 'framework' principles, while Level 2 should contain technical implementing measures to be adopted by the Commission with the assistance of a committee.

(7) The Stockholm European Council of 23 and 24 March 2001 endorsed the final report of the Committee of Wise Men and the proposed four-level approach to make the regulatory process for Community securities legislation more efficient and transparent.

1 OJ L 124, 5.5.1989, p. 8.

2 OJ L 184, 6.7.2001, p. 1.

发行可转让证券所公布的招募说明书的编制、审查与发布要求的第89/298/EEC号指令》[1]（1989年4月17日），由此开始实施一项片面而复杂的相互承认机制，然而该机制无法达成本指令所制定的单一护照目标。上述指令应予完善、更新并集合成单一的文本。

（2）然而，第80/390/EEC号指令也被整合到了《欧洲议会与欧盟理事会关于证券获准在证券交易所正式上市以及应公布的与该等证券有关的信息的第2001/34/EC号指令》[2]（2001年5月28日）当中，第2001/34/EC号指令汇编了与上市证券有关的若干指令。

（3）然而，为了保持一致，宜将第2001/34/EC号指令中源于第80/390/EEC号指令的条款与第89/298/EEC号指令归并，并对第2001/34/EC号指令作出相应修正。

（4）欧盟委员会《风险资本行动计划》和《落实金融市场框架：行动计划》两份通报以时间表形式指明了内部市场的改革进程，本指令是实现内部市场改革至关重要的法律文件之一，通过向发行人授予单一护照，促进欧共体各界，包括中小企业（SME）及创业企业尽可能广泛地获取投资资本。

（5）2000年7月17日，欧盟理事会成立了欧洲证券市场监督专家委员会。专家委员会在2000年11月9日发布的首份报告中强调，目前仍缺乏对“公开发行证券”的一致定义，以致相同的发行活动在部分成员国被视为私募，而在其他成员国则被视为公募；现行制度也阻碍企业在全欧共体范围内募集资金，因而无法真正受益于一个流动而一体化的大规模金融市场。

（6）在2001年2月15日的最终报告中，专家委员会建议采用基于四级立法程序的新的立法技术，即框架原则、实施细则、合作与执法。第一级的立法，即指令，应只阐述宏观的“框架性”原则，第二级的立法应当阐述欧盟委员会在各个委员会的协助下制定的技术性实施细则。

（7）2001年3月23日至24日于斯德哥尔摩举行的欧洲理事会会议同意并支持了专家委员会的最终报告及其所建议的四级立法程序，以保证欧共体证券领域立法的监管程序更高的效率和透明度。

1　1989年5月5日《欧盟公报》L124，第8页。

2　2001年7月6日《欧盟公报》L184，第1页。

(8) The resolution of the European Parliament of 5 February 2002 on the implementation of financial services legislation also endorsed the Committee of Wise Men's final report, on the basis of the solemn declaration made before Parliament the same day by the Commission and the letter of 2 October 2001 addressed by the Internal Market Commissioner to the chairman of Parliament's Committee on Economic and Monetary Affairs with regard to the safeguards for the European Parliament's role in this process.

(9) According to the Stockholm European Council, Level 2 implementing measures should be used more frequently to ensure that technical provisions can be kept up to date with market and supervisory developments and deadlines should be set for all stages of Level 2.

(10) The aim of this Directive and its implementing measures is to ensure investor protection and market efficiency, in accordance with high regulatory standards adopted in the relevant international fora.

(11) Non-equity securities issued by a Member State or by one of a Member State's regional or local authorities, by public international bodies of which one or more Member States are members, by the European Central Bank or by the central banks of the Member States are not covered by this Directive and thus remain unaffected by this Directive; the abovementioned issuers of such securities may, however, if they so choose, draw up a prospectus in accordance with this Directive.

(12) Full coverage of equity and non-equity securities offered to the public or admitted to trading on regulated markets as defined by Council Directive 93/22/EEC of 10 May 1993 on investment services in the securities field [1], and not only securities which have been admitted to the official lists of stock exchanges, is also needed to ensure investor protection. The wide definition of securities in this Directive, which includes warrants and covered warrants and certificates, is only valid for this Directive and consequently in no way affects the various definitions of financial instruments used in national legislation for other purposes, such as taxation. Some of the securities defined in this Directive entitle the holder to acquire transferable securities or to receive a cash amount through a cash settlement determined by reference to other instruments, notably transferable securities, currencies, interest rates or yields, commodities or other indices or measures. Depositary receipts and convertible notes, e.g. securities convertible at the option of the investor, fall within the definition of non- equity securities set out in this Directive.

1 OJ L 141, 11.6.1993, p. 27. Directive as last amended by Directive 000/64/EC of the European Parliament and of the Council (OJ L290, 17.11.2000, p. 27).

（8）基于欧盟委员会2002年2月5日向欧洲议会作出的庄严声明和内部市场委员于2001年10月2日就确保欧洲议会在上述立法的监管程序中的作用致欧洲议会经济和货币事务委员会主席的信函，《欧洲议会关于实施金融服务立法的决议》（2002年2月5日）也同意和支持专家委员会的最终报告。

（9）根据欧洲理事会斯德哥尔摩会议的决议，应更多地使用第二级立法即实施细则，以确保技术性条款能反映市场和监管的最新发展动态，同时，应为第二级立法的每一阶段工作设定完成期限。

（10）本指令及其实施细则的宗旨为依照相关国际组织制定的高监管标准来确保投资者保护和市场效率。

（11）由某一欧盟成员国或其地区或地方政府部门、国际公共机构（其一个或多个成员为欧盟成员国）、欧洲中央银行或欧盟各成员国的中央银行发行的非股权证券不属于本指令的管辖范围，因此不受本指令影响；然而，上述证券的发行人可以自愿选择遵循本指令编制招募说明书。

（12）为确保对投资者的保护，欧盟的监管有必要全面覆盖《欧洲经济共同体理事会关于证券领域投资服务的第93/22/EEC号指令》[1]（1993年5月10日）所定义的向公众发行或获准在受监管市场交易的股权与非股权证券，而不限于已获准在证券交易所正式上市的证券。本指令中对证券的宽泛定义（包括权证以及备兑权证与证书）仅就本指令有效，绝不影响成员国为其他目的（如税收）而在国内立法中对各种金融工具所做定义。本指令所定义的部份证券的持有人凭该等证券有权获得可转让证券，或有权凭该等证券参照其他工具（特别是可转让证券、货币、利率或收益率、商品或其他指数或指标）进行现金结算从而获得现金。存托凭证及可转换票据（如投资者可行使选择权进行转换的证券）均在本指令所定义的非股权证券范围内。

1 1993年6月11日《欧盟公报》L141，第27页。该指令由欧洲议会与欧盟理事会第2000/64/EC号指令（2000年11月17日《欧盟公报》L290，第27页）作出最新修正。

(13) Issuance of securities having a similar type and/or class in the case of non-equity securities issued on the basis of an offering programme, including warrants and certificates in any form, as well as the case of securities issued in a continuous or repeated manner, should be understood as covering not only identical securities but also securities that belong in general terms to one category. These securities may include different products, such as debt securities, certificates and warrants, or the same product under the same programme, and may have different features notably in terms of seniority, types of underlying, or the basis on which to determine the redemption amount or coupon payment.

(14) The grant to the issuer of a single passport, valid throughout the Community, and the application of the country of origin principle require the identification of the home Member State as the one best placed to regulate the issuer for the purposes of this Directive.

(15) The disclosure requirements of the present Directive do not prevent a Member State or a competent authority or an exchange through its rule book to impose other particular requirements in the context of admission to trading of securities on a regulated market (notably regarding corporate governance). Such requirements may not directly or indirectly restrict the drawing up, the content and the dissemination of a prospectus approved by a competent authority.

(16) One of the objectives of this Directive is to protect investors. It is therefore appropriate to take account of the different requirements for protection of the various categories of investors and their level of expertise. Disclosure provided by the prospectus is not required for offers limited to qualified investors. In contrast, any resale to the public or public trading through admission to trading on a regulated market requires the publication of a prospectus.

(17) Issuers, offerors or persons asking for the admission to trading on a regulated market of securities which are exempted from the obligation to publish a prospectus will benefit from the single passport if they comply with this Directive.

(18) The provision of full information concerning securities and issuers of those securities promotes, together with rules on the conduct of business, the protection of investors. Moreover, such information provides an effective means of increasing confidence in securities and thus of contributing to the proper functioning and development of securities markets. The appropriate way to make this information available is to publish a prospectus.

(19) Investment in securities, like any other form of investment, involves risk. Safeguards for the protection of the interests of actual and potential investors are required in all Member States in order to enable them to make an informed assessment of such

(13)对于按发行方案发行的非股权证券(包括任何形式的权证与证书)以及持续或重复发行的证券而言,“类似类型和/或类别的证券的发行”的范围应理解为不仅涵盖相同的证券,还应涵盖大致属于同一类别的证券。该等证券可包括不同品种的证券(如债务证券、证书及权证)或同一计划下的同一产品,也可包括主要在以下方面具有不同特征的产品:清偿优先权、标的物类型或赎回金额或息票支付的计算依据。

(14)向发行人发放全欧共体有效的单一护照和实施发行人母国监管原则,均要求认定母国是最适合负责依据本指令对发行人进行监管的国家。

(15)本指令的披露要求并不妨碍成员国或主管部门或交易所通过其规则手册就证券获准进入受监管市场交易施加其他特定要求(特别是公司治理方面的要求)。此等要求不得直接或间接对提交主管部门批准的招募说明书的编制、内容及传播作出限制性规定。

(16)本指令的目标之一是保护投资者。因此,应顾及各类投资者的不同保护要求及其专业水平。仅以合格投资者为对象的要约不必通过发布招募说明书的方式披露信息。反之,以公众为对象的转售或获准在受监管市场进行的任何公开交易,都应公布招募说明书。

(17)豁免公布招募说明书义务的证券发行人、要约人或请求获准在受监管市场交易其证券的人,只要遵守本指令均可获得单一护照。

(18)关于证券及证券发行人信息充分披露的条款以及业务行为规则共同促进了对投资者的保护。此外,上述信息有效地增强了公众对证券的信心,从而促进了证券市场的稳健运行及发展,而提供信息的适当方式即为公布招募说明书。

(19)证券投资和任何其他形式投资一样,均存在风险。所有成员国均应采取保障措施,保护实际或潜在投资者的利益,使其能对证券投资风险作出知情评估,从而在充分了解事实的情形下作出投资决定。

risks and thus to take investment decisions in full knowledge of the facts.

(20) Such information, which needs to be sufficient and as objective as possible as regards the financial circumstances of the issuer and the rights attaching to the securities, should be provided in an easily analysable and comprehensible form. Harmonisation of the information contained in the prospectus should provide equivalent investor protection at Community level.

(21) Information is a key factor in investor protection; a summary conveying the essential characteristics of, and risks associated with, the issuer, any guarantor and the securities should be included in the prospectus. To ensure easy access to this information, the summary should be written in non-technical language and normally should not exceed 2 500 words in the language in which the prospectus was originally drawn up.

(22) Best practices have been adopted at international level in order to allow cross-border offers of equities to be made using a single set of disclosure standards established by the International Organisation of Securities Commissions (IOSCO); the IOSCO disclosure standards [1] will upgrade information available for the markets and investors and at the same time will simplify the procedure for Community issuers wishing to raise capital in third countries. The Directive also calls for tailored disclosure standards to be adopted for other types of securities and issuers.

(23) Fast-track procedures for issuers admitted to trading on a regulated market and frequently raising capital on these markets require the introduction at Community level of a new format of prospectuses for offering programmes or mortgage bonds and a new registration document system. Issuers may choose not to use those formats and therefore to draft the prospectus as a single document.

(24) The content of a base prospectus should, in particular, take into account the need for flexibility in relation to the information to be provided about the securities.

(25) Omission of sensitive information to be included in a prospectus should be allowed through a derogation granted by the competent authority in certain circumstances in order to avoid detrimental situations for an issuer.

(26) A clear time limit should be set for the validity of a prospectus in order to avoid outdated information.

(27) Investors should be protected by ensuring publication of reliable information. The issuers whose securities are admitted to trading on a regulated market are subject to an ongoing disclosure obligation but are not required to publish updated information regularly. Further to this obligation, issuers should, at least annually, list all relevant information published or made available to the public over the preceding 12 months,

1 International disclosure standards for cross-border offering and nitial listings by foreign issuers, Part I, International Organisation of ecurities Commissions, September 1998.

(20)上述信息应当充分,尽可能客观地反映发行人的财务状况以及与证券有关的权利,并以易于分析和理解的形式列报。对欧共体各成员国关于招募说明书信息的规定进行协调时,应力求对欧共体各成员国投资者提供同等的保护。

(21)信息是投资者保护的关键因素;招募说明书应包含一份摘要,简述发行人、任何担保人及证券的基本特征以及相关风险。为确保此信息易于理解,上述摘要应以非技术性语言撰写,且按起草的源语言计算,正常情形下篇幅不得超过2500字。

(22)国际上已经形成了相关的最佳实践,使发行人能通过国际证监会组织(IOSCO)制定的一套统一披露标准跨境发行股票;国际证监会组织的披露标准[1]加强提供给市场和投资者的信息,同时简化欧共体发行人在第三国募集资金的程序。本指令也呼吁针对其他类型的证券及发行人量身定制相应的披露标准。

(23)要针对获准在受监管市场交易其证券且经常在该等市场募集资金的发行人建立快速通道程序,需要在欧共体层面出台一套全新的发行方案的招募说明书格式或抵押债券招募说明书格式,并引入新的注册文件系统。发行人可以选择不使用该等格式,而以单一文件形式起草招募说明书。

(24)基本招募说明书的内容尤应考虑到证券信息的提供需要一定的灵活度这一事实。

(25)某些情形下,经主管部门豁免,招募说明书可省略敏感信息,以避免发生对发行人造成损害的情况。

(26)应为招募说明书设定明确的有效期限,避免信息过时。

(27)应确保所公布信息的可靠性以保护投资者。证券获准在受监管市场交易的发行人有持续披露义务,但不必定期公布更新的信息。鉴于上述持续披露义务,发行人应至少每年列报一次前12个月期间内公布过的或向公众公开过的所有相关信息,包括其他欧共体立法所制定的各种报告规定所要求提供的信息。此举将能确保发行人定期公布相互一致且易于理解的信息。为避免加重某些发行人的负担,不得要求最低

1 国际证监会组织《跨境发行与外国发行人首次上市的国际披露标准》(1998年9月)第一部分。

including information provided to the various reporting requirements laid down in other Community legislation. This should make it possible to ensure the publication of consistent and easily understandable information on a regular basis. To avoid excessive burdens for certain issuers, issuers of non-equity securities with high minimum denomination should not be required to meet this obligation.

(28) It is necessary for the annual information to be provided by issuers whose securities are admitted to trading on a regulated market to be appropriately monitored by Member States in accordance with their obligations under the provisions of Community and national law concerning the regulation of securities, issuers of securities and securities markets.

(29) The opportunity of allowing issuers to incorporate by reference documents containing the information to be disclosed in a prospectus — provided that the documents incorporated by reference have been previously filed with or accepted by the competent authority — should facilitate the procedure of drawing up a prospectus and lower the costs for the issuers without endangering investor protection.

(30) Differences regarding the efficiency, methods and timing of the checking of the information given in a prospectus not only make it more difficult for undertakings to raise capital or to obtain admission to trading on a regulated market in more than one Member State but also hinder the acquisition by investors established in one Member State of securities offered by an issuer established in another Member State or admitted to trading in another Member State. These differences should be eliminated by harmonising the rules and regulations in order to achieve an adequate degree of equivalence of the safeguards required in each Member State to ensure the provision of information which is sufficient and as objective as possible for actual or potential securities holders.

(31) To facilitate circulation of the various documents making up the prospectus, the use of electronic communication facilities such as the Internet should be encouraged. The prospectus should always be delivered in paper form, free of charge to investors on request.

(32) The prospectus should be filed with the relevant competent authority and be made available to the public by the issuer, the offeror or the person asking for admission to trading on a regulated market, subject to European Union provisions relating to data protection.

(33) It is also necessary, in order to avoid loopholes in Community legislation which would undermine public confidence and therefore prejudice the proper functioning of financial markets, to harmonise advertisements.

(34) Any new matter liable to influence the assessment of the investment, arising after the publication of the prospectus but before the closing of the offer or the start of

面额较高的非股权证券发行人遵守此项义务。

(28)对于证券获准在受监管市场交易的发行人应提供的年度信息,成员国有必要依照其在欧共体法律和成员国国内法律关于证券、证券发行人以及证券市场的监管规定中的义务进行适当监控。

(29)如能允许发行人在招募说明书中引用含有待披露信息的文件(前提是引用的文件在此之前已向主管部门提交过或已为主管部门所接受),招募说明书的编制将更为便利,并且不影响投资者保护即可降低发行人的成本。

(30)鉴于成员国审核招募说明书信息的效率、方法与时间各不相同,不仅使企业筹募资金以及证券获准在一个以上成员国受监管市场交易的难度加大,也阻碍在某一成员国设立的投资者购买在另一成员国设立的发行人所发行的证券或在另一成员国获准交易的证券。应通过协调各成员国的规则和规章来弥合差异,使各个成员国规定实施的保障措施达到充分的等效程度,从而确保发行人向实际或潜在的证券持有人提供充分且尽可能客观的信息。

(31)为方便构成招募说明书的各种文件的流通,应鼓励使用如互联网之类的电子通讯手段。任何时候一经请求招募说明书即应以纸质形式向投资者免费提供。

(32)在遵守欧盟数据保护规定的前提下,发行人、要约人或请求获准在受监管市场交易其证券的人均应向相关主管部门提交并向公众提供招募说明书。

(33)为避免欧共体立法出现漏洞造成公众对市场的信心受打击,从而损害金融市场的稳健运行,有必要对广告的相关规定进行协调。

(34)在招募说明书公布后、发行截止前或证券开始在受监管市场交易前,如出现任何新增事项可能影响到投资评估,则应披露给投资者,供其作出恰当评估,因此需

trading on a regulated market, should be properly evaluated by investors and therefore requires the approval and dissemination of a supplement to the prospectus.

(35) The obligation for an issuer to translate the full prospectus into all the relevant official languages discourages cross-border offers or multiple trading. To facilitate cross-border offers, where the prospectus is drawn up in a language that is customary in the sphere of international finance, the host or home Member State should only be entitled to require a summary in its official language(s).

(36) The competent authority of the host Member State should be entitled to receive a certificate from the competent authority of the home Member State which states that the prospectus has been drawn up in accordance with this Directive. In order to ensure that the purposes of this Directive will be fully achieved, it is also necessary to include within its scope securities issued by issuers governed by the laws of third countries.

(37) A variety of competent authorities in Member States, having different responsibilities, may create unnecessary costs and overlapping of responsibilities without providing any additional benefit. In each Member State one single competent authority should be designated to approve prospectuses and to assume responsibility for supervising compliance with this Directive. Under strict conditions, a Member State should be allowed to designate more than one competent authority, but only one will assume the duties for international cooperation. Such an authority or authorities should be established as an administrative authority and in such a form that their independence from economic actors is guaranteed and conflicts of interest are avoided. The designation of a competent authority for prospectus approval should not exclude cooperation between that authority and other entities, with a view to guaranteeing efficient scrutiny and approval of prospectuses in the interest of issuers, investors, markets participants and markets alike. Any delegation of tasks relating to the obligations provided for in this Directive and in its implementing measures should be reviewed, in accordance with Article 31, five years after the date of entry into force of this Directive and should, except for publication on the Internet of approved prospectuses, and the filing of prospectuses as mentioned in Article 14, end eight years after the entry into force of this Directive.

(38) A common minimum set of powers for the competent authorities will guarantee the effectiveness of their supervision. The flow of information to the markets required by Directive 2001/34/EC should be ensured and action against breaches should be taken by competent authorities.

(39) For the purposes of carrying out their duties, cooperation between competent authorities of the Member States is required.

(40) Technical guidance and implementing measures for the rules laid down in this Directive may from time to time be necessary to take into account developments on

要针对该事项对招募说明书进行补充，补充文件应提交批准并予以传播。

(35)要求发行人将招募说明书全文翻译为所有相关的官方语言，并不利于跨境发行或交叉上市交易。为促进跨境向公众发行证券活动的开展，招募说明书系以国际金融行业惯用语言编制的，东道国或母国仅有权要求发行人提供以该国的一种或多种官方语言编制的摘要。

(36)东道国主管部门有权从母国主管部门处获得关于招募说明书系根据本指令编制的证明。为确保本指令宗旨全面实现，也有必要将受第三国法律管辖的发行人所发行的证券纳入其适用范围。

(37)各成员国主管部门繁多，且其职责各异，可能会造成不必要的成本负担和职责重叠，同时却不带来任何额外收益。因此，各成员国应指定单一的主管部门来负责批准招募说明书，并承担监管本指令的合规情况的责任。成员国有权按严格的条件指定一个以上的主管部门，但其中仅能有一个主管部门负责国际合作。该等一个或多个主管部门应为行政管理部门，其组建形式应保证其独立于经济主体并避免利益冲突。指定负责招募说明书批准的单一主管部门，不应影响该主管部门为保证高效审查和批准招募说明书(从而保护发行人、投资者、市场参与者及市场利益)而与其他实体的合作。应在本指令生效5年后，根据第31条的规定对与本指令及其实施细则中规定的义务相关的任何职责委托进行审评。此外，除了在互联网上公布获批的招募说明书和第14条所述的提交招募说明书的义务外，所有委托的职责均应于本指令生效8年后终止。

(38)授予各主管部门一系列共同和必不可少的权力，将有助于保证监管的有效性。应确保第2001/34/EC号指令规定的应予披露的信息确实向市场发布，主管部门应对违法违规情况采取相应的行动。

(39)为履行其职责，各成员国主管部门应相互合作。

(40)考虑到金融市场的发展，有必要就本指令的规则不时制定技术性指引和实施细则。因此，欧盟委员会应有权制定相关实施细则，前提是此等实施细则不对本指

financial markets. The Commission should accordingly be empowered to adopt implementing measures, provided that these do not modify the essential elements of this Directive and provided that the Commission acts in accordance with the principles set out in this Directive, after consulting the European Securities Committee established by Commission Decision 2001/528/EC [1].

(41) In exercising its implementing powers in accordance with this Directive, the Commission should respect the following principles:

— the need to ensure confidence in financial markets among small investors and small and medium-sized enterprises (SMEs) by promoting high standards of transparency in financial markets,

— the need to provide investors with a wide range of competing investment opportunities and a level of disclosure and protection tailored to their circumstances,

— the need to ensure that independent regulatory authorities enforce the rules consistently, especially as regards the fight against white-collar crime,

— the need for a high level of transparency and consultation with all market participants and with the European Parliament and the Council,

— the need to encourage innovation in financial markets if they are to be dynamic and efficient,

— the need to ensure systemic stability of the financial system by close and reactive monitoring of financial innovation,

— the importance of reducing the cost of, and increasing access to, capital,

— the need to balance, on a long-term basis, the costs and benefits to market participants (including SMEs and small investors) of any implementing measures,

— the need to foster the international competitiveness of the Community's financial markets without prejudice to a much needed extension of international cooperation,

— the need to achieve a level playing field for all market participants by establishing Community legislation every time it is appropriate,

— the need to respect differences in national financial markets where these do not unduly impinge on the coherence of the single market,

— the need to ensure coherence with other Community legislation in this area, as imbalances in information and a lack of transparency may jeopardise the operation of the markets and above all harm consumers and small investors.

(42) The European Parliament should be given a period of three months from the first transmission of draft implementing measures to allow it to examine them and to give its opinion. However, in urgent and duly justified cases, this period may be shortened. If,

1 OJ L 191, 13.7.2001, p. 45.

令的基本要素进行改动，并且欧盟委员会在行事时应先咨询根据欧盟委员会第2001/528/EC号决定[1]设立的欧洲证券委员会的意见，并遵循本指令规定的原则。

(41)欧盟委员会在根据本指令行使实施权时应遵守下列原则：

——有必要推行高标准的金融市场透明度，确保小型投资者与中小企业(SMEs)对金融市场的信心；

——有必要向投资者提供多样化的竞争性投资机会，以及与其实际情况相吻合的信息披露与保护水平；

——有必要确保独立监管机构执行相关规则(特别是打击白领犯罪的规则)的一致性；

——有必要保持高水平的透明度，并征求所有市场参与者以及欧洲议会和欧盟理事会的意见；

——有必要鼓励创新，使金融市场具有活力和效率；

——有必要对金融创新进行密切、灵活的监控，确保金融系统的稳定；

——有必要降低资本成本和拓宽融资渠道；

——采取任何实施细则均需实现市场参与者(包括中小型企业和小型投资者)成本和效益的长期平衡；

——有必要在不影响国际合作深化的前提下，培育欧共体金融市场的国际竞争力；

——有必要适时制定适用于全欧共体的法规，为所有市场参与者提供公平的竞争环境；

——有必要在不过度冲击单一市场一致性的前提下尊重各成员国国内金融市场的差异；

——有必要确保此领域法律与其他欧共体法律的一致性，以防止信息的不对等和透明度的缺失危害市场运行，尤其是防止因此损及消费者和小型投资者的利益。

(42)欧洲议会应在实施细则草案首次递交之后3个月内进行审核并提出意见。但在紧急并有正当理由的情形下，可以缩短该期限。欧洲议会在该等缩短期限内通过了任何决议的，欧盟委员会应对细则草案重新进行审核。

1 2001年7月13日《欧盟公报》L191，第45页。

within that period, a resolution is passed by the European Parliament, the Commission should re–examine the draft measures.

(43) Member States should lay down a system of sanctions for breaches of the national provisions adopted pursuant to this Directive and should take all the measures necessary to ensure that these sanctions are applied. The sanctions thus provided for should be effective, proportional and dissuasive.

(44) Provision should be made for the right of judicial review of decisions taken by Member States' competent authorities in respect of the application of this Directive.

(45) In accordance with the principle of proportionality, it is necessary and appropriate for the achievement of the basic objective of ensuring the completion of a single securities market to lay down rules on a single passport for issuers. This Directive does not go beyond what is necessary in order to achieve the objectives pursued in accordance with the third paragraph of Article 5 of the Treaty.

(46) The assessment made by the Commission of the application of this Directive should focus in particular on the process of approval of prospectuses by the competent authorities of the Member States, and more generally on the application of the home–country principle, and whether or not problems of investor protection and market efficiency might result from this application; the Commission should also examine the functioning of Article 10.

(47) For future developments of this Directive, consideration should be given to the matter of deciding which approval mechanism should be adopted to enhance further the uniform application of Community legislation on prospectuses, including the possible establishment of a European Securities Unit.

(48) This Directive respects the fundamental rights and observes the principles recognised in particular by the Charter of Fundamental Rights of the European Union.

(49) The measures necessary for the implementation of this Directive should be adopted in accordance with Council Decision 1999/468/EC of 28 June 1999 laying down the procedures for the exercise of implementing powers conferred on the Commission [1].

---

1 OJ L 184, 17.7.1999, p. 23.

(43)各成员国应对违反其依本指令制定的本国规定的行为建立处罚制度,并采取一切必要措施确保处罚的执行。因此,所规定的处罚应是有效、成比例并具有威慑作用的。

(44)应对相关司法审查权作出规定,以对成员国主管部门适用本指令所做的决定进行司法审查。

(45)根据比例原则,为实现完善单一证券市场这一基本目标,就发行人的单一护照制定规则确属必要且适当。本指令仅作出实现《条约》第5条第3款规定的目标的必要规定。

(46)欧盟委员会针对本指令的适用所做的评价,应特别着重于成员国主管部门批准招募说明书的程序,广义而言,即特别着重于母国原则的适用,以及适用母国原则是否会造成投资者保护与市场效率方面的问题;欧盟委员会还应审查第10条规定的运行。

(47)将来如对本指令进行修改,应当考虑宜采用何种批准机制以进一步推进欧共体关于招募说明书的立法统一适用的问题,其中包括设立欧洲证券处的可能性。

(48)本指令遵守并奉行《欧盟基本权利宪章》所认可的基本权利和原则。

(49)应依照《欧盟理事会关于制定欧盟委员会行使其被授予的实施权之程序的第1999/468/EC号决定》[1](1999年6月28日)制定本指令所需的实施细则。

1 1999年7月17日《欧盟公报》L184,第23页。

HAVE ADOPTED THIS DIRECTIVE:

CHAPTER I GENERAL PROVISIONS

Article 1 Purpose and scope

1. The purpose of this Directive is to harmonise requirements for the drawing up, approval and distribution of the prospectus to be published when securities are offered to the public or admitted to trading on a regulated market situated or operating within a Member State.

2. This Directive shall not apply to:

(a) units issued by collective investment undertakings other than the closed-end type;

(b) non-equity securities issued by a Member State or by one of a Member State's regional or local authorities, by public international bodies of which one or more Member States are members, by the European Central Bank or by the central banks of the Member States;

(c) shares in the capital of central banks of the Member States;

(d) securities unconditionally and irrevocably guaranteed by a Member State or by one of a Member State's regional or local authorities;

(e) securities issued by associations with legal status or non-profit-making bodies, recognised by a Member State, with a view to their obtaining the means necessary to achieve their non-profit-making objectives;

(f) non-equity securities issued in a continuous or repeated manner by credit institutions provided that these securities:

(i) are not subordinated, convertible or exchangeable;

(ii) do not give a right to subscribe to or acquire other types of securities and that they are not linked to a derivative instrument;

(iii) materialise reception of repayable deposits;

(iv) are covered by a deposit guarantee scheme under Directive 94/19/EC of the European Parliament and of the Council on deposit-guarantee schemes [1];

(g) non-fungible shares of capital whose main purpose is to provide the holder with a right to occupy an apartment, or other form of immovable property or a part thereof and where the shares cannot be sold on without this right being given up;

(h) securities included in an offer where the total consideration of the offer is less than EUR 2 500 000, which limit shall be calculated over a period of 12 months;

(i) 'bostadsobligationer' issued repeatedly by credit institutions in Sweden whose

1 OJ L 135, 31.5.1994, p. 5.

兹通过本指令如下：

第一章 总 则

第1条 宗旨与范围

1. 本指令旨在协调向公众发行证券或证券获准在位于某成员国或在某成员国境内运行的受监管市场交易时所应公布的招募说明书相关的编制、批准与发布要求。

2.本指令不适用于：

(a)非封闭式集合投资计划所发行的单位；

(b)由某一欧盟成员国或其地区或地方政府部门、国际公共机构(其一个或多个成员为欧盟成员国)、欧洲中央银行或欧盟成员国中央银行所发行的非股权证券；

(c)构成欧盟成员国中央银行资本的股份；

(d)由某一欧盟成员国或其某个地区或地方政府部门提供无条件且不可撤销担保的证券；

(e)由具有法律地位的协会或非营利性机构所发行的成员国认可的证券,以使其能获得实现非营利性目标所必要的资源；

(f)由信贷机构持续或重复发行的非股权证券,前提是该等证券：

(i)并非次级、可转换或可交换证券；

(ii)并不赋予持有人认购或购买其他类型证券的权利,且不与衍生品工具挂钩；

(iii)作为应偿还之存款的接收凭证；

(iv)属于《欧洲议会与欧盟理事会关于存款担保计划的第94/19/EC号指令》[1]中的存款担保计划覆盖范围；

(g)不可替代的股份,该等股份主要旨在令其持有人有权占有某套公寓或其他形式的不动产或某中的一部分,并且唯有放弃该占有权方能出售该股份；

(h)总对价少于250万欧元(以12个月为期计算该限额)的要约中包含的证券；

(i)由瑞典的信贷机构重复发行、主要目的为发放抵押贷款的“抵押债券”,前

1 1994年5月31日《欧盟公报》L135,第5页。

main purpose is to grant mortgage loans, provided that

(i) the 'bostadsobligationer' issued are of the same series;

(ii) the 'bostadsobligationer' are issued on tap during a specified issuing period;

(iii) the terms and conditions of the 'bostadsobligationer' are not changed during the issuing period;

(iv) the sums deriving from the issue of the said 'bostadsobligationer', in accordance with the articles of association of the issuer, are placed in assets which provide sufficient coverage for the liability deriving from securities;

(j) non-equity securities issued in a continuous or repeated manner by credit institutions where the total consideration of the offer is less than EUR 50 000 000, which limit shall be calculated over a period of 12 months, provided that these securities:

(i) are not subordinated, convertible or exchangeable;

(ii) do not give a right to subscribe to or acquire other types of securities and that they are not linked to a derivative instrument.

3. Notwithstanding paragraph 2 (b)(d)(h)(i) and (j) an issuer, an offeror or a person asking for admission to trading on a regulated market shall be entitled to draw up a prospectus in accordance with this Directive when securities are offered to the public or admitted to trading.

Article 2 Definitions

1. For the purposes of this Directive, the following definitions shall apply:

(a) 'securities' means transferable securities as defined by Article 1(4) of Directive 93/22/EEC with the exception of money market instruments as defined by Article 1(5) of Directive 93/22/EEC, having a maturity of less than 12 months. For these instruments national legislation may be applicable;

(b) 'equity securities' means shares and other transferable securities equivalent to shares in companies, as well as any other type of transferable securities giving the right to acquire any of the aforementioned securities as a consequence of their being converted or the rights conferred by them being exercised, provided that securities of the latter type are issued by the issuer of the underlying shares or by an entity belonging to the group of the said issuer;

(c) 'non-equity securities' means all securities that are not equity securities;

(d) 'offer of securities to the public' means a communication to persons in any form and by any means, presenting sufficient information on the terms of the offer and the securities to be offered, so as to enable an investor to decide to purchase or subscribe to these securities. This definition shall also be applicable to the placing of securities through financial intermediaries;

(e) 'qualified investors' means:

提是：

(i)发行的“抵押债券”属于同一系列；

(ii)该“抵押债券”是在规定的发行期内根据需要随时发行的债券；

(iii)发行期内该“抵押债券”的条款与条件并无变更；

(iv)根据发行人的公司章程，发行上述“抵押债券”所得各项金额记入资产，而该等资产能为证券所产生的债务提供足够的担保；

(j)由信贷机构持续或重复发行的，要约总对价少于5000万欧元(以12个月为期计算该限额)的非股权证券，前提是该等证券；

(i)并非次级、可转换或可交换的证券；

(ii)并不赋予持有人认购或购买其他类型证券的权利，且不与衍生品工具挂钩；

3.尽管有第2款第b项、第d项、第h项、第i项及第j项的规定，发行人、要约人或请求获准在受监管市场交易其证券的人，均有权在证券向公众发行或获准交易时根据本指令编制招募说明书。

第2条　定义

1.本指令适用下列定义：

(a)“证券”指第93/22/EEC号指令第1条第4款所定义的可转让证券，但第93/22/EEC号指令第1条第5款所定义的期限不到12个月的货币市场工具除外。此等工具可适用成员国的国内立法。

(b)“股权证券”指：股票；相当于公司股票的其他可转让证券；以及具有下列特征的任何其他类型的可转让证券：该等可转让证券经转换后或其所赋予的权利行使后，持有人将有权购买股票或相当于公司股票的其他可转让证券，前提是此类证券由标的股票的发行人所发行，或由与该等发行人同属一个集团的实体所发行；

(c)“非股权证券”指所有并非股权证券的证券；

(d)“向公众发行证券”指以任何形式和方式向他人传播与要约的条款和待要约证券有关的充分信息，以便投资者决定是否购买或认购该等证券。此定义也适用于通过金融中介机构进行的证券配售。

(e)“合格投资者”指：

(i) legal entities which are authorised or regulated to operate in the financial markets, including: credit institutions, investment firms, other authorised or regulated financial institutions, insurance companies, collective investment schemes and their management companies, pension funds and their management companies, commodity dealers, as well as entities not so authorised or regulated whose corporate purpose is solely to invest in securities;

(ii) national and regional governments, central banks, international and supranational institutions such as the International Monetary Fund, the European Central Bank, the European Investment Bank and other similar international organisations;

(iii) other legal entities which do not meet two of the three criteria set out in paragraph (f);

(iv) certain natural persons: subject to mutual recognition, a Member State may choose to authorise natural persons who are resident in the Member State and who expressly ask to be considered as qualified investors if these persons meet at least two of the criteria set out in paragraph 2;

(v) certain SMEs: subject to mutual recognition, a Member State may choose to authorise SMEs which have their registered office in that Member State and who expressly ask to be considered as qualified investors;

(f) 'small and medium-sized enterprises' means companies, which, according to their last annual or consolidated accounts, meet at least two of the following three criteria: an average number of employees during the financial year of less than 250, a total balance sheet not exceeding EUR 43 000 000 and an annual net turnover not exceeding EUR 50 000 000;

(g) 'credit institution' means an undertaking as defined by Article 1(1)(a) of Directive 2000/12/EC of the European Parliament and of the Council of 20 March 2000 relating to the taking up and pursuit of the business of credit institutions [1];

(h) 'issuer' means a legal entity which issues or proposes to issue securities;

(i) 'person making an offer' (or 'offeror') means a legal entity or individual which offers securities to the public;

(j) 'regulated market' means a market as defined by Article 1(13) of Directive 93/22/EEC;

(k) 'offering programme' means a plan which would permit the issuance of non-equity securities, including warrants in any form, having a similar type and/or class, in a continuous or repeated manner during a specified issuing period;

(l) 'securities issued in a continuous or repeated manner' means issues on tap or at

1 OJ L 126, 26.5.2000, p. 1. Directive as last amended by Directive 000/28/EC (OJ L 275, 27.10.2000, p. 37).

(i)其在金融市场的运营得到核准或受到监管的法律实体，包括：信贷机构、投资公司，其他获核准或受监管的金融机构、保险公司、集合投资计划及其管理公司、养老金及其管理公司、商品交易商，以及未获该等核准或不受该等监管而以证券投资为唯一经营目的的实体；

(ii)国家与地区政府、中央银行以及国际与超国家机构，例如，国际货币基金组织、欧洲中央银行、欧洲投资银行及其他类似的国际组织；

(iii)其他不符合第f项所列3项标准中两项的法律实体；

(iv)某些自然人：在遵守相互承认原则的前提下，成员国可核准居住在该国并明确请求被视为合格投资者的自然人成为合格投资者，但该等自然人应至少符合第2款所列标准中的两项；

(v)某些中小企业：在遵守相互承认原则的前提下，成员国可核准注册地在该国并明确请求被视为合格投资者的中小企业成为合格投资者；

(f)“中小企业”指根据其最新年度或合并财务报表，至少符合下列3项标准中两项的公司：在相应的会计年度，平均雇员人数少于250人，资产负债表总额不超过4300万欧元，且年度净营业额不超过5000万欧元；

(g)“信贷机构”指《欧洲议会与欧盟理事会关于开办和经营信贷机构业务的第2000/12/EC号指令》[1](2000年3月20日)第1条第1款第a项所定义的企业；

(h)“发行人”指发行或拟发行证券的法律实体；

(i)“发出要约的人”(或“要约人”)指向公众发行证券的法律实体或个人；

(j)“受监管市场”指第93/22/EEC号指令第1条第13款所定义的市场；

(k)“发行方案”指类型和/或类别相似的非股权证券(包括任何形式的权证)在规定的发行期间持续或重复发行的计划；

(l)“持续或重复发行的证券”指根据需要随时发行的或在12个月内至少单独发行

1　2000年5月26日《欧盟公报》L126，第1页。该指令由第2000/28/EC号指令(2000年10月27日《欧盟公报》L275，第37页)作出最新修正。

least two separate issues of securities of a similar type and/or class over a period of 12 months;

(m) 'home Member State' means:

(i) for all Community issuers of securities which are not mentioned in (ii) the Member State where the issuer has its registered office;

(ii) for any issues of non-equity securities whose denomination per unit amounts to at least EUR 1 000, and for any issues of non-equity securities giving the right to acquire any transferable securities or to receive a cash amount, as a consequence of their being converted or the rights conferred by them being exercised, provided that the issuer of the non-equity securities is not the issuer of the underlying securities or an entity belonging to the group of the latter issuer, the Member State where the issuer has its registered office, or where the securities were or are to be admitted to trading on a regulated market or where the securities are offered to the public, at the choice of the issuer, the offeror or the person asking for admission, as the case may be. The same regime shall be applicable to non-equity securities in a currency other than euro, provided that the value of such minimum denomination is nearly equivalent to EUR 1 000;

(iii) for all issuers of securities incorporated in a third country, which are not mentioned in (ii) the Member State where the securities are intended to be offered to the public for the first time after the date of entry into force of this Directive or where the first application for admission to trading on a regulated market is made, at the choice of the issuer, the offeror or the person asking for admission, as the case may be, subject to a subsequent election by issuers incorporated in a third country if the home Member State was not determined by their choice;

(n) 'host Member State' means the State where an offer to the public is made or admission to trading is sought, when different from the home Member State;

(o) 'collective investment undertaking other than the closedend type' means unit trusts and investment companies:

(i) the object of which is the collective investment of capital provided by the public, and which operate on the principle of risk-spreading;

(ii) the units of which are, at the holder's request, repurchased or redeemed, directly or indirectly, out of the assets of these undertakings;

(p) 'units of a collective investment undertaking' means securities issued by a collective investment undertaking as representing the rights of the participants in such an undertaking over its assets;

(q) 'approval' means the positive act at the outcome of the scrutiny of the completeness of the prospectus by the home Member State's competent authority including the consistency of the information given and its comprehensibility;

过两次的相似类型和/或类别的证券；

(m)“母国”：

(i)对于所有第ii目中未述及的欧共体证券发行人，母国指发行人注册地所在的成员国；

(ii)对于单位面值最低1000欧元的非股权证券的发行，以及符合特定条件(该证券使其持有人有权购买任何可转让证券，或使其在该证券转让后或在其所赋予的权利行使后可收取一笔现金，前提是该证券的发行人既非标的证券的发行人，也不与后者同属一个集团)的非股权证券的发行，根据发行人、要约人或准入请求人(具体为何者视情况而定)的选择，母国指发行人注册地所在的成员国，或证券已经或即将获准在其受监管市场交易的成员国，或证券向公众发行所在的成员国。同样的制度也适用于非欧元的非股权证券，前提是其最低面值约等值于1000欧元；

(iii)对于第ii目未述及的所有在第三国成立的证券发行人，根据发行人、要约人或准入请求人(具体为何者视情况而定)的选择，母国指本指令生效日后证券拟进行的首次向公众发行所在的成员国，或首次提出在受监管市场证券交易准入申请所在的成员国。但是，母国的认定并非根据在第三国成立的发行人的选择作出的，该发行人可在之后另作选择；

(n)“东道国”，如不同于母国，则指证券在其境内向公众发行的成员国，或申请人寻求在其境内获准交易其证券的成员国；

(o)“非封闭式集合投资计划”指符合以下条件的单位信托基金及投资公司：

(i)其目标是以公众提供的资本进行集合投资，并以风险分散为运营原则；

(ii)其投资单位可应单位持有人的请求直接或间接地从该等计划资产中回购或赎回；

(p)“集合投资计划份额”指由集合投资计划所发行的且代表计划参与者对计划资产的权利的证券；

(q)“批准”指母国主管部门根据对招募说明书完整性(包括所提供信息的一致性和可理解性)的审查结果做出的正面行动；

(r) 'base prospectus' means a prospectus containing all relevant information as specified in Articles 5, 7 and 16 in case there is a supplement, concerning the issuer and the securities to be offered to the public or admitted to trading, and, at the choice of the issuer, the final terms of the offering.

2. For the purposes of paragraph 1(e)(iv) the criteria are as follows:

(a) the investor has carried out transactions of a significant size on securities markets at an average frequency of, at least, 10 per quarter over the previous four quarters;

(b) the size of the investor's securities portfolio exceeds EUR 0.5 million;

(c) the investor works or has worked for at least one year in the financial sector in a professional position which requires knowledge of securities investment.

3. For the purposes of paragraphs 1(e)(iv) and (v) the following shall apply:

Each competent authority shall ensure that appropriate mechanisms are in place for a register of natural persons and SMEs considered as qualified investors, taking into account the need to ensure an adequate level of data protection. The register shall be available to all issuers. Each natural person or SME wishing to be considered as a qualified investor shall register and each registered investor may decide to opt out at any moment.

4. In order to take account of technical developments on financial markets and to ensure uniform application of this Directive, the Commission shall, in accordance with the procedure set out in Article 24(2) adopt implementing measures concerning the definitions referred to in paragraph 1, including adjustment of the figures used for the definition of SMEs, taking into account Community legislation and recommendations as well as economic developments and disclosure measures relating to the registration of individual qualified investors.

Article 3 Obligation to publish a prospectus

1. Member States shall not allow any offer of securities to be made to the public within their territories without prior publication of a prospectus.

2. The obligation to publish a prospectus shall not apply to the following types of offer:

(a) an offer of securities addressed solely to qualified investors; and/or

(b) an offer of securities addressed to fewer than 100 natural or legal persons per Member State, other than qualified investors; and/or

(c) an offer of securities addressed to investors who acquire securities for a total consideration of at least EUR 50 000 per investor, for each separate offer; and/or

(d) an offer of securities whose denomination per unit amounts to at least EUR 50 000; and/or

(e) an offer of securities with a total consideration of less than EUR 100 000, which

(r)“基本招募说明书”指包含第5条、第7条所有相关信息的招募说明书,针对发行人和待向公众发行的证券或待获准交易的证券提供补充文件的,则基本招募说明书还应包含第16条规定的所有相关信息,此外,也可根据发行人的选择纳入要约最终条款的信息;

2.第1款第e项第iv目所涉标准如下:

(a)在前4个季度内,投资者在证券市场达成较大金额交易的频率为每季度至少10次;

(b)投资者的证券组合规模超过50万欧元;

(c)投资者目前或曾经在金融行业的专业职位上工作至少满一年,该职位要求具备证券投资知识。

3.第1款第e项第iv目和第v目适用以下规定:

各主管部门应确保具备对被视为合格投资者的自然人和中小企业进行注册的适当机制,同时还应考虑需做到足够的数据保护。所有发行人均可查阅该注册档案。希望被视为合格投资者的自然人或中小企业均应进行注册,而已注册的投资者可随时自行决定注销注册。

4.为反映金融市场的技术发展动态并确保本指令的统一适用,欧盟委员会应依照第24条第2款所述程序,在考虑到欧共体立法和建议、经济发展以及与合格投资者个人注册相关的披露措施的情形下,就第1款所述定义制定相关实施细则(包括对界定中小企业的数据标准进行调整)。

第3条　公布招募说明书的义务

1.成员国不得允许任何未事先公布招募说明书的证券在其境内向公众发行。

2.下列类型的要约不受公布招募说明书义务的约束:

(a)证券要约只针对合格投资者发出;和/或

(b)每一成员国中的被要约方人数(包括自然人或法人,但不包括合格投资者)不超过100名;和/或

(c)作为被要约方的每名投资者,在每笔要约中购买证券的总对价至少达5万欧元;和/或

(d)证券要约单位面值最低等值于5万欧元;和/或

(e)证券要约总对价少于10万欧元(以12个月为期计算该限额)。

limit shall be calculated over a period of 12 months.

However, any subsequent resale of securities which were previously the subject of one or more of the types of offer mentioned in this paragraph shall be regarded as a separate offer and the definition set out in Article 2 (1)(d) shall apply for the purpose of deciding whether that resale is an offer of securities to the public. The placement of securities through financial intermediaries shall be subject to publication of a prospectus if none of the conditions (a) to (e) are met for the final placement.

3. Member States shall ensure that any admission of securities to trading on a regulated market situated or operating within their territories is subject to the publication of a prospectus.

Article 4 Exemptions from the obligation to publish a prospectus

1. The obligation to publish a prospectus shall not apply to offers of securities to the public of the following types of securities:

(a) shares issued in substitution for shares of the same class already issued, if the issuing of such new shares does not involve any increase in the issued capital;

(b) securities offered in connection with a takeover by means of an exchange offer, provided that a document is available containing information which is regarded by the competent authority as being equivalent to that of the prospectus, taking into account the requirements of Community legislation;

(c) securities offered, allotted or to be allotted in connection with a merger, provided that a document is available containing information which is regarded by the competent authority as being equivalent to that of the prospectus, taking into account the requirements of Community legislation;

(d) shares offered, allotted or to be allotted free of charge to existing shareholders, and dividends paid out in the form of shares of the same class as the shares in respect of which such dividends are paid, provided that a document is made available containing information on the number and nature of the shares and the reasons for and details of the offer;

(e) securities offered, allotted or to be allotted to existing or former directors or employees by their employer which has securities already admitted to trading on a regulated market or by an affiliated undertaking, provided that a document is made available containing information on the number and nature of the securities and the reasons for and details of the offer.

2. The obligation to publish a prospectus shall not apply to the admission to trading on a regulated market of the following types of securities:

(a) shares representing, over a period of 12 months, less than 10 per cent of the number of shares of the same class already admitted to trading on the same regulated

然而,本款所述的一个或多个类型要约所涉标的证券,如在要约后进行转售,则该转售应被视为一笔单独的要约,在该情形下,判定转售是否属于向公众发行证券时,应适用第2条第1款第d项的定义。通过金融中介机构配售证券的,如果最终配售并不满足本款第a项到第e项的条件,则应公布招募说明书。

3.成员国应确保,获准进入位于其境内的或在其境内运行的受监管市场交易的证券,都应受公布招募说明书义务的约束。

第4条　公布招募说明书义务的豁免

1.下列类型的证券向公众发行,不受公布招募说明书义务的约束:

(a)所涉股票发行的目的是取代已发行的同一类别股票,前提是发行上述新股不会造成已发行股本的增加;

(b)收购交易中以交换要约方式进行要约的证券,前提是所提供的文件含有主管部门认为与招募说明书等效(和欧共体立法的要求相比)的信息;

(c)兼并交易中所要约、配售或待配售的证券,前提是所提供的文件含有主管部门认为与招募说明书等效(和欧共体立法的要求相比)的信息;

(d)向现有股东免费要约、配售或待配售的股票,该股票的股息以同一类别的股票来支付,前提是所提供的文件含有该股票数量和性质以及要约的理由和详情;

(e)已获准在受监管市场交易证券的雇主或关联企业,向现任或前任董事或雇员要约、配售或待配售的证券,前提是所提供的文件说明了该等证券的数量和性质以及要约的理由和详情;

2.下列类型证券请求获准在受监管市场交易时,不受公布招募说明书义务的约束:

(a)申请核准的股票在12个月内的要约数量,少于已获准在同一受监管市场交易的与其同一类别的股票数量的10%;

market;

(b) shares issued in substitution for shares of the same class already admitted to trading on the same regulated market, if the issuing of such shares does not involve any increase in the issued capital;

(c) securities offered in connection with a takeover by means of an exchange offer, provided that a document is available containing information which is regarded by the competent authority as being equivalent to that of the prospectus, taking into account the requirements of Community legislation;

(d) securities offered, allotted or to be allotted in connection with a merger, provided that a document is available containing information which is regarded by the competent authority as being equivalent to that of the prospectus, taking into account the requirements of Community legislation;

(e) shares offered, allotted or to be allotted free of charge to existing shareholders, and dividends paid out in the form of shares of the same class as the shares in respect of which such dividends are paid, provided that the said shares are of the same class as the shares already admitted to trading on the same regulated market and that a document is made available containing information on the number and nature of the shares and the reasons for and details of the offer;

(f) securities offered, allotted or to be allotted to existing or former directors or employees by their employer or an affiliated undertaking, provided that the said securities are of the same class as the securities already admitted to trading on the same regulated market and that a document is made available containing information on the number and nature of the securities and the reasons for and detail of the offer;

(g) shares resulting from the conversion or exchange of other securities or from the exercise of the rights conferred by other securities, provided that the said shares are of the same class as the shares already admitted to trading on the same regulated market;

(h) securities already admitted to trading on another regulated market, on the following conditions:

(i) that these securities, or securities of the same class, have been admitted to trading on that other regulated market for more than 18 months;

(ii) that, for securities first admitted to trading on a regulated market after the date of entry into force of this Directive, the admission to trading on that other regulated market was associated with an approved prospectus made available to the public in conformity with Article 14;

(iii) that, except where (ii) applies, for securities first admitted to listing after 30 June 1983, listing particulars were approved in accordance with the requirements of Directive 80/390/EEC or Directive 2001/34/ EC;

(b)股票发行的目的是取代已获准在同一受监管市场交易的同一类别股票，前提是发行上述新股不会造成已发行股本的增加；

(c)收购交易中以交换要约方式进行要约的证券，前提是所提供的文件含有主管部门认为与招募说明书等效(和欧共体立法的要求相比)的信息；

(d)兼并交易中所要约、配售或待配售的证券，前提是所提供的文件含有主管部门认为与招募说明书等效(和欧共体立法的要求相比)的信息；

(e)向现有股东免费要约、配售或待配售的股票，该股票的股息以同一类别的股票来支付，前提是上述股票与获准在同一受监管市场交易的股票属于同一类别，且所提供的文件含有该股票的数量和性质以及要约的理由和详情；

(f)雇主或关联企业向现任或前任董事或雇员要约、配售或待配售的证券，前提是上述证券与获准在同一受监管市场交易的股票属于同一类别，且所提供的文件说明了该等股票的数量和性质以及要约的理由和详情；

(g) 由于其他证券的转换或交换或其他证券所赋予权利的行使而产生的股票，前提是上述股票与已获准在同一受监管市场交易的股票属于同一类别；

(h)符合下列条件的已获准在另一受监管市场交易的证券：

(i)该等证券或与其同一类别的证券已获准在该另一受监管市场交易达18个月以上；

(ii)对于在本指令生效后首次获准在某一受监管市场交易的证券，其获准在该另一受监管市场交易时已依照第14条的规定向公众公布了获得批准的招募说明书；

(iii)除了适用第ii目的情形外，在1983年6月30日以后首次获准上市的证券，其上市具体信息已根据第80/390/EEC号指令或第2001/34/EC号指令获得批准；

(iv) that the ongoing obligations for trading on that other regulated market have been fulfilled;

(v) that the person seeking the admission of a security to trading on a regulated market under this exemption makes a summary document available to the public in a language accepted by the competent authority of the Member State of the regulated market where admission is sought;

(vi) that the summary document referred to in (v) is made available to the public in the Member State of the regulated market where admission to trading is sought in the manner set out in Article 14(2); and

(vii) that the contents of the summary document shall comply with Article 5(2). Furthermore the document shall state where the most recent prospectus can be obtained and where the financial information published by the issuer pursuant to his ongoing disclosure obligations is available.

3. In order to take account of technical developments on financial markets and to ensure uniform application of this Directive, the Commission shall, in accordance with the procedure referred to in Article 24(2) adopt implementing measures concerning paragraphs 1(b) 1(c) 2(c) and 2(d) notably in relation to the meaning of equivalence.

CHAPTER II DRAWING UP OF THE PROSPECTUS

Article 5 The prospectus

1. Without prejudice to Article 8(2) the prospectus shall contain all information which, according to the particular nature of the issuer and of the securities offered to the public or admitted to trading on a regulated market, is necessary to enable investors to make an informed assessment of the assets and liabilities, financial position, profit and losses, and prospects of the issuer and of any guarantor, and of the rights attaching to such securities. This information shall be presented in an easily analysable and comprehensible form.

2. The prospectus shall contain information concerning the issuer and the securities to be offered to the public or to be admitted to trading on a regulated market. It shall also include a summary. The summary shall, in a brief manner and in nontechnical language, convey the essential characteristics and risks associated with the issuer, any guarantor and the securities, in the language in which the prospectus was originally drawn up. The summary shall also contain a warning that:

(a) it should be read as an introduction to the prospectus;

(b) any decision to invest in the securities should be based on consideration of the prospectus as a whole by the investor;

(c) where a claim relating to the information contained in a prospectus is brought

(iv)为在该另一受监管市场交易所承担的持续义务得到履行；

(v)寻求依赖此项豁免获得准入受监管市场交易证券的人，向公众公布一份摘要文件，且该文件以其寻求准入的受监管市场所在成员国主管部门能接受的语言撰写；

(vi)第v目所述摘要文件按第14条第2款规定的方式，向其寻求准入的受监管市场所在成员国的公众公布；及

(vii)摘要文件内容应符合第5条第2款的规定。此外，该文件应说明获取最新的招募说明书的渠道，以及于何处可查阅发行人根据其持续披露义务所公布的财务信息。

3.为反映金融市场的技术发展动态并确保本指令的统一适用，欧盟委员会应依照第24条第2款所述程序，就第1款第b项、第1款第c项、第2款第c项及第2款第d项制定相关实施细则，特别是针对"等效"的含义制定相关实施细则。

第二章 招募说明书的编制

第5条 招募说明书

1.在不影响第8条第2款的情形下，招募说明书应根据发行人的特性以及证券向公众发行或获准在受监管市场交易的特性，涵盖所有必要的信息，以使投资者能对发行人和任何担保人的资产与负债、财务状况、损益和前景以及证券所附带的权利作出知情评估。该等信息应以易于分析和理解的形式列报。

2.招募说明书应包含有关发行人以及待向公众发行或待获准在受监管市场交易的证券的信息。招募说明书还应包括一份摘要。摘要应以最初编制招募说明书时所使用的非技术性语言简要传达发行人、任何担保人以及证券的基本特征与风险。摘要还应包含下列警示：

(a)摘要应被理解为对招募说明书的介绍；
(b)任何投资证券的决定，均应基于投资者对招募说明书全文的考虑作出；

(c)如就招募说明书中的信息向法院提起权利主张，根据成员国国内立法，原告投

before a court, the plaintiff investor might, under the national legislation of the Member States, have to bear the costs of translating the prospectus before the legal proceedings are initiated; and

(d) civil liability attaches to those persons who have tabled the summary including any translation thereof, and applied for its notification, but only if the summary is misleading, inaccurate or inconsistent when read together with the other parts of the prospectus.

Where the prospectus relates to the admission to trading on a regulated market of non-equity securities having a denomination of at least EUR 50 000, there shall be no requirement to provide a summary except when requested by a Member State as provided for in Article 19(4).

3. Subject to paragraph 4, the issuer, offeror or person asking for the admission to trading on a regulated market may draw up the prospectus as a single document or separate documents. A prospectus composed of separate documents shall divide the required information into a registration document, a securities note and a summary note. The registration document shall contain the information relating to the issuer. The securities note shall contain the information concerning the securities offered to the public or to be admitted to trading on a regulated market.

4. For the following types of securities, the prospectus can, at the choice of the issuer, offeror or person asking for the admission to trading on a regulated market consist of a base prospectus containing all relevant information concerning the issuer and the securities offered to the public or to be admitted to trading on a regulated market:

(a) non-equity securities, including warrants in any form, issued under an offering programme;

(b) non-equity securities issued in a continuous or repeated manner by credit institutions,

(i) where the sums deriving from the issue of the said securities, under national legislation, are placed in assets which provide sufficient coverage for the liability deriving from securities until their maturity date;

(ii) where, in the event of the insolvency of the related credit institution, the said sums are intended, as a priority, to repay the capital and interest falling due, without prejudice to the provisions of Directive 2001/24/EC of the European Parliament and of the Council of 4 April 2001 on the reorganisation and winding up of credit institutions.[1]

The information given in the base prospectus shall be supplemented, if necessary, in accordance with Article 16, with updated information on the issuer and on the securities to be offered to the public or to be admitted to trading on a regulated market.

1 OJ L 125, 5.5.2001, p. 15.

资者可能应在法律诉讼程序开始前承担招募说明书的翻译费用;及

(d)编制摘要(包括其任何译文)并申请对该摘要作出相关通知的人,只有当结合招募说明书其他部分理解,摘要具有误导性、不正确或不一致时才承担民事责任。

面值最低5万欧元的非股权证券请求获准在受监管市场交易所应公布的招募说明书,不必提供摘要,除非成员国根据第19条第4款的规定提出该等要求。

3.在遵守第4款规定的前提下,发行人、要约人或请求获准在受监管市场交易其证券的人,可编制仅由一份单一文件构成的招募说明书,或由多份独立文件组成的招募说明书。由多份独立文件组成的招募说明书应将所需包含的信息分为注册文件、证券说明及摘要说明3份文件。注册文件应包含与发行人相关的信息。证券说明应包含与向公众发行的证券或待获准在受监管市场交易的证券相关的信息。

4.下列类型证券的发行人、要约人或请求获准在受监管市场交易的人,可以选择招募说明书仅由一份基本招募说明书构成,该基本招募说明书包含与发行人以及向公众发行的证券或待获准在受监管市场交易的证券相关的所有信息;

(a)根据发行方案发行的非股权证券,包括任何形式的权证;

(b)下列情形中,由信贷机构持续或重复发行的非股权证券,

(i)根据成员国国内立法,发行上述证券所得各项金额记入资产,而该等资产能为证券于到期日前产生的债务提供足够的担保;

(ii)在不影响《欧洲议会与欧盟理事会关于信贷机构的重组和停业清理的第2001/24/EC号指令》[1](2001年4月4日)的规定的情形下,相关信贷机构资不抵债的,上述各项金额将优先用于偿还到期的本金与利息。

如有必要,应根据第16条的规定,在基本招募说明书中补充关于发行人、待向公众发行或待获准在受监管市场交易的证券的最新信息。

1 2001年5月5日《欧盟公报》L125,第15页。

If the final terms of the offer are not included in either the base prospectus or a supplement, the final terms shall be provided to investors and filed with the competent authority when each public offer is made as soon as practicable and if possible in advance of the beginning of the offer. The provisions of Article 8(1)(a) shall be applicable in any such case.

5. In order to take account of technical developments on financial markets and to ensure uniform application of this Directive, the Commission shall, in accordance with the procedure referred to in Article 24(2) adopt implementing measures concerning the format of the prospectus or base prospectus and supplements.

Article 6 Responsibility attaching to the prospectus

1. Member States shall ensure that responsibility for the information given in a prospectus attaches at least to the issuer or its administrative, management or supervisory bodies, the offeror, the person asking for the admission to trading on a regulated market or the guarantor, as the case may be. The persons responsible shall be clearly identified in the prospectus by their names and functions or, in the case of legal persons, their names and registered offices, as well as declarations by them that, to the best of their knowledge, the information contained in the prospectus is in accordance with the facts and that the prospectus makes no omission likely to affect its import.

2. Member States shall ensure that their laws, regulation and administrative provisions on civil liability apply to those persons responsible for the information given in a prospectus.

However, Member States shall ensure that no civil liability shall attach to any person solely on the basis of the summary, including any translation thereof, unless it is misleading, inaccurate or inconsistent when read together with the other parts of the prospectus.

Article 7 Minimum information

1. Detailed implementing measures regarding the specific information which must be included in a prospectus, avoiding duplication of information when a prospectus is composed of separate documents, shall be adopted by the Commission in accordance with the procedure referred to in Article 24(2) . The first set of implementing measures shall be adopted by 1 July 2004.

2. In particular, for the elaboration of the various models of prospectuses, account shall be taken of the following:

(a) the various types of information needed by investors relating to equity securities as compared with non-equity securities; a consistent approach shall be taken with regard to information required in a prospectus for securities which have a similar economic rationale, notably derivative securities;

最终的要约条款并未包括在基本招募说明书或补充文件中的，每次公开发行时均应将最终的要约条款尽早提供给投资者，并提交主管部门，如有可能，应在要约开始前提供。任何上述情形下均可适用第8条第1款第a项的规定。

5.为反映金融市场的技术发展动态并确保本指令的统一适用，欧盟委员会应依照第24条第2款所述程序，就招募说明书或基本招募说明书与补充文件的格式制定相关实施细则。

第6条　与招募说明书相关的责任

1.成员国应确保，招募说明书所含信息的相关责任至少由下列主体承担（具体指何者视情况而定）：发行人或其董事会、管理机构或监事会；要约人；请求获准在受监管市场交易其证券的人；或担保人。招募说明书中应清楚标明责任人的姓名与职能或（如责任人为法人）名称和注册地以及责任人所做声明，以表明据责任人所知，招募说明书所含信息与事实相符、不存在可能影响其含义的任何疏漏。

2.成员国应确保，其关于民事责任的法律、法规和规章适用于对招募说明书中的信息负责的人。

然而，成员国应确保，除非结合招募说明书其他部分理解，摘要具有误导性、不正确或不一致，否则不得仅以摘要（包括相关译文）为依据而使任何人承担民事责任。

第7条　必不可少的信息

1.欧盟委员会应依照第24条第2款所述程序，就招募说明书应包含的具体信息制定详细的实施细则，在招募说明书由多份独立文件组成的情形下，该等实施细则可以避免不同文件信息的重复。应于2004年7月1日前制定首套实施细则。

2.尤其是，制定招募说明书的各种模板时：

（a）关于股权证券：应考虑投资者需要哪些类型信息（相对于非股权证券而言）；对具有类似经济原理的不同证券（特别是衍生证券）的招募说明书，应采取一致的模式来确定其应包含的信息；

(b) the various types and characteristics of offers and admissions to trading on a regulated market of non-equity securities. The information required in a prospectus shall be appropriate from the point of view of the investors concerned for non-equity securities having a denomination per unit of at least EUR 50 000;

(c) the format used and the information required in prospectuses relating to non-equity securities, including warrants in any form, issued under an offering programme;

(d) the format used and the information required in prospectuses relating to non-equity securities, in so far as these securities are not subordinated, convertible, exchangeable, subject to subscription or acquisition rights or linked to derivative instruments, issued in a continuous or repeated manner by entities authorised or regulated to operate in the financial markets within the European Economic Area;

(e) the various activities and size of the issuer, in particular SMEs. For such companies the information shall be adapted to their size and, where appropriate, to their shorter track record;

(f) if applicable, the public nature of the issuer.

3. The implementing measures referred to in paragraph 1 shall be based on the standards in the field of financial and non-financial information set out by international securities commission organisations, and in particular by IOSCO and on the indicative Annexes to this Directive.

Article 8 Omission of information

1. Member States shall ensure that where the final offer price and amount of securities which will be offered to the public cannot be included in the prospectus:

(a) the criteria, and/or the conditions in accordance with which the above elements will be determined or, in the case of price, the maximum price, are disclosed in the prospectus; or

(b) the acceptances of the purchase or subscription of securities may be withdrawn for not less than two working days after the final offer price and amount of securities which will be offered to the public have been filed.

The final offer price and amount of securities shall be filed with the competent authority of the home Member State and published in accordance with the arrangements provided for in Article 14(2).

2. The competent authority of the home Member State may authorise the omission from the prospectus of certain information provided for in this Directive or in the implementing measures referred to in Article 7(1) if it considers that:

(a) disclosure of such information would be contrary to the public interest; or

(b) disclosure of such information would be seriously detrimental to the issuer, provided that the omission would not be likely to mislead the public with regard to facts

(b)关于非股权证券:应考虑不同类型的要约和不同类型的受监管市场交易准入,及其相应的特征。在判断要求招募说明书所应包含的信息是否适当时,应从单位面值最低5万欧元的非股权证券投资者的角度来衡量;

(c)应考虑根据发行方案发行的非股权证券(包括任何形式的权证)的招募说明书所采用的格式和所应包含的信息;

(d)应考虑非股权证券的招募说明书所采用的格式和所应包含的信息,只要该等证券不属于下列情形:次级证券;可转换;可交换;赋予持有人认购权;赋予持有人收购权;与衍生品工具相挂钩;由在欧洲经济区金融市场运营的获核准实体或受监管实体持续或重复发行;

(e)应考虑发行人(特别是中小企业)的各种活动与规模。对该等公司而言,信息应与其规模和较短的经营记录(如适用)相适应;

(f)应考虑发行人的公共属性(如适用)。

3.第1款所述实施细则应以国际证券委员会组织,尤其是国际证监会组织(IOSCO)规定的金融与非金融信息领域的标准,以及本指令的指示性附录为基础。

第8条　不包含的信息

1.成员国应确保在下列情形下,招募说明书中不得包含待向公众发行的证券的最终要约价格与数量:

(a)招募说明书中披露了决定上述要素所依据的标准和/或条件或最高价格;或

(b)待向公众发行的证券最终要约价格和数量提交后至少两个工作日内,发行人可撤销对证券购买或认购的接受。

证券的最终要约价格和数量应提交母国主管部门,并根据第14条第2款规定的安排予以公布。

2.母国主管部门可许可在招募说明书中省略本指令或其第7条第1款所述实施细则规定的某些信息,如果该主管部门认为:

(a)该等信息的披露违反公共利益;或

(b)该等信息的披露会对发行人造成严重损害,前提是省略该等信息不太可能就下列内容误导公众:对发行人、要约人或担保人(如有)以及招募说明书中的证券赋予

and circumstances essential for an informed assessment of the issuer, offeror or guarantor, if any, and of the rights attached to the securities to which the prospectus relates; or

(c) such information is of minor importance only for a specific offer or admission to trading on a regulated market and is not such as will influence the assessment of the financial position and prospects of the issuer, offeror or guarantor, if any.

3. Without prejudice to the adequate information of investors, where, exceptionally, certain information required by implementing measures referred to in Article 7(1) to be included in a prospectus is inappropriate to the issuer's sphere of activity or to the legal form of the issuer or to the securities to which the prospectus relates, the prospectus shall contain information equivalent to the required information. If there is no such information, this requirement shall not apply.

4. In order to take account of technical developments on financial markets and to ensure uniform application of this Directive, the Commission shall, in accordance with the procedure referred to in Article 24(2) adopt implementing measures concerning paragraph 2.

Article 9 Validity of a prospectus, base prospectus and registration document

1. A prospectus shall be valid for 12 months after its publication for offers to the public or admissions to trading on a regulated market, provided that the prospectus is completed by any supplements required pursuant to Article 16.

2. In the case of an offering programme, the base prospectus, previously filed, shall be valid for a period of up to 12 months.

3. In the case of non-equity securities referred to in Article 5(4)(b) the prospectus shall be valid until no more of the securities concerned are issued in a continuous or repeated manner.

4. A registration document, as referred to in Article 5(3) previously filed, shall be valid for a period of up to 12 months provided that it has been updated in accordance with Article 10(1). The registration document accompanied by the securities note, updated if applicable in accordance with Article 12, and the summary note shall be considered to constitute a valid prospectus.

Article 10 Information

1. Issuers whose securities are admitted to trading on a regulated market shall at least annually provide a document that contains or refers to all information that they have published or made available to the public over the preceding 12 months in one or more Member States and in third countries in compliance with their obligations under Community and national laws and rules dealing with the regulation of securities, issuers of securities and securities markets. Issuers shall refer at least to the information required pursuant to company law directives, Directive 2001/34/EC and Regulation (EC) No 1606/

的权利作出知情评估至关重要的事实和情况；或

(c)该等信息对特定要约或获准在受监管市场交易而言属于次要信息，并不会影响对发行人、要约人或担保人(如有)财务状况与前景的评估。

3.在不影响提供给投资者的充分信息的情况下，如出现下述特例情形，则招募说明书应以等效的信息替代要求提供的信息：即第7条第1款所述实施细则规定的招募说明书应包含的某些信息，考虑到发行人的活动领域、发行人的法律形式或招募说明书中的证券的特殊性，公开披露不适当。不存在该等特例信息的，本项规定不适用。

4.为反映金融市场的技术发展动态并确保本指令的统一适用，欧盟委员会应依照第24条第2款所述程序，就第2款制定相关实施细则。

第9条　招募说明书的效力、基本招募说明书与注册文件

1.通过第16条规定的补充文件予以完善后，向公众发行证券或为获准在受监管市场交易证券所应公布的招募说明书应在其公布后生效，有效期为12个月。

2.对于发行方案，先前提交的基本招募说明书的有效期最多为12个月。

3.对于第5条第4款第b项所述的非股权证券，招募说明书的有效期截至该等证券不再持续或重复发行。

4.第5条第3款所述的先前提交的注册文件，如根据第10条第1款完成了更新，其有效期最长可为12个月。附证券说明的注册文件(如适用，已根据第12条更新)以及摘要说明应被视为有效的招募说明书的一部分。

第10条　信息

1. 获准在受监管市场交易其证券的发行人应至少每年提供一次包含或提及下列信息的一份清单性质的文件：发行人基于欧共体及成员国关于证券、证券发行人和证券市场监管的法律和规则中所规定的义务，于前12个月在一个或多个成员国以及第三国所公布的或向公众提供的所有信息。发行人在该文件中应至少提及公司法指令、第2001/34/EC号指令以及《欧洲议会与欧盟理事会关于适用国际会计准则的第1606/

2002 of the European Parliament and of the Council of 19 July 2002 on the application of international accounting standards [1].

2. The document shall be filed with the competent authority of the home Member State after the publication of the financial statement. Where the document refers to information, it shall be stated where the information can be obtained.

3. The obligation set out in paragraph 1 shall not apply to issuers of non-equity securities whose denomination per unit amounts to at least EUR 50 000.

4. In order to take account of technical developments on financial markets and to ensure uniform application of this Directive, the Commission may, in accordance with the procedure referred to in Article 24 (2) adopt implementing measures concerning paragraph 1. These measures will relate only to the method of publication of the disclosure requirements mentioned in paragraph 1 and will not entail new disclosure requirements. The first set of implementing measures shall be adopted by 1 July 2004.

Article 11 Incorporation by reference

1. Member States shall allow information to be incorporated in the prospectus by reference to one or more previously or simultaneously published documents that have been approved by the competent authority of the home Member State or filed with it in accordance with this Directive, in particular pursuant to Article 10, or with Titles IV and V of Directive 2001/34/EC. This information shall be the latest available to the issuer. The summary shall not incorporate information by reference.

2. When information is incorporated by reference, a cross-reference list must be provided in order to enable investors to identify easily specific items of information.

3. In order to take account of technical developments on financial markets and to ensure uniform application of this Directive, the Commission shall, in accordance with the procedure referred to in Article 24 (2) adopt implementing measures concerning the information to be incorporated by reference. The first set of implementing measures shall be adopted by 1 July 2004.

Article 12 Prospectuses consisting of separate documents

1. An issuer which already has a registration document approved by the competent authority shall be required to draw up only the securities note and the summary note when securities are offered to the public or admitted to trading on a regulated market.

2. In this case, the securities note shall provide information that would normally be provided in the registration document if there has been a material change or recent development which could affect investors' assessments since the latest updated registration document or any supplement as provided for in Article 16 was approved. The securities and summary notes shall be subject to a separate approval.

1 OJ L 243, 11.9.2002, p. 1.

2002号(欧共体)条例》[1](2002年7月19日)所要求公布或提供的信息。

2.该等文件应于财务报表公布后提交给母国主管部门。该等文件提及上述信息时,应说明在何处可获得相关信息。

3.第1款中所规定的义务不适用于单位面值最低5万欧元的非股权证券发行人。

4.为反映金融市场的技术发展动态并确保本指令的统一适用,欧盟委员会可依照第24条第2款所述程序,就第1款制定相关实施细则。此等细则仅涉及第1款要求披露的信息的公布方法,并不涉及新的披露要求。应于2004年7月1日前制定首套实施细则。

第11条　以引用的方式纳入

1.成员国应允许招募说明书通过引用一份或多份已于先前发布的或同时发布的文件,纳入相关信息。这些文件应已由母国主管部门批准,或根据本指令(特别是第10条)或第2001/34/EC号指令第四编和第五编已提交母国主管部门。该等信息应为发行人可获得的最新信息。摘要不得通过引用的方式纳入相关信息。

2.以引用的方式纳入相关信息时应提供交叉引用信息清单,以便投资者能轻易识别具体的引用信息。

3.为反映金融市场的技术发展动态并确保本指令的统一适用,欧盟委员会应依照第24条第2款所述程序,就引用的信息制定相关实施细则。应于2004年7月1日前制定首套实施细则。

第12条　由多份独立文件组成的招募说明书

1.发行人注册文件已获主管部门批准的,其证券向公众发行或获准在受监管市场交易时,只需要编制证券说明和摘要说明。

2.在下述情形下,证券说明应提供注册文件一般会提供的信息:自最新的注册文件或根据第16条补充的任何文件获得批准后,发生了可能会影响投资者评估的重大变化或最新发展。该等证券说明与摘要说明应另行获得批准。

1　2002年9月11日《欧盟公报》L243,第1页。

3. Where an issuer has only filed a registration document without approval, the entire documentation, including updated information, shall be subject to approval.

CHAPTER III ARRANGEMENTS FOR APPROVAL AND PUBLICATION OF THE PROSPECTUS

Article 13 Approval of the prospectus

1. No prospectus shall be published until it has been approved by the competent authority of the home Member State.

2. This competent authority shall notify the issuer, the offeror or the person asking for admission to trading on a regulated market, as the case may be, of its decision regarding the approval of the prospectus within 10 working days of the submission of the draft prospectus.

If the competent authority fails to give a decision on the prospectus within the time limits laid down in this paragraph and paragraph 3, this shall not be deemed to constitute approval of the application.

3. The time limit referred to in paragraph 2 shall be extended to 20 working days if the public offer involves securities issued by an issuer which does not have any securities admitted to trading on a regulated market and who has not previously offered securities to the public.

4. If the competent authority finds, on reasonable grounds, that the documents submitted to it are incomplete or that supplementary information is needed, the time limits referred to in paragraphs 2 and 3 shall apply only from the date on which such information is provided by the issuer, the offeror or the person asking for admission to trading on a regulated market.

In the case referred to in paragraph 2 the competent authority should notify the issuer if the documents are incomplete within 10 working days of the submission of the application.

5. The competent authority of the home Member State may transfer the approval of a prospectus to the competent authority of another Member State, subject to the agreement of that authority. Furthermore, this transfer shall be notified to the issuer, the offeror or the person asking for admission to trading on a regulated market within three working days from the date of the decision taken by the competent authority of the home Member State. The time limit referred to in paragraph 2 shall apply from that date.

6. This Directive shall not affect the competent authority's liability, which shall continue to be governed solely by national law.

Member States shall ensure that their national provisions on the liability of competent authorities apply only to approvals of prospectuses by their competent authority or

3.发行人只提交了未经批准的注册文件的，含有更新信息的整套文件均须经主管部门批准。

第三章 招募说明书的批准与公布安排

第13条 招募说明书的批准

1.未经母国主管部门批准的招募说明书不得公布。

2.母国主管部门应于招募说明书草案呈报后10个工作日内，根据实际情形向发行人、要约人或请求获准在受监管市场交易其证券的人（具体为何者视情况而定）发出通知，告知其对招募说明书的批准决定。

主管部门未在本款和第3款规定的时限内作出与招募说明书相关的决定的，申请不得被视为已获批准。

3.公开发行证券的发行人从未获得在受监管市场的证券交易准入，并且之前没有向公众发行过证券的，第2款所述时限可以延长至20个工作日。

4.主管部门基于合理的理由认定，向其呈报的文件不完整或需补充信息的，第2款及第3款所述的时限仅从发行人、要约人或请求获准在受监管市场交易其证券的人提供该等信息之日起适用。

在第2款所述情形下，文件不完整的，主管部门应于申请呈报后10个工作日内通知发行人。

5.经另一成员国主管部门同意，母国主管部门可将招募说明书的批准权委托给该另一成员国主管部门。母国主管部门作此决定后3个工作日内，应通知发行人、要约人或请求获准在受监管市场交易其证券的人该项委托授权。第2款所述时限自该日起适用。

6.本指令不对主管部门的法律责任造成任何影响，主管部门继续仅受成员国国内法律管辖。

成员国应确保，其关于主管部门法律责任的国内规定只适用于该国一个或多个主管部门对招募说明书的批准。

authorities.

7. In order to take account of technical developments on financial markets and to ensure uniform application of this Directive, the Commission may, in accordance with the procedure referred to in Article 24 (2) adopt implementing measures concerning the conditions in accordance with which time limits may be adjusted.

Article 14 Publication of the prospectus

1. Once approved, the prospectus shall be filed with the competent authority of the home Member State and shall be made available to the public by the issuer, offeror or person asking for admission to trading on a regulated market as soon as practicable and in any case, at a reasonable time in advance of, and at the latest at the beginning of, the offer to the public or the admission to trading of the securities involved. In addition, in the case of an initial public offer of a class of shares not already admitted to trading on a regulated market that is to be admitted to trading for the first time, the prospectus shall be available at least six working days before the end of the offer.

2. The prospectus shall be deemed available to the public when published either:

(a) by insertion in one or more newspapers circulated throughout, or widely circulated in, the Member States in which the offer to the public is made or the admission to trading is sought; or

(b) in a printed form to be made available, free of charge, to the public at the offices of the market on which the securities are being admitted to trading, or at the registered office of the issuer and at the offices of the financial intermediaries placing or selling the securities, including paying agents; or

(c) in an electronic form on the issuer's website and, if applicable, on the website of the financial intermediaries placing or selling the securities, including paying agents; or

(d) in an electronic form on the website of the regulated market where the admission to trading is sought; or

(e) in electronic form on the website of the competent authority of the home Member State if the said authority has decided to offer this service.

A home Member State may require issuers which publish their prospectus in accordance with (a) or (b) also to publish their prospectus in an electronic form in accordance with (c).

3. In addition, a home Member State may require publication of a notice stating how the prospectus has been made available and where it can be obtained by the public.

4. The competent authority of the home Member State shall publish on its website over a period of 12 months, at its choice, all the prospectuses approved, or at least the list of prospectuses approved in accordance with Article 13, including, if applicable, a hyperlink to the prospectus published on the website of the issuer, or on the website of

7.为反映金融市场的技术发展动态并确保本指令的统一适用,欧盟委员会应*依照第24条第2款所述程序,就时限调整的条件制定相关实施细则。

第14条　招募说明书的公布

1.招募说明书一经批准即应提交给母国主管部门,并由发行人、要约人或请求获准在受监管市场交易其证券的人在切实可行的范围内尽快向公众公布，公布时间应在所涉证券向公众发行或获准交易之前的合理时间内（最晚不得迟于向公众发行或获准交易之时）。此外,首次公开发行从未获准在受监管市场交易的某类别股票的,其首次获准交易时,招募说明书应在要约结束前至少提前6个工作日公布。

2.招募说明书以下列任何一种方式公布时,应被视为已向公众提供:

(a)在下述成员国全境内流通或在其境内广泛流通的一份或多份报纸上公布:证券在其境内向公众发行的成员国,或申请人寻求在其境内获准交易其证券的成员国;或

(b)在证券获准交易的市场的办公地点,或在发行人的注册地,以及在配售或出售证券的金融中介机构(包括代理付款人)的办公地点,以印刷品形式免费向公众提供;或

(c)在发行人的网站及配售或出售证券的金融中介机构(包括代理付款人)的网站(如有)上,以电子文件形式公布;或

(d)在收到核准证券交易的请求的受监管市场的网站上,以电子文件形式公布;或

(e)在母国主管部门的网站上以电子文件形式公布,如其决定提供此项公布招募说明书的服务。

母国可以要求按第a项或第b项公布招募说明书的发行人,除报纸或印刷品外还依第c项以电子文件形式公布招募说明书。

3.此外,母国可要求公布一份通知,说明招募说明书已按何种方式提供以及公众可于何处获取。

4.母国主管部门应于其网站上公布所有获得批准的招募说明书,或者至少公布清单列明按第13条获得批准的所有招募说明书,究竟采用何者由主管部门自行决定,其中应包括链接到公布于发行人网站或受监管市场网站的招募说明书的超链接（如适

---

* 英文为may,但文中其他相同表述为shall,疑误,译文已按shall处理。——译者注

the regulated market.

5. In the case of a prospectus comprising several documents and/or incorporating information by reference, the documents and information making up the prospectus may be published and circulated separately provided that the said documents are made available, free of charge, to the public, in accordance with the arrangements established in paragraph 2. Each document shall indicate where the other constituent documents of the full prospectus may be obtained.

6. The text and the format of the prospectus, and/or the supplements to the prospectus, published or made available to the public, shall at all times be identical to the original version approved by the competent authority of the home Member State.

7. Where the prospectus is made available by publication in electronic form, a paper copy must nevertheless be delivered to the investor, upon his request and free of charge, by the issuer, the offeror, the person asking for admission to trading or the financial intermediaries placing or selling the securities.

8. In order to take account of technical developments on financial markets and to ensure uniform application of the Directive, the Commission shall, in accordance with the procedure referred to in Article 24 (2) adopt implementing measures concerning paragraphs 1, 2, 3 and 4. The first set of implementing measures shall be adopted by 1 July 2004.

Article 15 Advertisements

1. Any type of advertisements relating either to an offer to the public of securities or to an admission to trading on a regulated market shall observe the principles contained in paragraphs 2 to 5. Paragraphs 2 to 4 shall apply only to cases where the issuer, the offeror or the person applying for admission to trading is covered by the obligation to draw up a prospectus.

2. Advertisements shall state that a prospectus has been or will be published and indicate where investors are or will be able to obtain it.

3. Advertisements shall be clearly recognisable as such. The information contained in an advertisement shall not be inaccurate, or misleading. This information shall also be consistent with the information contained in the prospectus, if already published, or with the information required to be in the prospectus, if the prospectus is published afterwards.

4. In any case, all information concerning the offer to the public or the admission to trading on a regulated market disclosed in an oral or written form, even if not for advertising purposes, shall be consistent with that contained in the prospectus.

5. When according to this Directive no prospectus is required, material information provided by an issuer or an offeror and addressed to qualified investors or special categories of investors, including information disclosed in the context of meetings relating

用)，公布期应为12个月。

5.对于由多份文件组成的招募说明书，和/或以引用的方式纳入相关信息的招募说明书，其构成文件与信息可与招募说明书分开公布和流通，前提是应根据第2款的安排免费向公众提供。每份文件均应指出可在何处获取构成完整招募说明书的其他文件。

6.发行人公布的或向公众提供的招募说明书文本和格式和/或补充文件，任何时候均应与母国主管部门所批准的原始版本完全相同。

7.招募说明书以电子形式公布的，经投资者请求，发行人、要约人、请求获准在受监管市场交易其证券的人或配售或出售证券的金融中介机构，均应免费向投资者提供纸质复件。

8.为反映金融市场的技术发展动态并确保本指令的统一适用，欧盟委员会应依照第24条第2款所述程序，就第1款、第2款、第3款及第4款制定相关实施细则。应于2004年7月1日前制定首套实施细则。

第15条　广告

1.与证券向公众发行或受监管市场的交易准入相关的任何类型的广告，均应遵守第2款至第5款所包含的原则。第2款至第4款应只适用于发行人、要约人、请求获准在受监管市场交易其证券的人负有编制招募说明书义务的情形。

2.广告应说明招募说明书已经公布或将要公布，并说明投资者现在或未来可于何处取得招募说明书。

3.广告本身应清晰可辨。广告所含信息不得含有不准确内容，亦不得具误导性。广告信息也应与已经公布的(如适用)招募说明书信息一致，招募说明书公布在后的，广告信息应与按规定应在招募说明书中公布的信息一致。

4.任何以口头或书面形式披露的与向公众发行或受监管市场的交易准入有关的信息，即使并非用于广告之目的，也应与招募说明书所含的信息一致。

5.相关发行根据本指令规定不必公布招募说明书的，由发行人或要约人提供的、以合格投资者或特殊类别的投资者为对象的重大信息(包括与证券要约相关的会议中所披露的信息)，应披露给所有该等要约或发行的专门对象，即上述合格投资者或

to offers of securities, shall be disclosed to all qualified investors or special categories of investors to whom the offer is exclusively addressed. Where a prospectus is required to be published, such information shall be included in the prospectus or in a supplement to the prospectus in accordance with Article 16(1).

6. The competent authority of the home Member State shall have the power to exercise control over the compliance of advertising activity, relating to a public offer of securities or an admission to trading on a regulated market, with the principles referred to in paragraphs 2 to 5.

7. In order to take account of technical developments on financial markets and to ensure uniform application of this Directive, the Commission shall, in accordance with the procedure referred to in Article 24(2) adopt implementing measures concerning the dissemination of advertisements announcing the intention to offer securities to the public or the admission to trading on a regulated market, in particular before the prospectus has been made available to the public or before the opening of the subscription, and concerning paragraph 4. The first set of implementing measures shall be adopted by the Commission by 1 July 2004.

Article 16 Supplements to the prospectus

1. Every significant new factor, material mistake or inaccuracy relating to the information included in the prospectus which is capable of affecting the assessment of the securities and which arises or is noted between the time when the prospectus is approved and the final closing of the offer to the public or, as the case may be, the time when trading on a regulated market begins, shall be mentioned in a supplement to the prospectus. Such a supplement shall be approved in the same way in a maximum of seven working days and published in accordance with at least the same arrangements as were applied when the original prospectus was published. The summary, and any translations thereof, shall also be supplemented, if necessary to take into account the new information included in the supplement.

2. Investors who have already agreed to purchase or subscribe for the securities before the supplement is published shall have the right, exercisable within a time limit which shall not be shorter than two working days after the publication of the supplement, to withdraw their acceptances.

CHAPTER IV CROSS-BORDER OFFERS AND ADMISSION TO TRADING

Article 17 Community scope of approvals of prospectuses

1. Without prejudice to Article 23, where an offer to the public or admission to trading on a regulated market is provided for in one or more Member States, or in a

特殊类别的投资者。按规定应公布招募说明书的，招募说明书或依照第16条第1款所公布的招募说明书的补充文件应将上述信息包括在内。

6.母国主管部门应有权对广告活动的合规施加控制，确保与证券向公众发行或获准在受监管市场交易相关的广告活动遵守第2款至第5款所述的原则。

7.为反映金融市场的技术发展动态并确保本指令的统一适用，欧盟委员会应依照第24条第2款所述程序，就与第4款相关的下述广告传播活动制定实施细则：宣布向公众发行证券意图的广告，宣布获得在受监管市场交易准入的广告（特别是在招募说明书向公众公布或在认购开始之前）。应于2004年7月1日前制定首套实施细则。

第16条　招募说明书的补充文件

1.与招募说明书所含信息相关的每项重要的新要素、重大错误或重大不准确内容足以影响投资者对证券的评估的，并且在招募说明书获得批准后和向公众发行截止前或者在招募说明书获得批准后和开始在受监管市场交易前（视具体情况而定）发生或被发现的，均应在招募说明书的补充文件中述及。上述补充文件应最长在7个工作日内以同样的方式得到批准，并至少按照与原始招募说明书公布时所采用的同样安排予以公布。如有必要反映补充文件所含的新信息，则摘要及其译文也应加以补充。

2.在补充文件公布前已同意购买或认购证券的投资者，有权在不短于补充文件公布后的两个工作日内撤销该购买或认购承诺。

第四章　跨境要约和交易准入

第17条　欧共体招募说明书批准的范围

1.在不影响第23条的规定的情形下，如证券被允许在一个或多个成员国或某个非母国的成员国向公众发行或在其受监管市场交易，则母国批准的招募说明书及其任

Member State other than the home Member State, the prospectus approved by the home Member State and any supplements thereto shall be valid for the public offer or the admission to trading in any number of host Member States, provided that the competent authority of each host Member State is notified in accordance with Article 18. Competent authorities of host Member States shall not undertake any approval or administrative procedures relating to prospectuses.

2. If there are significant new factors, material mistakes or inaccuracies, as referred to in Article 16, arising since the approval of the prospectus, the competent authority of the home Member State shall require the publication of a supplement to be approved as provided for in Article 13(1). The competent authority of the host Member State may draw the attention of the competent authority of the home Member State to the need for any new information.

Article 18 Notification

1. The competent authority of the home Member State shall, at the request of the issuer or the person responsible for drawing up the prospectus and within three working days following that request or, if the request is submitted together with the draft prospectus, within one working day after the approval of the prospectus provide the competent authority of the host Member State with a certificate of approval attesting that the prospectus has been drawn up in accordance with this Directive and with a copy of the said prospectus. If applicable, this notification shall be accompanied by a translation of the summary produced under the responsibility of the issuer or person responsible for drawing up the prospectus. The same procedure shall be followed for any supplement to the prospectus.

2. The application of the provisions of Article 8(2) and (3) shall be stated in the certificate, as well as its justification.

CHAPTER V USE OF LANGUAGES AND ISSUERS INCORPORATED IN THIRD COUNTRIES

Article 19 Use of languages

1. Where an offer to the public is made or admission to trading on a regulated market is sought only in the home Member State, the prospectus shall be drawn up in a language accepted by the competent authority of the home Member State.

2. Where an offer to the public is made or admission to trading on a regulated market is sought in one or more Member States excluding the home Member State, the prospectus shall be drawn up either in a language accepted by the competent authorities of those Member States or in a language customary in the sphere of international finance, at the choice of the issuer, offeror or person asking for admission, as the case may be. The competent authority of each host Member State may only require that the summary be

何补充文件对于在任何东道国(数量不限)进行的公开发行或交易准入均有效,前提是各东道国主管部门应根据第18条的规定收到相关通知。东道国主管部门不承担有关招募说明书的任何批准或行政程序。

2.在招募说明书获得批准后出现了第16条所述的重要的新要素、重大错误或重大不准确的,母国主管部门应要求补充文件的公布须按第13条第1款的规定获得批准。东道国主管部门可提请母国主管部门注意对任何新信息的需要。

第18条　通知

1.经发行人或负责编制招募说明书的人的请求,母国主管部门应在请求提出后的3个工作日内,或如果该项请求是与招募说明书草案一同呈报的,则在招募说明书获得通过后的1个工作日内,向东道国主管部门提供一份证明招募说明书系根据本指令编制的批准证书,并提供上述招募说明书的复件。此通知应随附摘要翻译(如有),与摘要翻译制作相关的责任由发行人或负责编制招募说明书的人承担。对招募说明书的任何补充均应根据相同程序进行。

2.证书应说明第8条第2款及第3款规定的适用及其理由。

第五章　语言的使用以及在第三国成立的发行人

第19条　语言的使用

1.对于请求仅在母国向公众发行或在母国受监管市场交易的证券,招募说明书应以母国主管部门接受的语言编制。

2.对于请求在母国以外的一个或多个成员国向公众发行或在其受监管市场交易的证券,招募说明书应根据发行人、要约人或交易准入请求人(具体指何者视情况而定)的选择,以该等成员国主管部门接受的语言或国际金融行业惯用语言编制。各东道国的主管部门只可要求将摘要翻译成其一种或多种官方语言。

translated into its official language(s).

For the purpose of the scrutiny by the competent authority of the home Member State, the prospectus shall be drawn up either in a language accepted by this authority or in a language customary in the sphere of international finance, at the choice of the issuer, offeror or person asking for admission to trading, as the case may be.

3. Where an offer to the public is made or admission to trading on a regulated market is sought in more than one Member State including the home Member State, the prospectus shall be drawn up in a language accepted by the competent authority of the home Member State and shall also be made available either in a language accepted by the competent authorities of each host Member State or in a language customary in the sphere of international finance, at the choice of the issuer, offeror, or person asking for admission to trading, as the case may be. The competent authority of each host Member State may only require that the summary referred to in Article 5(2) be translated into its official language(s).

4. Where admission to trading on a regulated market of non-equity securities whose denomination per unit amounts to at least EUR 50 000 is sought in one or more Member States, the prospectus shall be drawn up either in a language accepted by the competent authorities of the home and host Member States or in a language customary in the sphere of international finance, at the choice of the issuer, offeror or person asking for admission to trading, as the case may be. Member States may choose to require in their national legislation that a summary be drawn up in their official language(s).

Article 20 Issuers incorporated in third countries

1. The competent authority of the home Member State of issuers having their registered office in a third country may approve a prospectus for an offer to the public or for admission to trading on a regulated market, drawn up in accordance with the legislation of a third country, provided that:

(a) the prospectus has been drawn up in accordance with international standards set by international securities commission organisations, including the IOSCO disclosure standards;

(b) the information requirements, including information of a financial nature, are equivalent to the requirements under this Directive.

2. In the case of an offer to the public or admission to trading on a regulated market of securities, issued by an issuer incorporated in a third country, in a Member State other than the home Member State, the requirements set out in Articles 17, 18 and 19 shall apply.

3. In order to ensure uniform application of this Directive, the Commission may adopt implementing measures in accordance with the procedure referred to in Article 24 (2),

为母国主管部门审查之目的，招募说明书应依照发行人、要约人或交易准入请求人（具体指何者视情况而定）的选择，以母国主管部门接受的语言或国际金融行业惯用语言编制。

3.对于在包括母国在内的一个或多个成员国向公众发行的证券，或寻求获准在该国受监管市场交易的证券，招募说明书应依照发行人、要约人或交易准入请求人（具体指何者视情况而定）的选择，以母国主管部门接受的语言编写，且应以各东道国主管部门接受的语言或国际金融行业惯用语言公开。各东道国的主管部门仅可要求将第5条第2款所述摘要翻译成其一种或多种官方语言。

4.对于请求获准在一个或多个成员国受监管市场交易的投资单位面值最低达5万欧元的非股权证券，招募说明书应依照发行人、要约人或交易准入请求人（具体指何者视情况而定）的选择，以母国及东道国接受的语言或国际金融行业惯用语言编制。成员国可在其国内立法中规定以其一种或多种官方语言编制摘要。

第20条　在第三国成立的发行人

1.对于注册地位于第三国的发行人，其母国主管部门可以批准为向公众发行或为在受监管市场的交易准入而根据第三国立法编制的招募说明书，前提是：

（a）招募说明书根据国际证券委员会组织设定的国际标准（包括国际证监会组织的披露标准）编制；

（b）信息（包括财务信息）要求与本指令中的要求等效。

2.在第三国成立的发行人在非母国成员国发行的证券，其向公众发行或在受监管市场的交易准入应适用第17条、第18条及第19条规定的要求。

3.为确保本指令的统一适用，欧盟委员会应依照第24条第2款所述程序制定相关实施细则，该等实施细则应说明，如第三国的国内法律或惯例或程序以国际组织设定

stating that a third country ensures the equivalence of prospectuses drawn up in that country with this Directive, by reason of its national law or of practices or procedures based on international standards set by international organisations, including the IOSCO disclosure standards.

CHAPTER VI COMPETENT AUTHORITIES

Article 21 Powers

1. Each Member State shall designate a central competent administrative authority responsible for carrying out the obligations provided for in this Directive and for ensuring that the provisions adopted pursuant to this Directive are applied.

However, a Member State may, if so required by national law, designate other administrative authorities to apply Chapter Ⅲ.

These competent authorities shall be completely independent from all market participants.

If an offer of securities is made to the public or admission to trading on a regulated market is sought in a Member State other than the home Member State, only the central competent administrative authority designated by each Member State shall be entitled to approve the prospectus.

2. Member States may allow their competent authority or authorities to delegate tasks. Except for delegation of the publication on the Internet of approved prospectuses and the filing of prospectuses as mentioned in Article 14, any delegation of tasks relating to the obligations provided for in this Directive and in its implementing measures shall be reviewed, in accordance with Article 31 by 31 December 2008, and shall end on 31 December 2011. Any delegation of tasks to entities other than the authorities referred to in paragraph 1 shall be made in a specific manner stating the tasks to be undertaken and the conditions under which they are to be carried out.

These conditions shall include a clause obliging the entity in question to act and be organised in such a manner as to avoid conflict of interest and so that information obtained from carrying out the delegated tasks is not used unfairly or to prevent competition. In any case, the final responsibility for supervising compliance with this Directive and with its implementing measures and for approving the prospectus shall lie with the competent authority or authorities designated in accordance with paragraph 1.

Member States shall inform the Commission and the competent authorities of other Member States of any arrangements entered into with regard to delegation of tasks, including the precise conditions regulating such delegation.

3. Each competent authority shall have all the powers necessary for the performance of its functions. A competent authority that has received an application for approving a

的国际标准(包括国际证监会组织的披露标准)为基础,则该国编制的招募说明书与本指令中的招募说明书等效。

第六章　主管部门

第21条　主管部门的权力

1.各成员国应指定一个中央行政主管部门负责履行本指令所规定的义务,并确保根据本指令所制定的国内规定得到适用。

然而,成员国的法律有所要求的,成员国可指定其他行政部门负责第三章的适用。

该等主管部门应完全独立于所有市场参与者。

对于在非母国的成员国向公众发行的证券或获准在非母国成员国的受监管市场交易的证券,唯有各成员国所指定的中央行政主管部门有权批准招募说明书。

2.成员国可允许其一个或多个主管部门委托其他实体代为履行职责。除了委托第14条所述的在网上公布获得批准的招募说明书以及提交招募说明书的职责之外,任何其他与本指令规定的义务有关的职责委托均应根据第31条规定于2008年12月31日以前进行审评,并应于2011年12月31日前终止。任何向第1款所述主管部门以外的实体所做的职责委托,均应明确指明需承担的职责以及履行该等职责的条件。

该等条件应包括下述条款:受托实体有义务采取避免利益冲突的行为和组织方式,以便履行受托职责时所获信息不会被不正当使用或妨碍竞争。任何情形下,监管本指令及其实施细则的合规情况以及批准招募说明书的最终责任均应由根据第1款规定所指定的一个或多个主管部门承担。

成员国应通知欧盟委员会以及其他成员国主管部门其就职责委托所设置的任何安排,包括规范职责委托的确切条件。

3.各主管部门均应有履行其职能所必要的一切权力。收到招募说明书批准申请的主管部门,至少有权:

prospectus shall be empowered at least to:

(a) require issuers, offerors or persons asking for admission to trading on a regulated market to include in the prospectus supplementary information, if necessary for investor protection;

(b) require issuers, offerors or persons asking for admission to trading on a regulated market, and the persons that control them or are controlled by them, to provide information and documents;

(c) require auditors and managers of the issuer, offeror or person asking for admission to trading on a regulated market, as well as financial intermediaries commissioned to carry out the offer to the public or ask for admission to trading, to provide information;

(d) suspend a public offer or admission to trading for a maximum of 10 consecutive working days on any single occasion if it has reasonable grounds for suspecting that the provisions of this Directive have been infringed;

(e) prohibit or suspend advertisements for a maximum of 10 consecutive working days on any single occasion if it has reasonable grounds for believing that the provisions of this Directive have been infringed;

(f) prohibit a public offer if it finds that the provisions of this Directive have been infringed or if it has reasonable grounds for suspecting that they would be infringed;

(g) suspend or ask the relevant regulated markets to suspend trading on a regulated market for a maximum of 10 consecutive working days on any single occasion if it has reasonable grounds for believing that the provisions of this Directive have been infringed;

(h) prohibit trading on a regulated market if it finds that the provisions of this Directive have been infringed;

(i) make public the fact that an issuer is failing to comply with its obligations.

Where necessary under national law, the competent authority may ask the relevant judicial authority to decide on the use of the powers referred to in points (d) to (h) above.

4. Each competent authority shall also, once the securities have been admitted to trading on a regulated market, be empowered to:

(a) require the issuer to disclose all material information which may have an effect on the assessment of the securities admitted to trading on regulated markets in order to ensure investor protection or the smooth operation of the market;

(b) suspend or ask the relevant regulated market to suspend the securities from trading if, in its opinion, the issuer's situation is such that trading would be detrimental to investors' interests;

(c) ensure that issuers whose securities are traded on regulated markets comply with

(a)在对投资者保护必要的情形下,要求发行人、要约人或请求获准在受监管市场交易其证券的人在招募说明书中添加补充信息;

(b)要求发行人、要约人或请求获准在受监管市场交易其证券的人以及其控制人或被控制人提供信息和文件;

(c)要求发行人、要约人或请求获准在受监管市场交易其证券的人的审计师和经理人提供信息,并要求受发行人、要约人或请求获准在受监管市场交易其证券的人委托负责向公众发行或请求交易准入事宜的金融中介机构提供信息;

(d)有合理理由怀疑出现违反本指令规定的情形的,暂停证券公开发行或交易准入,每次暂停时间最长为连续10个工作日;

(e)有合理理由确信出现违反本指令规定的情形的,禁止或暂停广告,每次禁止或暂停时间最长为连续10个工作日;

(f)认定本指令的规定遭到违反,或有合理理由怀疑其可能遭到违反的情形下,禁止公开发行;

(g)有合理理由确信出现违反本指令规定的情形的,暂停或要求相关受监管市场暂停证券在受监管市场的交易,每次暂停时间最长为连续10个工作日;

(h)认定本指令的规定遭到违反的,禁止证券在受监管市场交易;

(i)对发行人未能遵守其义务的事实予以公布。

根据成员国国内法律,必要时主管部门可要求相关司法部门就上述第d项至第h项所述权力的使用作出裁决。

4.证券获准在受监管市场交易后,各主管部门还有权:

(a)要求发行人披露所有可能影响获准在受监管市场交易的证券之评估的重大信息,以确保对投资者的保护或市场的平稳运行;

(b)在其认为根据发行人的状况交易会对投资者利益造成损害的情形下,暂停或要求相关受监管市场暂停证券交易;

(c)确保在受监管市场交易的证券的发行人遵守第2001/34/EC号指令第102条和

the obligations provided for in Articles 102 and 103 of Directive 2001/34/EC and that equivalent information is provided to investors and equivalent treatment is granted by the issuer to all securities holders who are in the same position, in all Member States where the offer to the public is made or the securities are admitted to trading;

(d) carry out on-site inspections in its territory in accordance with national law, in order to verify compliance with the provisions of this Directive and its implementing measures. Where necessary under national law, the competent authority or authorities may use this power by applying to the relevant judicial authority and/or in cooperation with other authorities.

5. Paragraphs 1 to 4 shall be without prejudice to the possibility for a Member State to make separate legal and administrative arrangements for overseas European territories for whose external relations that Member State is responsible.

Article 22 Professional secrecy and cooperation between authorities

1. The obligation of professional secrecy shall apply to all persons who work or have worked for the competent authority and for entities to which competent authorities may have delegated certain tasks. Information covered by professional secrecy may not be disclosed to any other person or authority except in accordance with provisions laid down by law.

2. Competent authorities of Member States shall cooperate with each other whenever necessary for the purpose of carrying out their duties and making use of their powers. Competent authorities shall render assistance to competent authorities of other Member States. In particular, they shall exchange information and cooperate when an issuer has more than one home competent authority because of its various classes of securities, or where the approval of a prospectus has been transferred to the competent authority of another Member State pursuant to Article 13(5). They shall also closely cooperate when requiring suspension or prohibition of trading for securities traded in various Member States in order to ensure a level playing field between trading venues and protection of investors. Where appropriate, the competent authority of the host Member State may request the assistance of the competent authority of the home Member State from the stage at which the case is scrutinised, in particular as regards a new type or rare forms of securities. The competent authority of the home Member State may ask for information from the competent authority of the host Member State on any items specific to the relevant market.

Without prejudice to Article 21, the competent authorities of Member States may consult with operators of regulated markets as necessary and, in particular, when deciding to suspend, or to ask a regulated market to suspend or prohibit trading.

3. Paragraph 1 shall not prevent the competent authorities from exchanging

第103条规定的义务，并确保在证券向公众发行或获准交易所在的成员国内，发行人向投资者提供等效信息并对处于同等状况的所有证券持有人给予同等待遇；

(d)根据成员国国内法律在其境内开展现场检查，以核查本指令的规定及其实施细则的合规情况。根据成员国国内法律，必要时成员国的一个或多个主管部门可通过向相关司法部门提出申请和/或与其他主管部门合作行使此项权力。

5.第1款至第4款不影响成员国对海外欧洲领地制定独立的法律和行政安排，该等领地的对外关系责任由该成员国承担。

第22条　职业保密和主管部门之间的合作

1.职业保密义务适用于主管部门或接受主管部门职责委托的实体的现任或前任工作人员。职业保密义务所涵盖的信息不得向任何人或部门披露，但成员国国内法律允许的除外。

2.成员国主管部门应在必要时相互合作，以履行其职责并运用其权力。主管部门应向其他成员国的主管部门提供协助。特别在发行人因其不同类别的证券而有超过一个母国时，或当批准招募说明书的权力根据第13条第5款的规定委托给另一成员国的主管部门时，各主管部门应交换信息并相互合作。要求暂停或禁止在多个成员国交易的证券的交易活动时，各主管部门还应紧密合作，以确保交易场所彼此有公平的竞争环境并保护投资者。在适当情形下，特别是当个案涉及新型证券或形式罕见的证券时，东道国主管部门可请求母国主管部门从个案审查阶段即开始提供协助。母国主管部门可请求东道国主管部门提供相关市场中任何特定事项的信息。

在不影响第21条的规定的情形下，成员国主管部门可在必要时，特别是在决定暂停或请求受监管市场暂停或禁止交易时，征求受监管市场运营者的意见。

3.第1款不妨碍各主管部门交换保密信息。所交换的信息受职业保密义务约束，接

confidential information. Information thus exchanged shall be covered by the obligation of professional secrecy, to which the persons employed or formerly employed by the competent authorities receiving the information are subject.

Article 23 Precautionary measures

1. Where the competent authority of the host Member State finds that irregularities have been committed by the issuer or by the financial institutions in charge of the public offer or that breaches have been committed of the obligations attaching to the issuer by reason of the fact that the securities are admitted to trading on a regulated market, it shall refer these findings to the competent authority of the home Member State.

2. If, despite the measures taken by the competent authority of the home Member State or because such measures prove inadequate, the issuer or the financial institution in charge of the public offer persists in breaching the relevant legal or regulatory provisions, the competent authority of the host Member State, after informing the competent authority of the home Member State, shall take all the appropriate measures in order to protect investors. The Commission shall be informed of such measures at the earliest opportunity.

CHAPTER VII IMPLEMENTING MEASURES

Article 24 Committee procedure

1. The Commission shall be assisted by the European Securities Committee, instituted by Decision 2001/528/EC (hereinafter referred to as 'the Committee').

2. Where reference is made to this paragraph, Articles 5 and 7 of Decision 1999/468/EC shall apply, having regard to the provisions of Article 8 thereof and provided that the implementing measures adopted in accordance with this procedure do not modify the essential provisions of this Directive.

The period laid down in Article 5(6) of Decision 1999/468/EC shall be set at three months.

3. The Committee shall adopt its rules of procedure.

4. Without prejudice to the implementing measures already adopted, on the expiry of a four-year period following the entry into force of this Directive the application of its provisions providing for the adoption of technical rules and decisions in accordance with the procedure referred to in paragraph 2 shall be suspended. On a proposal from the Commission, the European Parliament and the Council may renew the provisions concerned in accordance with the procedure laid down in Article 251 of the Treaty and, to that end, shall review them prior to the expiry of the four-year period.

Article 25 Sanctions

1. Without prejudice to the right of Member States to impose criminal sanctions and without prejudice to their civil liability regime, Member States shall ensure, in conformity

收信息的主管部门的前任或现任雇员均应遵守该项义务。

第23条　预防措施

1.东道国主管部门认定发行人或负责公开发行的金融机构犯有不法行为或发行人违反了因证券获准在受监管市场交易而产生的义务的，应将此等认定结果移交母国主管部门处理。

2. 尽管母国主管部门已采取措施或由于事实证明采取的措施不充分，发行人或负责公开发行的金融机构继续违反相关法律规章的，东道国主管部门应在通知母国主管部门相关情况后，采取一切适当措施以保护投资者。东道国主管部门应尽早向欧盟委员会通知此等措施。

第七章　实施细则

第24条　委员会程序

1.根据第2001/528/EC号决定成立的欧洲证券委员会（以下简称证券委员会）应协助欧盟委员会工作。

2.根据第1999/468/EC号决定第8条规定，引用本款内容时应适用该决定的第5条和第7条，前提是依照该程序制定的实施细则不对本指令的基本条款做出改动。

第1999/468/EC号决定第5条第6款所规定的期限应设定为3个月。

3.证券委员会应制定其程序规则。

4.在不影响已制定的实施细则的情形下，在本指令生效4年期限届满之后，本指令中要求根据第2款所述程序制定技术性规则和决定的规定应暂停适用。经欧盟委员会提议，欧洲议会与欧盟理事会可依照《条约》第251条规定的程序展延所涉条款，为此，欧洲议会与欧盟理事会应在4年期满前对该等条款进行审评。

第25条　罚则

1.在不影响成员国刑事处罚权及实施民事责任制度的情形下，各成员国应确保根据其国内法律，对违反本指令实施过程中制定的国内规定的相关责任人采取适当的

with their national law, that the appropriate administrative measures can be taken or administrative sanctions be imposed against the persons responsible, where the provisions adopted in the implementation of this Directive have not been complied with. Member States shall ensure that these measures are effective, proportionate and dissuasive.

2. Member States shall provide that the competent authority may disclose to the public every measure or sanction that has been imposed for infringement of the provisions adopted pursuant to this Directive, unless the disclosure would seriously jeopardise the financial markets or cause disproportionate damage to the parties involved.

Article 26 Right of appeal

Member States shall ensure that decisions taken pursuant to laws, regulations and administrative provisions adopted in accordance with this Directive are subject to the right to appeal to the courts.

CHAPTER VIII TRANSITIONAL AND FINAL PROVISIONS

Article 27 Amendments

With effect from the date set out in Article 29, Directive 2001/34/EC is hereby amended as follows:

1. Articles 3, 20 to 41, 98 to 101, 104 and 108(2)(c)(ii) shall be deleted;

2. in Article 107(3) the first subparagraph shall be deleted;

3. in Article 108(2)(a) the words 'the conditions of establishment, the control and circulation of listing particulars to be published for admission' shall be deleted;

4. Annex I shall be deleted.

Article 28 Repeal

With effect from the date indicated in Article 29, Directive 89/298/EEC shall be repealed. References to the repealed Directive shall be construed as references to this Directive.

Article 29 Transposition

Member States shall bring into force the laws, regulations and administrative provisions necessary to comply with this Directive not later than 1 July 2005. They shall forthwith inform the Commission thereof. When Member States adopt those measures they shall contain a reference to this Directive or shall be accompanied by such a reference on the occasion of their official publication. The methods for making such reference shall be laid down by Member States.

Article 30 Transitional provision

1. Issuers which are incorporated in a third country and whose securities have already been admitted to trading on a regulated market shall choose their competent

行政措施或行政处罚。各成员国应确保此等措施有效、成比例且具有威慑作用。

2.成员国应规定，对于违反依本指令制定的国内规定而采取的各项行政措施或实施的各项处罚，主管部门可向公众披露，但上述披露会严重危害金融市场或对所涉各方造成不成比例损害的除外。

第26条 行政诉讼权

成员国应确保，依照按本指令制定的法律、法规和规章所作的任何决定可由相对人向法院提起行政诉讼。

第八章 过渡规定和最终条款

第27条 修正

特此对第2001/34/EC号指令作如下修正，所作修正自第29条规定的日期起生效：

1.删除第3条、第20条至第41条、第98条至第101条、第104条以及第108条第2款第c项第ii目；

2.删除第107条第3款第1项；

3.删除第108条第2款第a项中的“为获得准入而公布的上市具体信息的制定、控制及流通条件”；

4.删除附件一。

第28条 废止

自第29条规定的日期起，第89/298/EEC号指令应予废止。引用该等已废止指令时，应视为指代本指令。

第29条 转化

各成员国应于2005年7月1日前实施必要的法律、法规和规章以使本指令得到遵守，并立即就此通知欧盟委员会。成员国制定该等法律、法规和规章时，应在其中对本指令予以援引，或在官方正式公布该等法律、法规和规章时予以援引。援引的具体方式，由成员国决定。

第30条 过渡规定

1.在第三国成立且证券获准在受监管市场交易的发行人应根据第2条第1款第m项第iii目选择其主管部门，并于2005年12月31日前通知其选择的母国主管部门该

authority in accordance with Article 2(1)(m)(iii) and notify their decision to the competent authority of their chosen home Member State by 31 December 2005.

2. By way of derogation from Article 3, Member States which have used the exemption in Article 5(a) of Directive 89/298/EEC may continue to allow credit institutions or other financial institutions equivalent to credit institutions which are not covered by Article 1(2)(j) of this Directive to offer debt securities or other transferable securities equivalent to debt securities issued in a continuous or repeated manner within their territory for five years following the date of entry into force of this Directive.

3. By way of derogation from Article 29, the Federal Republic of Germany shall comply with Article 21(1) by 31 December 2008.

Article 31 Review

Five years after the date of entry into force of this Directive, the Commission shall make an assessment of the application of this Directive and present a report to the European Parliament and the Council, accompanied where appropriate by proposals for its review.

Article 32 Entry into force

This Directive shall enter into force on the day of its publication in the Official Journal of the European Union.

Article 33 Addressees

This Directive is addressed to the Member States.

Done at Brussels, 4 November 2003.

For the European Parliament	For the Council
The President	*The President*
P. COX	G. ALEMANNO

ANNEX I PROSPECTUS

I.Summary

The summary shall provide in a few pages the most important information included in the prospectus, covering at least the following items:

A. identity of directors, senior management, advisers and auditors

B. offer statistics and expected timetable

C. key information concerning selected financial data; capitalisation and indebtedness; reasons for the offer and use of proceeds; risk factors

D. information concerning the issuer

— history and development of the issuer

— business overview

等决定。

2.作为第3条规定的例外，已实施第89/298/EEC号指令第5条第a款豁免的成员国，可继续允许信贷机构或本指令第1条第2款第j项范围以外的其他等同于信贷机构的金融机构在本指令生效后5年内，于其境内持续或重复地要约债务证券或其他等同于债务证券的可转让证券。

3.作为第29条规定的例外，德意志联邦共和国遵守第21条第1款规定的期限为2008年12月31日。

第31条　审评

本指令生效5年后，欧盟委员会应对本指令的适用情况进行评价，并向欧洲议会与欧盟理事会提交评价报告，并在适当时随附其审评建议。

第32条　生效

本指令自公布于《欧盟公报》之日起生效。

第33条　对象

本指令对象为各成员国。

2003年11月4日于布鲁塞尔通过。

欧洲议会议长　　　　　　　　欧盟理事会主席

考克斯　　　　　　　　　　　阿莱曼诺

附录一　招募说明书

I.摘要

摘要应以少量页数的篇幅说明招募说明书所包含的最重要的信息，至少应包含下列事项：

A.董事、高级管理人员、顾问及审计师的身份信息

B.向公众发行的统计数据和预期时间表

C.择要列示的财务数据的关键信息；资本和负债；向公众发行的理由和募集资金用途；风险因素

D.发行人信息

——发行人历史与发展

——业务概况

E. operating and financial review and prospects

— research and development, patents and licences, etc.

— trends

F. directors, senior management and employees

G. major shareholders and related-party transactions

H. financial information

— consolidated statement and other financial information

— significant changes

I. details of the offer and admission to trading

— offer and admission to trading

— plan for distribution

— markets

— selling shareholders

— dilution (equity securities only)

— expenses of the issue

J. additional information

— share capital

— memorandum and articles of association

— documents on display

II.Identity of directors, senior management, advisers and auditors

The purpose is to identify the company representatives and other individuals involved in the company's offer or admission to trading; these are the persons responsible for drawing up the prospectus as required by Article 5 of the Directive and those responsible for auditing the financial statements.

III. Offer statistics and expected timetable

The purpose is to provide key information regarding the conduct of any offer and the identification of important dates relating to that offer.

A. Offer statistics

B. Method and expected timetable

IV. Key information

The purpose is to summarise key information about the company's financial condition, capitalisation and risk factors. If the financial statements included in the document are restated to reflect material changes in the company's group structure or accounting policies, the selected financial data must also be restated.

A. Selected financial data

B. Capitalisation and indebtedness

C. Reasons for the offer and use of proceeds

E.经营与财务状况审评及前景
——研发、专利与许可等
——趋势
F.董事、高级管理人员及职员
G.主要股东和关联交易
H.财务信息
——合并财务报表及其他财务信息
——重大变更
I.与向公众发行以及交易准入相关的详情
——向公众发行与交易准入
——分销计划
——市场
——售股股东
——稀释(仅指股权证券)
——发行费用
J.额外信息
——股本
——公司章程大纲和细则
——备查文件

II.董事、高级管理人员、顾问及审计师的身份信息

旨在识别公司代表人以及其他参与公司证券向公众发行或交易准入的个人身份;该等人员承担根据本指令第5条要求的编制招募说明书及审计财务报表的责任。

III.向公众发行的统计数据与预期时间表

旨在提供与向公众发行相关的关键信息,并标明与向公众发行相关的重要日期。

A.向公众发行的统计数据
B.方法与预期时间表

IV关键信息

旨在总结关于公司财务状况、资本与风险因素的关键信息。文件所含财务报表已作重述,以反映公司集团结构或会计政策的重大变更的,择要列示的财务数据亦应重述。

A.择要列示的财务数据
B.资本与负债
C.向公众发行的理由与募集资金用途

D. Risk factors

V.Information on the company

The purpose is to provide information about the company's business operations, the products it makes or the services it provides, and the factors which affect the business. It is also intended to provide information regarding the adequacy and suitability of the company's properties, plant and equipment, as well as its plans for future capacity increases or decreases.

A. History and development of the company

B. Business overview

C. Organisational structure

D. Property, plant and equipment

VI. Operating and financial review and prospects

The purpose is to provide the management's explanation of factors that have affected the company's financial condition and results of operations for the historical periods covered by the financial statements, and management's assessment of factors and trends which are expected to have a material effect on the company's financial condition and results of operations in future periods.

A. Operating results

B. Liquidity and capital resources

C. Research and development, patents and licences, etc.

D. Trends

VII. Directors, senior management and employees

The purpose is to provide information concerning the company's directors and managers that will allow investors to assess their experience, qualifications and levels of remuneration, as well as their relationship with the company.

A. Directors and senior management

B. Remuneration

C. Board practices

D. Employees

E. Share ownership

VIII.Major shareholders and related-party transactions

The purpose is to provide information regarding the major shareholders and others that may control or have an influence on the company. It also provides information regarding transactions the company has entered into with persons affiliated with the company and whether the terms of such transactions are fair to the company.

A. Major shareholders

B. Related-party transactions

D.风险因素

V.公司信息

旨在提供关于公司业务运营、所制造产品或所提供服务以及对业务造成影响的因素的信息。同时旨在说明公司财产、厂房和设备的充分性与适合性，及其未来产能增减计划。

A.公司历史及发展

B.业务概况

C.组织结构

D.财产、厂房与设备

VI.经营与财务状况审评及前景

旨在提供管理层对财务报表涵盖的历史时期内影响公司财务状况以及经营成果的因素的解释，以及管理层对预计未来会对公司财务状况及经营成果造成重大影响的因素与趋势的评估。

A.经营成果

B.流动资金与资本资源

C.研发、专利与许可等

D.趋势

VII.董事、高级管理人员及职员

旨在提供与公司董事与管理层相关的信息，使投资者能对其经验、资历及薪酬水平及其与公司的关系进行评估。

A.董事与高级管理人员

B.薪酬

C.董事会惯例

D.职员

E.持股状况

VIII.主要股东和关联交易

旨在提供主要股东及其他可能控制公司或对公司产生影响之人的相关信息。同时提供公司与公司关联人所订立的交易的信息，并说明该等交易的条款对公司而言是否公平。

A.主要股东

B.关联交易

C. Interests of experts and advisers

IX. Financial information

The purpose is to specify which financial statements must be included in the document, as well as the periods to be covered, the age of the financial statements and other information of a financial nature. The accounting and auditing principles that will be accepted for use in preparation and audit of the financial statements will be determined in accordance with international accounting and auditing standards.

A. Consolidated statements and other financial information

B. Significant changes

X. Details of the offer and admission to trading details

The purpose is to provide information regarding the offer and the admission to trading of securities, the plan for distribution of the securities and related matters.

A. Offer and admission to trading

B. Plan for distribution

C. Markets

D. Holders of securities who are selling

E. Dilution (for equity securities only)

F. Expenses of the issue

XI. Additional information

The purpose is to provide information, most of which is of a statutory nature, that is not covered elsewhere in the prospectus.

A. Share capital

B. Memorandum and articles of association

C. Material contracts

D. Exchange controls

E. Taxation

F. Dividends and paying agents

G. Statement by experts

H. Documents on display

I. Subsidiary information

ANNEX II REGISTRATION DOCUMENT

I. Identity of directors, senior management, advisers and auditors

The purpose is to identify the company representatives and other individuals involved in the company's offer or admission to trading; these are the persons responsible for drawing up the prospectus and those responsible for auditing the financial statements.

C.专家与顾问的权益

IX.财务信息

旨在说明文件中应当包含的财务报表，以及财务报表应涵盖的报告期、账龄以及其他财务信息。拟用于编制和审计财务报表的会计和审计原则应根据国际会计及审计准则确定。

A.合并财务报表及其他财务信息

B.重大变更

X.向公众发行与交易准入的详情

旨在提供关于向公众发行和证券交易准入、证券分销计划及相关事项的信息。

A.向公众发行与交易准入

B.分销计划

C.市场

D.出售证券的持有人

E.稀释(仅适用于股权证券)

F.发行费用

XI.额外信息

旨在提供不涵盖在招募说明书范围内的信息(大部分属于法定信息)。

A.股本

B.公司章程大纲和细则

C.重大合同

D.外汇管制

E.税务

F.股息与代理付款人

G.专家声明

H.备查文件

I.子公司信息

附录二　注册文件

I.董事、高级管理人员、顾问及审计师的身份信息

旨在识别公司代表人及其他参与公司证券向公众发行或交易准入的个人的身份；该等人员承担编制招募说明书及审计财务报表的责任。

II.Key information about the issuer

The purpose is to summarise key information about the company's financial condition, capitalisation and risk factors. If the financial statements included in the document are restated to reflect material changes in the company's group structure or accounting policies, the selected financial data must also be restated.

A. Selected financial data

B. Capitalisation and indebtedness

C. Risk factors

III.Information on the company

The purpose is to provide information about the company's business operations, the products it makes or the services it provides and the factors which affect the business. It is also intended to provide information regarding the adequacy and suitability of the company's properties, plants and equipment, as well as its plans for future capacity increases or decreases.

A. History and development of the company

B. Business overview

C. Organisational structure

D. Property, plants and equipment

IV.Operating and financial review and prospects

The purpose is to provide the management's explanation of factors that have affected the company's financial condition and results of operations for the historical periods covered by the financial statements, and management's assessment of factors and trends which are expected to have a material effect on the company's financial condition and results of operations in future periods.

A. Operating results

B. Liquidity and capital resources

C. Research and development, patents and licences, etc.

D. Trends

V.Directors, senior management and employees

The purpose is to provide information concerning the company's directors and managers that will allow investors to assess their experience, qualifications and levels of remuneration, as well as their relationship with the company.

A. Directors and senior management

B. Remuneration

C. Board practices

D. Employees

E. Share ownership

II.发行人的关键信息

旨在总结关于公司财务状况、资本与风险因素的关键信息。如文件所含财务报表已作重述，以反映公司集团结构或会计政策的重大变更，则择要列示的财务数据亦应重述。

A.择要列示的财务数据

B.资本与负债

C.风险因素

III.公司信息

旨在提供关于公司业务运营、所制造的产品或所提供的服务以及对业务造成影响的因素的信息。同时旨在说明公司财产、厂房与设备的充分性与适合性，及其未来产能增减计划。

A.公司历史及发展

B.业务概况

C.组织结构

D.财产、厂房与设备

IV.经营与财务状况审评及前景

旨在提供管理层对于财务报表所涵盖的历史时期内影响公司财务状况以及经营成果的因素的解释，以及管理层对未来会对公司财务状况及经营成果造成重大影响的因素与趋势的评估。

A.经营成果

B.流动资金与资本资源

C.研发、专利与许可等

D.趋势

V.董事、高级管理人员及职员

旨在提供有关公司董事与管理层的信息，使投资者能对其经验、资历及薪酬水平及其与公司的关系进行评估。

A.董事与高级管理人员

B.薪酬

C.董事会惯例

D.职员

E.持股状况

VI. Major shareholders and related-party transactions

The purpose is to provide information regarding the major shareholders and others that may control or have an influence on the company. It also provides information regarding transactions the company has entered into with persons affiliated with the company and whether the terms of such transactions are fair to the company.

A. Major shareholders

B. Related-party transactions

C. Interests of experts and advisers

VII. Financial information

The purpose is to specify which financial statements must be included in the document, as well as the periods to be covered, the age of the financial statements and other information of a financial nature. The accounting and auditing principles that will be accepted for use in preparation and audit of the financial statements will be determined in accordance with international accounting and auditing standards.

A. Consolidated statements and other financial information

B. Significant changes

VIII. Additional information

The purpose is to provide information, most of which is of a statutory nature, that is not covered elsewhere in the prospectus.

A. Share capital

B. Memorandum and articles of association

C. Material contracts

D. Statement by experts

E. Documents on display

F. Subsidiary information

ANNEX III SECURITIES NOTE

I. Identity of directors, senior management, advisers and auditors

The purpose is to identify the company representatives and other individuals involved in the company's offer or admission to trading; these are the persons responsible for drawing up the prospectus and those responsible for auditing the financial statements.

II. Offer statistics and expected timetable

The purpose is to provide key information regarding the conduct of any offer and the identification of important dates relating to that offer.

A. Offer statistics

B. Method and expected timetable

VI.主要股东和关联交易

旨在提供主要股东及其他可能控制公司或对公司有所影响的人的相关信息。同时提供公司与公司关联人所订立的交易的信息,并说明该等交易的条件对公司而言是否公平。

A.主要股东

B.关联交易

C.专家与顾问的权益

VII.财务信息

旨在说明文件中应当包含哪些财务报表,以及财务报表所应涵盖的报告期、账龄以及其他财务信息。拟用于编制和审计财务报表的会计与审计原则,应根据国际会计及审计标准确定。

A.合并财务报表及其他财务信息

B.重大变更

VIII.额外信息

旨在提供不涵盖在招募说明书范围内的信息(大部分属于法定信息)。

A.股本

B.公司章程大纲和细则

C.重大合同

D.专家声明

E.备查文件

F.子公司信息

附录三 证券说明

I.董事、高级管理人员、顾问及审计师的身份信息

旨在识别公司代表人及其他参与公司证券向公众发行或交易准入的个人的身份;该等人员承担编制招募说明书以及审计财务报表的责任。

II. 向公众发行的统计数据与预期时间表

旨在提供与向公众发行有关的关键信息以及标明与向公众发行有关的重要日期。

A.向公众发行的统计数据

B.方法与预期时间表

III.Key information about the issuer

The purpose is to summarise key information about the company's financial condition, capitalisation and risk factors. If the financial statements included in the document are restated to reflect material changes in the company's group structure or accounting policies, the selected financial data must also be restated.

A. Capitalisation and indebtedness

B. Reasons for the offer and use of proceeds

C. Risk factors

IV.Interests of experts

The purpose is to provide information regarding transactions the company has entered into with experts or advisers employed on a contingent basis.

V.Details of the offer and admission to trading

The purpose is to provide information regarding the offer and the admission to trading of securities, the plan for distribution of the securities and related matters.

A. Offer and admission to trading

B. Plan for distribution

C. Markets

D. Selling securities holders

E. Dilution (for equity securities only)

F. Expenses of the issue

VI.Additional information

The purpose is to provide information, most of which is of a statutory nature, that is not covered elsewhere in the prospectus.

A. Exchange controls

B. Taxation

C. Dividends and paying agents

D. Statement by experts

E. Documents on display

ANNEX IV SUMMARY NOTE

The summary note shall provide in a few pages the most important information included in the prospectus, covering at least the following items:

— identity of directors, senior management, advisers and auditors

— offer statistics and expected timetable

— key information concerning selected financial data; capitalisation and indebtedness; reasons for the offer and use of proceeds; risk factors

— information concerning the issuer

III.发行人关键信息

旨在总结关于公司财务状况、资本与风险因素的关键信息。如文件所含财务报表已作重述,以反映公司集团结构或会计政策的重大变更,则择要列示的财务数据亦应重述。

A.资产与负债

B.向公众发行的理由与募集资金用途

C.风险因素

IV.专家的权益

旨在提供公司与其暂时聘用的专家或顾问之间所订立的交易信息。

V.向公众发行与交易准入的详情

旨在提供关于证券向公众发行和交易准入、证券分销计划及相关事项的信息。

A.向公众发行与交易准入

B.分销计划

C.市场

D.出售证券的持有人

E.稀释(仅指股权证券)

F.发行费用

VI.额外信息

旨在提供不涵盖在招募说明书范围内的信息(大部分属于法定信息)。

A.外汇管制

B.税务

C.股息与代理付款人

D.专家声明

E.备查文件

附录四　摘 要 说 明

摘要应以少量页数的篇幅说明招募说明书所包含的最重要的信息,至少应包含下列事项:

——董事、高级管理人员、顾问及审计师的身份信息

——向公众发行的统计数据与预期时间表

——择要列示的财务数据的关键信息;资本和负债;向公众发行的理由和募集资金用途;风险因素

——发行人信息

  - — history and development of the issuer
  - — business overview
- — operating and financial review and prospects
  - — research and development, patents and licences, etc.
  - — trends
- — directors, senior management and employees
- — major shareholders and related-party transactions
- — financial information
  - — consolidated statement and other financial information
  - — significant changes
- — details on the offer and admission to trading
  - — offer and admission to trading
  - — plan for distribution
  - — markets
  - — selling shareholders
  - — dilution (for equity securities only)
  - — expenses of the issue
- — additional information
  - — share capital
  - — memorandum and articles of incorporation
  - — documents available for inspection

——发行人历史与发展

——业务概况

——经营与财务状况审评及前景

——研发、专利与许可等

——趋势

——董事、高级管理人员及职员

——主要股东和关联交易

——财务信息

——合并财务报表及其他财务信息

——重大变更

——与向公众发行以及交易准入相关的详情

——向公众发行与交易准入

——分销计划

——市场

——售股股东

——稀释(仅适用于股权证券)

——发行费用

——额外信息

——股本

——公司章程大纲和细则

——备查文件

DIRECTIVE 2008/11/EC OF THE EUROPEAN PARLIAMENT AND OF THE COUNCIL

欧洲议会与欧盟理事会第2008/11/EC号指令

DIRECTIVE 2008/11/EC OF THE EUROPEAN PARLIAMENT AND OF THE COUNCIL

of 11 March 2008
amending Directive 2003/71/EC on the prospectus to be published when securities are offered to the public or admitted to trading, as regards the implementing powers conferred on the Commission
(Text with EEA relevance)

THE EUROPEAN PARLIAMENT AND THE COUNCIL OF THE EUROPEAN UNION,

Having regard to the Treaty establishing the European Community, and in particular Articles 44 and 95 thereof,

Having regard to the proposal from the Commission,

Having regard to the opinion of the European Economic and Social Committee1 [1],

Having regard to the opinion of the European Central Bank [2],

Acting in accordance with the procedure laid down in Article 251 of the Treaty [3],

Whereas:

(1) Directive 2003/71/EC of the European Parliament and of the Council [4] provides that certain measures are to be adopted in accordance with Council Decision 1999/468/EC of 28 June 1999 laying down the procedures for the exercise of implementing powers conferred on the Commission [5].

(2) Council Decision 1999/468/EC has been amended by Decision 2006/512/EC, which introduced the regulatory procedure with scrutiny for the adoption of measures of

1 OJ C 161, 13.7.2007, p. 45.

2 OJ C 39, 23.2.2007, p. 1.

3 Opinion of the European Parliament of 14 November 2007 (not yet ublished in the Official Journal) and Council Decision of 3 March 2008.

4 OJ L 345, 31.12.2003, p. 64.

5 OJ L 184, 17.7.1999, p. 23. Decision as amended by Decision 006/512/EC (OJ L 200, 22.7.2006, p. 11).

欧洲议会与欧盟理事会
第2008/11/EC号指令

（本指令于2008年3月11日通过，修正《关于向公众发行
证券或证券获准交易时所应公布的招募说明书的第2003/71/EC号指令》
中关于授予欧盟委员会的实施权的规定）
（欧洲经济区适用文本）

欧洲议会与欧盟理事会，

根据《欧洲共同体条约》（以下简称《条约》），特别是其中的第44条及第95条，

根据欧盟委员会的提议，
根据欧洲经济与社会委员会的意见，[1]
根据欧洲中央银行的意见，[2]
依照《条约》第251条规定的程序，[3]
鉴于：

（1）欧洲议会与欧盟理事会第2003/71/EC号指令[4]规定，应根据《欧盟理事会关于制定欧盟委员会行使其被授予的实施权之程序的第1999/468/EC号决定》[5]（1999年6月28日）制定某些细则。

（2）第1999/468/EC号决定经第2006/512/EC号决定修正，后者出台了制定具有一般适用范围的细则时须经欧盟理事会与欧洲议会审查的监管程序，该等程序旨在对

1 2007年7月13日《欧盟公报》C161，第45页。
2 2007年2月23日《欧盟公报》C39，第1页。
3 2007年11月14日欧洲议会意见（尚未在《欧盟公报》公布）以及2008年3月3日欧盟理事会决定。
4 2003年12月31日《欧盟公报》L345，第64页。
5 1999年7月17日《欧盟公报》L184，第23页。该决定经第2006/512/EC号决定（2006年7月22日《欧盟公报》L200，第11页）修正。

general scope and designed to amend non – essential elements of a basic instrument adopted in accordance with the procedure referred to in Article 251 of the Treaty, inter alia, by deleting some of those elements or by supplementing the instrument with new non–essential elements.

(3) In accordance with the statement by the European Parliament, the Council and the Commission [1] concerning Decision 2006/512/EC, for the regulatory procedure with scrutiny to be applicable to instruments adopted in accordance with the procedure referred to in Article 251 of the Treaty which are already in force, those instruments must be adjusted in accordance with the applicable procedures.

(4) The Commission should be empowered to adopt the measures necessary for the implementation of Directive 2003/71/EC in order to take account of technical developments in financial markets and ensure the uniform application of that Directive. Those measures are designed to adapt definitions and elaborate upon or supplement the provisions of Directive 2003/71/EC by detailed specification of the form and contents of a prospectus. Since those measures are of general scope and are designed to amend non–essential elements of Directive 2003/71/EC by supplementing it with new non–essential elements, they must be adopted in accordance with the regulatory procedure with scrutiny provided for in Article 5a of Decision 1999/468/EC.

(5) Directive 2003/71/EC provides for a time restriction concerning the implementing powers conferred on the Commission. In their statement concerning Decision 2006/512/EC, the European Parliament, the Council and the Commission stated that Decision 2006/512/EC provides a horizontal and satisfactory solution to the European Parliament's wish to scrutinise the implementation of instruments adopted under the co–decision procedure and that, accordingly, implementing powers should be conferred on the Commission without time limit. The European Parliament and the Council also declared that they would ensure that the proposals aimed at repealing the provisions in the instruments that provide for a time limit on the delegation of implementing powers to the Commission are adopted as rapidly as possible. Following the introduction of the regulatory procedure with scrutiny, the provision establishing that time restriction in Directive 2003/71/EC should be deleted.

(6) The Commission should, at regular intervals, evaluate the functioning of the provisions concerning the implementing powers conferred on it in order to allow the European Parliament and the Council to determine whether the extent of those powers and the procedural requirements imposed on the Commission are appropriate and ensure both efficiency and democratic accountability.

---

1 OJ C 255, 21.10.2006, p. 1.

依照《条约》第251条所述程序制定的基础法律文件中的非基本要素进行修正，包括但不限于删除部分该等要素或在基础法律文件中补充新的非基本要素。

（3）根据《欧洲议会、欧盟理事会和欧盟委员会关于第2006/512/EC号决定的声明》[1]，针对依照《条约》第251条所述程序制定且已生效的法律文件适用须经欧盟理事会和欧洲议会审查的监管程序时，该等法律文件必须根据适用的程序进行调整。

（4）欧盟委员会应有权制定实施第2003/71/EC号指令所必要的细则，以反映金融市场的技术发展动态并确保本指令的统一适用。该等细则旨在通过对招募说明书格式和内容作出具体规定，从而调整第2003/71/EC号指令的定义、对其进行详尽的说明或对其规定进行补充。由于该等细则属于一般适用范围的细则，并且旨在通过在第2003/71/EC号指令中补充新的非基本要素而对其非基本要素进行修正，因此，制定该等细则时必须遵循第1999/468/EC号决定第5a条规定的须经欧盟理事会和欧洲议会审查的监管程序。

（5）第2003/71/EC号指令就授予欧盟委员会的实施权设定了时间限制。在其《关于第2006/512/EC号指令的声明》中，欧洲议会、欧盟理事会及欧盟委员会声明，第2006/512/EC号决定提供了一个横向的完善的解决方案，使欧洲议会能实现其对依照共同决定程序制定的法律文件的实施进行审查的意愿，因此，不必再对授予欧盟委员会的实施权施加时间限制。欧洲议会和欧盟理事会同时宣布将确保其提案尽快通过，废止相关法律文件中就向欧盟委员会授予的实施权设定时限的条款。须经欧盟理事会和欧洲议会审查的监管程序开始实施后，第2003/71/EC号指令中设定该等时限的条款应予删除。

（6）欧盟委员会应定期评价授予其实施权的条款的运行情况，以便欧洲议会与欧盟理事会判定该等权力的范围及对欧盟委员会施加的程序性要求是否适当，确保效率和民主问责两者兼备。

1　2006年10月21日《欧盟公报》C255，第1页。

(7) Directive 2003/71/EC should therefore be amended accordingly.

(8) Since the amendments made to Directive 2003/71/EC by this Directive are technical in nature and concern committee procedure only, they do not need to be transposed by the Member States. It is therefore not necessary to lay down provisions to that effect,

HAVE ADOPTED THIS DIRECTIVE:

Article 1 Amendments

Directive 2003/71/EC is hereby amended as follows:

1. Articles 2(4) 4(3) 5(5) 7(1) 8(4) 11(3) 13(7) 14(8) and 15(7) shall be amended as follows:

(a) the words 'in accordance with the procedure referred to in Article 24(2) ' shall be deleted;

(b) the following sentence shall be added:

'Those measures, designed to amend non-essential elements of this Directive by supplementing it, shall be adopted in accordance with the regulatory procedure with scrutiny referred to in Article 24(2a) .';

2. Article 20(3) shall be replaced by the following:

'3.In order to ensure uniform application of this Directive, the Commission shall adopt implementing measures aimed at establishing general equivalence criteria, based on the requirements laid down in Articles 5 and 7. Those measures, designed to amend non-essential elements of this Directive by supplementing it, shall be adopted in accordance with the regulatory procedure with scrutiny referred to in Article 24(2a) .

On the basis of the above criteria, the Commission may adopt implementing measures in accordance with the regulatory procedure referred to in Article 24 (2) stating that a third country ensures the equivalence of prospectuses drawn up in that country with this Directive by reason of its national law or of practices or procedures based on international standards set by international organisations, including the IOSCO disclosure standards.';

3. Article 24 shall be amended as follows:

(a) the following paragraph shall be inserted:

'2a.Where reference is made to this paragraph, Article 5a(1) to (4) and Article 7 of Decision 1999/468/EC shall apply, having regard to the provisions of Article 8 thereof.';

(b) paragraphs 3 and 4 shall be replaced by the following:

'3.By 31 December 2010 and, thereafter, at least every three years, the Commission shall review the provisions concerning its implementing powers and present a report to the European Parliament and to the Council on the functioning of those powers. The report shall examine, in particular, the need for the Commission to propose amendments to this Directive in order to ensure the appropriate scope of the implementing powers conferred

(7)因此,第2003/71/EC号指令应做出相应修正。

(8)本指令对第2003/71/EC号指令的修正属于技术性的修正,仅涉及欧盟委员会程序,各成员国不必对其进行转化。因此,不必就成员国的转化作出规定。

兹通过本指令如下:

第1条　修正

特此对第2003/71/EC号指令修正如下:

1.对第2条第4款、第4条第3款、第5条第5款、第7条第1款、第8条第4款、第11条第3款、第13条第7款、第14条第8款和第15条第7款修正如下:

(a)删除"依照第24条第2款所述程序";

(b)增加如下内容:

"该等旨在通过对本指令进行补充而修正其非基本要素的细则,应依照第24条第2款第a项所述的须经欧盟理事会和欧洲议会审查的监管程序制定。"

2.第20条第3款替以如下内容:

"3.为确保本指令的统一适用,欧盟委员会应依照第5条和第7条的要求,制定旨在建立一般性的等效标准的实施细则。该等旨在通过对本指令进行补充而修正其非基本要素的实施细则,应依照第24条第2a款所述的须经欧盟理事会与欧洲议会审查的监管程序制定。

基于上述标准,欧盟委员会可依照第24条第2款所述的监管程序制定实施细则,声明由于第三国国内的法律或其国内遵照国际组织设定的国际标准(包括国际证监会组织的披露标准)适用的惯例或程序,第三国能确保在其国内编制的招募说明书与本指令下的招募说明书等效。"

3.对第24条修正如下:

(a)插入下列条款:

"2a.根据第1999/468/EC号决定第8条规定引用本款内容时,应适用该决定第5a条第1款至第4 款和第7条。"

(b)第3款和第4款替以如下内容:

"3.在2010年12月31日前,欧盟委员会应对关于其实施权的条款进行审评,并就该等权力的运行向欧洲议会与欧盟理事会提交一份报告,此后应至少每3年进行一次审评和报告。报告应着重审查欧盟委员会是否有必要对本指令提出修正案,以确保授予欧盟委员会的实施权维持在适当的范围之内。作出是否有必要进行修正的结论时,应附上详细的理由说明。必要时,报告应附上关于修正授予欧盟委员会实施权的条款的

on the Commission. The conclusion as to whether or not amendment is necessary shall be accompanied by a detailed statement of reasons. If necessary, the report shall be accompanied by a legislative proposal to amend the provisions conferring implementing powers on the Commission.'

Article 2 Entry into force

This Directive shall enter into force on the day following its publication in the *Official Journal of the European Union.*

Article 3 Addressees

This Directive is addressed to the Member States.

Done at Strasbourg, 11 March 2008.

For the European Parliament
The President
H.-G. PÖTTERING

For the Council
The President
J. LENARČIČ

立法提案。”

第2条　生效

本条例应于《欧盟公报》公布，公布的次日生效。

第3条　对象

本指令对象为各成员国。

2008年3月11日于斯特拉斯堡通过。

欧洲议会议长　　　　欧盟理事会主席

波特林　　　　莱纳茨

DIRECTIVE 2003/6/EC OF THE EUROPEAN PARLIAMENT AND OF THE COUNCIL

欧洲议会与欧盟理事会第2003/6/EC号指令

DIRECTIVE 2003/6/EC OF THE EUROPEAN PARLIAMENT AND OF THE COUNCIL

of 28 January 2003
on insider dealing and market manipulation (market abuse)

THE EUROPEAN PARLIAMENT AND THE COUNCIL OF THE EUROPEAN UNION,

Having regard to the Treaty establishing the European Community, and in particular Article 95 thereof,

Having regard to the proposal from the Commission [1],

Having regard to the opinion of the European Economic and Social Committee [2],

Having regard to the opinion of the European Central Bank [3],

Acting in accordance with the procedure laid down in Article 251 [4],

Whereas:

(1) A genuine Single Market for financial services is crucial for economic growth and job creation in the Community.

(2) An integrated and efficient financial market requires market integrity. The smooth functioning of securities markets and public confidence in markets are prerequisites for economic growth and wealth. Market abuse harms the integrity of financial markets and public confidence in securities and derivatives.

(3) The Commission Communication of 11 May 1999 entitled 'Implementing the framework for financial markets: action plan' identifies a series of actions that are needed

1 OJ C 240 E, 28.8.2001, p. 265.

2 OJ C 80, 3.4.2002, p. 61.

3 OJ C 24, 26.1.2002, p. 8.

4 Opinion of the European Parliament of 14 March 2002 (not yet ublished in the Official Journal) Council Common Position of 19 uly 2002 (OJ C 228 E, 25.9.2002, p. 19) and Decision of the uropean Parliament of 24 October 2002 (not yet published in the fficial Journal).

欧洲议会与欧盟理事会
第2003/6/EC号指令

[本指令于2003年1月28日通过，
关于内幕交易和市场操纵(市场滥用)]

欧洲议会与欧盟理事会，

根据《欧洲共同体条约》(以下简称《条约》)，特别是其中的第95条，

根据欧盟委员会的提议，[1]
根据欧洲经济与社会委员会的意见，[2]
根据欧洲中央银行的意见，[3]
依照第251条规定的程序，[4]
鉴于：
(1)真正单一的金融服务市场对于欧共体的经济增长和创造就业机会至关重要。

(2)诚信是一体化和高效率的金融市场的题中之义。证券市场的平稳运行和公众对市场的信心是经济增长和繁荣的先决条件。市场滥用将损害金融市场的诚信度并打击公众对证券和衍生品的信心。

(3)欧盟委员会于1999年5月11日发布的名为《落实金融市场框架:行动计划》的通报明确了为完善单一的金融服务市场所应采取的一系列行动。2000年4月于里斯本

1 2001年8月28日《欧盟公报》C240 E，第265页。

2 2002年4月3日《欧盟公报》C80，第61页。

3 2002年1月26日《欧盟公报》C24，第8页。

4 2002年3月14日欧洲议会意见(尚未在《欧盟公报》公布)、2002年7月19日欧盟理事会共同立场(2002年9月25日《欧盟公报》C228 E，第19页)以及2002年10月24日欧洲议会决定(尚未在《欧盟公报》公布)。

in order to complete the single market for financial services. The Lisbon European Council of April 2000 called for the implementation of that action plan by 2005. The action plan stresses the need to draw up a Directive against market manipulation.

(4) At its meeting on 17 July 2000, the Council set up the Committee of Wise Men on the Regulation of European Securities Markets. In its final report, the Committee of Wise Men proposed the introduction of new legislative techniques based on a four-level approach, namely framework principles, implementing measures, cooperation and enforcement. Level 1, the Directive, should confine itself to broad general 'framework' principles while Level 2 should contain technical implementing measures to be adopted by the Commission with the assistance of a committee.

(5) The Resolution adopted by the Stockholm European Council of March 2001 endorsed the final report of the Committee of Wise Men and the proposed four-level approach to make the regulatory process for Community securities legislation more efficient and transparent.

(6) The Resolution of the European Parliament of 5 February 2002 on the implementation of financial services legislation also endorsed the Committee of Wise Men's report, on the basis of the solemn declaration made before Parliament the same day by the Commission and the letter of 2 October 2001 addressed by the Internal Market Commissioner to the chairman of Parliament's Committee on Economic and Monetary Affairs with regard to the safeguards for the European Parliament's role in this process.

(7) The measures necessary for the implementation of this Directive should be adopted in accordance with Council Decision 1999/468/EC of 28 June 1999 laying down the procedures for the exercise of implementing powers conferred on the Commission [1].

(8) According to the Stockholm European Council, Level 2 implementing measures should be used more frequently, to ensure that technical provisions can be kept up to date with market and supervisory developments, and deadlines should be set for all stages of Level 2 work.

(9) The European Parliament should be given a period of three months from the first transmission of draft implementing measures to allow it to examine them and to give its opinion. However, in urgent and duly justified cases, this period may be shortened. If, within that period, a resolution is passed by the European Parliament, the Commission should re-examine the draft measures.

(10) New financial and technical developments enhance the incentives, means and opportunities for market abuse: through new products, new technologies, increasing cross-border activities and the Internet.

1 OJ L 184, 17.7.1999, p. 23.

举行的欧洲理事会会议呼吁在2005年之前落实该项《行动计划》。《行动计划》强调了制定一项反市场操纵指令的必要性。

（4）欧盟理事会在2000年7月17日的会议中成立了欧洲证券市场监管专家委员会。在其提交的最终报告中，专家委员会建议采用基于四级立法程序的新的立法技术，即框架原则、实施细则、合作与执法。第一级立法，即指令应只阐述宏观的、一般性的“框架性”原则，第二级立法应当阐述欧盟委员会在各个委员会的协助下制定的技术性实施细则。

（5）2001年3月于斯德哥尔摩举行的欧州理事会会议通过的决议同意并支持了专家委员会的最终报告及其建议的四级立法程序，以保证欧共体证券领域立法程序更高的效率和透明度。

（6）基于欧盟委员会2002年2月5日向欧洲议会作出的庄严声明和内部市场委员于2001年10月2日就确保欧洲议会在上述立法程序中的作用致经济和货币事务委员会主席的信函，《欧洲议会关于实施金融服务立法的决议》（2002年2月5日）也同意和支持专家委员会的报告。

（7）应依照《欧盟理事会关于制定欧盟委员会行使其被授予的实施权之程序的第1999/468/EC号决定》[1]（1999年6月28日）制定本指令所需实施细则。

（8）根据欧洲理事会斯德哥尔摩会议的决议，应更多地使用第二级的立法即实施细则，以确保技术性条款能反映市场和监管方面的最新发展动态，同时，应为第二级立法的每一阶段工作设定完成期限。

（9）欧洲议会应在实施细则草案首次递交之后3个月内进行审核并提出意见。但在紧急并有正当理由的情形下，可以缩短该期限。欧洲议会在该等缩短期限内通过了任何决议的，欧盟委员会应对细则草案重新进行审核。

（10）新的金融发展和技术进步，增加了通过新产品、新技术、日益增多的跨境活动和互联网进行的市场滥用的动机、手段和机会。

1 1999年7月17日《欧盟公报》L184，第23页。

(11) The existing Community legal framework to protect market integrity is incomplete. Legal requirements vary from one Member State to another, leaving economic actors often uncertain over concepts, definitions and enforcement. In some Member States there is no legislation addressing the issues of price manipulation and the dissemination of misleading information.

(12) Market abuse consists of insider dealing and market manipulation. The objective of legislation against insider dealing is the same as that of legislation against market manipulation: to ensure the integrity of Community financial markets and to enhance investor confidence in those markets. It is therefore advisable to adopt combined rules to combat both insider dealing and market manipulation. A single Directive will ensure throughout the Community the same framework for allocation of responsibilities, enforcement and cooperation.

(13) Given the changes in financial markets and in Community legislation since the adoption of Council Directive 89/592/EEC of 13 November 1989 coordinating regulations on insider dealing [1], that Directive should now be replaced, to ensure consistency with legislation against market manipulation. A new Directive is also needed to avoid loopholes in Community legislation which could be used for wrongful conduct and which would undermine public confidence and therefore prejudice the smooth functioning of the markets.

(14) This Directive meets the concerns expressed by the Member States following the terrorist attacks on 11 September 2001 as regards the fight against financing terrorist activities.

(15) Insider dealing and market manipulation prevent full and proper market transparency, which is a prerequisite for trading for all economic actors in integrated financial markets.

(16) Inside information is any information of a precise nature which has not been made public, relating, directly or indirectly, to one or more issuers of financial instruments or to one or more financial instruments. Information which could have a significant effect on the evolution and forming of the prices of a regulated market as such could be considered as information which indirectly relates to one or more issuers of financial instruments or to one or more related derivative financial instruments.

(17) As regards insider dealing, account should be taken of cases where inside information originates not from a profession or function but from criminal activities, the preparation or execution of which could have a significant effect on the prices of one or more financial instruments or on price formation in the regulated market as such.

1 OJ L 334, 18.11.1989, p. 30.

(11)欧共体保护市场诚信度的现有法律框架并不完善。由于成员国的法律要求各异,经济主体对于各种概念、定义和执法活动往往感到无所适从。在部分成员国,有关价格操纵和误导性信息散布的立法尚付之阙如。

(12)市场滥用包括内幕交易和市场操纵。反内幕交易的立法宗旨与反市场操纵的立法宗旨并无二致,两者均旨在确保欧共体金融市场的诚信度以及增强投资者对该等市场的信心。因此,通过组合规则同时打击内幕交易和市场操纵行为是明智之举。单一指令有助于确保欧共体范围内在责任分配、执法和合作方面适用统一的框架。

(13)自通过《欧洲经济共同体理事会协调关于内幕交易监管的法规的第89/592/EEC号指令》[1](1989年11月13日)以来,金融市场和欧共体立法均发生了变化,有鉴于此,原指令应被取代,以确保市场操纵立法的一致性。同时应制定新的指令,避免欧共体立法中相关漏洞被不当利用,削弱公众对市场的信心,从而影响市场的平稳运行。

(14)本指令顺应了2001年9月11日恐怖袭击过后各成员国在打击资助恐怖活动的斗争中所表现的关注。

(15)内幕交易和市场操纵妨碍市场实现充分而适当的透明度,而这正是所有经济主体在一体化的金融市场进行交易的前提条件。

(16)内幕信息是与一个或多个金融工具发行人或与一项或多项金融工具直接或间接相关的任何尚未公开的确切信息。对某一受监管市场的价格演变和形成有重大影响的信息可视为与一个或多个金融工具发行人或与一项或多项相关衍生金融工具间接相关的信息。

(17)在界定内幕交易之时,应考虑到以下情形,即内幕信息并非来自于其职业或职务,而是源自犯罪活动,且该犯罪活动的准备或实施可能会对一项或多项金融工具的价格或受监管市场中的价格形成造成重大影响。

1 1989年11月18日《欧盟公报》L334,第30页。

(18) Use of inside information can consist in the acquisition or disposal of financial instruments by a person who knows, or ought to have known, that the information possessed is inside information. In this respect, the competent authorities should consider what a normal and reasonable person would know or should have known in the circumstances. Moreover, the mere fact that market makers, bodies authorised to act as counterparties, or persons authorised to execute orders on behalf of third parties with inside information confine themselves, in the first two cases, to pursuing their legitimate business of buying or selling financial instruments or, in the last case, to carrying out an order dutifully, should not in itself be deemed to constitute use of such inside information.

(19) Member States should tackle the practice known as 'front running', including 'front running' in commodity derivatives, where it constitutes market abuse under the definitions contained in this Directive.

(20) A person who enters into transactions or issues orders to trade which are constitutive of market manipulation may be able to establish that his reasons for entering into such transactions or issuing orders to trade were legitimate and that the transactions and orders to trade were in conformity with accepted practice on the regulated market concerned. A sanction could still be imposed if the competent authority established that there was another, illegitimate, reason behind these transactions or orders to trade.

(21) The competent authority may issue guidance on matters covered by this Directive, e.g. definition of inside information in relation to derivatives on commodities or implementation of the definition of accepted market practices relating to the definition of market manipulation. This guidance should be in conformity with the provisions of the Directive and the implementing measures adopted in accordance with the comitology procedure.

(22) Member States should be able to choose the most appropriate way to regulate persons producing or disseminating research concerning financial instruments or issuers of financial instruments or persons producing or disseminating other information recommending or suggesting investment strategy, including appropriate mechanisms for self-regulation, which should be notified to the Commission.

(23) Posting of inside information by issuers on their internet sites should be in accordance with the rules on transfer of personal data to third countries as laid down in Directive 95/46/EC of the European Parliament and of the Council of 24 October 1995 on the protection of individuals with regard to the processing of personal data and on the movement of such data [1].

(24) Prompt and fair disclosure of information to the public enhances market

1 OJ L 281, 23.11.1995, p. 31.

(18)知悉或理应知悉所掌握的信息为内幕信息的人购买或处置金融工具,即可构成对内幕信息的利用。有鉴于此,主管部门应考虑在该等情况下,一个正常而理性的人知悉或理应知悉的信息内容。此外,仅有以下事实本身并不足以构成对该等内幕信息的利用:做市商或获准作为对手方的机构从事其合法买入或卖出金融工具的行为,或获准代表第三方利用内幕信息执行指令的人员尽职地执行某项指令的行为。

(19)当所谓"抢跑交易"(包括商品衍生品的"抢跑交易")的做法构成本指令所定义的市场滥用时,各成员国应予以规制。

(20)所参与的交易或发出的交易指令构成市场操纵的人,可能能够证明其从事上述行为的理由是合法的,且交易和交易指令与相关受监管市场上公认的惯例相符。但只要主管部门证实在此等交易或交易指令背后存在其他非法理由,仍可对行为人施以处罚。

(21)主管部门可就本指令管辖范围内的事项发布指引,如对与商品衍生品有关的内幕信息进行定义或落实与市场操纵的定义有关的公认市场惯例的定义。该等指引应与本指令的规定以及根据专家委员会程序所制定的实施细则相符。

(22)各成员国应该能够选择最合适的方式(包括适当的自律机制)对以下人员进行监管,并通知欧盟委员会其所选择的方式:制作或传播关于金融工具或金融工具发行人的研究结果的人;或制作或传播其他包含投资战略建议或提议的信息的人。

(23)发行人在其网站上发布内幕信息时应遵守《欧洲议会与欧盟理事会关于处理个人资料时对个人的保护以及该等资料的自由流动的第95/46/EC号指令》[1](1995年10月24日)所制定的将个人数据转交第三国的规则。

(24)及时、公允地向公众披露信息有助于增强市场诚信度,而发行人的选择性披

1 1995年11月23日《欧盟公报》L281,第31页。

integrity, whereas selective disclosure by issuers can lead to a loss of investor confidence in the integrity of financial markets. Professional economic actors should contribute to market integrity by various means. Such measures could include, for instance, the creation of 'grey lists', the application of 'window trading' to sensitive categories of personnel, the application of internal codes of conduct and the establishment of 'Chinese walls'. Such preventive measures may contribute to combating market abuse only if they are enforced with determination and are dutifully controlled. Adequate enforcement control would imply for instance the designation of compliance officers within the bodies concerned and periodic checks conducted by independent auditors.

(25) Modern communication methods make it possible for financial market professionals and private investors to have more equal access to financial information, but also increase the risk of the spread of false or misleading information.

(26) Greater transparency of transactions conducted by persons persons closely associated with them discharging managerial responsibilities within issuers and, where applicable, persons closely associated with them, constitutes a preventive measure against market abuse. The publication of those transactions on at least an individual basis can also be a highly valuable source of information to investors.

(27) Market operators should contribute to the prevention of market abuse and adopt structural provisions aimed at preventing and detecting market manipulation practices. Such provisions may include requirements concerning transparency of transactions concluded, total disclosure of price regularisation agreements, a fair system of order pairing, introduction of an effective atypical-order detection scheme, sufficiently robust financial instrument reference price fixing schemes and clarity of rules on the suspension of transactions.

(28) This Directive should be interpreted, and implemented by Member States, in a manner consistent with the requirements for effective regulation in order to protect the interests of holders of transferable securities carrying voting rights in a company (or which may carry such rights as a consequence of the exercise of rights or conversion) when the company is subject to a public takeover bid or other proposed change of control. In particular, this Directive does not in any way prevent a Member State from putting or having in place such measures as it sees fit for these purposes.

(29) Having access to inside information relating to another company and using it in the context of a public takeover bid for the purpose of gaining control of that company or proposing a merger with that company should not in itself be deemed to constitute insider dealıng.

(30) Since the acquisition or disposal of financial instruments necessarily involves a prior decision to acquire or dispose taken by the person who undertakes one or other of

露则可能导致投资者对金融市场诚信度丧失信心。专业经济主体应通过各种方式维护市场诚信度。该等措施可包括建立“灰名单”,对敏感类人员适用“窗口交易”,适用内部行为守则以及建立“隔离墙”等。上述防范措施唯有得到坚决地执行和尽职地控制,方能发挥打击市场滥用的作用。适当的执行控制包括在相关机构内选任合规官,以及通过独立的审计师进行定期检查。

(25)现代通信方式一方面使金融市场专业人士和私人投资者彼此的金融信息查阅权更为公平,但另一方面也加深了虚假或误导性信息传播的风险。

(26)增加发行人内部履行管理职责的人以及与其密切相关的人(如有)所开展交易的透明度,是打击市场滥用的一项预防性措施。逐一公布该等交易,对投资者获得信息意义重大。

(27)市场经营者应致力于防范市场滥用,并制定旨在防范和发现市场操纵行为的架构性规定。该等规定可涉及如下事项:成交交易的透明度、价格调整协议的完整披露、公允的指令配对系统、有效的非典型指令监测机制的引入、充分完善的金融工具参考定价机制以及交易暂停规则的阐明。

(28)本指令应由各成员国予以解释和实施,其采取的方式应与公司发生公开收购要约或面临其他控制权变动时,为保护公司有表决权的可转让证券(或可能因行权或转换而具有表决权的证券)持有人的利益而进行有效监管的要求一致。本指令不以任何方式妨碍成员国为实现上述目的而采取或落实其认为适当的措施。

(29)接触到与其他公司相关的内幕信息并将之用于公开收购要约,以期获得对该公司的控制权或兼并该公司的,该等行为本身不应被视为构成内幕交易。

(30)金融工具的购买或处置必然涉及从事该等交易的人之前作出的购买或处置决定,因此,购买或处置本身不应被视为构成对内幕信息的利用。

these operations, the carrying out of this acquisition or disposal should not be deemed in itself to constitute the use of inside information.

(31) Research and estimates developed from publicly available data should not be regarded as inside information and, therefore, any transaction carried out on the basis of such research or estimates should not be deemed in itself to constitute insider dealing within the meaning of this Directive.

(32) Member States and the European System of Central Banks, national central banks or any other officially designated body, or any person acting on their behalf, should not be restricted in carrying out monetary, exchange rate or public debt management policy.

(33) Stabilisation of financial instruments or trading in own shares in buy-back programmes can be legitimate, in certain circumstances, for economic reasons and should not, therefore, in themselves be regarded as market abuse. Common standards should be developed to provide practical guidance.

(34) The widening scope of financial markets, the rapid change and the range of new products and developments require a wide application of this Directive to financial instruments and techniques involved, in order to guarantee the integrity of Community financial markets.

(35) Establishing a level playing field in Community financial markets requires wide geographical application of the provisions covered by this Directive. As regards derivative instruments not admitted to trading but falling within the scope of this Directive, each Member State should be competent to sanction actions carried out on its territory or abroad which concern underlying financial instruments admitted to trading on a regulated market situated or operating within its territory or for which a request for admission to trading on such a regulated market has been made. Each Member State should also be competent to sanction actions carried out on its territory which concern underlying financial instruments admitted to trading on a regulated market in a Member State or for which a request for admission to trading on such a market has been made.

(36) A variety of competent authorities in Member States, having different responsibilities, may create confusion among economic actors. A single competent authority should be designated in each Member State to assume at least final responsibility for supervising compliance with the provisions adopted pursuant to this Directive, as well as international collaboration. Such an authority should be of an administrative nature guaranteeing its independence of economic actors and avoiding conflicts of interest. In accordance with national law, Member States should ensure appropriate financing of the competent authority. That authority should have adequate arrangements for consultation concerning possible changes in national legislation such as a

(31)利用公开数据得出的研究和估算结果不应被视为内幕信息,因此任何基于该等研究或估算结果所开展的交易本身亦不得被视为构成本指令所定义的内幕交易。

(32)各成员国和欧洲中央银行体系、成员国中央银行或任何其他官方指定机构或任何代表上述实体行事的人在执行货币、汇率或公共债务管理政策时不应受到限制。

(33)在某些情况下,出于经济原因而对金融工具进行稳定操作或在回购计划中交易自身股票可以是合法的,因此该等行为本身不应被视为市场滥用。应制定相关通用标准对此提供实践指引。

(34)金融市场范围的日益扩大,新型产品层出不穷、日益增多,都要求本指令广泛适用于相关金融工具和金融技术,以保证欧共体金融市场的诚信度。

(35)在欧共体金融市场建立公平竞争的环境,需要保证本指令能在广泛的地域得到适用。对未获准交易但属于本指令管辖范围内的衍生品工具而言,各成员国应有权对在其境内或境外开展的涉及以下金融工具的活动实施处罚:已获准在位于其境内或在其境内运营的受监管市场交易的标的金融工具,或已申请在上述受监管市场交易的标的金融工具。各成员国还应有权对在其境内开展的涉及获准在某成员国受监管市场交易或申请在上述市场交易的标的金融工具的活动实施处罚。

(36)各成员国主管部门繁多,且其职责各异,可能会造成经济主体的困惑。各成员国应指定单一的主管部门来至少承担监管依本指令制定的国内规定的合规情况及国际合作的最终责任。该部门应为行政管理部门,以保证其独立于经济主体并避免利益冲突。根据成员国国内法律,成员国应确保主管部门有适当的经费来源。该部门应对国内立法可能发生的变更做好充分的咨询安排,如设立由发行人、金融服务供应商及消费者代表组成的咨询委员会,以充分了解其意见和关注的问题。

consultative committee composed of representatives of issuers, financial services providers and consumers, so as to be fully informed of their views and concerns.

(37) A common minimum set of effective tools and powers for the competent authority of each Member State will guarantee contribute at their level to supervisory effectiveness. Market undertakings and all economic actors should also market integrity. In this sense, the designation of a single competent authority for market abuse does not exclude collaboration links or delegation under the responsibility of the competent authority, between that authority and market undertakings with a view to guaranteeing efficient supervision of compliance with the provisions adopted pursuant to this Directive.

(38) In order to ensure that a Community framework against market abuse is sufficient, any infringement of the prohibitions or requirements laid down pursuant to this Directive will have to be promptly detected and sanctioned. To this end, sanctions should be sufficiently dissuasive and proportionate to the gravity of the infringement and to the gains realised and should be consistently applied.

(39) Member States should remain alert, in determining the administrative measures and sanctions, to the need to ensure a degree of uniformity of regulation from one Member State to another.

(40) Increasing cross-border activities require improved cooperation and a comprehensive set of provisions for the exchange of information between national competent authorities. The organisation of supervision and of investigatory powers in each Member State should not hinder cooperation between the competent national authorities.

(41) Since the objective of the proposed action, namely to prevent market abuse in the form of insider dealing and market manipulation, cannot be sufficiently achieved by the Member States and can therefore, by reason of the scale and effects of the measures, be better achieved at Community level, the Community may adopt measures, in accordance with the principle of subsidiarity as set out in Article 5 of the Treaty. In accordance with the principle of proportionality, as set out in that Article, this Directive does not go beyond what is necessary in order to achieve that objective.

(42) Technical guidance and implementing measures for the rules laid down in this Directive may from time to time be necessary to take account of new developments on financial markets. The Commission should accordingly be empowered to adopt implementing measures, provided that these do not modify the essential elements of this Directive and the Commission acts according to the principles set out in this Directive, after consulting the European Securities Committee established by Commission Decision 2001/528/EC [1].

1 OJ L 191, 13.7.2001, p. 45.

(37)授予各成员国主管部门一套共同和必不可少的有效监管手段与权力，将有助于保证监管的有效性。市场组织以及所有经济主体也应各尽其力，为市场诚信度作出贡献。在此意义上，指定单一的市场滥用主管部门并不排除在其职权范围内与市场组织进行合作或向市场组织委托授权，以保证对依本指令制定的国内规定的合规情况进行有效监管，但主管部门仍需对此自负其责。

(38)为确保欧共体反市场滥用框架的充分性，任何违反根据本指令而制定的要求或禁止性规定的行为，均应予以及时发现和处罚。为此，处罚应具有充分的威慑作用并与违规行为的严重性以及所实现的收益成比例，同时其适用应有一致性。

(39)在决定采取行政措施和处罚时，各成员国应随时注意以确保各成员国之间形成某种程度上统一的监管水平。

(40)跨境活动的日益频繁要求各国家级主管部门之间加强合作，并制定一套全面的信息交换规定。各成员国的监管和调查权的组织形式不应妨碍各国家级主管部门之间的合作。

(41)由于行动计划提出的目标，即防范以内幕交易和市场操纵形式出现的市场滥用，单靠成员国不足以实现，而考虑到相关措施的适用范围和效用，该等目标更容易在欧共体层面获得实现，因此，欧共体可依照《条约》第5条规定的辅助性原则制定相关细则。根据该条规定的比例原则，本指令仅作出实现上述目标的必要规定。

(42)就本指令的规则制定技术性指引和实施细则时，应不时考虑金融市场的最新发展。为此，欧盟委员会应有权制定相关实施细则，前提是此等实施细则不对本指令的基本要素作出改动，并且欧盟委员会在行事时应咨询根据欧盟委员会第2001/528/EC号决定[1]成立的欧洲证券委员会的意见，并遵循本指令所规定的原则。

1 2001年7月13日《欧盟公报》L191，第45页。

(43) In exercising its implementing powers in accordance with this Directive, the Commission should respect the following principles:

— the need to ensure confidence in financial markets among investors by promoting high standards of transparency in financial markets,

— the need to provide investors with a wide range of competing investments and a level of disclosure and protection tailored to their circumstances,

— the need to ensure that independent regulatory authorities enforce the rules consistently, especially as regards the fight against economic crime,

— the need for high levels of transparency and consultation with all market participants and with the European Parliament and the Council,

— the need to encourage innovation in financial markets if they are to be dynamic and efficient,

— the need to ensure market integrity by close and reactive monitoring of financial innovation,

— the importance of reducing the cost of, and increasing access to, capital,

— the balance of costs and benefits to market participants on a long-term basis (including small and medium-sized businesses and small investors) in any implementing measures,

— the need to foster the international competitiveness of EU financial markets without prejudice to a much needed extension of international cooperation,

— the need to achieve a level playing field for all market participants by establishing EU-wide regulations every time it is appropriate,

— the need to respect differences in national markets where these do not unduly impinge on the coherence of the single market,

— the need to ensure coherence with other Community legislation in this area, as imbalances in information and a lack of transparency may jeopardise the operation of the markets and above all harm consumers and small investors.

(44) This Directive respects the fundamental rights and observes the principles recognised in particular by the Charter of Fundamental Rights of the European Union and in particular by Article 11 thereof and Article 10 of the European Convention on Human Rights. In this regard, this Directive does not in any way prevent Member States from applying their constitutional rules relating to freedom of the press and freedom of expression in the media.

HAVE ADOPTED THIS DIRECTIVE:

Article 1

For the purposes of this Directive:

1. 'Inside information' shall mean information of a precise nature which has not

(43)根据本指令行使其实施权时,欧盟委员会应遵守下列原则:

——有必要推行高标准的金融市场透明度,确保投资者对金融市场的信心;

——有必要向投资者提供多样化的竞争性投资机会,以及与其实际情况相吻合的信息披露与保护水平;

——有必要确保独立监管机构执行相关规则(特别是打击经济犯罪的规则)的一致性;

——有必要保持高水平的透明度,并征求所有市场参与者以及欧洲议会和欧盟理事会的意见;

——有必要鼓励创新,使金融市场具有活力和效率;

——有必要对金融创新进行密切、灵活的监控,确保市场诚信度;

——有必要降低资本成本和拓宽融资渠道;

——采取任何实施细则均需实现市场参与者(包括中小型企业和小型投资者)成本和效益的长期平衡;

——有必要在不影响国际合作深化的前提下,培育欧共体金融市场的国际竞争力;

——有必要适时制定适用于全欧盟的法规,为所有市场参与者提供公平的竞争环境;

——有必要在不过度冲击单一市场一致性的前提下尊重各成员国金融市场的差异;

——有必要确保此领域法律与其他欧共体法律的一致性,以防止信息的不对等和透明度的缺失危害市场运行,尤其是防止因此损及消费者和小型投资者的利益。

(44)本指令遵守并奉行《欧盟基本权利宪章》所认可的基本权利和原则,尤其是《欧盟基本权利宪章》第11条规定以及《欧盟人权公约》第10条规定所认可的关于人权的基本权利和原则。有鉴于此,本指令不以任何方式禁止各成员国实施关于新闻自由和媒体言论自由的宪法规定。

兹通过本指令如下:

第1条

就本指令而言:

1."内幕信息" 指与一个或多个金融工具发行人或与一项或多项金融工具直接或

been made public, relating, directly or indirectly, to one or more issuers of financial instruments or to one or more financial instruments and which, if it were made public, would be likely to have a significant effect on the prices of those financial instruments or on the price of related derivative financial instruments.

In relation to derivatives on commodities, 'inside information' shall mean information of a precise nature which has not been made public, relating, directly or indirectly, to one or more such derivatives and which users of markets on which such derivatives are traded would expect to receive in accordance with accepted market practices on those markets.

For persons charged with the execution of orders concerning financial instruments, 'inside information' shall also mean information conveyed by a client and related to the client's pending orders, which is of a precise nature, which relates directly or indirectly to one or more issuers of financial instruments or to one or more financial instruments, and which, if it were made public, would be likely to have a significant effect on the prices of those financial instruments or on the price of related derivative financial instruments.

2. 'Market manipulation' shall mean:

(a) transactions or orders to trade:

— which give, or are likely to give, false or misleading signals as to the supply of, demand for or price of financial instruments, or

— which secure, by a person, or persons acting in collaboration, the price of one or several financial instruments at an abnormal or artificial level,

unless the person who entered into the transactions or issued the orders to trade establishes that his reasons for so doing are legitimate and that these transactions or orders to trade conform to accepted market practices on the regulated market concerned;

(b) transactions or orders to trade which employ fictitious devices or any other form of deception or contrivance;

(c) dissemination of information through the media, including the Internet, or by any other means, which gives, or is likely to give, false or misleading signals as to financial instruments, including the dissemination of rumours and false or misleading news, where the person who made the dissemination knew, or ought to have known, that the information was false or misleading. In respect of journalists when they act in their professional capacity such dissemination of information is to be assessed, without prejudice to Article 11, taking into account the rules governing their profession, unless those persons derive, directly or indirectly, an advantage or profits from the dissemination of the information in question.

In particular, the following instances are derived from the core definition given in points (a)(b) and (c) above:

间接相关的尚未公开的确切信息，且该等信息一旦公开，将很可能对该等金融工具的价格或相关衍生金融工具的价格造成重大影响。

对于商品衍生品而言，"内幕信息" 指与一项或多项衍生品直接或间接相关的尚未公开的确切信息，且该等衍生品交易市场的用户均预期根据该等市场的公认市场惯例收到该等信息。

对于负责执行金融工具指令的人而言，"内幕信息" 还指客户提供的且与客户待执行的指令相关的与一个或多个金融工具发行人或一项或多项金融工具直接或间接相关的尚未公开的确切信息，且该等信息一旦公开，将可能对该等金融工具的价格或相关衍生金融工具的价格造成重大影响。

2."市场操纵"指：

(a)符合以下情况的交易或交易指令：

——发出或可能发出关于金融工具的供应、需求或价格的虚假或误导性信号，或

——一人或多人串通确保一项或数项金融工具的价格，导致该价格处于异常或人为的水平，

但是，达成交易或发出交易指令的人能够证明其如此行为的理由是合法的并证明此等交易或交易指令符合所涉受监管市场的公认市场惯例的除外；

(b)采用虚假手段或任何其他形式的欺骗或诡计开展的交易或签发的交易指令；

(c)在明知或应知信息具有虚假或误导性的情形下，通过媒体(包括互联网)或以任何其他方式传播信息(包括散布谣言和虚假或误导性消息)，且该信息发出了或可能发出关于金融工具的虚假或误导性信号。在不影响第11条的规定的情形下，认定新闻工作者系以专业身份传播上述信息的，须考虑到其职业规范，但该等人从所涉信息的传播中直接或间接获取好处或利益的除外，不得获得该等认定。

根据上述第a目、第b目和第c目给出的核心定义，市场操作主要有以下几种情形：

— conduct by a person, or persons acting in collaboration, to secure a dominant position over the supply of or demand for a financial instrument which has the effect of fixing, directly or indirectly, purchase or sale prices or creating other unfair trading conditions,

— the buying or selling of financial instruments at the close of the market with the effect of misleading investors acting on the basis of closing prices,

— taking advantage of occasional or regular access to the traditional or electronic media by voicing an opinion about a financial instrument (or indirectly about its issuer) while having previously taken positions on that financial instrument and profiting subsequently from the impact of the opinions voiced on the price of that instrument, without having simultaneously disclosed that conflict of interest to the public in a proper and effective way.

The definitions of market manipulation shall be adapted so as to ensure that new patterns of activity that in practice constitute market manipulation can be included.

3. 'Financial instrument' shall mean:

— transferable securities as defined in Council Directive 93/22/EEC of 10 May 1993 on investment services in the securities field [1],

— units in collective investment undertakings,

— money market instruments,

— financial futures contracts, including equivalent cash-settled instruments,

— forward interest-rate agreements,

— interest rate, currency and equity swaps,

— options to acquire or dispose of any instrument falling into these categories, including equivalent cash-settled instruments. This category includes in particular options on currency and on interest rates,

— derivatives on commodities,

— any other instrument admitted to trading on a regulated market in a Member State or for which a request for admission to trading on such a market has been made.

4. 'Regulated market' shall mean a market as defined by Article 1(13) of Directive 93/22/EEC.

5. 'Accepted market practices' shall mean practices that are reasonably expected in one or more financial markets and are accepted by the competent authority in accordance with guidelines adopted by the Commission in accordance with the procedure laid down in Article 17(2).

6. 'Person' shall mean any natural or legal person.

---

1 OJ L 141, 11.6.1993, p. 27. Directive as last amended by European arliament and Council Directive 2000/64/EC (OJ L 290,17.11.2000, p. 27).

——一人或多人串通行事以确保取得对某项金融工具供需的支配地位,从而得以直接或间接地决定买入或卖出价格或创造其他不公平交易条件,

——在临近收市时买卖金融工具,以误导投资者基于收盘价行事,

——已持有某项金融工具头寸的人,定期或不定期地利用其接触传统媒体或电子媒体的机会,发表关于该金融工具的意见(或间接发表关于其发行人的意见),并从该等意见所造成的对金融工具价格的影响中获益,但其没有同时以适当有效的方式向公众披露该等利益冲突。

市场操纵的定义应适时调整,以确保将实践中出现的新形式的市场操纵活动纳入市场操纵的定义之中。

3.“金融工具”指:

——《欧洲经济共同体理事会关于证券领域投资服务的第93/22/EEC号指令》[1](1993年5月10日)所定义的可转让证券,

——集合投资计划的单位,

——货币市场工具,

——金融期货合约,包括等效的现金结算工具,

——远期利率协议,

——利率、货币和股权互换,

——购买或处置任何上述类别工具(包括等效的现金结算工具)的期权。本类别主要包括货币和利率期权,

——商品衍生品,

——任何其他获准在某成员国受监管市场交易的工具,或已申请在上述市场交易的工具。

4.“受监管市场”指第93/22/EEC号指令第1条第13款所定义的市场。

5.“公认市场惯例”指在一个或多个金融市场被合理预期的,且主管部门根据欧盟委员会依第17条第2款所述的须经欧盟理事会和欧洲议会审查的监管程序制定的指引予以认可的惯例。

6.“人”指任何自然人或法人。

---

1 1993年6月11日《欧盟公报》L141,第27页。该指令由欧洲议会与欧盟理事会第2000/64/EC号指令(2000年11月17日《欧盟公报》L290,第27页)作出最新修正。

7. 'Competent authority' shall mean the competent authority designated in accordance with Article 11.

In order to take account of developments on financial markets and to ensure uniform application of this Directive in the Community, the Commission, acting in accordance with the procedure laid down in Article 17(2) shall adopt implementing measures concerning points 1, 2 and 3 of this Article.

Article 2

1. Member States shall prohibit any person referred to in the second subparagraph who possesses inside information from using that information by acquiring or disposing of, or by trying to acquire or dispose of, for his own account or for the account of a third party, either directly or indirectly, financial instruments to which that information relates.

The first subparagraph shall apply to any person who possesses that information:

(a) by virtue of his membership of the administrative, management or supervisory bodies of the issuer; or

(b) by virtue of his holding in the capital of the issuer; or

(c) by virtue of his having access to the information through the exercise of his employment, profession or duties; or

(d) by virtue of his criminal activities.

2. Where the person referred to in paragraph 1 is a legal person, the prohibition laid down in that paragraph shall also apply to the natural persons who take part in the decision to carry out the transaction for the account of the legal person concerned.

3. This Article shall not apply to transactions conducted in the discharge of an obligation that has become due to acquire or dispose of financial instruments where that obligation results from an agreement concluded before the person concerned possessed inside information.

Article 3

Member States shall prohibit any person subject to the prohibition laid down in Article 2 from:

(a) disclosing inside information to any other person unless such disclosure is made in the normal course of the exercise of his employment, profession or duties;

(b) recommending or inducing another person, on the basis of inside information, to acquire or dispose of financial instruments to which that information relates.

Article 4

Member States shall ensure that Articles 2 and 3 also apply to any person, other than the persons referred to in those Articles, who possesses inside information while that person knows, or ought to have known, that it is inside information.

7."主管部门"指依照第11条指定的主管部门。

为反映金融市场的发展动态并确保本指令在欧共体的统一适用,欧盟委员会应依照第17条第2款规定的程序,就本条第1项、第2项和第3项制定实施细则。

第2条

1.主管部门应禁止第2项所述的持有内幕信息的任何人将该信息用于为其自身账户或第三方账户直接或间接地购买或处置,或试图购买或处置与该信息相关的金融工具。

第1项适用于因以下情况而持有该等信息的任何人:

(a)担任发行人的董事会、管理机构或监事会的成员;或

(b)持有发行人的股份;或

(c)其因工作、职业或职责的关系而有权接触该等信息;或

(d)从事犯罪活动。

2.第1款所述的人为法人的,第1款规定的禁令还应适用于参与决定为所涉法人账户进行交易的自然人。

3.本条规定不适用于为履行已到期的义务而达成的购买或处置金融工具的交易,前提是该等义务产生于所涉人员获得内幕信息之前缔结的协议。

第3条

各成员国应禁止受到第2条的禁止性规定约束的任何人从事以下活动:

(a)向任何其他人披露内幕信息,但在正常地履行其工作、职业或职责的过程中所做的披露除外;

(b)基于内幕信息建议或劝诱其他人购买或处置与该信息相关的金融工具。

第4条

除第2条和第3条所述人员外,各成员国还应确保该等条款同样适用于任何明知或应知其所持信息为内幕信息的其他人。

Article 5

Member States shall prohibit any person from engaging in market manipulation.

Article 6

1. Member States shall ensure that issuers of financial instruments inform the public as soon as possible of inside information which directly concerns the said issuers.

Without prejudice to any measures taken to comply with the provisions of the first subparagraph, Member States shall ensure that issuers, for an appropriate period, post on their Internet sites all inside information that they are required to disclose publicly.

2. An issuer may under his own responsibility delay the public disclosure of inside information, as referred to in paragraph 1, such as not to prejudice his legitimate interests provided that such omission would not be likely to mislead the public and provided that the issuer is able to ensure the confidentiality of that information. Member States may require that an issuer shall without delay inform the competent authority of the decision to delay the public disclosure of inside information.

3. Member States shall require that, whenever an issuer, or a person acting on his behalf or for his account, discloses any inside information to any third party in the normal exercise of his employment, profession or duties, as referred to in Article 3(a) he must make complete and effective public disclosure of that information, simultaneously in the case of an intentional disclosure and promptly in the case of a non-intentional disclosure.

The provisions of the first subparagraph shall not apply if the person receiving the information owes a duty of confidentiality, regardless of whether such duty is based on a law, on regulations, on articles of association or on a contract.

Member States shall require that issuers, or persons acting on their behalf or for their account, draw up a list of those persons working for them, under a contract of employment or otherwise, who have access to inside information. Issuers and persons acting on their behalf or for their account shall regularly update this list and transmit it to the competent authority whenever the latter requests it.

4. Persons discharging managerial responsibilities within an issuer of financial instruments and, where applicable, persons closely associated with them, shall, at least, notify to the competent authority the existence of transactions conducted on their own account relating to shares of the said issuer, or to derivatives or other financial instruments linked to them. Member States shall ensure that public access to information concerning such transactions, on at least an individual basis, is readily available as soon as possible.

5. Member States shall ensure that there is appropriate regulation in place to ensure that persons who produce or disseminate research concerning financial instruments or issuers of financial instruments and persons who produce or disseminate other information

第5条

各成员国应禁止任何人从事市场操纵行为。

第6条

1.各成员国应确保金融工具的发行人尽快通知公众直接涉及该发行人的内幕信息。

在不影响根据第1项采取的任何措施的情形下，各成员国应确保发行人在一段适当的期间内通过其互联网网站发布应向公众披露的所有内幕信息。

2.发行人可在自负责任的情形下推迟公开披露第1款所述的内幕信息，以避免对其合法利益造成影响，前提是上述不作为不可能对公众造成误导，且发行人能够确保该等信息的保密性。各成员国可要求发行人立即通知主管部门推迟公开披露内幕信息的决定。

3.各成员国应规定，如果发行人或为其自身账户或为第三方账户行事的人如第3条第a款所述，在正常履行其工作、职业或职责的过程中向第三方披露任何内幕信息，则必须在故意披露的同时或在非故意披露之后立即完整、有效地公开披露该等信息。

信息接收者负有保密义务的，不论该义务是法律、法规、公司章程或合同规定的义务，均不适用第1项规定。

各成员国应规定发行人或代表其利益或为其利益行事的人，编制一份根据雇佣合同或因其他原因而有机会接触内幕信息的工作人员名单。发行人和或代表其利益或为其利益行事的人应定期更新该名单，并在主管部门需要的任何时间内递交。

4.金融工具发行人内部承担管理责任的人以及与其密切关联的人(如适用)，通过自身账户交易上述发行人的股票或与其相关联的衍生品或其他金融工具的，至少应向主管部门通知该等交易的存在。各成员国应确保公众可以尽快方便地查阅有关交易的信息，至少能够逐一查阅具体的交易信息。

5.各成员国应确保制定有适当的法规，确保以下人员在向其他渠道分送或向公众公布时，合理谨慎地确保相关信息得到公允列报，并披露其利益或说明与该信息所涉金融工具有关的利益冲突：制作或传播关于金融工具或金融工具发行人的研究结果

recommending or suggesting investment strategy, intended for distribution channels or for the public, take reasonable care to ensure that such information is fairly presented and disclose their interests or indicate conflicts of interest concerning the financial instruments to which that information relates. Details of such regulation shall be notified to the Commission.

6. Member States shall ensure that market operators adopt structural provisions aimed at preventing and detecting market manipulation practices.

7. With a view to ensuring compliance with paragraphs 1 to 5, the competent authority may take all necessary measures to ensure that the public is correctly informed.

8. Public institutions disseminating statistics liable to have a significant effect on financial markets shall disseminate them in a fair and transparent way.

9. Member States shall require that any person professionally arranging transactions in financial instruments who reasonably suspects that a transaction might constitute insider dealing or market manipulation shall notify the competent authority without delay.

10. In order to take account of technical developments on financial markets and to ensure uniform application of this Directive, the Commission shall adopt, in accordance with the procedure referred to in Article 17(2) implementing measures concerning:

— the technical modalities for appropriate public disclosure of inside information as referred to in paragraphs 1 and 3,

— the technical modalities for delaying the public disclosure of inside information as referred to in paragraph 2,

— the technical modalities designed to favour a common approach in the implementation of the second sentence of paragraph 2,

— the conditions under which issuers, or entities acting on their behalf, are to draw up a list of those persons working for them and having access to inside information, as referred to in paragraph 3, together with the conditions under which such lists are to be updated,

— the categories of persons who are subject to a duty of disclosure as referred to in paragraph 4 and the characteristics of a transaction, including its size, which trigger that duty, and the technical arrangements for disclosure to the competent authority,

— technical arrangements, for the various categories of person referred to in paragraph 5, for fair presentation of research and other information recommending investment strategy and for disclosure of particular interests or conflicts of interest as referred to in paragraph 5. Such arrangements shall take into account the rules, including self-regulation, governing the profession of journalist,

— technical arrangements governing notification to the competent authority by the persons referred to in paragraph 9.

的人，以及制作或传播其他包含投资战略提议或建议的信息的人。应通知欧盟委员会上述法规的详细内容。

6.各成员国应确保市场经营者制定架构性规定，以防范和发现市场操纵行为。

7.为确保第1款至第5款得到遵守，主管部门可制定所有必要的实施细则以确保公众获得准确的信息。

8.公共机构应公允、透明地发布可能对金融市场造成重大影响的统计信息。

9.各成员国应规定，任何专业从事金融工具交易安排的人，一旦合理怀疑某项交易可能构成内幕交易或市场操纵，均应立即通知主管部门。

10.为反映金融市场的技术发展动态并确保本指令的统一适用，欧盟委员会应依照第17条第2款所述程序，就以下方面制定相关实施细则：

——第1款和第3款所述的适当地向公众披露内幕信息的技术模式，

——第2款所述的推迟向公众披露内幕信息的技术模式，

——以共同的方法实施第2款第2句的技术模式，

——发行人或代表其行事的实体在何等情形下应按第3款编制一份有机会接触内幕信息的工作人员名单，以及在何等情形下应对该等名单进行更新，

——需要遵守第4款所述披露义务的人员类别和触发该项披露义务的交易的特征（包括其规模）以及向主管部门披露交易的技术性安排，

——针对以下事项所做的技术性安排：第5款所述的各类别人员；对研究结果和其他包含投资战略建议的信息的公允列报；以及对第5款所述的特殊利益或利益冲突的披露。上述安排应考虑新闻工作者的职业规范，包括自律规则，

——第9款所述人员向主管部门通知信息时应遵守的技术性安排。

Article 7

This Directive shall not apply to transactions carried out in pursuit of monetary, exchange-rate or public debt-management policy by a Member State, by the European System of Central Banks, by a national central bank or by any other officially designated body, or by any person acting on their behalf. Member States may extend this exemption to their federated States or similar local authorities in respect of the management of their public debt.

Article 8

The prohibitions provided for in this Directive shall not apply to trading in own shares in 'buy-back' programmes or to the stabilisation of a financial instrument provided such trading is carried out in accordance with implementing measures adopted in accordance with the procedure laid down in Article 17(2).

Article 9

This Directive shall apply to any financial instrument admitted to trading on a regulated market in at least one Member State, or for which a request for admission to trading on such a market has been made, irrespective of whether or not the transaction itself actually takes place on that market.

Articles 2, 3 and 4 shall also apply to any financial instrument not admitted to trading on a regulated market in a Member State, but whose value depends on a financial instrument as referred to in paragraph 1.

Article 6(1) to (3) shall not apply to issuers who have not requested or approved admission of their financial instruments to trading on a regulated market in a Member State.

Article 10

Each Member State shall apply the prohibitions and requirements provided for in this Directive to:

(a) actions carried out on its territory or abroad concerning financial instruments that are admitted to trading on a regulated market situated or operating within its territory or for which a request for admission to trading on such market has been made;

(b) actions carried out on its territory concerning financial instruments that are admitted to trading on a regulated market in a Member State or for which a request for admission to trading on such market has been made.

Article 11

Without prejudice to the competences of the judicial authorities, each Member State shall designate a single administrative authority competent to ensure that the provisions adopted pursuant to this Directive are applied.

Member States shall establish effective consultative arrangements and procedures

第7条

本指令不适用于成员国、欧洲中央银行体系、成员国中央银行或任何其他官方指定机构或任何代表上述实体行事的人在执行货币、汇率或公共债务管理政策时所开展的交易。各成员国可将此项豁免延展适用于其联邦各州或类似的地方机构对其各自公共债务进行的管理。

第8条

本指令的禁止性规定不适用于对金融工具进行稳定操作或在回购计划中交易自身股票的行为，前提是上述交易应按依照第17条第2款规定的程序制定的实施细则进行。

第9条

本指令适用于已获准在至少一个成员国受监管市场交易的任何金融工具，或已申请在上述市场交易的任何金融工具，不论交易本身是否实际发生在该市场。

第2条、第3条和第4条也适用于未获准在成员国受监管市场交易，但其价值取决于第1款所述金融工具的任何金融工具。

第6条第1款至第3款不适用于尚未申请在成员国受监管市场交易其金融工具或申请尚未获得批准的发行人。

第10条

各成员国应将本指令的要求和禁止性规定适用于：

(a)在其境内或境外开展的涉及以下金融工具的活动：获准在位于其境内的或在其境内运行的受监管市场交易的金融工具，或已申请在上述市场交易的金融工具；

(b)在其境内开展的涉及以下金融工具的活动：获准在某成员国受监管市场交易的金融工具，或已申请在上述市场交易的金融工具。

第11条

在不影响司法部门的职权的情形下，各成员国应指定单一的行政主管部门，负责确保根据本指令制定的国内规定得到实施。

各成员国应当就其国内立法可能发生的变更，建立与市场参与者之间进行有效

with market participants concerning possible changes in national legislation. These arrangements may include consultative committees within each competent authority, the membership of which should reflect as far as possible the diversity of market participants, be they issuers, providers of financial services or consumers.

Article 12

1. The competent authority shall be given all supervisory and investigatory powers that are necessary for the exercise of its functions. It shall exercise such powers:

(a) directly; or

(b) in collaboration with other authorities or with the market undertakings; or

(c) under its responsibility by delegation to such authorities or to the market undertakings; or

(d) by application to the competent judicial authorities.

2. Without prejudice to Article 6(7) the powers referred to in paragraph 1 of this Article shall be exercised in conformity with national law and shall include at least the right to:

(a) have access to any document in any form whatsoever, and to receive a copy of it;

(b) demand information from any person, including those who are successively involved in the transmission of orders or conduct of the operations concerned, as well as their principals, and if necessary, to summon and hear any such person;

(c) carry out on-site inspections;

(d) require existing telephone and existing data traffic records;

(e) require the cessation of any practice that is contrary to the provisions adopted in the implementation of this Directive;

(f) suspend trading of the financial instruments concerned;

(g) request the freezing and/or sequestration of assets;

(h) request temporary prohibition of professional activity.

3. This Article shall be without prejudice to national legal provisions on professional secrecy.

Article 13

The obligation of professional secrecy shall apply to all persons who work or who have worked for the competent authority or for any authority or market undertaking to whom the competent authority has delegated its powers, including auditors and experts instructed by the competent authority. Information covered by professional secrecy may not be disclosed to any other person or authority except by virtue of provisions laid down by law.

Article 14

1. Without prejudice to the right of Member States to impose criminal sanctions,

的磋商安排和程序。此等安排可包括在各主管部门内设立咨询委员会,咨询委员会的成员应尽可能广泛地代表各类市场参与者,包括发行人、金融服务供应商和消费者等。

第12条

1.各主管部门应被授予履行其职能所必要的所有监管和调查权。主管部门应通过如下方式行使该等权力:

(a)直接行使;或

(b)与其他部门或市场组织共同行使;或

(c)通过委托授权由上述部门或市场组织行使,但由主管部门自行承担有关责任;或

(d)通过向有管辖权的司法部门提出申请来行使。

2.在不影响第6条第7款的前提下,本条第1款所述的权力应根据各成员国国内法律行使,且该等权力至少应包括:

(a)查阅并复印任何形式的任何文件;

(b)要求任何人(包括先后参与指令发送或进行所涉操作的人及其委托人)提供信息,并在必要时传唤任何上述人员并听取陈述;

(c)开展现场调查;

(d)要求提供现存的电话记录和数据流通记录;

(e)要求终止违反本指令实施过程中制定的国内规定的任何做法;

(f)暂停所涉金融工具的交易;

(g)申请冻结和/或扣押资产;

(h)申请临时禁止专业活动。

3.本条规定不影响各成员国关于职业保密的国内法律规定。

第13条

职业保密义务应适用于各主管部门或获得该主管部门委托授权的任何部门或市场组织的前任或现任工作人员,包括根据主管部门指示行事的审计师和专家。职业保密义务所涵盖的信息不得向任何人或部门披露,但法律另有规定的除外。

第14条

1.在不影响各成员国刑事处罚权的情形下,各成员国应确保根据其国内法律,对

Member States shall ensure, in conformity with their national law, that the appropriate administrative measures can be taken or administrative sanctions be imposed against the persons responsible where the provisions adopted in the implementation of this Directive have not been complied with. Member States shall ensure that these measures are effective, proportionate and dissuasive.

2. In accordance with the procedure laid down in Article17(2) the Commission shall, for information, draw up a list of the administrative measures and sanctions referred to in paragraph 1.

3. Member States shall determine the sanctions to be applied for failure to cooperate in an investigation covered by Article 12.

4. Member States shall provide that the competent authority may disclose to the public every measure or sanction that will be imposed for infringement of the provisions adopted in the implementation of this Directive, unless such disclosure would seriously jeopardise the financial markets or cause disproportionate damage to the parties involved.

Article 15

Member States shall ensure that an appeal may be brought before a court against the decisions taken by the competent authority.

Article 16

1. Competent authorities shall cooperate with each other whenever necessary for the purpose of carrying out their duties, making use of their powers whether set out in this Directive or in national law. Competent authorities shall render assistance to competent authorities of other Member States. In particular, they shall exchange information and cooperate in investigation activities.

2. Competent authorities shall, on request, immediately supply any information required for the purpose referred to in paragraph 1. Where necessary, the competent authorities receiving any such request shall immediately take the necessary measures in order to gather the required information. If the requested competent authority is not able to supply the required information immediately, it shall notify the requesting competent authority of the reasons. Information thus supplied shall be covered by the obligation of professional secrecy to which the persons employed or formerly employed by the competent authorities receiving the information are subject.

The competent authorities may refuse to act on a request for information where:

— communication might adversely affect the sovereignty, security or public policy of the Member State addressed,

— judicial proceedings have already been initiated in respect of the same actions and against the same persons before the authorities of the Member State addressed, or

— where a final judgment has already been delivered in relation to such persons for

违反本指令实施过程中制定的国内规定的相关责任人采取适当的行政措施或行政处罚。各成员国应确保此等措施有效、成比例且具有威慑作用。

2.欧盟委员会应依照第17条第2款规定的程序，编制一份第1款所述的行政措施和处罚清单，供成员国参考。

3.对于第12条所规定的调查不予合作的情形，各成员国应确定适用的处罚。

4.各成员国应规定，针对违反本指令实施过程中制定的国内规定的行为而施加的所有措施或处罚，主管部门均有权向公众披露，但上述披露会严重损害金融市场或对所涉各方造成不成比例的损害的除外。

第15条

各成员国应确保主管部门作出的决定可向法院提起行政诉讼。

第16条

1.各主管部门之间在必要时应相互合作，以履行其在本指令或成员国国内法律下的职责并行使相关权力。主管部门应向其他成员国主管部门提供协助，尤其在调查活动中，应相互交换信息并合作。

2.主管部门收到请求时，应立即提供为实现第1款所述之目的所需的任何信息。必要时，收到任何上述请求的主管部门均应立即采取必要措施以收集请求提供的信息。收到请求的主管部门无法立即提供所请求的信息的，应将理由告知提出信息请求的主管部门。按上述规定提供的信息应受到职业保密义务的约束，接收信息的主管部门的现任或前任雇员均须遵守该项职业保密义务。

主管部门可拒绝下列情况的信息请求：

——提供信息可能对被请求国的主权、安全或公共政策造成不利影响；

——被请求国有关部门已针对同一行为和行为人启动司法程序，或

——被请求国已针对同一行为就相关行为人作出终审判决。

the same actions in the Member State addressed.

In any such case, they shall notify the requesting competent authority accordingly, providing as detailed information as possible on those proceedings or the judgment.

Without prejudice to Article 226 of the Treaty, a competent authority whose request for information is not acted upon within a reasonable time or whose request for information is rejected may bring that non-compliance to the attention of the Committee of European Securities Regulators, where discussion will take place in order to reach a rapid and effective solution.

Without prejudice to the obligations to which they are subject in judicial proceedings under criminal law, the competent authorities which receive information pursuant to paragraph 1 may use it only for the exercise of their functions within the scope of this Directive and in the context of administrative or judicial proceedings specifically related to the exercise of those functions. However, where the competent authority communicating information consents thereto, the authority receiving the information may use it for other purposes or forward it to other States' competent authorities.

3. Where a competent authority is convinced that acts contrary to the provisions of this Directive are being, or have been, carried out on the territory of another Member State or that acts are affecting financial instruments traded on a regulated market situated in another Member State, it shall give notice of that fact in as specific a manner as possible to the competent authority of the other Member State. The competent authority of the other Member State shall take appropriate action. It shall inform the notifying competent authority of the outcome and, so far as possible, of significant interim developments. This paragraph shall not prejudice the competences of the competent authority that has forwarded the information. The competent authorities of the various Member States that are competent for the purposes of Article 10 shall consult each other on the proposed follow-up to their action.

4. A competent authority of one Member State may request that an investigation be carried out by the competent authority of another Member State, on the latter's territory.

It may further request that members of its own personnel be allowed to accompany the personnel of the competent authority of that other Member State during the course of the investigation.

The investigation shall, however, be subject throughout to the overall control of the Member State on whose territory it is conducted.

The competent authorities may refuse to act on a request for an investigation to be conducted as provided for in the first subparagraph, or on a request for its personnel to be accompanied by personnel of the competent authority of another Member State as provided for in the second subparagraph, where such an investigation might adversely affect the

在任何上述情况下,被请求国主管部门应相应通知提出请求的主管部门,并尽可能详细地提供关于该等程序或判决的信息。

在不影响《条约》第226条的情形下,主管部门提出的信息请求未在合理的时间内落实或者请求被拒的,该主管部门可将该等情况提请欧洲证券监管机构委员会注意,双方将就此进行商议以达成一项迅速有效的解决方案。

在不影响其在刑事司法程序中所应遵守的义务的情形下,根据第1款接收信息的主管部门仅可将该等信息用于履行本指令范围内的职能,以及在与该等职能之行使具体相关的行政或司法程序中使用该等信息。但是,经提供信息的主管部门同意,接收信息的主管部门亦可将信息用于其他目的或转交其他成员国的主管部门。

3.主管部门确信在另一成员国境内正在发生或已发生违反本指令的行为,或存在正在影响另一成员国境内受监管市场上交易的金融工具的行为的,应当以尽可能具体的方式通知该等其他成员国的主管部门该等事实。收到通知的主管部门应当采取适当的行动,并应将其行动的结果通知向其转发信息的主管部门,在可能的范围内还应通知其行动的重要阶段性进展。本款规定不影响转发信息的主管部门的职权。就第10条而言有管辖权的各成员国主管部门应就其拟采取的跟进措施开展相互磋商。

4.成员国主管部门可请求另一成员国主管部门在其境内代为开展调查。

成员国主管部门可进一步请求另一成员国主管部门,在调查过程中允许其人员陪同调查。

但整个调查应始终处于调查地所在成员国的全面控制之下。

在以下情况下,主管部门可拒绝落实第1项所述的调查请求或第2项所述的由另一成员国主管部门人员陪同其人员进行调查的请求:上述调查可能会对本国的主权、安全或公共政策造成不利影响;或本国的相关部门已针对同一行为和同一行为人启动司法程序;或在本国已针对同一行为的有关行为人作出终审判决。在上述情况下,

sovereignty, security or public policy of the State addressed, or where judicial proceedings have already been initiated in respect of the same actions and against the same persons before the authorities of the State addressed or where a final judgment has already been delivered in relation to such persons for the same actions in the State addressed. In such case, they shall notify the requesting competent authority accordingly, providing information, as detailed as possible, on those proceedings or judgment.

Without prejudice to the provisions of Article 226 of the Treaty, a competent authority whose application to open an inquiry or whose request for authorisation for its officials to accompany those of the other Member State's competent authority is not acted upon within a reasonable time or is rejected may bring that non-compliance to the attention of the Committee of European Securities Regulators, where discussion will take place in order to reach a rapid and effective solution.

5. In accordance with the procedure laid down in Article 17(2) the Commission shall adopt implementing measures on the procedures for exchange of information and cross-border inspections as referred to in this Article.

Article 17

1. The Commission shall be assisted by the European Securities Committee instituted by Decision 2001/528/EC (hereinafter referred to as the 'Committee').

2. Where reference is made to this paragraph, Articles 5 and 7 of Decision 1999/468/EC shall apply, having regard to the provisions of Article 8 thereof, provided that the implementing measures adopted according to this procedure do not modify the essential provisions of this Directive.

The period laid down in Article 5(6) of Decision 1999/468/EC shall be set at three months.

3. The Committee shall adopt its rules of procedure.

4. Without prejudice to the implementing measures already adopted, on the expiry of a four-year period following the entry into force of this Directive, the application of its provisions requiring the adoption of technical rules and decisions in accordance with paragraph 2 shall be suspended. On a proposal from the Commission, the European Parliament and the Council may renew the provisions concerned in accordance with the procedure laid down in Article 251 of the Treaty and, to that end, they shall review them prior to the expiry of the period referred to above.

Article 18

Member States shall bring into force the laws, regulations and administrative provisions necessary to comply with this Directive not later than 12 October 2004. They shall forthwith inform the Commission thereof.

When Member States adopt those measures, they shall contain a reference to this

相关主管部门均应将相关情况通知提出请求的成员国主管部门,并尽可能详细地提供关于该等程序或判决的信息。

在不影响《条约》第226条的情形下,主管部门提出的信息请求未在合理的时间内落实或请求被拒的,该主管部门可将该等情况提请欧洲证券监管机构委员会注意,双方将在此进行商议以达成一项迅速有效的解决方案。

5.欧盟委员会应依照第17条第2款规定的程序,就本条所述的信息交换和跨境调查程序制定相关实施细则。

第17条

1.根据第2001/528/EC号指令成立的欧洲证券委员会(以下简称证券委员会)应协助欧盟委员会开展工作。

2.根据第1999/468/EC号决定第8条的规定,引用本款内容时,应适用该决定第5条和第7条的规定,前提是依照此程序制定的实施细则不对本指令的基本要素做出改动。

第1999/468/EC号决定第5条第6款所规定的期限应设定为3个月。

3.证券委员会应制定其议事规则。

4.在不影响已制定的实施细则的情形下,在本指令生效4年期限届满之后,本指令中要求根据第2款制定技术性规则和决定的规定应暂停适用。经欧盟委员会提议,欧洲议会与欧盟理事会可依照《条约》第251条规定的程序展延所涉条款,为此,欧洲议会与欧盟理事会应在上述期限届满前对该等条款进行审评。

第18条

各成员国应在2004年10月12日前实施必要的法律、法规和规章以使本指令得到遵守,并立即就此通知欧盟委员会。

成员国制定该等法律、法规和规章时,应在其中对本指令予以援引,或在官方正

Directive or be accompanied by such a reference on the occasion of their official publication. Member States shall determine how such reference is to be made.

Article 19

Article 11 shall not prejudge the possibility for a Member State to make separate legal and administrative arrangements for overseas European territories for whose external relations that Member State is responsible.

Article 20

Directive 89/592/EEC and Article 68(1) and Article 81(1) of Directive 2001/34/EC of the European Parliament and of the Council of 28 May 2001 on the admission of securities to official stock exchange listing and on information to be published on those securities [1] shall be repealed with effect from the date of entry into force of this Directive.

Article 21

This Directive shall enter into force on the day of its publication in the Official Journal of the European Union.

Article 22

This Directive is addressed to the Member States.

Done at Brussels, 28 January 2003.

For the Parliament	*For the Council*
The President	*The President*
P. COX	G. PAPANDREOU

1 OJ L 184, 6.7.2001, p. 1.

式公布该等法律、法规和规章时予以援引。援引的具体方式,由成员国决定。

第19条

适用第11条时，不应就成员国为其海外欧洲领地制定独立的法律和行政管理安排的可能性作出预先判断,该等领地的对外关系责任由该成员国承担。

第20条

第89/592/EEC号指令以及《欧洲议会与欧盟理事会关于证券获准在证券交易所正式上市以及应公布的与该等证券有关的信息的第2001/34/EC号指令》[1]（2001年5月28日)的第68条第1款和第81条第1款于本指令生效之日废止。

第21条

本指令应于《欧盟公报》公布,并于公布当日生效。

第22条

本指令对象为各成员国。

2003年1月28日于布鲁塞尔通过。

欧洲议会议长　　　　欧盟理事会主席

考克斯　　　　帕潘德里欧

1　2001年7月6日《欧盟公报》L184,第1页。

DIRECTIVE 2008/26/EC OF THE EUROPEAN PARLIAMENT AND OF THE COUNCIL

欧洲议会与欧盟理事会第2008/26/EC号指令

DIRECTIVE 2008/26/EC OF THE EUROPEAN PARLIAMENT AND OF THE COUNCIL

of 11 March 2008

amending Directive 2003/6/EC on insider dealing and market manipulation (market abuse) as regards the implementing powers conferred on the Commission

THE EUROPEAN PARLIAMENT AND THE COUNCIL OF THE EUROPEAN UNION,

Having regard to the Treaty establishing the European Community, and in particular Article 95 thereof,

Having regard to the proposal of the Commission,

Having regard to the opinion of the European Economic and Social Committee [1],

Having regard to the opinion of the European Central Bank [2],

Acting in accordance with the procedure laid down in Article 251 of the Treaty [3],

Whereas:

(1) Directive 2003/6/EC of the European Parliament and of the Council [4] provides that certain measures are to be adopted in accordance ith Council Decision 1999/468/EC of 28 June 1999 laying down the procedures for the exercise of implementing powers conferred on the Commission [5].

(2) Decision 1999/468/EC has been amended by Decision 2006/512/EC which introduced the regulatory procedure with scrutiny for the adoption of measures of general scope and designed to amend non-essential elements of a basic instrument adopted in accordance with the procedure referred to in Article 251 of the Treaty, inter alia, by

1 OJ C 161, 13.7.2007, p. 45.

2 OJ C 39, 23.2.2007, p. 1.

3 Opinion of the European Parliament of 14 November 2007 (not yet ublished in the Official Journal) and Council Decision of 3 March 2008.

4 OJ L 96, 12.4.2003, p. 16.

5 OJ L 184, 17.7.1999, p. 23. Decision as amended by Decision 006/512/EC (OJ L 200, 22.7.2006, p. 11).

欧洲议会与欧盟理事会
第2008/26/EC号指令

[本指令于2008年3月11日通过，修正《关于内幕交易和市场操纵（市场滥用）的第2003/6/EC号指令》中关于授予欧盟委员会的实施权的规定]

欧洲议会与欧盟理事会，

根据《欧洲共同体条约》(以下简称《条约》)，特别是其中的第95条，

根据欧盟委员会的提议，

根据欧洲经济与社会委员会的意见，[1]

根据欧洲中央银行的意见，[2]

依照《条约》第251条规定的程序，[3]

鉴于：

(1)欧洲议会与欧盟理事会第2003/6/EC号指令[4]规定，应根据《欧盟理事会关于制定欧盟委员会行使其被授予的实施权之程序的第1999/468/EC号决定》[5](1999年6月28日)制定某些实施细则。

(2)第1999/468/EC号决定经第2006/512/EC号决定修正，后者出台了制定具有一般适用范围的细则时须经欧盟理事会与欧洲议会审查的监管程序，该等程序旨在对依照《条约》第251条所述程序制定的基础法律文件中的非基本要素进行修正，包括但不限于删除部分该等要素或在基础法律文件中补充新的非基本要素。

1 2007年7月13日《欧盟公报》C161，第45页。

2 2007年2月23日《欧盟公报》C39，第1页。

3 欧洲议会2007年11月14日欧洲议会意见(尚未在《欧盟公报》公布)以及2008年3月3日欧盟理事会决定。

4 2003年4月12日《欧盟公报》L96，第16页。

5 1999年7月17日《欧盟公报》L184，第23页。该决定经第2006/512/EC号决定(2006年7月22日《欧盟公报》L200，第11页)修正。

deleting some of those elements or by supplementing the instrument with new non-essential elements.

(3) In accordance with the statement by the European Parliament, the Council and the Commission [1] concerning Decision 2006/512/EC, for the regulatory procedure with scrutiny to be applicable to instruments adopted in accordance with the procedure referred to in Article 251 of the Treaty which are already in force, those instruments must be adjusted in accordance with the applicable procedures.

(4) The Commission should be empowered to adopt the measures necessary for the implementation of Directive 2003/6/EC in order to take account of technical developments in financial markets and ensure the uniform application of that Directive. Those measures are designed to adapt definitions; elaborate upon or supplement the provisions of that Directive by technical modalities for disclosure of inside information, insider lists, reporting of managerial and suspicious transactions to competent authorities; and present the research in a fair manner. Since those measures are of general scope and are designed to amend non-essential elements of Directive 2003/6/EC by supplementing it with new non-essential elements, they must be adopted in accordance with the regulatory procedure with scrutiny provided for in Article 5a of Decision 1999/468/EC.

(5) Directive 2003/6/EC provides for a time restriction concerning the implementing powers conferred on the Commission. In their statement concerning Decision 2006/512/EC, the European Parliament, the Council and the Commission stated that Decision 2006/512/EC provides a horizontal and satisfactory solution to the European Parliament's wish to scrutinise the implementation of instruments adopted under the co-decision procedure and that, accordingly, implementing powers should be conferred on the Commission without time limit. The European Parliament and the Council also declared that they would make sure that the proposals aimed at repealing the provisions in the instruments that provide for a time limit on the delegation of implementing powers to the Commission are adopted as rapidly as possible. Following the introduction of the regulatory procedure with scrutiny, the provision establishing that time restriction in Directive 2003/6/EC should be deleted.

(6) The Commission should, at regular intervals, evaluate the functioning of the provisions concerning the implementing powers conferred on it in order to allow the European Parliament and the Council to determine whether the extent of those powers and the procedural requirements imposed on the Commission are appropriate and ensure both efficiency and democratic accountability.

(7) Directive 2003/6/EC should therefore be amended accordingly.

1 OJ C 255, 21.10.2006, p. 1.

（3）根据《欧洲议会、欧盟理事会和欧盟委员会关于第2006/512/EC号决定的声明》[1]，在将须经欧盟理事会与欧洲议会审查的监管程序适用于依照《条约》第251条所述程序制定且已生效的法律文件时，该等法律文件必须根据适用的程序进行调整。

（4）欧盟委员会应有权制定实施第2003/6/EC号指令所必要的细则，以反映金融市场的技术发展动态并确保该指令的统一适用。该等实施细则用于：修改定义；细化或补充该指令关于内幕信息披露的技术模式、内幕人士清单、向主管部门报告管理层的交易以及可疑的交易等的规定；以及以公平的方式列报研究结果。由于该等实施细则属于具有一般适用范围的实施细则，并且旨在通过在第2003/6/EC号指令中补充新的非基本要素而对其非基本要素进行修正，因此，制定该等实施细则时必须遵循第1999/468/EC号决定第5a条规定的须经欧盟理事会与欧洲议会审查的监管程序。

（5）第2003/6/EC号指令就授予欧盟委员会的实施权设定了时间限制。在其《关于第2006/512/EC号决定的声明》中，欧洲议会、欧盟理事会以及欧盟委员会声明，第2006/512/EC号决定提供了一个横向和完善的解决方案，使得欧洲议会能够实现其对根据共同决定程序制定的法律文件的实施情况进行审查的意愿，因此，不必再对授予欧盟委员会的实施权施加时间限制。欧洲议会和欧盟理事会同时宣布，它们将确保其提案尽快通过，废止相关法律文件中就向欧盟委员会授予的实施权设定时限的条款。须经欧盟理事会和欧洲议会审查的监管程序开始实施后，第2003/6/EC号指令中设定期限的条款应予删除。

（6）欧盟委员会应定期评价关于授予其实施权的条款的运行情况，以便欧洲议会和欧盟理事会判定该等权力的范围及对欧盟委员会施加的程序性要求是否适当，确保效率和民主问责两者兼备。

（7）因此，第2003/6/EC号指令应作出相应修正。

---

1 2006年10月21日《欧盟公报》C255，第1页。

(8) Since the amendments made to Directive 2003/6/EC by this Directive are technical in nature and concern committee procedure only, they do not need to be transposed by the Member States. It is therefore not necessary to lay down provisions to that effect,

HAVE ADOPTED THIS DIRECTIVE:

Article 1 Amendments

Directive 2003/6/EC is hereby amended as follows:

1. Article 1 shall be amended as follows:

(a) in the first paragraph, point 5 shall be replaced by the following:

'5. "Accepted market practices" shall mean practices that are reasonably expected in one or more financial markets and are accepted by the competent authority in accordance with guidelines adopted by the Commission in accordance with the regulatory procedure with scrutiny laid down in Article 17(2a).';

(b) the second paragraph shall be amended as follows:

(i) the words 'acting in accordance with the procedure laid down in Article 17(2)' shall be deleted;

(ii) the following sentence shall be added:

'Those measures, designed to amend non-essential elements of this Directive by supplementing it, shall be adopted in accordance with the regulatory procedure with scrutiny referred to in Article 17(2a).';

2. Article 6(10) shall be amended as follows:

(a) the words 'in accordance with the procedure referred to in Article 17(2)' shall be deleted;

(b) the following subparagraph shall be added:

'Those measures, designed to amend non-essential elements of this Directive by supplementing it, shall be adopted in accordance with the regulatory procedure with scrutiny referred to in Article 17(2a).';

3. Article 8 shall be amended as follows:

(a) the words 'adopted in accordance with the procedure laid down in Article 17(2)' shall be deleted;

(b) the following sentence shall be added:

'Those measures, designed to amend non-essential elements of this Directive by supplementing it, shall be adopted in accordance with the regulatory procedure with scrutiny referred to in Article 17(2a).';

4. Article 16(5) shall be replaced by the following:

'5.In accordance with the regulatory procedure laid down in Article 17 (2) the Commission shall adopt implementing measures on the working procedures for exchange of

(8)本指令对第2003/6/EC号指令的修正属于技术性的修正,且仅涉及欧盟委员会程序,各成员国不必对其进行转化。因此,不必就成员国的转化作出规定。

兹通过本指令如下:

第1条　修正

特此对第2003/6/EC号指令修正如下:

1.对第1条修正如下:

(a)第1款第5项应替以如下规定:

"5.'公认市场惯例'指在一个或多个金融市场被合理预期的,且主管部门根据欧盟委员会依第17条第2a款所述的须经欧盟理事会和欧洲议会审查的监管程序制定的指引认可的惯例。"

(b)对第2款修正如下:

(i)删除"依照第17条第2款规定的程序,"

(ii)增加如下内容:

"该等旨在通过补充本指令而修正其非基本要素的实施细则,应依照第17条第2a款所述的须经欧盟理事会和欧洲议会审查的监管程序制定。"

2.对第6条第10款修正如下:

(a)删除"依照第17条第2款规定的程序,"

(b)增加如下内容:

"该等旨在通过补充本指令而修正其非基本要素的实施细则,应依照第17条第2a款所述的须经欧盟理事会和欧洲议会审查的监管程序制定。"

3.对第8条修正如下:

(a)删除"依照第17条第2款规定的程序,"

(b)增加如下内容:

"该等旨在通过补充本指令而修正其非基本要素的实施细则,应依照第17条第2a款所述的须经欧盟理事会和欧洲议会审查的监管程序制定。"

4.第16条第5款应替以如下规定:

"5.欧盟委员会应当依照第17条第2款所述监管程序,就本条所述信息交流和跨境检查程序制定相关实施细则。"

information and cross-border inspections as referred to in this Article.';

5. Article 17 shall be amended as follows:

(a) the following paragraph shall be inserted:

'2a.Where reference is made to this paragraph, Article 5a(1) to (4) and Article 7 of Decision 1999/468/EC shall apply, having regard to the provisions of Article 8 thereof.';

(b) paragraphs 3 and 4 shall be replaced by the following:

'3.By 31 December 2010, and, thereafter, at least every three years, the Commission shall review the provisions concerning its implementing powers and present a report to the European Parliament and to the Council on the functioning of those powers. The report shall examine, in particular, the need for the Commission to propose amendments to this Directive in order to ensure the appropriate scope of the implementing powers conferred on the Commission. The conclusion as to whether or not amendment is necessary shall be accompanied by a detailed statement of reasons. If necessary, the report shall be accompanied by a legislative proposal to amend the provisions conferring implementing powers on the Commission'.

Article 2 Entry into force

This Directive shall enter into force on the day following its publication in the *Official Journal of the European Union.*

Article 3 Addressees

This Directive is addressed to the Member States.

Done at Strasbourg, 11 March 2008.

For the European Parliament
The President
H.-G. PÖTTERING

For the Council
The President
J. LENARČIČ

5.对第17条修正如下：

(a)插入以下款项：

“2a. 根据第1999/468/EC号决定第8条的规定，引用本款内容时，应适用该决定的第5a条第1款至第4款和第7条的规定。”

(b)第3款和第4款应替以如下规定：

“3.在2010年12月31日前，欧盟委员会应对关于其实施权的条款进行审评，并就该等权力的行使向欧洲议会与欧盟理事会提交一份报告，此后应至少每三年进行一次审评和报告。报告应着重审查欧盟委员会是否有必要对本指令提出修正案，以确保授予欧盟委员会的实施权维持在适当的范围之内。作出是否有必要进行修正的结论时，应附上详细的理由说明。必要时，报告应附上关于修正授予欧盟委员会实施权的条款的立法提案。”

第2条　生效

本条例应于《欧盟公报》公布，公布的次日生效。

第3条　对象

本指令对象为各成员国。

2008年3月11日于斯特拉斯堡通过。

欧洲议会议长　　　　欧盟理事会主席

波特林　　　　莱纳茨

DIRECTIVE 2004/109/EC OF THE EUROPEAN PARLIAMENT AND OF THE COUNCIL

欧洲议会与欧盟理事会第2004/109/EC号指令

DIRECTIVE 2004/109/EC OF THE EUROPEAN PARLIAMENT AND OF THE COUNCIL

of 15 December 2004

on the harmonisation of transparency requirements in relation to information about issuers whose securities are admitted to trading on a regulated market and amending Directive 2001/34/EC

THE EUROPEAN PARLIAMENT AND THE COUNCIL OF THE EUROPEAN UNION,

Having regard to the Treaty establishing the European Community, and in particular Articles 44 and 95 thereof,

Having regard to the proposal from the Commission,

Having regard to the opinion of the European Economic and Social Committee [1],

Having regard to the opinion of the European Central Bank [2],

Acting in accordance with the procedure laid down in Article 251 of the Treaty [3],

Whereas:

(1) Efficient, transparent and integrated securities markets contribute to a genuine single market in the Community and foster growth and job creation by better allocation of capital and by reducing costs. The disclosure of accurate, comprehensive and timely information about security issuers builds sustained investor confidence and allows an informed assessment of their business performance and assets. This enhances both investor protection and market efficiency.

(2) To that end, security issuers should ensure appropriate transparency for investors

1 OJ C 80, 30.3.2004, p. 128.

2 OJ C 242, 9.10.2003, p. 6.

3 Opinion of the European Parliament of 30 March 2004 (not yet ublished in the Official Journal) and Council Decision of 2 ecember 2004.

欧洲议会与欧盟理事会
第2004/109/EC号指令

（本指令于2004年12月15日通过，修正第2001/34/EC号指令，
协调关于证券获准在受监管市场交易的发行人的信息透明度要求）

欧洲议会与欧盟理事会，

根据《欧洲共同体条约》（以下简称《条约》），特别是其中的第44条和第95条，

根据欧盟委员会的提议，
根据欧洲经济与社会委员会的意见，[1]
根据欧洲中央银行的意见，[2]
依照《条约》第251条[3]规定的程序，
鉴于：

（1）高效、透明和一体化的证券市场，有助于欧共体真正单一市场的形成，并且通过更好地配置资本和降低成本，可以促进经济增长和创造就业机会。披露准确、全面和及时的证券发行人信息不仅能建立持续的投资者信心，亦能帮助投资者对发行人业绩和资产作出知情评估，从而加强对投资者的保护，提高市场效率。

（2）为此，证券发行人应通过定期的信息发布确保发行人面对投资者的适当透明

1 2004年3月30日《欧盟公报》C80，第128页。
2 2003年10月9日《欧盟公报》C242，第6页。
3 2004年3月30日欧洲议会意见（尚未在《欧盟公报》公布）和2004年12月2日欧盟理事会决定。

through a regular flow of information. To the same end, shareholders, or natural persons or legal entities holding voting rights or financial instruments that result in an entitlement to acquire existing shares with voting rights, should also inform issuers of the acquisition of or other changes in major holdings in companies so that the latter are in a position to keep the public informed.

(3) The Commission Communication of 11 May 1999, entitled 'Implementing the framework for financial markets: Action Plan', identifies a series of actions that are needed in order to complete the single market for financial services. The Lisbon European Council of March 2000 calls for the implementation of that Action Plan by 2005. The Action Plan stresses the need to draw up a Directive upgrading transparency requirements. That need was confirmed by the Barcelona European Council of March 2002.

(4) This Directive should be compatible with the tasks and duties conferred upon the European System of Central Banks (ESCB) and the Member States' central banks by the Treaty and the Statute of the European System of Central Banks and of the European Central Bank; particular attention in this regard needs to be given to the Member States' central banks whose shares are currently admitted to trading on a regulated market, in order to guarantee the pursuit of primary Community law objectives.

(5) Greater harmonisation of provisions of national law on periodic and ongoing information requirements for security issuers should lead to a high level of investor protection throughout the Community. However, this Directive does not affect existing Community legislation on units issued by collective investment undertakings other than the closed-end type, or on units acquired or disposed of in such undertakings.

(6) Supervision of an issuer of shares, or of debt securities the denomination per unit of which is less than EUR 1 000, for the purposes of this Directive, would be best effected by the Member State in which the issuer has its registered office. In that respect, it is vital to ensure consistency with Directive 2003/71/EC of the European Parliament and of the Council of 4 November 2003 on the prospectus to be published when securities are offered to the public or admitted to trading. [1]Along the same lines, some flexibility should be introduced allowing third country issuers and Community companies issuing only securities other than those mentioned above a choice of home Member State.

(7) A high level of investor protection throughout the Community would enable barriers to the admission of securities to regulated markets situated or operating within a Member State to be removed. Member States other than the home Member State should no longer be allowed to restrict admission of securities to their regulated markets by imposing

1 OJ L 345, 31.12.2003, p. 64.

度。出于同一目的,股东或持有表决权的自然人或法人实体或者持有赋予购买附带表决权的现有股票权利的金融工具的自然人或法人实体,作出公司大额股份购买或其他变更时,应通知发行人,以便发行人不断地向公众提供最新的信息。

(3)欧盟委员会1999年5月11日发布的名为《落实金融市场框架:行动计划》的通报明确了为完善单一的金融服务市场所应采取的一系列行动。2000年3月于里斯本举行的欧洲理事会会议呼吁在2005年之前落实该项《行动计划》。《行动计划》强调制定一项指令来提高透明度要求的必要性。2002年3月在巴塞罗那举行的欧洲理事会会议确认了此必要性。

(4)本指令应与《条约》以及《欧洲中央银行体系及欧洲中央银行章程》授予欧洲中央银行体系(ESCB)以及成员国中央银行的职责和任务相兼容;为此,应特别关注其股票目前获准在受监管市场交易的成员国中央银行,以保证达成欧共体法律的首要宗旨。

(5)进一步协调成员国国内法律关于证券发行人定期和持续信息披露要求的规定,将促进对欧共体全境内投资者的高标准保护。然而,本指令不影响涉及非封闭式集合投资计划发行的单位或投资人所购买或处置的非封闭式集合投资计划单位的现有欧共体立法。

(6)就本指令而言,由发行人注册地所在的成员国实施的监管,是对股票发行人或单位面值低于1000欧元的债务证券的发行人最有效的监管。因此,确保本指令与《欧洲议会与欧盟理事会关于向公众发行证券或证券获准交易时所应公布的招募说明书的第2003/71/EC号指令》[1](2003年11月4日)相互一致,至关重要。同理,应保留一定的灵活性,允许仅发行非属上述证券范围内证券的第三国发行人和欧共体公司选择其母国。

(7)为欧共体投资者设置高标准保护,能消除证券在位于某成员国境内或在某成员国境内运营的受监管市场的准入障碍。然而,非母国成员国不得再对证券获准在受监管市场交易的发行人施加更严格的定期和持续信息披露要求,不得企图利用该等手段限制国内受监管市场的证券准入。

1 2003年12月31日《欧盟公报》L345,第64页。

more stringent requirements on periodic and ongoing information about issuers whose securities are admitted to trading on a regulated market.

(8) The removal of barriers on the basis of the home Member State principle under this Directive should not affect areas not covered by this Directive, such as rights of shareholders to intervene in the management of an issuer. Nor should it affect the home Member State's right to request the issuer to publish, in addition, parts of or all regulated information through newspapers.

(9) Regulation (EC) No 1606/2002 of the European Parliament and of the Council of 19 July 2002 on the application of international accounting standards [1] has already paved the way for a convergence of financial reporting standards throughout the Community for issuers whose securities are admitted to trading on a regulated market and who are required to prepare consolidated accounts. Thus, a specific regime for security issuers beyond the general system for all companies, as laid down in the Company Law Directives, is already established. This Directive builds on this approach with regard to annual and interim financial reporting, including the principle of providing a true and fair view of an issuer's assets, liabilities, financial position and profit or loss. A condensed set of financial statements, as part of a half-yearly financial report, also represents a sufficient basis for giving such a true and fair view of the first six months of an issuer's financial year.

(10) An annual financial report should ensure information over the years once the issuer's securities have been admitted to a regulated market. Making it easier to compare annual financial reports is only of use to investors in securities markets if they can be sure that this information will be published within a certain time after the end of the financial year. As regards debt securities admitted to trading on a regulated market prior to1 January 2005 and issued by issuers incorporated in a third country, the home Member State may under certain conditions allow issuers not to prepare annual financial reports in accordance with the standards required under this Directive.

(11) This Directive introduces more comprehensive half-yearly financial reports for issuers of shares admitted to trading on a regulated market. This should allow investors to make a more informed assessment of the issuer's situation.

(12) A home Member State may provide for exemptions from half-yearly reporting by issuers of debt securities in the case of:

— credit institutions acting as small-size issuers of debt securities, or

— issuers already existing on the date of the entry into force of this Directive who exclusively issue debt securities unconditionally and irrevocably guaranteed by the home

1 OJ L 243, 11.9.2002, p. 1.

(8)根据本指令的母国原则消除上述准入障碍时,不应对本指令范围之外的事项(如发行人股东干预公司管理的权利)产生影响。母国要求发行人额外通过报刊公布部分或全部受监管信息的权利,也不受影响。

(9)针对证券获准在受监管市场交易且应制作合并财务报表的发行人,《欧洲议会与欧盟理事会关于适用国际会计准则的第1606/2002号(欧共体)条例》[1](2002年7月19日)已为其财务报告标准在欧共体内的趋同打下基础。因此,在《公司法指令》规定的、对所有公司均适用的一般制度之外,又建立了一套专门针对证券发行人的特定体制。本指令以该体制为基础,对年度和中期财务报告作出规定,其中包括真实公允地反映发行人资产、负债、财务状况和损益的原则。半年度财务报告中的简要财务报表,也能真实公允地反映发行人会计年度上半年的情况。

(10)发行人证券从开始获准在受监管市场交易后历年的信息应通过年度财务报告提供。不同年度的财务报告应易于比较,应使证券市场投资者确信财务报告将于会计年度结束后的一定时期内公布,才能发挥投资者需要的比较作用。对于2005年1月1日前获准在受监管市场交易并由在第三国成立的发行人发行的债务证券,某些条件下母国可允许发行人不按本指令规定的标准制作年度财务报告。

(11)本指令为股票获准在受监管市场交易的发行人出台了关于更全面的半年度财务报告的规定,使投资者能对发行人状况作出更为知情的评估。

(12)在下列情形中,母国可作出豁免债务证券发行人半年度财务报告的规定:

——信贷机构以小型发行人身份发行债务证券,或

——发行人在本指令生效当日业已存在,仅发行由母国或母国某个地区或地方政府部门提供无条件且不可撤销担保的债务证券,或

1 2002年9月11日《欧盟公报》L243,第1页。

Member State or by one of its regional or local authorities, or

— during a transitional period of ten years, only in respect of those debt securities admitted to trading on a regulated market prior to 1 January 2005 which may be purchased by professional investors only. If such an exemption is given by the home Member State, it may not be extended in respect of any debt securities admitted to a regulated market thereafter.

(13) The European Parliament and the Council welcome the Commission's commitment rapidly to consider enhancing the transparency of the remuneration policies, total remuneration paid, including any contingent or deferred compensation, and benefits in kind granted to each member of administrative, management or supervisory bodies under its Action Plan for 'Modernising Company Law and Enhancing Corporate Governance in the European Union' of 21 May 2003 and the Commission's intention to make a Recommendation on this topic in the near future.

(14) The home Member State should encourage issuers whose shares are admitted to trading on a regulated market and whose principal activities lie in the extractive industry to disclose payments to governments in their annual financial report. The home Member State should also encourage an increase in the transparency of such payments within the framework established at various international financial fora.

(15) This Directive will also make half-yearly reporting mandatory for issuers of only debt securities on regulated markets. Exemptions should only be provided for wholesale markets on the basis of a denomination per unit starting at EUR 50 000, as under Directive 2003/71/EC. Where debt securities are issued in another currency, exemptions should only be possible where the denomination per unit in such a currency is, at the date of the issue, at least equivalent to EUR 50 000.

(16) More timely and more reliable information about the share issuer's performance over the financial year also requires a higher frequency of interim information. A requirement should therefore be introduced to publish an interim management statement during the first six months and a second interim management statement during the second six months of a financial year. Share issuers who already publish quarterly financial reports should not be required to publish interim management statements.

(17) Appropriate liability rules, as laid down by each Member State under its national law or regulations, should be applicable to the issuer, its administrative, management or supervisory bodies, or persons responsible within the issuer. Member States should remain free to determine the extent of the liability.

(18) The public should be informed of changes to major holdings in issuers whose shares are traded on a regulated market situated or operating within the Community. This information should enable investors to acquire or dispose of shares in full knowledge of

——在10年过渡期间，仅对2005年1月1日前获准在受监管市场交易且仅可由专业投资者购买的债务证券作出该等豁免规定。母国给予的豁免范围不得延伸至在该日期后获准在受监管市场交易的任何债务证券。

(13)对于《欧盟公司法现代化和加强欧盟公司治理之行动计划》(2003年5月21日)中的董事会、管理机构或监事会成员薪酬政策、支付的总报酬(包括任何或有或递延薪酬)以及实物福利的透明度的加强，欧盟委员会迅速承诺予以审议并有意近期内就此议题发布建议，对此欧洲议会与欧盟理事会欣然接受。

(14)对于股票获准在受监管市场交易的以采掘业为主业的发行人，母国应鼓励其在年度财务报告中披露支付给政府的款项。母国还应鼓励在各个国际金融组织建立的框架下提高支付给政府的款项的透明度。

(15)同时，对于仅发行在受监管市场交易的债务证券的发行人，本指令将强制其提供半年度报告。唯有在达到第2003/71/EC号指令规定的单位面值5万欧元起的大额市场上始得豁免。债务证券以其他货币发行且发行当日以该货币表示的单位面值最低等值于5万欧元的始得豁免。

(16)为提供更及时和可靠的股票发行人在每一会计年度的业绩信息，还应要求发行人提供更频繁的中期信息。因此，应要求发行人在会计年度上半年期间公布第一次中期管理说明书，并在下半年公布第二次中期管理说明书。不应要求已公布过季度财务报告的股票发行人公布中期管理说明书。

(17)各成员国依其国内法律或规章制定的适当的法律责任规则应可适用于发行人、其董事会、管理机构或监事会或发行人的公司负责人。成员国应有裁量权可自行确定法律责任范围。

(18)发行人股票在位于欧共体境内或在欧共体境内运营的受监管市场交易的，发生大额股票变动时应告知公众。该等信息将允许投资者在全面了解投票结构变更的情形下购买或处置股票；该等信息还将加强对股票发行人的有效控制，提高整体市

changes in the voting structure; it should also enhance effective control of share issuers and overall market transparency of important capital movements. Information about shares or financial instruments as determined by Article 13, lodged as collateral, should be provided in certain circumstances.

(19) Articles 9 and 10(c) should not apply to shares provided to or by the members of the ESCB in carrying out their functions as monetary authorities provided that the voting rights attached to such shares are not exercised; the reference to a 'short period' in Article 11 should be understood with reference to credit operations carried out in accordance with the Treaty and the European Central Bank (ECB) legal acts, in particular the ECB Guidelines on monetary policy instruments and procedures and TARGET, and to credit operations for the purpose of performing equivalent functions in accordance with national provisions.

(20) In order to avoid unnecessary burdens for certain market participants and to clarify who actually exercises influence over an issuer, there is no need to require notification of major holdings of shares, or other financial instruments as determined by Article 13 that result in an entitlement to acquire shares with regard to market makers or custodians, or of holdings of shares or such financial instruments acquired solely for clearing and settlement purposes, within limits and guarantees to be applied throughout the Community. The home Member State should be allowed to provide limited exemptions as regards holdings of shares in trading books of credit institutions and investment firms.

(21) In order to clarify who is actually a major holder of shares or other financial instruments in the same issuer throughout the Community, parent undertakings should not be required to aggregate their own holdings with those managed by undertakings for collective investment in transferable securities (UCITS) or investment firms, provided that such undertakings or firms exercise voting rights independently from their parent undertakings and fulfil certain further conditions.

(22) Ongoing information to holders of securities admitted to trading on a regulated market should continue to be based on the principle of equal treatment. Such equal treatment only relates to shareholders in the same position and does not therefore prejudice the issue of how many voting rights may be attached to a particular share. By the same token, holders of debt securities ranking pari passu should continue to benefit from equal treatment, even in the case of sovereign debt. Information to holders of shares and/or debt securities in general meetings should be facilitated. In particular, holders of shares and/or debt securities situated abroad should be more actively involved in that they should be able to mandate proxies to act on their behalf. For the same reasons, it should be decided in a general meeting of holders of shares and/or debt securities whether the use of modern information and communication technologies should become a reality. In

场透明度，便于投资者知悉重要的资本流动。提供股票或第13条规定的金融工具作为抵押品的，某些情形下也应提供相关信息。

（19）第9条和第10条第c款不应适用于欧洲中央银行体系成员履行其货币管理当局职能时所获得或提供的股票，前提是上述股票附带的表决权未予行使；第11条述及的“短期”应以下列信贷业务期限为准：依据《条约》和欧洲中央银行（ECB）法律文件，尤其是《欧洲中央银行关于货币政策工具和程序以及欧洲间实时全额自动结算系统（TARGET）的指引》开展的信贷业务；以及为依照成员国规定履行同等职能而开展的信贷业务。

（20）为避免给特定市场参与者带来不必要的负担，也为了澄清对发行人施加实际影响的主体，不必要求发行人对以下事项作出通知：做市商或托管人持有的大额股票或大额的第13条确定的附股票买入权的其他金融工具；或，持有仅为清算和结算目的购买的股票或上述金融工具，只要持有数额不超过在全欧共体范围适用的限额和担保额。母国应可向信贷机构和投资公司提供有限豁免，使其不必就在交易账户中持有的份额作出通知。

（21）为了澄清在全欧共体范围内实际持有同一发行人大额股票或其他金融工具的持有人的认定标准，计算持股数额时不必要求母公司自身的持股与可转让证券集合投资计划（UCITS）或投资公司管理的持股合并计算，前提是该等计划或公司独立于其母公司行使表决权并满足某些其他条件。

（22）向获准在受监管市场交易的证券的持有人进行的持续信息披露，应继续遵守平等待遇原则。上述平等待遇只涉及处于相同情况的股东，不对某一特定股票可附带的表决权数量问题产生影响。同理，类别相同的债务证券持有人，即使是主权债务持有人，也应继续受到平等的待遇。应当为通过股东（债务证券持有人）大会向股票和/或债务证券持有人披露信息创造便利条件。尤其是位于国外的股票和/或债务证券持有人应当更积极地参与，因为其能够委托代理人代表代其行事。同理，应当在股东大会和/或债务证券持有人大会上决定是否应为此目的充分运用现代信息通信技术。在此情形下，发行人应落实相关安排，以便在能识别股票和/或债务证券持有人身份的情形下，有效通知该等持有人其所持有的股票和/或债务证券。

that case, issuers should put in place arrangements in order effectively to inform holders of their shares and/or debt securities, insofar as it is possible for them to identify those holders.

(23) Removal of barriers and effective enforcement of new Community information requirements also require adequate control by the competent authority of the home Member State. This Directive should at least provide for a minimum guarantee for the timely availability of such information. For this reason, at least one filing and storage system should exist in each Member State.

(24) Any obligation for an issuer to translate all ongoing and periodic information into all the relevant languages in all the Member States where its securities are admitted to trading does not foster integration of securities markets, but has deterrent effects on cross-border admission of securities to trading on regulated markets. Therefore, the issuer should in certain cases be entitled to provide information drawn up in a language that is customary in the sphere of international finance. Since a particular effort is needed to attract investors from other Member States and third countries, Member States should no longer prevent shareholders, persons exercising voting rights, or holders of financial instruments, from making the required notifications to the issuer in a language that is customary in the sphere of international finance.

(25) Access for investors to information about issuers should be more organised at a Community level in order to actively promote integration of European capital markets. Investors who are not situated in the issuer's home Member State should be put on an equal footing with investors situated in the issuer's home Member State, when seeking access to such information. This could be achieved if the home Member State ensures compliance with minimum quality standards for disseminating information throughout the Community, in a fast manner on a non-discriminatory basis and depending on the type of regulated information in question. In addition, information which has been disseminated should be available in the home Member State in a centralised way allowing a European network to be built up, accessible at affordable prices for retail investors, while not leading to unnecessary duplication of filing requirements for issuers. Issuers should benefit from free competition when choosing the media or operators for disseminating information under this Directive.

(26) In order to further simplify investor access to corporate information across Member States, it should be left to the national supervisory authorities to formulate guidelines for setting up electronic networks, in close consultation with the other parties concerned, in particular security issuers, investors, market participants, operators of regulated markets and financial information providers.

(27) So as to ensure the effective protection of investors and the proper operation of

(23)消除障碍和有效执行新的欧共体信息要求时,还需母国主管部门实施适当的控制。本指令至少应作出使上述信息的及时提供获得最低保障的相关规定。为此,每一成员国至少应设置一套信息提交存储系统。

(24)要求发行人将定期和持续披露的信息全部翻译成授予其证券交易准入的各成员国的所有相关语言,不仅无法促进证券市场一体化,还适得其反,对证券跨境获准在受监管市场交易构成障碍。因此,某些情形下,发行人应有权提供以国际金融行业惯用语言编制的信息。由于从其他成员国和第三国吸引投资者本身已需付出额外努力,成员国不应再阻碍股东、表决权行使人或金融工具持有人以国际金融行业惯用语言向发行人发送规定的通知。

(25)应更多地在欧共体层级规划投资者查阅发行人信息的方式,以积极推动欧洲资本市场的一体化。位于发行人母国境外的投资者寻求获得上述信息时应获得与发行人母国投资者平等的待遇。要实现平等待遇,母国主管部门应确保信息传播最低质量标准在欧共体全境内得到遵守,根据受监管信息类别,使信息快速、无差别待遇地传播。此外,应能在母国集中查阅已传播的信息,因此需要建立一个欧洲网络,接入该网络查阅信息的价格应为零售投资者能承担的水平,同时还应避免对发行人施加不必要的重复提交信息要求。发行人在选择传播本指令中的信息的媒体或运营商时,应从媒体或运营商的自由竞争中获益。

(26)为进一步简化投资者在各成员国查阅公司信息的程序,各国家级监管机构应与其他所涉当事方(特别是证券发行人、投资者、市场参与者、受监管市场运营者以及金融信息提供方)紧密磋商,制定建立电子网络的指引。

(27)为确保对投资者的有效保护以及受监管市场的稳健运行,对于不在成员国

regulated markets, the rules relating to information to be published by issuers whose securities are admitted to trading on a regulated market should also apply to issuers which do not have a registered office in a Member State and which do not fall within the scope of Article 48 of the Treaty. It should also be ensured that any additional relevant information about Community issuers or third country issuers, disclosure of which is required in a third country but not in a Member State, is made available to the public in the Community.

(28) A single competent authority should be designated in each Member State to assume final responsibility for supervising compliance with the provisions adopted pursuant to this Directive, as well as for international cooperation. Such an authority should be of an administrative nature, and its independence from economic players should be ensured in order to avoid conflicts of interest. Member States may however designate another competent authority for examining that information referred to in this Directive is drawn up in accordance with the relevant reporting framework and taking appropriate measures in case of discovered infringements; such an authority need not be of an administrative nature.

(29) Increasing cross-border activities require improved cooperation between ational competent authorities, including a comprehensive set of provisions for the exchange of information and for precautionary measures. The organisation of the regulatory and supervisory tasks in each Member State should not hinder efficient cooperation between the competent national authorities.

(30) At its meeting on 17 July 2000, the Council set up the Committee of Wise Men on the Regulation of European securities markets. In its final report, that Committee proposed the introduction of new legislative techniques based on a four-level approach, namely essential principles, technical implementing measures, cooperation amongst national securities regulators, and enforcement of Community law. This Directive should confine itself to broad 'framework' principles, while implementing measures to be adopted by the Commission with the assistance of the European Securities Committee established by Commission Decision 2001/528/EC [1] should lay down the technical details.

(31) The Resolution adopted by the Stockholm European Council of March 2001 endorsed the final report of the Committee of Wise Men and the proposed four-level approach to make the regulatory process for Community securities legislation more efficient and transparent.

(32) According to that Resolution, implementing measures should be used more frequently, to ensure that technical provisions can be kept up to date with market and

1 OJ L 191, 13.7.2001, p. 45. Decision as amended by Decision 004/8/EC (OJ L 3, 7.1.2004, p. 33).

注册且不属于《条约》第48条范围的发行人，也应适用与证券获准在受监管市场交易的发行人应公布的信息有关的规则。还应确保，按第三国规定应披露但成员国不要求披露的关于欧共体发行人或第三国发行人的任何额外相关信息均能在欧共体内公开获得。

(28)各成员国应指定单一的主管部门承担监管依本指令制定的国内合规情况及国际合作的最终责任。该主管部门应为行政管理部门，应保证其独立于经济参与者以避免发生利益冲突。然而，成员国可指定另一主管部门负责核查本指令要求提供的信息是否按照相关的报告框架编制，在发现违规之时采取适当的措施；该部门不必是行政管理部门。

(29)日益增多的跨境活动要求国家级主管部门之间加强合作，包括为信息交换和预防措施制定一套全面的规定。各成员国规制和监管工作的组织不应妨碍国家级主管部门之间的有效合作。

(30)欧盟理事会在2000年7月17日的会议中成立了欧洲证券市场监管专家委员会。在其提交的最终报告中，专家委员会建议采用基于四级立法程序的新的立法技术，即基本原则、技术性实施细则、国家级证券监管机构之间的合作以及欧共体法律的执行。本指令应仅建立宏观的"框架性"原则，由欧盟委员会在欧盟委员会第2001/528/EC号决定[1]设立的欧洲证券委员会协助下制定相关技术性实施细则。

(31)2001年3月在斯德哥尔摩举行的欧洲理事会会议上通过的决议同意并支持了专家委员会的最终报告及其建议的四级立法程序，以保证欧共体证券领域的立法程序更高的效率和透明度。

(32)根据该项决议，应更多地使用实施细则，以确保技术性规定能够反映市场和监管方面的最新发展动态，同时，应为实施规则的每一阶段工作设定完成期限。

---

1 2001年7月31日《欧盟公报》L191，第45页。该决定经第2004/8/EC号决定（2004年1月7日《欧盟公报》L3，第33页）修正。

supervisory developments, and deadlines should be set for all stages of implementing rules.

(33) The Resolution of the European Parliament of 5 February 2002 on the implementation of financial services legislation also endorsed the Committee of Wise Men's report, on the basis of the solemn declaration made before the European Parliament the same day by the President of the Commission and the letter of 2 October 2001 addressed by the Internal Market Commissioner to the Chairman of the Parliament's Committee on Economic and Monetary Affairs with regard to safeguards for the European Parliament's role in this process.

(34) The European Parliament should be given a period of three months from the first transmission of draft implementing measures to allow it to examine them and to give its opinion. However, in urgent and duly justified cases, that period may be shortened. If, within that period, a Resolution is passed by the European Parliament, the Commission should re-examine the draft measures.

(35) Technical implementing measures for the rules laid down in this Directive may be necessary to take account of new developments on securities markets. The Commission should accordingly be empowered to adopt implementing measures, provided that they do not modify the essential elements of this Directive and provided that the Commission acts in accordance with the principles set out therein, after consulting the European Securities Committee.

(36) In exercising its implementing powers in accordance with this Directive, the Commission should respect the following principles:

— the need to ensure confidence in financial markets among investors by promoting high standards of transparency in financial markets;

— the need to provide investors with a wide range of competing investments and a level of disclosure and protection tailored to their circumstances;

— the need to ensure that independent regulatory authorities enforce the rules consistently, especially as regards the fight against economic crime;

— the need for high levels of transparency and consultation with all market participants and with the European Parliament and the Council;

— the need to encourage innovation in financial markets if they are to be dynamic and efficient;

— the need to ensure market integrity by close and reactive monitoring of financial innovation;

— the importance of reducing the cost of, and increasing access to, capital;

— the balance of costs and benefits to market participants on a long-term basis, including small and medium-sized businesses and small investors, in any implementing measures;

(33)基于欧盟委员会2002年2月5日向欧洲议会作出的庄严声明和内部市场委员于2001年10月2日就确保欧洲议会在上述立法程序中的作用致欧洲议会经济和货币事务委员会主席的信函,《欧洲议会关于实施金融服务立法的决议》(2002年2月5日)也同意和支持专家委员会的最终报告。

(34)欧洲议会应在实施细则草案首次递交之后3个月内进行审核并提出意见。但在紧急并有正当理由的情形下,可以缩短该期限。如果欧洲议会在该等缩短期限内通过了任何决议,欧盟委员会应对细则草案重新进行审核。

(35)考虑到金融市场的发展,有必要就本指令的规则不时制定技术性实施细则。因此,欧盟委员会应有权制定相关实施细则,前提是此等实施细则不对本指令的基本要素进行改动,并且欧盟委员在行事时应先咨询欧洲证券委员会的意见,并遵循本指令所规定的原则。

(36)欧盟委员会在根据本指令行使实施权时应遵守下列原则:

——有必要推行高标准的金融市场透明度,确保投资者对金融市场的信心;

——有必要向投资者提供多样化的竞争性投资机会,以及与其实际情况相吻合的信息披露与保护水平;

——有必要确保独立的监管机构执行相关规则(特别是打击经济犯罪的规则)的一致性;

——有必要保持高水平的透明度,并征求所有市场参与者以及欧洲议会与欧盟理事会的意见;

——有必要鼓励创新,使金融市场具有活力和效率;

——有必要对金融创新进行密切、灵活的监控,确保市场诚信度;

——有必要降低资本成本和拓宽融资渠道;

——采取任何实施细则均需实现市场参与者(包括中小型企业和小型投资者)成本和效益的长期平衡;

— the need to foster the international competitiveness of Community financial markets without prejudice to a much needed extension of international cooperation;

— the need to achieve a level playing field for all market participants by establishing Community-wide regulations wherever appropriate;

— the need to respect differences in national markets where these do not unduly impinge on the coherence of the single market;

— the need to ensure coherence with other Community legislation in this area, as imbalances in information and a lack of transparency may jeopardise the operation of the markets and above all harm consumers and small investors.

(37) In order to ensure that the requirements set out in this Directive or the measures implementing this Directive are fulfilled, any infringement of those requirements or measures should be promptly detected and, if necessary, subject to penalties. To that end, measures and penalties should be sufficiently dissuasive, proportionate and consistently enforced. Member States should ensure that decisions taken by the competent national authorities are subject to the right of appeal to the courts.

(38) This Directive aims to upgrade the current transparency requirements for security issuers and investors acquiring or disposing of major holdings in issuers whose shares are admitted to trading on a regulated market. This Directive replaces some of the requirements set out in Directive 2001/34/EC of the European Parliament and of the Council of 28 May 2001 on the admission of securities to official stock exchange listing and on information to be published on those securities. In order to gather transparency requirements in a single act it is necessary to amend it accordingly. Such an amendment however should not affect the ability of Member States to impose additional requirements under Articles 42 to 63 of Directive 2001/34/EC, which remain valid.

(39) This Directive is in line with Directive 95/46/EC of the European Parliament and of the Council of 24 October 1995 on the protection of individuals with regard to the processing of personal data and on the free movement of such data [1].

(40) This Directive respects fundamental rights and observes the principles recognised in particular by the Charter of the Fundamental Rights of the European Union.

(41) Since the objectives of this Directive, namely to ensure investor confidence through equivalent transparency throughout the Community and thereby to complete the internal market, cannot be sufficiently achieved by the Member States on the basis of the existing Community legislation and can therefore be better achieved at Community level, the Community may adopt measures, in accordance with the principle of subsidiarity as

1 OJ L 281, 23.11.1995, p. 31. Directive as amended by Regulation (EC) No 1882/2003 (OJ L 284, 31.10.2003, p. 1).

——有必要在不影响国际合作深化的前提下，培育欧共体金融市场的国际竞争力；

——有必要适时制定适用于全欧共体的法规，为所有市场参与者提供公平的竞争环境；

——有必要在不过度冲击单一市场一致性的前提下尊重各成员国国内市场的差异；

——有必要确保此领域法律与其他欧共体法律的一致性，以防止信息的不对等和透明度的缺失危害市场运行，尤其是防止因此损及消费者和小型投资者的利益。

(37)为确保本指令设定的要求或本指令的实施细则得到落实，应及时发现任何违反该等要求或细则的行为并在必要时实施处罚。为此，措施和处罚的执行应有足够的威慑作用，并应成比例地和一致地执行。成员国应确保对于国家级主管部门所做的决定可由相对人向法院提起行政诉讼。

(38)本指令旨在强化现有的证券发行人透明度要求，另外，对于发行人股票获准在受监管市场交易的，大额购买或处置该等股份的投资者的透明度要求亦应通过本指令得到加强。本指令取代了《欧洲议会与欧盟理事会关于证券获准在证券交易所正式上市以及应公布的与该等证券有关的信息的第2001/34/EC号指令》(2001年5月28日)的部分要求。为把透明度要求归集在一份单一的法律文件中，有必要对其进行相应的修正。但上述修正不应影响成员国依据第2001/34/EC号指令第42条至第63条(该等条款仍然有效)的规定施加额外要求。

(39)本指令与《欧洲议会与欧盟理事会关于处理个人资料时对个人的保护以及该等资料的自由流动的第95/46/EC号指令》[1](1995年10月24日)一致。

(40)本指令尤其遵守和奉行《欧盟基本权利宪章》所认可的基本权利和原则。

(41)本指令的目标在于通过全欧共体同等的透明度确保投资者信心，从而完善内部市场，该等目标单靠成员国基于现有的欧共体立法不足以实现，而在欧共体这一层级更容易实现，因此，欧共体可依据《条约》第5条规定的辅助性原则制定相关细则。依照《条约》第5条规定的比例原则，本指令仅作出实现上述目标所必要的规定。

---

1 1995年11月23日《欧盟公报》L281，第31页。该指令经第1882/2003号(欧共体)条例(2003年10月31日《欧盟公报》L284，第1页)修正。

set out in Article 5 of the Treaty. In accordance with the principle of proportionality, as set out in that Article, this Directive does not go beyond what is necessary in order to achieve these objectives.

(42) The measures necessary for implementing this Directive should be adopted in accordance with Council Decision 1999/468/EC of 28 June 1999 laying down the procedures for the exercise of implementing powers conferred on the Commission [1].

HAVE ADOPTED THIS DIRECTIVE:

CHAPTER I GENERAL PROVISIONS

Article 1 Subject matter and scope

1. This Directive establishes requirements in relation to the disclosure of periodic and ongoing information about issuers whose securities are already admitted to trading on a regulated market situated or operating within a Member State.

2. This Directive shall not apply to units issued by collective investment undertakings other than the closed-end type, or to units acquired or disposed of in such collective investment undertakings.

3. Member States may decide not to apply the provisions mentioned in Article 16(3) and in paragraphs 2, 3 and 4 of Article 18 to securities which are admitted to trading on a regulated market issued by them or their regional or local authorities.

4. Member States may decide not to apply Article 17 to their national central banks in their capacity as issuers of shares admitted to trading on a regulated market if this admission took place before 20 January 2005.

Article 2 Definitions

1. For the purposes of this Directive the following definitions shall apply:

(a) 'securities' means transferable securities as defined in Article 4(1) point 18, of Directive 2004/39/EC of the European Parliament and of the Council of 21 April 2004 on markets in financial instruments [2] with the exception of money market instruments, as defined in Article 4(1) point 19, of that Directive having a maturity of less than 12 months, for which national legislation may be applicable;

(b) 'debt securities' means bonds or other forms of transferable securitised debts, with the exception of securities which are equivalent to shares in companies or which, if converted or if the rights conferred by them are exercised, give rise to a right to acquire shares or securities equivalent to shares;

(c) 'regulated market' means a market as defined in Article 4(1) point 14, of

1 OJ L 184, 17.7.1999, p. 23.

2 OJ L 145, 30.4.2004, p. 1.

(42)应根据《欧盟理事会关于制定欧盟委员会行使其被授予的实施权之程序的第1999/468/EC号决定》[1](1999年6月28日)制定本指令所需实施细则。

兹通过本指令如下:

第一章 总 则

第1条 宗旨与范围

1.对于证券获准在位于某成员国境内或在某成员国境内运营的受监管市场交易的发行人,本指令规定了其定期和持续信息披露的要求。

2.本指令不适用于非封闭式集合投资计划发行的单位或投资人购买或处置的非封闭式集合投资计划单位。

3.成员国可决定不对其发行的或其地区或地方政府部门发行的获准在受监管市场交易的证券适用第16条第3款以及第18条第2款、第3款和第4款所述的规定。

4.任何成员国的中央银行以发行人身份发行的股票获准在受监管市场交易的,只要准入日期早于2005年1月20日,该成员国可决定不对其适用第17条规定。

第2条 定义

1.本指令适用下列定义:

(a)"证券"指《欧洲议会与欧盟理事会关于金融工具市场的第2004/39/EC号指令》[2](2004年4月21日)第4条第1款第18项所定义的可转让证券,但该指令第4条第1款第19项所定义的距到期日不足12个月的货币市场工具除外,此等证券可适用成员国国内立法;

(b)"债务证券"指债券或其他形式的可转让证券化债务,但不包括以下两类证券:等同于公司股票的证券;或经转换后或其所赋予的权利一经行使,持有人即有权购买股票或等同于股票的证券;

(c)"受监管市场"指第2004/39/EC号指令第4条第1款第14项所定义的市场;

1 1999年7月17日《欧盟公报》L184,第23页。
2 2004年4月30日《欧盟公报》L145,第1页。

Directive 2004/39/EC;

(d) 'issuer' means a legal entity governed by private or public law, including a State, whose securities are admitted to trading on a regulated market, the issuer being, in the case of depositary receipts representing securities, the issuer of the securities represented;

(e) 'shareholder' means any natural person or legal entity governed by private or public law, who holds, directly or indirectly:

(i) shares of the issuer in its own name and on its own account;

(ii) shares of the issuer in its own name, but on behalf of another natural person or legal entity;

(iii) depositary receipts, in which case the holder of the depositary receipt shall be considered as the shareholder of the underlying shares represented by the depositary receipts;

(f) 'controlled undertaking' means any undertaking

(i) in which a natural person or legal entity has a majority of the voting rights; or

(ii) of which a natural person or legal entity has the right to appoint or remove a majority of the members of the administrative, management or supervisory body and is at the same time a shareholder in, or member of, the undertaking in question; or

(iii) of which a natural person or legal entity is a shareholder or member and alone controls a majority of the shareholders' or members' voting rights, respectively, pursuant to an agreement entered into with other shareholders or members of the undertaking in question; or

(iv) over which a natural person or legal entity has the power to exercise, or actually exercises, dominant influence or control;

(g) 'collective investment undertaking other than the closed-end type' means unit trusts and investment companies:

(i) the object of which is the collective investment of capital provided by the public, and which operate on the principle of risk spreading; and

(ii) the units of which are, at the request of the holder of such units, repurchased or redeemed, directly or indirectly, out of the assets of those undertakings;

(h) 'units of a collective investment undertaking' means securities issued by a collective investment undertaking and representing rights of the participants in such an undertaking over its assets;

(i) 'home Member State' means

(i) in the case of an issuer of debt securities the denomination per unit of which is less than EUR 1 000 or an issuer of shares:

— where the issuer is incorporated in the Community, the Member State in which it

(d)“发行人”指证券获准在受监管市场交易的受私法或公法管辖的法人实体(包括国家);以存托凭证代表证券时,“发行人”指标的证券的发行人;

(e)“股东”指受私法或公法管辖的任何自然人或法人实体,该等实体直接或间接地:

(i)以其名义并在其自身账户中持有发行人的股票;

(ii)以其名义但代表其他自然人或法人实体持有发行人的股票;

(iii)持有存托凭证,在该等情形下,存托凭证的持有人应被视为存托凭证的标的股票的持有人;

(f)“受控企业”指符合以下条件的任何企业:

(i)某个自然人或法人实体持有其大多数表决权;或

(ii)某个自然人或法人实体有权任免其大多数董事会、管理机构或监事会成员,并且该自然人或法人实体同时身为该企业的股东或成员;或

(iii)作为该企业股东或成员的某个自然人或法人实体根据与该企业其他股东或其他成员所达成的协议,单独控制了全体股东或成员的多数表决权;或

(iv)某一自然人或法人实体有权对该企业发挥支配性影响或控制,或实际上发挥该等影响或控制;

(g)“非封闭式集合投资计划”指符合以下条件的单位信托基金和投资公司:

(i)其宗旨为以公众提供的资本进行集合投资,并以风险分散为运营原则;

(ii)其单位可应单位持有人的请求直接或间接地从该等资产中回购或赎回;

(h)“集合投资计划份额”指集合投资计划发行的且代表计划参与者对计划资产的权利的证券;

(i)“母国”:

(i)对于单位面值低于1000欧元的债务证券发行人或股票发行人:

——如发行人在欧共体境内成立,则指发行人注册地所在的成员国;

has its registered office;

— where the issuer is incorporated in a third country, the Member State in which it is required to file the annual information with the competent authority in accordance with Article 10 of Directive 2003/71/EC.

The definition of 'home' Member State shall be applicable to debt securities in a currency other than Euro, provided that the value of such denomination per unit is, at the date of the issue, less than EUR 1 000, unless it is nearly equivalent to EUR 1 000;

(ii) for any issuer not covered by (i), the Member State chosen by the issuer from among the Member State in which the issuer has its registered office and those Member States which have admitted its securities to trading on a regulated market on their territory. The issuer may choose only one Member State as its home Member State. Its choice shall remain valid for at least three years unless its securities are no longer admitted to trading on any regulated market in the Community;

(j) 'host Member State' means a Member State in which securities are admitted to trading on a regulated market, if different from the home Member State;

(k) 'regulated information' means all information which the issuer, or any other person who has applied for the admission of securities to trading on a regulated market without the issuer's consent, is required to disclose under this Directive, under Article 6 of Directive 2003/6/EC of the European Parliament and of the Council of 28 January 2003 on insider dealing and market manipulation (market abuse) [1], or under the laws, regulations or administrative provisions of a Member State adopted under Article 3(1) of this Directive;

(l) 'electronic means' are means of electronic equipment for the processing (including digital compression) storage and transmission of data, employing wires, radio, optical technologies, or any other electromagnetic means;

(m) 'management company' means a company as defined in Article 1a(2) of Council Directive 85/611/EEC of 20 December 1985 on the coordination of laws, regulations and administrative provisions relating to undertakings for collective investment in transferable securities (UCITS) [2];

(n) 'market maker' means a person who holds himself out on the financial markets on a continuous basis as being willing to deal on own account by buying and selling financial instruments against his proprietary capital at prices defined by him;

(o) 'credit institution' means an undertaking as defined in Article 1(1)(a) of Directive 2000/12/EC of the European Parliament and of the Council of 20 March 2000 relating to the taking up and pursuit of the business of credit institutions [3];

1 OJ L 96, 12.4.2003, p. 16.

2 OJ L 375, 31.12.1985, p. 3. Directive as last amended by Directive 2004/39/EC.

3 OJ L 126, 26.5.2000, p. 1. Directive as last amended by Commission Directive 2004/69/EC (OJ L 125, 28.4.2004, p. 44).

——如发行人在第三国成立，则指依照第2003/71/EC号指令第10条接收发行人应提交的年度信息的主管部门成员国。

“母”国的定义应能适用于非欧元的债务证券，前提是发行当日单位面值低于1000欧元，约等值于1000欧元的除外；

(ii)对于第i目涵盖范围之外的任何发行人，指发行人从下列成员国中选择的国家：其注册地所在的成员国和核准证券在其境内受监管市场交易的成员国。发行人仅可选择一个成员国作为母国。选择的有效期至少为3年，除非证券不再获准在欧共体内的任何受监管市场交易；

(j)“东道国”如不同于母国则指证券获准在其受监管市场交易的成员国；

(k)“受监管信息”指发行人或未经发行人同意自行申请了证券获准在受监管市场交易的其他人按照下列各项披露的信息：本指令、《欧洲议会与欧盟理事会关于内幕交易和市场操纵（市场滥用）的第2003/6/EC号指令》[1]（2003年1月28日）第6条或成员国依据本指令第3条第1款制定的法律、法规或规章；

(l)“电子手段”指利用电子设备对数据进行处理（包括数码压缩）、存储和传输的手段，处理过程中采用了电线、无线电、光学技术或任何其他电磁手段；

(m)“管理公司”指《欧洲经济共同体理事会协调关于可转让证券集合投资计划（UCITS）的法律、法规和规章的第85/611/EEC号指令》[2]（1985年12月20日）第1a条第2款所定义的公司；

(n)“做市商”指在金融市场中持续地以自营商身份自居，即其愿意以自有资本依自己的报价不断买入卖出金融工具的人；

(o)“信贷机构”指《欧洲议会与欧盟理事会关于开办和经营信贷机构业务的第2000/12/EC号指令》[3]（2000年3月20日）第1条第1款第a项所定义的企业；

1 2003年4月12日《欧盟公报》L96，第16页。

2 1985年12月31日《欧盟公报》L375，第3页。该指令由第2004/39/EC号指令作出最新修正。

3 2000年5月26日《欧盟公报》L126，第1页。该指令由第2004/69/EC号指令（2004年4月28日《欧盟公报》L125，第44页）作出最新修正。

(p) 'securities issued in a continuous or repeated manner' means debt securities of the same issuer on tap or at least two separate issues of securities of a similar type and/or class.

2. For the purposes of the definition of 'controlled undertaking' in paragraph 1(f)(ii) the holder's rights in relation to voting, appointment and removal shall include the rights of any other undertaking controlled by the shareholder and those of any natural person or legal entity acting, albeit in its own name, on behalf of the shareholder or of any other undertaking controlled by the shareholder.

3. In order to take account of technical developments on financial markets and to ensure the uniform application of paragraph 1, the Commission shall, in accordance with the procedure referred to in Article 27(2) adopt implementing measures concerning the definitions set out in paragraph 1.

The Commission shall, in particular:

(a) establish, for the purposes of paragraph 1(i)(ii) the procedural arrangements in accordance with which an issuer may make the choice of the home Member State;

(b) adjust, where appropriate for the purposes of the choice of the home Member State referred to in paragraph 1(i)(ii) the three-year period in relation to the issuer's track record in the light of any new requirement under Community law concerning admission to trading on a regulated market;

(c) establish, for the purposes of paragraph 1(l) an indicative list of means which are not to be considered as electronic means, thereby taking into account Annex V to Directive 98/34/EC of the European Parliament and of the Council of 22 June 1998 laying down a procedure for the provision of information in the field of technical standards and regulations [1].

Article 3 Integration of securities markets

1. The home Member State may make an issuer subject to requirements more stringent than those laid down in this Directive.

The home Member State may also make a holder of shares, or a natural person or legal entity referred to in Articles 10 or 13, subject to requirements more stringent than those laid down in this Directive.

2. A host Member State may not:

(a) as regards the admission of securities to a regulated market in its territory, impose disclosure requirements more stringent than those laid down in this Directive or in Article 6 of Directive 2003/6/EC;

(b) as regards the notification of information, make a holder of shares, or a natural person or legal entity referred to in Articles 10 or 13, subject to requirements more stringent than those laid down in this Directive.

1 OJ L 204, 21.7.1998, p. 37. Directive as last amended by the 2003 Act of Accession.

(p)"持续或重复发行的证券"指同一发行人根据需要随时发行的债务证券,或至少单独发行过两次的,其类型和/或类别相似的证券。

2.就第1款第f项第ii目对"受控企业"的定义而言,持股人的表决权和任免权应包括股东所控制的任何其他公司的权利,以及任何以其自身名义行事、代表股东行事或代表股东所控制的任何其他企业行事的自然人或法人实体的权利。

3.为反映金融市场的技术发展动态并确保第1款的统一适用,欧盟委员会应依照第27条第2款所述程序,就第1款的定义制定相关实施细则。

欧盟委员会尤应:

(a)为第1款第i项第ii目之目的,建立发行人可据以选择母国的程序性安排;

(b)对第1款第i项第ii目的母国选择适当的情形下,根据欧共体关于受监管市场交易准入法律中的任何新要求,调整对发行人的3年经营记录期;

(c)为第1款第l项之目的,建立一份指导性清单,列出不得被视为电子手段的手段,由此反映《欧洲议会与欧盟理事会制定技术标准和规章领域的信息提供程序的第98/34/EC号指令》[1](1998年6月22日)附录五的要求。

第3条　证券市场的一体化

1.母国可规定发行人应遵守比本指令所制定的要求更严格的要求。

母国还可规定持股人或第10条或第13条所述自然人或法人实体应遵守比本指令所制定的要求更严格的要求。

2.东道国不得:

(a)就证券在其境内受监管市场的准入,施加比本指令或第2003/6/EC号指令第6条所制定的要求更为严格的披露要求;

(b)规定持股人或第10条或第13条所述自然人或法人实体遵守比本指令所制定的要求更加严格的信息通知要求。

1　1998年7月21日《欧盟公报》L204,第37页。该指令由《2003年加入法案》作出最新修正。

CHAPTER II PERIODIC INFORMATION

Article 4 Annual financial reports

1. The issuer shall make public its annual financial report at the latest four months after the end of each financial year and shall ensure that it remains publicly available for at least five years.

2. The annual financial report shall comprise:

(a) the audited financial statements;

(b) the management report; and

(c) statements made by the persons responsible within the issuer, whose names and functions shall be clearly indicated, to the effect that, to the best of their knowledge, the financial statements prepared in accordance with the applicable set of accounting standards give a true and fair view of the assets, liabilities, financial position and profit or loss of the issuer and the undertakings included in the consolidation taken as a whole and that the management report includes a fair review of the development and performance of the business and the position of the issuer and the undertakings included in the consolidation taken as a whole, together with a description of the principal risks and uncertainties that they face.

3. Where the issuer is required to prepare consolidated accounts according to the Seventh Council Directive 83/349/ EEC of 13 June 1983 on consolidated accounts [1], the audited financial statements shall comprise such consolidated accounts drawn up in accordance with Regulation (EC) No 1606/2002 and the annual accounts of the parent company drawn up in accordance with the national law of the Member State in which the parent company is incorporated.

Where the issuer is not required to prepare consolidated accounts, the audited financial statements shall comprise the accounts prepared in accordance with the national law of the Member State in which the company is incorporated.

4. The financial statements shall be audited in accordance with Articles 51 and 51a of the Fourth Council Directive 78/660/EEC of 25 July 1978 on the annual accounts of certain types of companies [2] and, if the issuer is required to prepare consolidated accounts, in accordance with Article 37 of Directive 83/349/EEC.

The audit report, signed by the person or persons responsible for auditing the financial statements, shall be disclosed in full to the public together with the annual financial report.

---

1 OJ L 193, 18.7.1983, p. 1. Directive as last amended by Directive 2003/51/EC of the European Parliament and of the Council (OJ L 178, 17.7.2003, p. 16).

2 OJ L 222, 14.8.1978, p. 11. Directive as last amended by Directive 2003/51/EC.

第二章 定期披露的信息

第4条 年度财务报告

1.发行人最晚应于每个会计年度结束后4个月内公布年度财务报告,并确保维持该等报告至少在5年期间内均可公开获得。

2.年度财务报告应包括:

(a)经审计的财务报表;

(b)管理报告;及

(c)发行人内部相关负责人制作的说明书(应清楚注明该等负责人的姓名和职能),表明如下内容:就其所知,按适用的会计准则制作的财务报表真实公允地反映了发行人和合并报表覆盖的各个企业的资产、负债、财务状况和损益情况,管理报告则包含了对发行人和合并报表覆盖的各个企业的业务发展和业绩以及所处状况的公允审评,连同一份对其面临的主要风险和不确定因素的说明。

3.发行人有义务按照《欧洲经济共同体理事会关于合并财务报表的第83/349/EEC号第七指令》[1](1983年6月23日)制作合并财务报表的,经审计的财务报表应包括按照第1606/2002号(欧共体)条例编制的合并财务报表以及按其母公司成立所在地成员国国内法律编制的母公司年度财务报表。

发行人无义务制作合并财务报表的,经审计的财务报表应包含按照公司成立所在地成员国国内法律制作的财务报表。

4.财务报表的审计应按照《欧洲经济共同体理事会关于某些类型公司的年度财务报表的第78/660/EEC号第四指令》[2](1978年7月25日)第51条和第51a条进行,发行人有义务制作合并财务报表的,审计应依据第83/349/EEC号指令第37条进行。

由负责审计财务报表的一个或多个人签署的审计报告应连同年度财务报告一起完整地向公众披露。

1 1983年7月18日《欧盟公报》L193,第1页。该指令由欧洲议会与欧盟理事会第2003/51/EC号指令(2003年7月17日《欧盟公报》L178,第16页)作出最新修正。

2 1978年8月14日《欧盟公报》L222,第11页。该指令由第2003/51/EC号指令作出最新修正。

5. The management report shall be drawn up in accordance with Article 46 of Directive 78/660/EEC and, if the issuer is required to prepare consolidated accounts, in accordance with Article 36 of Directive 83/349/EEC.

6. The Commission shall, in accordance with the procedure referred to in Article 27 (2) adopt implementing measures in order to take account of technical developments in financial markets and to ensure the uniform application of paragraph 1. The Commission shall in particular specify the technical conditions under which a published annual financial report, including the audit report, is to remain available to the public.

Where appropriate, the Commission may also adapt the five-year period referred to in paragraph 1.

Article 5 Half-yearly financial reports

1. The issuer of shares or debt securities shall make public a half-yearly financial report covering the first six months of the financial year as soon as possible after the end of the relevant period, but at the latest two months thereafter. The issuer shall ensure that the half-yearly financial report remains available to the public for at least five years.

2. The half-yearly financial report shall comprise:

(a) the condensed set of financial statements;

(b) an interim management report; and

(c) statements made by the persons responsible within the issuer, whose names and functions shall be clearly indicated, to the effect that, to the best of their knowledge, the condensed set of financial statements which has been prepared in accordance with the applicable set of accounting standards gives a true and fair view of the assets, liabilities, financial position and profit or loss of the issuer, or the undertakings included in the consolidation as a whole as required under paragraph 3, and that the interim management report includes a fair review of the information required under paragraph 4.

3. Where the issuer is required to prepare consolidated accounts, the condensed set of financial statements shall be prepared in accordance with the international accounting standard applicable to the interim financial reporting adopted pursuant to the procedure provided for under Article 6 of Regulation (EC) No 1606/2002.

Where the issuer is not required to prepare consolidated accounts, the condensed set of financial statements shall at least contain a condensed balance sheet, a condensed profit and loss account and explanatory notes on these accounts. In preparing the condensed balance sheet and the condensed profit and loss account, the issuer shall follow the same principles for recognising and measuring as when preparing annual financial reports.

4. The interim management report shall include at least an indication of important events that have occurred during the first six months of the financial year, and their impact on the condensed set of financial statements, together with a description of the principal

5.管理报告应按照第78/660/EEC号指令第46条编制,发行人有义务制作合并财务报表的,管理报告应按照第83/349/EEC号指令第36条编制。

6.为反映金融市场的技术发展动态并确保第1款的统一适用,欧盟委员会应依照第27条第2款所述程序制定相关实施细则。欧盟委员会尤应对已公布的年度财务报告(包括审计报告)维持可公开获得所须符合的技术条件作出规定。

适当情形下,欧盟委员会还可调整第1款所述的5年期限。

第5条　半年度财务报告

1.股票或债务证券发行人最晚应于每个会计年度上半年结束后两个月内公布半年度财务报告,并确保维持该等报告至少在5年期间内均可公开获得。

2.半年度财务报告应包括:

(a)一套简要财务报表;

(b)一份中期管理报告;及

(c)发行人内部相关负责人制作的说明书(应清楚注明该等负责人姓名和职能),表明如下内容:就其所知,按适用的会计准则制作的一套简要财务报表真实公允地反映了发行人和按第3款要求合并报表覆盖的各个企业的资产、负债、财务状况和损益情况,中期管理报告则包含了对第4款要求的信息的公允审评。

3.发行人有义务制作合并财务报表的,简要财务报表应按照依第1606/2002号(欧共体)条例第6条程序制定的适用于中期财务报告的国际会计准则制作。

发行人无义务制作合并财务报表的,简要财务报表应至少包括一份简要资产负债表、简要损益表以及该等报表的注释。制作简要资产负债表及简要损益表时,发行人应遵从其制作年度财务报告时所采用的相同的确认和计量原则。

4.中期管理报告至少应包括对该会计年度前半年发生的重要事件及其对简要财务报表的影响说明,连同一份对该会计年度后半年的主要风险和不确定性的说明。对于股票发行人,中期管理报告还应包括重大关联交易。

risks and uncertainties for the remaining six months of the financial year. For issuers of shares, the interim management report shall also include major related parties transactions.

5. If the half-yearly financial report has been audited, the audit report shall be reproduced in full. The same shall apply in the case of an auditors' review. If the half-yearly financial report has not been audited or reviewed by auditors, the issuer shall make a statement to that effect in its report.

6. The Commission shall, in accordance with the procedure referred to in Article 27 (2) adopt implementing measures in order to take account of technical developments on financial markets and to ensure the uniform application of paragraphs 1 to 5 of this Article.

The Commission shall, in particular:

(a) specify the technical conditions under which a published half-yearly financial report, including the auditors' review, is to remain available to the public;

(b) clarify the nature of the auditors' review;

(c) specify the minimum content of the condensed balance sheet and profit and loss accounts and explanatory notes on these accounts, where they are not prepared in accordance with the international accounting standards adopted pursuant to the procedure provided for under Article 6 of Regulation (EC) No 1606/2002.

Where appropriate, the Commission may also adapt the five-year period referred to in paragraph 1.

Article 6 Interim management statements

1. Without prejudice to Article 6 of Directive 2003/6/EC, an issuer whose shares are admitted to trading on a regulated market shall make public a statement by its management during the first six-month period of the financial year and another statement by its management during the second six-month period of the financial year. Such statement shall be made in a period between ten weeks after the beginning and six weeks before the end of the relevant six-month period. It shall contain information covering the period between the beginning of the relevant six-month period and the date of publication of the statement. Such a statement shall provide:

— an explanation of material events and transactions that have taken place during the relevant period and their impact on the financial position of the issuer and its controlled undertakings, and

— a general description of the financial position and performance of the issuer and its controlled undertakings during the relevant period.

2. Issuers which, under either national legislation or the rules of the regulated market or of their own initiative, publish quarterly financial reports in accordance with such legislation or rules shall not be required to make public statements by the management provided for in paragraph 1.

5.半年度财务报告做过审计的,审计报告应全文收录。半年度财务报告经审计师做过审查的,审计报告也应全文收录。半年度财务报告未经审计师审计或审评的,发行人应在其报告中作出相关声明。

6.为反映金融市场的技术发展动态并确保本条第1款至第5款的统一适用,欧盟委员会应依照第27条第2款所述程序制定相关实施细则。

欧盟委员会尤应:

(a)对已公布的半年度财务报告(包括审计师的审查报告)维持可公开获得状态所须符合的技术条件作出规定。

(b)明确审计师审查的性质;

(c)简要资产负债表和损益表以及该等报表的注释并非按照依第1606/2002号(欧共体)条例第6条程序制定的国际会计准则制作的,应对其必不可少的内容作出规定。

适当情形下,欧盟委员会还可调整第1款所述的5年期限。

第6条　中期管理说明书

1.在不影响第2003/6/EC号指令第6条的情形下,股票获准在受监管市场交易的发行人应在每个会计年度上半年期间内公布一份管理说明书,在该会计年度下半年期间内公布另一份管理说明书。上述说明书应在相关半年期第十周至倒数第六周期间制作。说明书应涵盖自相关半年期开始至说明书公布之日的信息。上述说明书应提供:

——关于报告期内发生的重大事件和交易及其对发行人及其受控企业财务状况影响的解释,以及

——对发行人及其受控企业在报告期内财务状况和业绩的总体说明。

2. 发行人按照成员国国内立法或受监管市场规则要求或主动公布季度财务报表的,不必公布第1款规定的管理说明书。

3. The Commission shall provide a report to the European Parliament and the Council by 20 January 2010 on the transparency of quarterly financial reporting and statements by the management of issuers to examine whether the information provided meets the objective of allowing investors to make an informed assessment of the financial position of the issuer. Such a report shall include an impact assessment on areas where the Commission considers proposing amendments to this Article.

Article 7 Responsibility and liability

Member States shall ensure that responsibility for the information to be drawn up and made public in accordance with Articles 4, 5, 6 and 16 lies at least with the issuer or its administrative, management or supervisory bodies and shall ensure that their laws, regulations and administrative provisions on liability apply to the issuers, the bodies referred to in this Article or the persons responsible within the issuers.

Article 8 Exemptions

1. Articles 4, 5 and 6 shall not apply to the following issuers:

(a) a State, a regional or local authority of a State, a public international body of which at least one Member State is a member, the ECB, and Member States' national central banks whether or not they issue shares or other securities; and

(b) an issuer exclusively of debt securities admitted to trading on a regulated market, the denomination per unit of which is at least EUR 50 000 or, in the case of debt securities denominated in a currency other than Euro, the value of such denomination per unit is, at the date of the issue, equivalent to at least EUR 50 000.

2. The home Member State may choose not to apply Article 5 to credit institutions whose shares are not admitted to trading on a regulated market and which have, in a continuous or repeated manner, only issued debt securities provided that the total nominal amount of all such debt securities remains below EUR 100 000 000 and that they have not published a prospectus under Directive 2003/71/EC.

3. The home Member State may choose not to apply Article 5 to issuers already existing at the date of the entry into force of Directive 2003/71/EC which exclusively issue debt securities unconditionally and irrevocably guaranteed by the home Member State or by one of its regional or local authorities, on a regulated market.

3.欧盟委员会应在2010年1月20日前向欧洲议会与欧盟理事会提供一份关于发行人季度财务报告和管理说明书透明度的报告，以审查所提供的信息是否达到了令投资者得以对发行人财务状况作出知情评估的目标。上述报告应包括欧盟委员会考虑对本条规定提出修改建议的领域的影响评估。

第7条　职责和责任

成员国应至少确保，发行人或其董事会、管理机构或监事会对应按第4条、第5条、第6条以及第16条编制和公开的信息负责，并确保其关于发行人责任的法律、法规和规章适用于发行人、本条所述的董事会、管理机构或监事会或发行人内部的相关负责人。

第8条　豁免

1.第4条、第5条和第6条不适用于下列发行人：

(a)成员国、成员国的地区或地方政府部门、国际公共机构(其一个或多个成员为欧盟成员国)、欧洲中央银行以及各成员国的中央银行(不论其发行或不发行股票或其他证券)；及

(b)仅发行获准在受监管市场交易的债务证券的发行人，前提是证券单位面值最低应达5万欧元，非欧元债务证券单位面值则应在发行当日最低等值于5万欧元。

2.母国可选择不将第5条规定适用于股票未获准在受监管市场交易且仅持续或重复地发行债务证券的信贷机构，前提是所有上述债务证券的总面值始终低于1亿欧元且该等信贷机构未曾公布过第2003/71/EC号指令中的招募说明书。

3.母国可选择不将第5条规定适用于下述发行人，即其在第2003/71/EC号指令生效之日已经存在，且仅在受监管市场上发行由母国或母国某个地区或地方政府部门提供无条件且不可撤销担保的债务证券的发行人。

CHAPTER Ⅲ ONGOING INFORMATION

SECTION Ⅰ Information about major holdings

Article 9 Notification of the acquisition or disposal of major holdings

1. The home Member State shall ensure that, where a shareholder acquires or disposes of shares of an issuer whose shares are admitted to trading on a regulated market and to which voting rights are attached, such shareholder notifies the issuer of the proportion of voting rights of the issuer held by the shareholder as a result of the acquisition or disposal where that proportion reaches, exceeds or falls below the thresholds of 5%, 10%, 15%, 20%, 25%, 30%, 50% and 75%.

The voting rights shall be calculated on the basis of all the shares to which voting rights are attached even if the exercise thereof is suspended. Moreover this information shall also be given in respect of all the shares which are in the same class and to which voting rights are attached.

2. The home Member States shall ensure that the shareholders notify the issuer of the proportion of voting rights, where that proportion reaches, exceeds or falls below the thresholds provided for in paragraph 1, as a result of events changing the breakdown of voting rights, and on the basis of the information disclosed pursuant to Article 15. Where the issuer is incorporated in a third country, the notification shall be made for equivalent events.

3. The home Member State need not apply:

(a) the 30% threshold, where it applies a threshold of one-thirds;

(b) the 75% threshold, where it applies a threshold of two-thirds.

4. This Article shall not apply to shares acquired for the sole purpose of clearing and settling within the usual short settlement cycle, or to custodians holding shares in their custodian capacity provided such custodians can only exercise the voting rights attached to such shares under instructions given in writing or by electronic means.

5. This Article shall not apply to the acquisition or disposal of a major holding reaching or crossing the 5% threshold by a market maker acting in its capacity of a market maker, provided that:

(a) it is authorised by its home Member State under Directive 2004/39/EC; and

(b) it neither intervenes in the management of the issuer concerned nor exerts any influence on the issuer to buy such shares or back the share price.

6. Home Member States under Article 2(1)(i) may provide that voting rights held in the trading book, as defined in Article 2(6) of Council Directive 93/6/EEC of 15 March

第三章 持续披露的信息

第1节 大额持股信息

第9条 关于购买或处置大额股份的通知

1.母国应确保，发行人的股票获准在受监管市场交易且附带表决权的，当股东购买或处置该等发行人股票从而持有发行人表决权比例达到、超过或低于5%、10%、15%、20%、25%、30%、50%和75%时，应通知发行人其所持有的表决权比例。

表决权应按附带表决权的股票总数计算，而不论其表决权是否暂停行使。此外，还应就所有类别相同并附带表决权的股票提供此等信息。

2.母国应确保，由于表决权持有人之间持有比例发生变动的事件而使表决权达到、超过或低于第1款所设定的门槛时，股东应基于根据第15条披露的信息通知发行人其所持有的表决权比例。发行人在第三国成立的，应就同等事件发出通知。

3.母国不必适用：

(a)30%的门槛，如果已采用1/3的门槛；

(b)75%的门槛，如果已采用2/3的门槛。

4.本条规定不适用于仅为在惯常的短结算周期内清算和结算之目的所购买的股票，亦不适用于作为托管人持有股票的托管人，前提是该等托管人仅能按照以书面形式或电子手段提供的指示行使该等股票附带的表决权。

5.本条规定不适用于做市商以做市商身份购买或处置达到或超过5%门槛的大额股份，前提是：

(a)做市商根据第2004/39/EC号指令获得母国核准；且

(b)做市商既不干涉所涉发行人的管理，也不对发行人施加购买上述股票或降低股票价格的任何影响。

6.第2条第1款第i项中的母国可以规定，在本条中不得将信贷机构或投资公司在交易账户（定义见《欧洲经济共同体理事会关于投资公司和信贷机构的资本充足性的

1993 on the capital adequacy of investment firms and credit institutions [1], of a credit institution or investment firm shall not be counted for the purposes of this Article provided that:

(a) the voting rights held in the trading book do not exceed 5%, and

(b) the credit institution or investment firm ensures that the voting rights attaching to shares held in the trading book are not exercised nor otherwise used to intervene in the management of the issuer.

7. The Commission shall, in accordance with the procedure referred to in Article 27(2) adopt implementing measures in order to take account of technical developments on financial markets and to ensure the uniform application of paragraphs 2, 4 and 5 of this Article.

The Commission shall in particular specify the maximum length of the 'short settlement cycle' referred to in paragraph 4, as well as the appropriate control mechanisms by the competent authority of the home Member State. In addition, the Commission may draw up a list of the events referred to in paragraph 2.

Article 10 Acquisition or disposal of major proportions of voting rights

The notification requirements defined in paragraphs 1 and 2 of Article 9 shall also apply to a natural person or legal entity to the extent it is entitled to acquire, to dispose of, or to exercise voting rights in any of the following cases or a combination of them:

(a) voting rights held by a third party with whom that person or entity has concluded an agreement, which obliges them to adopt, by concerted exercise of the voting rights they hold, a lasting common policy towards the management of the issuer in question;

(b) voting rights held by a third party under an agreement concluded with that person or entity providing for the temporary transfer for consideration of the voting rights in question;

(c) voting rights attaching to shares which are lodged as collateral with that person or entity, provided the person or entity controls the voting rights and declares its intention of exercising them;

(d) voting rights attaching to shares in which that person or entity has the life interest;

(e) voting rights which are held, or may be exercised within the meaning of points (a) to (d) by an undertaking controlled by that person or entity;

(f) voting rights attaching to shares deposited with that person or entity which the person or entity can exercise at its discretion in the absence of specific instructions from the shareholders;

1 OJ L 141, 11.6.1993, p. 1. Directive as last amended by Directive 2004/39/EC.

第93/6/EEC号指令》[1]（1993年3月15日）第2 条第6款）中持有的表决权计算在内，前提是：

（a）在此等交易账户中所持有的表决权不超过5%，并且

（b）信贷机构或投资公司确保交易账户中的股票附带的表决权，既不行使也不被用于干涉发行人的管理。

7.为反映金融市场的技术发展动态并确保本条第2款、第4款和第5款的统一适用，欧盟委员会应依照第27条第2款所述程序制定相关实施细则。

欧盟委员会尤应指明第4款所述"短结算周期"的最长时长以及母国主管部门的适当控制机制。此外，欧盟委员会可就第2款所述事件编制一份清单。

第10条　购买或处置大额表决权

第9条第1款和第2款的通知规定还应适用于有权购买、处置或行使涉及以下一类或多类表决权的自然人或法人实体：

（a）与该等自然人或法人实体订有协议的第三方持有的表决权，该等协议规定各方有义务一致地行使其持有的表决权，以期对发行人的管理采取共同的长期政策；

（b）与该等自然人或法人实体订有协议的第三方持有的表决权，该等协议规定了以所涉表决权为对价的临时转让；

（c）以该等自然人或法人实体作为担保权人的股票担保品附带的表决权，前提是该等人士或实体控制了并宣称有意行使该等表决权；

（d）该等自然人或法人实体拥有终身权益的股票附带的表决权；

（e）该等自然人或法人实体所控制的企业所持有的表决权，或可在第a项至第d项定义范围内行使的表决权；

（f）存管于该等自然人或法人实体处的股票附带的表决权，且该等人士或实体可在股东未发出任何特殊指示的情形下自行行使该等表决权；

1　1993年6月11日《欧盟公报》L141，第1页。该指令由第2004/39/EC号指令作出最新修正。

(g) voting rights held by a third party in its own name on behalf of that person or entity;

(h) voting rights which that person or entity may exercise as a proxy where the person or entity can exercise the voting rights at its discretion in the absence of specific instructions from the shareholders.

Article 11

1. Articles 9 and 10(c) shall not apply to shares provided to or by the members of the ESCB in carrying out their functions as monetary authorities, including shares provided to or by members of the ESCB under a pledge or repurchase or similar agreement for liquidity granted for monetary policy purposes or within a payment system.

2. The exemption shall apply to the above transactions lasting for a short period and provided that the voting rights attaching to such shares are not exercised.

Article 12 Procedures on the notification and disclosure of major holdings

1. The notification required under Articles 9 and 10 shall include the following information:

(a) the resulting situation in terms of voting rights;

(b) the chain of controlled undertakings through which voting rights are effectively held, if applicable;

(c) the date on which the threshold was reached or crossed; and

(d) the identity of the shareholder, even if that shareholder is not entitled to exercise voting rights under the conditions laid down in Article 10, and of the natural person or legal entity entitled to exercise voting rights on behalf of that shareholder.

2. The notification to the issuer shall be effected as soon as possible, but not later than four trading days, the first of which shall be the day after the date on which the shareholder, or the natural person or legal entity referred to in Article 10,

(a) learns of the acquisition or disposal or of the possibility of exercising voting rights, or on which, having regard to the circumstances, should have learned of it, regardless of the date on which the acquisition, disposal or possibility of exercising voting rights takes effect; or

(b) is informed about the event mentioned in Article 9(2) .

3. An undertaking shall be exempted from making the required notification in accordance with paragraph 1 if the notification is made by the parent undertaking or, where the parent undertaking is itself a controlled undertaking, by its own parent undertaking.

4. The parent undertaking of a management company shall not be required to aggregate its holdings under Articles 9 and 10 with the holdings managed by the management company under the conditions laid down in Directive 85/611/ EEC, provided

(g)第三方以自身名义代表该等自然人或法人实体持有的表决权;

(h)可由该等自然人或法人实体以代理身份代表股东行使的表决权(该等人士或实体可在股东未发出任何特殊指示的情形下自行行使该等表决权)。

第11条

1.第9条和第10条第c款不适用于欧洲中央银行体系成员履行货币管理当局职能所获得或提供的股票,包括欧洲中央银行体系成员根据质押或回购协议或类似协议而获得或提供的股票,该等协议旨在出于货币政策之目的或在支付系统内提供流动性。

2.在不行使该等股票附带的表决权的前提下,上述短期交易应予豁免。

第12条　大额持股的通知和披露程序

1.第9条和第10条规定的通知应包含以下信息:

(a) 表决权经购买或处置后的状态;

(b) 通过何等受控企业链来有效持有表决权(如适用);

(c) 达到或超过表决权比例门槛的日期;及

(d) 股东的身份(即使股东无权依据第10条规定的条件行使表决权)以及有权代表该股东行使表决权的自然人或法人实体的身份。

2.应尽快且不得晚于4个交易日向发行人发出通知,其中第一个交易日指股东或第10条所述自然人或法人实体发生以下事件日期的次日;

(a)知悉表决权被购买或处置之日,或知悉表决权可能被行使之日;或者,不论表决权购买或处置于何日生效或于何日可以行使,鉴于相关情况应当知悉该等情况之日;或

(b)被告知第9条第2款所述事件之日。

3.豁免某个企业根据第1款发送规定的通知的条件是:通知应由其母公司发出;或者,母公司本身是受控企业的,通知应由母公司自身的母公司发出。

4.管理公司的母公司不必将其第9条和第10条中的股份与管理公司根据第85/611/EEC号指令的条件所管理的股份合并计算,前提是上述管理公司独立于母公司行使其表决权。

such management company exercises its voting rights independently from the parent undertaking.

However, Articles 9 and 10 shall apply where the parent undertaking, or another controlled undertaking of the parent undertaking, has invested in holdings managed by such management company and the management company has no discretion to exercise the voting rights attached to such holdings and may only exercise such voting rights under direct or indirect instructions from the parent or another controlled undertaking of the parent undertaking.

5. The parent undertaking of an investment firm authorised under Directive 2004/39/EC shall not be required to aggregate its holdings under Articles 9 and 10 with the holdings which such investment firm manages on a client-by-client basis within the meaning of Article 4(1) point 9, of Directive 2004/39/EC, provided that:

— the investment firm is authorised to provide such portfolio management under point 4 of Section A of Annex I to Directive 2004/39/EC;

— it may only exercise the voting rights attached to such shares under instructions given in writing or by electronic means or it ensures that individual portfolio management services are conducted independently of any other services under conditions equivalent to those provided for under Directive 85/611/EEC by putting into place appropriate mechanisms; and

— the investment firm exercises its voting rights independently from the parent undertaking.

However, Articles 9 and 10 shall apply where the parent undertaking, or another controlled undertaking of the parent undertaking, has invested in holdings managed by such investment firm and the investment firm has no discretion to exercise the voting rights attached to such holdings and may only exercise such voting rights under direct or indirect instructions from the parent or another controlled undertaking of the parent undertaking.

6. Upon receipt of the notification under paragraph 1, but no later than three trading days thereafter, the issuer shall make public all the information contained in the notification.

7. A home Member State may exempt issuers from the requirement in paragraph 6 if the information contained in the notification is made public by its competent authority, under the conditions laid down in Article 21, upon receipt of the notification, but no later than three trading days thereafter.

8. In order to take account of technical developments on financial markets and to ensure the uniform application of paragraphs 1, 2, 4, 5 and 6 of this Article, the Commission shall, in accordance with the procedure referred to in Article 27(2) adopt

然而，下列情形应适用第9条和第10条的规定：母公司或母公司的其他受控企业已投资于上述管理公司所管理的股份，且管理公司无权自行行使该等股份附带的表决权，只可在母公司或母公司其他受控企业的直接或间接指示下行使该等表决权。

5.根据第2004/39/EC号指令获得核准的投资公司的母公司不必将其第9条和第10条中的股份与该投资公司在第2004/39/EC号指令第4条第1款第9项定义范围内为客户提供一对一管理的股份合并计算，前提是：

——投资公司根据第2004/39/EC号指令附录一第A节第4项获准提供上述投资组合管理服务；

——该母公司仅可根据以书面形式或电子手段发出的指示行使该等股票附带的表决权；或者，该母公司设置适当的机制确保，个人投资组合管理服务按照相当于第85/611/EEC号指令的条件独立于任何其他服务开展；并且

——投资公司独立于母公司行使其表决权。

然而，下列情形应适用第9条和第10条：母公司或母公司的其他控股公司已投资于该投资公司所管理的股份，且投资公司无权自行行使该等股份附带的表决权，仅得在母公司或母公司其他受控企业的直接或间接指示下行使该等表决权。

6.发行人应最迟于接到第1款所述通知后3个交易日（含）内公布通知所含全部信息。

7.通知所含信息已由母国主管部门最迟于接到通知后3个交易日（含）内按照第21条规定的条件公布的，该母国可豁免发行人履行第6款的要求。

8.为反映金融市场的技术发展动态并确保本条第1款、第2款、第4款、第5款以及第6款的统一适用，欧盟委员会应依照第27条第2款所述程序制定相关实施细则：

implementing measures:

(a) to establish a standard form to be used throughout the Community when notifying the required information to the issuer under paragraph 1 or when filing information under Article 19(3);

(b) to determine a calendar of 'trading days' for all Member States;

(c) to establish in which cases the shareholder, or the natural person or legal entity referred to in Article 10, or both, shall effect the necessary notification to the issuer;

(d) to clarify the circumstances under which the shareholder, or the natural person or legal entity referred to in Article 10, should have learned of the acquisition or disposal;

(e) to clarify the conditions of independence to be complied with by management companies and their parent undertakings or by investment firms and their parent undertakings to benefit from the exemptions in paragraphs 4 and 5.

Article 13

1. The notification requirements laid down in Article 9 shall also apply to a natural person or legal entity who holds, directly or indirectly, financial instruments that result in an entitlement to acquire, on such holder's own initiative alone, under a formal agreement, shares to which voting rights are attached, already issued, of an issuer whose shares are admitted to trading on a regulated market.

2. The Commission shall, in accordance with the procedure referred to in Article 27 (2) adopt implementing measures in order to take account of technical developments in financial markets and to ensure the uniform application of paragraph 1. It shall in particular determine:

(a) the types of financial instruments referred to in paragraph 1 and their aggregation;

(b) the nature of the formal agreement referred to in paragraph 1;

(c) the contents of the notification to be made, establishing a standard form to be used throughout the Community for that purpose;

(d) the notification period;

(e) to whom the notification is to be made.

Article 14

1. Where an issuer of shares admitted to trading on a regulated market acquires or disposes of its own shares, either itself or through a person acting in his own name but on the issuer's behalf, the home Member State shall ensure that the issuer makes public the proportion of its own shares as soon as possible, but not later than four trading days following such acquisition or disposal where that proportion reaches, exceeds or falls below the thresholds of 5% or 10% of the voting rights. The proportion shall be calculated on the basis of the total number of shares to which voting rights are attached.

(a)针对按第1款通知发行人要求提供的信息或按第19条第3款提交信息，制定全欧共体通用的标准格式；

(b)设定适用于所有成员国的“交易日”日历；

(c)确定在何种情形下股东或第10条所述自然人或法人实体（或两者一起）应向发行人发出必要的通知；

(d)明确股东或第10条所述自然人或法人实体在何种情形下理应知悉股份购买或处置的情况；

(e)明确管理公司及其母公司，或投资公司及其母公司，为享有第4款和第5款豁免所须符合的独立性条件。

第13条

1.第9条规定的通知要求还适用于直接或间接持有符合以下条件的金融工具的自然人或法人实体：该等金融工具使其持有人有权单独自主地决定依据一份正式协议购买附带表决权的股票，且该等股票的发行人获得了股票在受监管市场交易的核准。

2.为反映金融市场的技术发展动态并确保第1款的统一适用，欧盟委员会应依照第27条第(2)款所述程序制定相关实施细则。欧盟委员会尤应确定：

(a)第1款所述金融工具的类型及其合并计算；

(b)第1款所述正式协议的性质；

(c)通知所需包含的内容，为此应制定一个全欧共体通用的标准格式；

(d)通知期限；

(e)通知对象。

第14条

1.股票获准在受监管市场交易的发行人自行（或由他人以该发行人名义代表该发行人）购买或处置发行人自身股票的，母国应确保发行人在自身持股比例达到、超过或低于5%或10%的表决权门槛时，尽快且最晚在该项购买或处置之后的4个交易日内公布该比例。该比例应按附带表决权的股票总数计算。

2. The Commission shall, in accordance with the procedure referred to in Article 27 (2) adopt implementing measures in order to take account of technical developments in financial markets and to ensure the uniform application of paragraph 1.

Article 15

For the purpose of calculating the thresholds provided for in Article 9, the home Member State shall at least require the disclosure to the public by the issuer of the total number of voting rights and capital at the end of each calendar month during which an increase or decrease of such total number has occurred.

Article 16 Additional information

1. The issuer of shares admitted to trading on a regulated market shall make public without delay any change in the rights attaching to the various classes of shares, including changes in the rights attaching to derivative securities issued by the issuer itself and giving access to the shares of that issuer.

2. The issuer of securities, other than shares admitted to trading on a regulated market, shall make public without delay any changes in the rights of holders of securities other than shares, including changes in the terms and conditions of these securities which could indirectly affect those rights, resulting in particular from a change in loan terms or in interest rates.

3. The issuer of securities admitted to trading on a regulated market shall make public without delay of new loan issues and in particular of any guarantee or security in respect thereof. Without prejudice to Directive 2003/6/EC, this paragraph shall not apply to a public international body of which at least one Member State is member.

SECTION II Information for holders of securities admitted to trading on a regulated market

Article 17 Information requirements for issuers whose shares are admitted to trading on a regulated market

1. The issuer of shares admitted to trading on a regulated market shall ensure equal treatment for all holders of shares who are in the same position.

2. The issuer shall ensure that all the facilities and information necessary to enable holders of shares to exercise their rights are available in the home Member State and that the integrity of data is preserved. Shareholders shall not be prevented from exercising their rights by proxy, subject to the law of the country in which the issuer is incorporated. In particular, the issuer shall:

(a) provide information on the place, time and agenda of meetings, the total number of shares and voting rights and the rights of holders to participate in meetings;

(b) make available a proxy form, on paper or, where applicable, by electronic

2.为反映金融市场的技术发展动态并确保第1款的统一适用,欧盟委员会应依照第27条第2款所述程序制定相关实施细则。

第15条

为计算第9条所制定的门槛,母国至少应规定发行人应向公众披露表决权和资本的总数,披露时间为上述总数发生增减的每一日历月月末。

第16条　额外信息

1.股票获准在受监管市场交易的发行人应立即公布各种类别股票附带的权利的任何变更,包括发行人自身发行的衍生证券所附带的使其持有人有权获取该发行人股票的权利的变更。

2.发行人的证券并非获准在受监管市场交易的股票的,应立即公布非股票证券持有人的任何权利变更,包括该等证券的条款和条件发生的可能对该等权利造成间接影响(尤其是贷款条款或利率的变更造成的影响)的变更。

3.发行人的证券获准在受监管市场交易的,应立即公布新贷款发放的信息,尤其是发放该等贷款时所提供的任何保证或担保。在不影响第2003/6/EC号指令的情形下,本款不适用于至少1名成员是欧共体成员国的国际公共机构。

第二节　获准在受监管市场交易证券的持有人信息

第17条　对股票获准在受监管市场交易的发行人的信息要求

1.股票获准在受监管市场交易的发行人应确保平等对待处于相同状况的所有持股人。

2.发行人应确保持股人行使其权利所需的所有设施和信息均可在母国获得,并且数据的完整性受到保护。在遵守发行人成立地所在国家的法律的前提下,股东通过代理行使其权利不应受到阻碍。发行人尤应:

(a)提供有关会议地点、时间和议程、股票和表决权总数以及持股人参加会议的权利的信息;

(b)以纸质形式或(如适用)通过电子手段向有权在股东会议上表决的所有人提

means, to each person entitled to vote at a shareholders' meeting, togetherwith the notice concerning the meeting or, on request, after an announcement of the meeting;

(c) designate as its agent a financial institution through which shareholders may exercise their financial rights; and

(d) publish notices or distribute circulars concerning the allocation and payment of dividends and the issue of new shares, including information on any arrangements for allotment, subscription, cancellation or conversion.

3. For the purposes of conveying information to shareholders, the home Member State shall allow issuers the use of electronic means, provided such a decision is taken in a general meeting and meets at least the following conditions:

(a) the use of electronic means shall in no way depend upon the location of the seat or residence of the shareholder or, in the cases referred to in Article 10(a) to (h) of the natural persons or legal entities;

(b) identification arrangements shall be put in place so that the shareholders, or the natural persons or legal entities entitled to exercise or to direct the exercise of voting rights, are effectively informed;

(c) shareholders, or in the cases referred to in Article 10(a) to (e) the natural persons or legal entities entitled to acquire, dispose of or exercise voting rights, shall be contacted in writing to request their consent for the use of electronic means for conveying information and, if they do not object within a reasonable period of time, their consent shall be deemed to be given. They shall be able to request, at any time in the future, that information be conveyed in writing, and

(d) any apportionment of the costs entailed in the conveyance of such information by electronic means shall be determined by the issuer in compliance with the principle of equal treatment laid down in paragraph 1.

4. The Commission shall, in accordance with the procedure provided for in Article 27(2) adopt implementing measures in order to take account of technical developments in financial markets, to take account of developments in information and communication technology and to ensure the uniform application of paragraphs 1, 2 and 3. It shall, in particular, specify the types of financial institution through which a shareholder may exercise the financial rights provided for in paragraph 2(c).

Article 18 Information requirements for issuers whose debt securities are admitted to trading on a regulated market

1. The issuer of debt securities admitted to trading on a regulated market shall ensure that all holders of debt securities ranking paripassu are given equal treatment in respect of all the rights attaching to those debt securities.

2. The issuer shall ensure that all the facilities and information necessary to enable

供代理委托书，代理委托书应与会议通知同时发出，或经要求在发出会议公告后提供；

(c)指定某个金融机构作为代理人，使股东能够通过该金融机构行使其财务权利；及

(d)就股息分配和支付以及新股发行，包括关于配售、认购、撤销或转换的任何安排的信息发布通知或派发通告。

3.母国应允许发行人使用电子手段将信息传送给股东，前提是该项决定在股东大会上作出且至少符合以下条件：

(a)电子手段的使用无论如何均不得因为股东或(在第10条第a款至第h款所述情形下)自然人或法人实体的住所地或居住地的不同而有差别待遇；

(b)应落实相应的身份信息识别安排，使股东或者有权行使或指令他人行使表决权的自然人或法人实体收到有效的通知；

(c)应书面联系股东或在第10条第a款至第e款所述情形下有权购买、处置或行使表决权的自然人或法人实体，为使用电子手段传送信息征求其同意，如果他们未在合理时间内提出反对意见，则应被视为已经表示同意。未来他们应能随时要求以书面形式传送信息；及

(d)通过电子手段传送信息的成本分摊应由发行人按照第1款规定的平等待遇原则决定。

4.为反映金融市场的技术发展动态以及信息通信技术的发展动态，并确保第1款、第2款和第3款的统一适用，欧盟委员会应依照第27条第2款所述程序制定相关实施细则。欧盟委员会尤应指明股东可以通过哪些类型金融机构行使第2款第c项规定的财务权利。

第18条　对债务证券获准在受监管市场交易的发行人的信息要求

1.债务证券获准在受监管市场交易的发行人应确保，就该等债务证券附带的所有权利平等地对待清偿顺位相同的债务证券的全部持有人。

2.发行人应确保，债务证券持有人行使其权利所需的所有设施和信息均可在母国

debt securities holders to exercise their rights are publicly available in the home Member State and that the integrity of data is preserved. Debt securities holders shall not be prevented from exercising their rights by proxy, subject to the law of country in which the issuer is incorporated. In particular, the issuer shall:

(a) publish notices, or distribute circulars, concerning the place, time and agenda of meetings of debt securities holders, the payment of interest, the exercise of any conversion, exchange, subscription or cancellation rights, and repayment, as well as the right of those holders to participate therein;

(b) make available a proxy form on paper or, where applicable, by electronic means, to each person entitled to vote at a meeting of debt securities holders, together with the notice concerning the meeting or, on request, after an announcement of the meeting; and

(c) designate as its agent a financial institution through which debt securities holders may exercise their financial rights.

3. If only holders of debt securities whose denomination per unit amounts to at least EUR 50 000 or, in the case of debt securities denominated in a currency other than Euro whose denomination per unit is, at the date of the issue, equivalent to at least EUR 50 000, are to be invited to a meeting, the issuer may choose as venue any Member State, provided that all the facilities and information necessary to enable such holders to exercise their rights are made available in that Member State.

4. For the purposes of conveying information to debt securities holders, the home Member State, or the Member State chosen by the issuer pursuant to paragraph 3, shall allow issuers the use of electronic means, provided such a decision is taken in a general meeting and meets at least the following conditions:

(a) the use of electronic means shall in no way depend upon the location of the seat or residence of the debt security holder or of a proxy representing that holder;

(b) identification arrangements shall be put in place so that debt securities holders are effectively informed;

(c) debt securities holders shall be contacted in writing to request their consent for the use of electronic means for conveying information and if they do not object within a reasonable period of time, their consent shall be deemed to be given. They shall be able to request, at any time in the future, that information be conveyed in writing; and

(d) any apportionment of the costs entailed in the conveyance of information by electronic means shall be determined by the issuer in compliance with the principle of equal treatment laid down in paragraph 1.

5. The Commission shall, in accordance with the procedure provided for in Article 27(2) adopt implementing measures in order to take account of technical developments in financial markets, to take account of developments in information and communication

公开获得，并且数据的完整性受到保护。在遵守发行人成立所在国家的法律的前提下，债务证券持有人通过代理行使其权利不应受到阻碍。发行人尤应：

(a)就下列事项发布通知或派发通告：债务证券持有人会议的地点、时间和议程；利息支付；任何转换、交换、认购或撤销权的行使；还款；以及该等证券持有人参加会议的权利；

(b)以纸质形式或(如适用)通过电子手段向有权在债务证券持有人会议上表决的所有人提供代理委托书格式，代理委托书格式应与会议通知同时发出，或经要求在发出会议公告后提供；及

(c)指定某个金融机构作为代理人，使债务证券持有人能够通过该金融机构行使其财务权利。

3.如果受邀参会的持有人仅限于单位面值最低5万欧元(或者，非欧元债务证券单位面值在发行当日最低等值于5万欧元)的债务证券持有人，则发行人可选择在任何成员国召开会议，前提是为上述持有人行使其权利所需的所有设施和信息均可在该成员国获得。

4.母国或发行人根据第3款选择的成员国应允许发行人使用电子手段将信息传送给债务证券持有人，前提是该项决定在债务证券持有人大会上作出且至少符合以下条件：

(a)电子手段的使用无论如何均不得因为债务证券持有人或其代理人的住所地或居住地的不同而有差别待遇；

(b)应落实相应的身份信息识别安排，使债务证券持有人收到有效的通知；

(c)应书面联系债务证券持有人，为使用电子手段传送信息征求其同意，如果他们未在合理时间内提出反对意见，则应被视为已经表示同意。未来他们应能随时要求以书面形式传送信息；及

(d)通过电子手段传送信息的成本分摊应由发行人按照第1款规定的平等待遇原则决定。

5.为反映金融市场的技术发展动态以及信息通信技术的发展动态，并确保第1款至第4款的统一适用，欧盟委员会应依照第27条第2款所述程序制定相关实施细则。欧盟委员会尤应指明债务证券持有人可以通过哪些类型金融机构行使其第2款第c项所

technology and to ensure the uniform application of paragraphs 1 to 4. It shall, in particular, specify the types of financial institution through which a debt security holder may exercise the financial rights provided for in paragraph 2(c).

CHAPTER IV GENERAL OBLIGATIONS

Article 19 Home Member State control

1. Whenever the issuer, or any person having requested, without the issuer's consent, the admission of its securities to trading on a regulated market, discloses regulated information, it shall at the same time file that information with the competent authority of its home Member State. That competent authority may decide to publish such filed information on its Internet site.

Where an issuer proposes to amend its instrument of incorporation or statutes, it shall communicate the draft amendment to the competent authority of the home Member State and to the regulated market to which its securities have been admitted to trading. Such communication shall be effected without delay, but at the latest on the date of calling the general meeting which is to vote on, or be informed of, the amendment.

2. The home Member State may exempt an issuer from the requirement under paragraph 1 in respect of information disclosed in accordance with Article 6 of Directive 2003/6/EC or Article 12(6) of this Directive.

3. Information to be notified to the issuer in accordance with Articles 9, 10, 12 and 13 shall at the same time be filed with the competent authority of the home Member State.

4. In order to ensure the uniform application of paragraphs 1, 2 and 3, the Commission shall, in accordance with the procedure referred to in Article 27 (2) adopt implementing measures.

The Commission shall, in particular, specify the procedure in accordance with which an issuer, a holder of shares or other financial instruments, or a person or entity referred to in Article 10, is to file information with the competent authority of the home Member State under paragraphs 1 or 3, respectively, in order to:

(a) enable filing by electronic means in the home Member State;

(b) coordinate the filing of the annual financial report referred to in Article 4 of this Directive with the filing of the annual information referred to in Article 10 of Directive 2003/71/ EC.

Article 20 Languages

1. Where securities are admitted to trading on a regulated market only in the home Member State, regulated information shall be disclosed in a language accepted by the competent authority in the home Member State.

2. Where securities are admitted to trading on a regulated market both in the home

规定的财务权利。

第四章　一般义务

第19条　母国的控制

1.发行人或未经发行人同意自行申请了证券获准在受监管市场交易的其他人披露受监管信息时,应同时将该信息提交母国主管部门。母国主管部门可决定在其网站上公布该等提交的信息。

发行人提议对其公司成立文件或章程作出修改的,应通知母国主管部门以及证券准入交易的受监管市场该等修改草案。该等通知应立即且最晚于对修改进行表决或告知的大会的召集日作出。

2.母国可就依据第2003/6/EC号指令第6条以及本指令第12条第6款披露的信息豁免发行人履行第1款的要求。

3.根据第9条、第10条、第12条和第13条向发行人发出的信息通知应同时提交母国主管部门。

4.为确保第1款、第2款和第3款的统一适用,欧盟委员会应依照第27条第2款所述程序制定相关实施细则。

欧盟委员会尤应规定发行人、股票或其他金融工具持有人或第10条所述的人或实体各自根据第1款或第3款向母国主管部门提交信息应遵循的程序,以便:

(a)可以用电子手段向母国提交信息;

(b)协调本指令第4条所述年度财务报告的提交以及第2003/71/EC号指令第10条所述年度信息的提交。

第20条　语言

1.证券仅获准在母国受监管市场交易的,受监管信息应以母国主管部门接受的语言披露。

2.证券同时获准在母国和一个或多个东道国受监管市场交易的,受监管信息应:

Member State and in one or more host Member States, regulated information shall be disclosed:

(a) in a language accepted by the competent authority in the home Member State; and

(b) depending on the choice of the issuer, either in a language accepted by the competent authorities of those host Member States or in a language customary in the sphere of international finance.

3. Where securities are admitted to trading on a regulated market in one or more host Member States, but not in the home Member State, regulated information shall, depending on the choice of the issuer, be disclosed either in a language accepted by the competent authorities of those host Member States or in a language customary in the sphere of international finance.

In addition, the home Member State may lay down in its law, regulations or administrative provisions that the regulated information shall, depending on the choice of the issuer, be disclosed either in a language accepted by its competent authority or in a language customary in the sphere of international finance.

4. Where securities are admitted to trading on a regulated market without the issuer's consent, the obligations under paragraphs 1, 2 and 3 shall be incumbent not upon the issuer, but upon the person who, without the issuer's consent, has requested such admission.

5. Member States shall allow shareholders and the natural person or legal entity referred to in Articles 9, 10 and 13 to notify information to an issuer under this Directive only in a language customary in the sphere of international finance. If the issuer receives such a notification, Member States may not require the issuer to provide a translation into a language accepted by the competent authorities.

6. By way of derogation from paragraphs 1 to 4, where securities whose denomination per unit amounts to at least EUR 50 000 or, in the case of debt securities denominated in a currency other than Euro equivalent to at least EUR 50 000 at the date of the issue, are admitted to trading on a regulated market in one or more Member States, regulated information shall be disclosed to the public either in a language accepted by the competent authorities of the home and host Member States or in a language customary in the sphere of international finance, at the choice of the issuer or of the person who, without the issuer's consent, has requested such admission.

7. If an action concerning the content of regulated information is brought before a court or tribunal in a Member State, responsibility for the payment of costs incurred in the translation of that information for the purposes of the proceedings shall be decided in accordance with the law of that Member State.

(a)以母国主管部门接受的语言披露；并且

(b)根据发行人的选择，以东道国主管部门接受的语言或国际金融行业惯用语言披露。

3.证券获准在一个或多个东道国受监管市场交易但未获准在母国受监管市场交易的，受监管信息应根据发行人的选择以东道国主管部门接受的语言或国际金融行业惯用语言披露。

此外，母国可在其法律、法规和规章中规定受监管信息根据发行人的选择以其主管部门接受的语言或国际金融行业惯用语言披露。

4.证券未经发行人同意而在受监管市场获准交易的，第1款、第2款和第3款的义务不应由发行人承担，而应由未经发行人同意自行请求获得上述准入的人来承担。

5.成员国应允许股东以及第9条、第10条和第13条所述自然人或法人实体仅以国际金融行业惯用语言按本指令向发行人发送信息通知。发行人收到上述通知的，成员国不得要求其将通知翻译成主管部门接受的语言。

6.作为第1款至第4款的例外，单位面值最低5万欧元的证券（或者，非欧元债务证券单位面值在发行当日最低等值于5万欧元的债务证券）获准在一个或多个成员国受监管市场交易的，受监管信息应根据发行人或未经发行人同意自行申请了准入的人的选择，以母国和东道国主管部门接受的语言或国际金融行业惯用语言披露。

7.如针对受监管信息内容向某一成员国的法院或特别法院提出诉讼，则应按该成员国国内法律裁定由哪一方负责支付用于诉讼程序的该等受监管信息的翻译费。

Article 21 Access to regulated information

1. The home Member State shall ensure that the issuer, or the person who has applied for admission to trading on a regulated market without the issuer's consent, discloses regulated information in a manner ensuring fast access to such information on a non-discriminatory basis and makes it available to the officially appointed mechanism referred to in paragraph 2. The issuer, or the person who has applied for admission to trading on a regulated market without the issuer's consent, may not charge investors any specific cost for providing the information. The home Member State shall require the issuer to use such media as may reasonably be relied upon for the effective dissemination of information to the public throughout the Community. The home Member State may not impose an obligation to use only media whose operators are established on its territory.

2. The home Member State shall ensure that there is at least one officially appointed mechanism for the central storage of regulated information. These mechanisms should comply with minimum quality standards of security, certainty as to the information source, time recording and easy access by end users and shall be aligned with the filing procedure under Article 19(1).

3. Where securities are admitted to trading on a regulated market in only one host Member State and not in the home Member State, the host Member State shall ensure disclosure of regulated information in accordance with the requirements referred to in paragraph 1.

4. In order to take account of technical developments in financial markets, to take account of developments in information and communication technology and to ensure the uniform application of paragraphs 1, 2 and 3, the Commission shall adopt implementing measures in accordance with the procedure referred to in Article 27(2).

The Commission shall in particular specify:

(a) minimum standards for the dissemination of regulated information, as referred to in paragraph 1;

(b) minimum standards for the central storage mechanism as referred to in paragraph 2.

The Commission may also specify and update a list of media for the dissemination of information to the public.

Article 22 Guidelines

1. The competent authorities of the Member States shall draw up appropriate guidelines with a view to further facilitating public access to information to be disclosed under Directive 2003/6/EC, Directive 2003/71/EC and this Directive.

The aim of those guidelines shall be the creation of:

(a) an electronic network to be set up at national level between national securities

第21条　查阅受监管信息

1.母国应确保,发行人或未经发行人同意自行申请了准入受监管市场交易的人披露受监管信息的方式应能保证所有投资者能无差别地迅速查阅其所披露的信息,并将该等信息提供给第2款所述的官方指定机制。发行人或未经发行人同意自行申请了准入受监管市场交易的人不得就信息的提供向投资者收取任何特殊费用。母国应要求发行人使用可合理信赖的媒体,以将信息有效地传播给全欧共体公众。母国不得施加仅能使用在其境内设立的运营商所运营的媒体的义务。

2.母国应确保至少有一个官方指定机制负责对受监管信息进行中央存储。此等机制应满足以下方面的最低质量标准:安全、信息来源确定、时间记录以及终端用户易于查阅,并应与第19条第1款中的提交程序一致。

3.证券仅获准在一个东道国受监管市场交易而未获准在母国受监管市场交易的,东道国应确保受监管信息按照第1款所述的要求进行披露。

4.为反映金融市场的技术发展动态以及信息通信技术的发展动态,并确保第1款、第2款和第3款的统一适用,欧盟委员会应依照第27条第2款所述程序制定相关实施细则。

欧盟委员会尤应规定:

(a)第1款所述的受监管信息传播的最低标准;

(b)第2款所述的中央存储机制的最低标准。

欧盟委员会还可列明和更新向公众传播信息的媒体名单。

第22条　指引

1.成员国主管部门应起草适当的指引,以进一步方便公众查阅根据第2003/6/EC号指令、第2003/71/EC号指令和本指令应予披露的信息。

该等指引旨在:

(a)在国家层面创设一个电子网络,连接国家级证券监管机构、受监管市场运营者

regulators, operators of regulated markets and national company registers covered by the First Council Directive 68/151/EEC of 9 March 1968 on coordination of safeguards which, for the protection of the interests of members and others, are required by Member States of companies within the meaning of the second paragraph of Article 48 [1] of the Treaty, with a view to making such safeguards equivalent throughout the Community [2]; and

(b) a single electronic network, or a platform of electronic networks across Member States.

2. The Commission shall review the results achieved under paragraph 1 by 31 December 2006 and may, in accordance with the procedure referred to in Article 27(2) adopt implementing measures to facilitate compliance with Articles 19 and 21.

Article 23 Third countries

1. Where the registered office of an issuer is in a third country, the competent authority of the home Member State may exempt that issuer from requirements under Articles 4 to 7 and Articles 12(6) 14, 15 and 16 to 18, provided that the law of the third country in question lays down equivalent requirements or such an issuer complies with requirements of the law of a third country that the competent authority of the home Member State considers as equivalent.

However, the information covered by the requirements laid down in the third country shall be filed in accordance with Article 19 and disclosed in accordance with Articles 20 and 21.

2. By way of derogation from paragraph 1, an issuer whose registered office is in a third country shall be exempted from preparing its financial statement in accordance with Article 4 or Article 5 prior to the financial year starting on or after 1 January 2007, provided such issuer prepares its financial statements in accordance with internationally accepted standards referred to in Article 9 of Regulation (EC) No 1606/2002.

3. The competent authority of the home Member State shall ensure that information disclosed in a third country which may be of importance for the public in the Community is disclosed in accordance with Articles 20 and 21, even if such information is not regulated information within the meaning of Article 2(1)(k).

4. In order to ensure the uniform application of paragraph 1, the Commission shall, in accordance with the procedure referred to in Article 27(2) adopt implementing measures

---

1 Editorial note: The title has been adjusted to take account of the renumbering of the Articles of the Treaty establishing the European Community in accordance with Article 12 of the Treaty of Amsterdam; the original reference was to Article 58 of the Treaty.

2 OJ L 65, 14.3.1968, p. 8. Directive as last amended by Directive 2003/58/EC of the European Parliament and of the Council (OJ L 221, 4.9.2003, p. 13).

以及《欧洲经济共同体理事会协调关于〈欧洲共同体条约〉第48条[1]第2款所定义的公司所在的成员国为保护成员和其他人利益所规定的保障措施以实现在全欧共体内提供等效保障的第68/151/EEC号第一指令》[2]（1968年3月9日）所涵盖的国家级公司注册处；及

（b）建立单一的电子网络或跨成员国的电子网络平台。

2.欧盟委员会应在2006年12月31日前对根据第1款获得的成果进行审评，并可依照第27条第2款所述程序制定相关实施细则以便于第19条和第21条得到遵守。

第23条　第三国

1.对于在第三国注册的发行人，母国主管部门可豁免其履行第4条至第7条和第12条第6款、第14条、第15条以及第16条至第18条的要求，前提是所涉第三国的法律制定了等效的要求或该发行人遵守的第三国法律规定被母国主管部门认为是等效的。

然而，第三国制定的要求所涵盖的信息应当按照第19条进行提交并按照第20条和第21条披露。

2.作为第1款的例外，在起始于2007年1月1日或更晚日期的会计年度之前，注册地位于第三国的发行人应免于依第4条或第5条制作财务报表，前提是该发行人根据第1606/2002号（欧共体）条例第9条所述国际公认标准制作其财务报表。

3.对于在第三国披露且可能对欧共体公众而言重要的信息，即使上述信息并非第2条第1款第k项所述的受监管信息，母国主管部门也应确保其根据第20条和第21条进行披露。

4.为确保第1款的统一适用，欧盟委员会应当依照第27条第2款所述程序制定能达到以下效果的实施细则：

1　已根据《阿姆斯特丹条约》第12条对《欧洲共同体条约》作出的条款重新编号调整标题；原文献索引是《欧洲共同体条约》第58条。——编者注

2　1968年3月14日《欧盟公报》L65，第8页。此指令由欧洲议会与欧盟理事会的第2003/58/EC号指令（2003年9月4日《欧盟公报》L221，第13页）作出最新修正。

(i) setting up a mechanism ensuring the establishment of equivalence of information required under this Directive, including financial statements and information, including financial statements, required under the law, regulations or administrative provisions of a third country;

(ii) stating that, by reason of its domestic law, regulations, administrative provisions, or of the practices or procedures based on the international standards set by international organisations, the third country where the issuer is registered ensures the equivalence of the information requirements provided for in this Directive.

The Commission shall, in accordance with the procedure referred to in Article 27(2) take the necessary decisions on the equivalence of accounting standards which are used by third country issuers under the conditions set out in Article 30(3) at the latest five years following the date referred to in Article 31. If the Commission decides that the accounting standards of a third country are not equivalent, it may allow the issuers concerned to continue using such accounting standards during an appropriate transitional period.

5. In order to ensure uniform application of paragraph 2, the Commission may, in accordance with the procedure referred to in Article 27(2) adopt implementing measures defining the type of information disclosed in a third country that is of importance to the public in the Community.

6. Undertakings whose registered office is in a third country which would have required an authorisation in accordance with Article 5(1) of Directive 85/611/EEC or, with regard to portfolio management under point 4 of section A of Annex I to Directive 2004/39/EC if it had its registered office or, only in the case of an investment firm, its head office within the Community, shall also be exempted from aggregating holdings with the holdings of its parent undertaking under the requirements laid down in Article 12 (4) and (5) provided that they comply with equivalent conditions of independence as management companies or investment firms.

7. In order to take account of technical developments in financial markets and to ensure the uniform application of paragraph 6, the Commission shall, in accordance with the procedure referred to in Article 27(2) adopt implementing measures stating that, by reason of its domestic law, regulations, or administrative provisions, a third country ensures the equivalence of the independence requirements provided for under this Directive and its implementing measures.

CHAPTER V COMPETENT AUTHORITIES

Article 24 Competent authorities and their powers

1. Each Member State shall designate the central authority referred to in Article 21(1)

(i)建立一项机制据以认定本指令要求披露的信息的等效性,包括财务报表和信息(包括第三国法律、法规或规章要求披露的财务报表);

(ii)说明如下内容:发行人注册所在地的第三国凭其国内法律、法规或规章,或凭其国内遵照国际组织设定的国际标准适用的惯例或程序,能确保该国信息要求与本指令的信息要求等效。

欧盟委员会应最晚在第31条所述日期后5年内依照第27条第2款所述程序就第三国发行人按第30条第3款所列条件使用的会计准则是否等效作出必要的认定。欧盟委员会认定第三国的会计准则不等效的,可允许所涉发行人在适当的过渡时期继续使用上述会计准则。

5.为确保第2款的统一适用,欧盟委员会可依照第27条第2款所述程序制定相关实施细则,就在第三国披露的、对欧共体公众有重要意义的信息的类型作出界定。

6.以下公司也应免于按照第12条第4款和第5款所述要求将股份与其母公司的股份合并计算,前提是该等公司符合与管理公司或投资公司独立性条件等效的条件:注册地位于第三国,或者,就第2004/39/EC号指令附录一第A节第4项中的投资组合管理而言,其注册地或(仅针对投资公司而言)总部位于欧共体境内的,应按第85/611/EEC号指令第5条第1款获得核准。

7.为反映金融市场的技术发展动态并确保第6款的统一适用,欧盟委员会应依照第27条第2款所述程序制定相关实施细则,说明第三国由于其国内的法律、法规或规章能确保独立性要求与本指令及其实施细则所规定的独立性要求等效。

第五章　主管部门

第24条　主管部门及其权力

1.各成员国应指定第2003/71/EC号指令第21条第1款所述的中央部门作为中央行

of Directive 2003/71/EC as central competent administrative authority responsible for carrying out the obligations provided for in this Directive and for ensuring that the provisions adopted pursuant to this Directive are applied. Member States shall inform the Commission accordingly.

However, for the purpose of paragraph 4(h) Member States may designate a competent authority other than the central competent authority referred to in the first subparagraph.

2. Member States may allow their central competent authority to delegate tasks. Except for the tasks referred to in paragraph 4(h) any delegation of tasks relating to the obligations provided for in this Directive and in its implementing measures shall be reviewed five years after the entry into force of this Directive and shall end eight years after the entry into force of this Directive. Any delegation of tasks shall be made in a specific manner stating the tasks to be undertaken and the conditions under which they are to be carried out.

Those conditions shall include a clause requiring the entity in question to be organised in a manner such that conflicts of interest are avoided and information obtained from carrying out the delegated tasks is not used unfairly or to prevent competition. In any case, the final responsibility for supervising compliance with the provisions of this Directive and implementing measures adopted pursuant thereto shall lie with the competent authority designated in accordance with paragraph 1.

3. Member States shall inform the Commission and competent authorities of other Member States of any arrangements entered into with regard to the delegation of tasks, including the precise conditions for regulating the delegations.

4. Each competent authority shall have all the powers necessary for the performance of its functions. It shall at least be empowered to:

(a) require auditors, issuers, holders of shares or other financial instruments, or persons or entities referred to in Articles 10 or 13, and the persons that control them or are controlled by them, to provide information and documents;

(b) require the issuer to disclose the information required under point (a) to the public by the means and within the time limits the authority considers necessary. It may publish such information on its own initiative in the event that the issuer, or the persons that control it or are controlled by it, fail to do so and after having heard the issuer;

(c) require managers of the issuers and of the holders of shares or other financial instruments, or of persons or entities referred to in Articles 10 or 13, to notify the information required under this Directive, or under national law adopted in accordance with this Directive, and, if necessary, to provide further information and documents;

(d) suspend, or request the relevant regulated market to suspend, trading in

政主管部门,负责履行本指令规定的义务以及确保根据本指令制定的国内规定的适用。成员国应向欧盟委员会通知其所指定的部门。

然而,就第4款第h项而言,成员国可指定一个非第一段所述的中央主管部门的主管部门。

2.成员国可允许其中央主管部门进行职责委托。除第4款第h项的职责外,任何与本指令及其实施细则规定的义务相关的职责委托均应在本指令生效后5年内进行审评,并在本指令生效8年后终止。任何职责委托均应以明确的方式进行,即应说明所委托的职责以及在何等条件下履行委托职责。

该等条件包括此等条款:所涉实体有义务以避免利益冲突的方式组建,以便履行受托职责过程中所获信息不会被不正当使用或妨碍竞争。任何情形下,监管本指令规定及其实施细则是否得到遵守的最终责任, 均应由根据第1款所指定的主管部门承担。

3.成员国应通知欧盟委员会及其他成员国主管部门就职责委托所达成的任何安排,包括规范职责委托的条件。

4.各主管部门应有履行其职能所必要的一切权力,至少应有权:

(a)要求审计师、发行人、股票或其他金融工具的持有人,或第10条或第13条所述的人或实体以及其控制人或被控制人提供信息和文件;

(b)要求发行人以该部门认为必要的方式并在必要的时间内披露第a目要求提供的信息。发行人或其被控制人或控制人未公布该等信息的,主管部门可在听取发行人的意见后主动予以公布;

(c)要求发行人和股票或其他金融工具的持有人的管理人或第10条或第13条所述的人或实体的管理人通知本指令要求披露的信息或依本指令制定的成员国国内法律要求披露的信息,并在必要时提供进一步的信息和文件;

(d)有合理理由怀疑发行人违反本指令或依据本指令制定的成员国国内法律的

securities for a maximum of ten days at a time if it has reasonable grounds for suspecting that the provisions of this Directive, or of national law adopted in accordance with this Directive, have been infringed by the issuer;

(e) prohibit trading on a regulated market if it finds that the provisions of this Directive, or of national law adopted in accordance with this Directive, have been infringed, or if it has reasonable grounds for suspecting that the provisions of this Directive have been infringed;

(f) monitor that the issuer discloses timely information with the objective of ensuring effective and equal access to the public in all Member States where the securities are traded and take appropriate action if that is not the case;

(g) make public the fact that an issuer, or a holder of shares or other financial instruments, or a person or entity referred to in Articles 10 or 13, is failing to comply with its obligations;

(h) examine that information referred to in this Directive is drawn up in accordance with the relevant reporting framework and take appropriate measures in case of discovered infringements; and

(i) carry out on-site inspections in its territory in accordance with national law, in order to verify compliance with the provisions of this Directive and its implementing measures. Where necessary under national law, the competent authority or authorities may use this power by applying to the relevant judicial authority and/or in cooperation with other authorities.

5. Paragraphs 1 to 4 shall be without prejudice to the possibility for a Member State to make separate legal and administrative arrangements for overseas European territories for whose external relations that Member State is responsible.

6. The disclosure to competent authorities by the auditors of any fact or decision related to the requests made by the competent authority under paragraph (4)(a) shall not constitute a breach of any restriction on disclosure of information imposed by contract or by any law, regulation or administrative provision and shall not involve such auditors in liability of any kind.

Article 25 Professional secrecy and cooperation between Member States

1. The obligation of professional secrecy shall apply to all persons who work or who have worked for the competent authority and for entities to which competent authorities may have delegated certain tasks. Information covered by professional secrecy may not be disclosed to any other person or authority except by virtue of the laws, regulations or administrative provisions of a Member State.

2. Competent authorities of the Member States shall cooperate with each other, whenever necessary, for the purpose of carrying out their duties and making use of their

规定的，暂停或要求相关受监管市场暂停证券交易，暂停时间不超过10天；

(e)认定本指令或依据本指令制定的成员国国内法律的规定遭到违反，或有合理理由怀疑本指令的规定遭到违反时，禁止在受监管市场交易；

(f)监控发行人及时披露信息，以确保证券交易活动所在成员国的公众能够有效平等地查阅信息，并在无法保证有效平等查阅信息时采取适当的行动；

(g)公开发行人、股票或其他金融工具的持有人或第10条或第13条所述的人或实体无法履行义务的事实；

(h)核查本指令所述信息是否根据相关的报告框架编制，并在发现违规行为时采取适当的措施；及

(i)根据成员国国内法律在其境内开展现场调查，以核实本指令规定及其实施细则是否得到遵守。必要时根据成员国国内法律，成员国的一个或多个主管部门可通过向相关司法部门提出申请和/或与其他部门合作的方式行使其权力。

5.第1款至第4款不影响成员国对海外欧洲领地制定独立的法律和行政安排，该等领地的对外关系责任由该成员国承担。

6.审计师向主管部门披露与主管部门根据第4款第a项所提要求相关的事实或决定，不构成对合同或任何法律、法规或规章施加的任何信息披露限制的违反，也不使审计师因此承受任何法律责任。

第25条　职业保密和主管部门之间的合作

1.职业保密义务适用于主管部门或接受主管部门职责委托的实体的现任或前任工作人员。属于职业保密范围内的信息不得向任何其他人或部门披露，成员国的法律、法规或规章允许的除外。

2.成员国主管部门应在必要时相互合作，以履行其职责以及运用其在本指令或依据本指令制定的成员国国内法律下的权力。主管部门应向其他成员国的主管部门提

powers, whether set out in this Directive or in national law adopted pursuant to this Directive. Competent authorities shall render assistance to competent authorities of other Member States.

3. Paragraph 1 shall not prevent the competent authorities from exchanging confidential information. Information thus exchanged shall be covered by the obligation of professional secrecy to which the persons employed or formerly employed by the competent authorities receiving the information are subject.

4. Member States may conclude cooperation agreements providing for the exchange of information with the competent authorities or bodies of third countries enabled by their respective legislation to carry out any of the tasks assigned by this Directive to the competent authorities in accordance with Article 24. Such an exchange of information is subject to guarantees of professional secrecy at least equivalent to those referred to in this Article. Such exchange of information shall be intended for the performance of the supervisory task of the authorities or bodies mentioned. Where the information originates in another Member State, it may not be disclosed without the express agreement of the competent authorities which have disclosed it and, where appropriate, solely for the purposes for which those authorities gave their agreement.

Article 26 Precautionary measures

1. Where the competent authority of a host Member State finds that the issuer or the holder of shares or other financial instruments, or the person or entity referred to in Article 10, has committed irregularities or infringed its obligations, it shall refer its findings to the competent authority of the home Member State.

2. If, despite the measures taken by the competent authority of the home Member State, or because such measures prove inadequate, the issuer or the security holder persists in infringing the relevant legal or regulatory provisions, the competent authority of the host Member State shall, after informing the competent authority of the home Member State, take, in accordance with Article 3(2) all the appropriate measures in order to protect investors. The Commission shall be informed of such measures at the earliest opportunity.

CHAPTER Ⅵ IMPLEMENTING MEASURES

Article 27 Committee procedure

1. The Commission shall be assisted by the European Securities Committee, instituted by Article 1 of Decision 2001/528/ EC.

2. Where reference is made to this paragraph, Articles 5 and 7 of Decision 1999/ 468/EC shall apply, having regard to the provisions of Article 8 thereof, provided that the implementing measures adopted in accordance with that procedure do not modify the

供协助。

3.第1款不得妨碍主管部门交换保密信息。所交换的信息受职业保密义务约束，接收信息的主管部门的现任或前任工作人员均须遵守该项义务。

4.成员国可与根据其各自立法能履行本指令按第24条委托给主管部门的任何职责的第三国主管部门或机构缔结合作协议，为信息交换制定相关规定。上述信息交换所受保障应至少与本条所述职业保密等效，并用于上述部门或机构监管职责的履行。对于来源于其他成员国的信息，未经披露该等信息的主管部门明确同意不得披露，并且，在适当时仅得为了该等部门同意的目的披露。

第26条　预防措施

1.东道国主管部门认定发行人或股票、其他金融工具的持有人或第10条所述的人或实体从事不法行为或违反其义务的，应将其认定结果移交母国主管部门处理。

2.尽管母国主管部门已采取措施或由于事实证明采取的措施不充分，发行人或证券持有人继续违反相关法律规章的，东道国主管部门应在通知母国主管部门相关情况后，根据第3条第2款采取一切适当措施以保护投资者。东道国主管部门应尽快通知欧盟委员会此等措施。

第六章　实施细则

第27条　委员会程序

1.欧盟委员会应在第2001/528/EC号指令第1条设立的欧洲证券委员会的协助下工作。

2.根据第1999/468/EC号决定第8条规定，引用本款内容时，应适用该决定第5条和第7条，前提是依照该程序制定的实施细则不对本指令的基本条款作出变更。

essential provisions of this Directive.

The period laid down in Article 5(6) of Decision 1999/468/EC shall be set at three months.

3. The Committee shall adopt its Rules of Procedure.

4. Without prejudice to the implementing measures already adopted by 20 January 2009 the application of the provisions of this Directive concerning the adoption of technical rules and decisions in accordance with the procedure referred to in paragraph 2 shall be suspended. On a proposal from the Commission, the European Parliament and the Council may renew the provisions concerned in accordance with the procedure laid down in Article 251 of the Treaty and, to that end, shall review them prior to the expiry of the four-year period.

Article 28 Penalties

1. Without prejudice to the right of Member States to impose criminal penalties, Member States shall ensure, in conformity with their national law, that at least the appropriate administrative measures may be taken or civil and/or administrative penalties imposed in respect of the persons responsible, where the provisions adopted in accordance with this Directive have not been complied with. Member States shall ensure that those measures are effective, proportionate and dissuasive.

2. Member States shall provide that the competent authority may disclose to the public every measure taken or penalty imposed for infringement of the provisions adopted in accordance with this Directive, save where such disclosure would seriously jeopardise the financial markets or cause disproportionate damage to the parties involved.

Article 29 Right of appeal

Member States shall ensure that decisions taken under laws, regulations, and administrative provisions adopted in accordance with this Directive are subject to the right of appeal to the courts.

CHAPTER VII TRANSITIONAL AND FINAL PROVISIONS

Article 30 Transitional provisions

1. By way of derogation from Article 5(3) of this Directive, the home Member State may exempt from disclosing financial statements in accordance with Regulation (EC) No 1606/2002 issuers referred to in Article 9 of that Regulation for the financial year starting on or after 1 January 2006.

2. Notwithstanding Article 12(2) a shareholder shall notify the issuer at the latest two months after the date in Article 31(1) of the proportion of voting rights and capital it holds, in accordance with Articles 9, 10 and 13, with issuers at that date, unless it has already made a notification containing equivalent information before that date.

第1999/468/EC号决定第5条第6款规定的期限应设定为3个月。

3.委员会应制定其程序规则。

4.在不影响2009年1月20日前已经通过的实施细则的情形下，应暂停适用本指令关于依照第2款所述程序制定的技术性工作和决定的条款。经欧盟委员会提议，欧洲议会与欧盟理事会可依照《条约》第251条规定的程序展延所涉条款，为此，还应在4年期限届满前对该等条款进行审评。

第28条　罚则

1.在不影响成员国刑事处罚权的情形下，本指令实施过程中制定的国内规定未能得到遵守的，成员国应确保按其国内法律对相关责任人采取适当的行政措施或施加民事和/或行政处罚。成员国应确保此等措施有效、成比例且具有威慑作用。

2.成员国应确保主管部门可向公众披露对违反依本指令制定的国内规定而采取的各项措施或实施的各项处罚，但上述披露会严重危害金融市场或对所涉各方造成不成比例损害的除外。

第29条　行政诉讼权

成员国应确保，依照按本指令制定的法律、法规或规章所作的任何决定，可由相对人向法院提起行政诉讼。

第七章　过渡规定和最终条款

第30条　过渡规定

1.作为本指令第5条第3款的例外，母国可豁免第1606/2002号(欧共体)条例第9条所述的发行人根据该条例披露起始于2006年1月1日或更晚日期的会计年度的财务报表。

2.尽管有第12条第2款的规定，股东最晚应于第31条第1款所述日期后两个月内向发行人通知其在该日根据第9条、第10条和第13条持有的发行人表决权和资本比例，在该日期前已发送包含同等信息的通知的除外。

Notwithstanding Article 12(6) an issuer shall in turn disclose the information received in those notifications no later than three months after the date in Article 31(1).

3. Where an issuer is incorporated in a third country, the home Member State may exempt such issuer only in respect of those debt securities which have already been admitted to trading on a regulated market in the Community prior to 1 January 2005 from drawing up its financial statements in accordance with Article 4(3) and its management report in accordance with Article 4(5) as long as

(a) the competent authority of the home Member State acknowledges that annual financial statements prepared by issuers from such a third country give a true and fair view of the issuer's assets and liabilities, financial position and results;

(b) the third country where the issuer is incorporated has not made mandatory the application of international accounting standards referred to in Article 2 of Regulation (EC) No 1606/2002; and

(c) the Commission has not taken any decision in accordance with Article 23(4)(ii) as to whether there is an equivalence between the abovementioned accounting standards and

— the accounting standards laid down in the law, regulations or administrative provisions of the third country where the issuer is incorporated, or

— the accounting standards of a third country such an issuer has elected to comply with.

4. The home Member State may exempt issuers only in respect of those debt securities which have already been admitted to trading on a regulated market in the Community prior to 1 January 2005 from disclosing half-yearly financial report in accordance with Article 5 for 10 years following 1 January 2005, provided that the home Member State had decided to allow such issuers to benefit from the provisions of Article 27 of Directive 2001/34/EC at the point of admission of those debt securities.

Article 31 Transposition

1. Member States shall take the necessary measures to comply with this Directive by 20 January 2007. They shall forthwith inform the Commission thereof.

When Member States adopt these measures, they shall contain a reference to this Directive or shall be accompanied by such reference on the occasion of their official publication. The methods of making such reference shall be laid down by Member States.

2. Where Member States adopt measures pursuant to Articles 3(1) 8(2) 8(3) 9(6) or 30, they shall immediately communicate those measures to the Commission and to the other Member States.

Article 32 Amendments

With effect from the date specified in Article 31(1) Directive 2001/34/EC shall be

尽管有第12条第6款的规定，发行人应披露在该等通知中接收到的信息，且最迟于第31条第1款所述日期后3个月(含)内披露。

3.发行人在第三国成立的，母国豁免的范围仅限于如下情形：债务证券在2005年1月1日前已获准在欧共体的受监管市场交易的，发行人可以不按照第4条第3款编制财务报表，也不必按照第4条第5款编制管理报告，前提是：

(a)母国主管部门认可，上述第三国发行人制作的年度财务报表真实公允地反映了发行人的资产和负债、财务状况和损益；

(b)发行人成立所在地的第三国未曾强制要求适用第1606/2002号(欧共体)条例第2条所述国际会计准则；并且

(c)欧盟委员会未曾根据第23条第4款第ii项就上述会计准则与下列准则是否等效作出认定：

——发行人成立所在地的第三国的法律、法规或规章所规定的会计准则，或

——上述发行人选择遵守的第三国会计准则。

4.母国豁免的范围仅限于如下情形：2005年1月1日前获准在欧共体的受监管市场交易的债务证券，在2005年1月1日后的10年期间内，其发行人不必按照第5条披露半年度财务报告，前提是母国已决定允许上述发行人就该等债务证券的准入享受第2001/34/EC号指令第27条的规定。

第31条　转化

1.各成员国应于2007年1月20日前实施必要的规定，以使本指令得到遵守，并立即就此通知欧盟委员会。

成员国制定该等规定时，应在其中对本指令予以援引，或在官方正式公布该等规定时予以援引。援引的具体方式，由成员国决定。

2.成员国根据第3条第1款、第8条第2款、第8条第3款、第9条第6款或第30条通过相关规定后，应立即通知欧盟委员会及其他成员国该等规定。

第32条　修正

应对第2001/34/EC号指令作如下修正，所作修正于第31条第1款规定的日期生效：

amended as follows:

(1) In Article 1, points (g) and (h) shall be deleted;

(2) Article 4 shall be deleted;

(3) In Article 6, paragraph 2 shall be deleted;

(4) In Article 8, paragraph 2 shall be replaced by the following:

'2.Member States may make the issuers of securities admitted to official listing subject to additional obligations, provided that those additional obligations apply generally for all issuers or for individual classes of issuers';

(5) Articles 65 to 97 shall be deleted;

(6) Articles 102 and 103 shall be deleted;

(7) In Article 107(3), the second subparagraph shall be deleted;

(8) In Article 108, paragraph 2 shall be amended as follows:

(a) in point (a), the words 'periodic information to be published by the companies of which shares are admitted' shall be deleted;

(b) point (b) shall be deleted;

(c) point (c)(iii) shall be deleted;

(d) point (d) shall be deleted.

References made to the repealed provisions shall be construed as being made to the provisions of this Directive.

Article 33 Review

The Commission shall by 30 June 2009 report on the operation of this Directive to the European Parliament and to the Council including the appropriateness of ending the exemption for existing debt securities after the 10-year period as provided for by Article 30(4) and its potential impact on the European financial markets.

Article 34 Entry into force

This Directive shall enter into force on the twentieth day following that of its publication in the *Official Journal of the European Union.*

Article 35 Addressees

This Directive is addressed to the Member States.

Done at Strasbourg, 15 December 2004.

For the European Parliament
The President
J. BORRELL FONTELLES

For the Council
The President A.
NICOLAÏ

（1）删除第1条第g项和第h项；
（2）删除第4条；
（3）删除第6条第2款；
（4）第8条第2款应替以如下内容：
“2.各成员国可要求证券获准正式上市的发行人履行额外的义务，前提是该等额外义务对全部发行人或个别类别发行人普遍适用”；

（5）删除第65条至第97条；
（6）删除第102条和第103条；
（7）删除第107条第3款第2项；
（8）对第108条第2款作如下修正：
（a）删去第a项中的“股票获准上市的公司须公布的定期信息”；

（b）删除第b项；
（c）删除第c项第iii目；
（d）删除第d项。
引用该等已废止条款时，应视为指代本指令的相关条款。

第33条　审评

欧盟委员会应在2009年6月30日前就本指令的实施向欧洲议会与欧盟理事会作报告，报告内容包括：第30条第4款中的10年期过后终止现有债务证券享有的豁免是否适当，以及此举可能对欧洲金融市场产生的影响。

第34条　生效

本指令自公布于《欧盟公报》后的第20日生效。

第35条　对象

本指令对象为各成员国。
2004年12月15日于斯特拉斯堡通过。

欧洲议会议长　　　　欧盟理事会主席

冯特勒斯　　　　尼古拉

COMMISSION DIRECTIVE 2007/14/EC

欧盟委员会第 2007/14/EC 号指令

COMMISSION DIRECTIVE 2007/14/EC

(of 8 March 2007 laying down detailed rules for the implementation of certain provisions of Directive 2004/109/EC on the harmonization of transparency requirements in relation to information about issuers whose securities are admitted to trading on a regulated market)

THE COMMISSION OF THE EUROPEAN COMMUNITIES,

Having regard to the Treaty establishing the European Community,

Having regard to Directive 2004/109/EC of the European Parliament and of the Council of 15 December 2004 on the harmonization of transparency requirements in relation to information about issuers whose securities are admitted to trading on a regulated market and amending Directive 2001/34/EC [1], and in particular Articles 2(3)(a), 5(6), first subparagraph, and 5(6)(c), 9(7), 12(8)(b) to (e), 13(2), 14(2), 21(4)(a), 23(4)(ii) and 23(7) thereof,

After consulting the Committee of European Securities Regulators (CESR) [2] for technical advice,

Whereas:

(1) Directive 2004/109/EC establishes the general principles for the harmonization of transparency requirements in respect of the holding of voting rights or financial instruments that result in an entitlement to acquire existing shares with voting rights. It seeks to ensure that, through the disclosure of accurate, comprehensive and timely information about security issuers, investor confidence is built up and sustained. By the same token, by requiring issuers to be informed of movements affecting major holdings in companies, it seeks to ensure that the latter are in a position to keep the public informed.

1 OJ L 390, 31.12.2004, p. 38.

2 CESR was established by Commission Decision 2001/527/EC of 6 June 2001 (OJ L 191, 13.7.2001, p. 43).

欧盟委员会
第 2007/14/EC 号指令

（本指令于 2007 年 3 月 8 日通过，系《协调关于证券获准在受监管市场交易的发行人的信息透明度要求的第 2004/109/EC 号指令》某些条款的实施细则）

欧盟委员会，

根据《欧洲共同体条约》(以下简称《条约》)，

根据《欧洲议会与欧盟理事会协调关于证券获准在受监管市场交易的发行人的信息透明度要求并修正〈第2001/34/EC号指令〉的第2004/109/EC号指令》[1](2004年12月15日)，尤其是其中的第2条第3款第a项、第5条第6款第1项和第5条第6款第c项、第9条第7款、第12条第8款第b项至第e项、第13条第2款、第14条第2款、第21条第4款第a项、第23条第4款第ii项以及第23条第7款，

在征求欧洲证券监管机构委员会(CESR)[2]的技术性建议后，

鉴于：

(1)为协调持有表决权或持有赋予购买附带表决权的现有股票权利的金融工具的透明度要求，第2004/109/EC号指令制定了一般性原则。该指令旨在确保通过准确、全面和及时披露证券发行人信息来建立和维持投资者信心。与此同理，该指令要求相关主体通知发行人公司的大额持股变更情况，以确保发行人能向公众提供最新信息。

1 2004 年 12 月 31 日《欧盟公报》L390，第 38 页。

2 欧洲证券监管机构委员会由欧盟委员会 2001 年 6 月 6 日的第 2001/527/EC 号决定（2001 年 7 月 13 日《欧盟公报》L191，第 43 页）设立。

(2) The rules for the implementation of the rules governing transparency requirements should likewise be designed to ensure a high level of investor protection, to enhance market efficiency, and to be applied in a uniform manner.

(3) As regards the procedural arrangements in accordance with which investors are to be informed of the issuer's choice of home Member State, it is appropriate that such choices be disclosed in accordance with the same procedure as regulated information under Directive 2004/109/EC.

(4) As regards the minimum content of the condensed set of half-yearly financial statements, where that set is not prepared in accordance with international accounting standards, this should be such as to avoid giving a misleading view of the assets, liabilities, financial position and profit or loss of the issuer. The content of half-yearly reports should be such as to ensure appropriate transparency for investors through a regular flow of information about the performance of the issuer, and that information should be presented in such a way that it is easy to compare it with the information provided in the annual report of the preceding year.

(5) Issuers of shares who prepare consolidated accounts in accordance with International Accounting Standards (IAS) and International Financial Reporting Standards (IFRS) should apply the same definition of related party transactions in annual and half-yearly reports under Directive 2004/109/EC. Issuers of shares who do not prepare consolidated accounts and are not required to apply IAS and IFRS should, in their half-yearly reports under Directive 2004/109/EC, apply the definition of related party transactions set out in Council Directive 78/660/EEC of 25 July 1978 based on Article 54 (3)(g) of the Treaty on the annual accounts of certain types of companies[1].

(6) For the purposes of benefiting from the exemption from the notification of major holdings under Directive 2004/109/EC in the case of shares acquired for the sole purpose of clearing and settling, the maximum length of the 'short settlement cycle' should be as short as possible.

(7) In order for the relevant competent authority to be able to monitor compliance as regards the derogation for market makers with respect to the notification of information about major holdings, the market maker seeking to benefit from that derogation should make known that it is acting or intends to act as market maker and for which shares or financial instruments.

(8) Conducting market making activities in full transparency is particularly important. Thus, the market maker should be capable upon request from the relevant

1 OJ L 222, 14.8.1978, p. 11. Directive as last amended by Directive 2006/46/EC of the European Parliament and of the Council (OJ L 224, 16.8.2006, p. 1).

(2)透明度要求的实施规则同样也应以确保高标准的投资者保护、提高市场效率和统一的适用为宗旨。

(3)投资者据以查阅发行人的母国选择信息的程序性安排,应按照第2004/109/EC号指令中的受监管信息的披露程序进行披露。

(4)非按照国际会计准则制作的一套简要半年度财务报表,至少应包含足以避免对发行人资产、负债、财务状况和损益造成误导的信息。半年度报告的内容应能通过发行人业绩信息的定期发布确保对投资者的适当透明度,同时,半年度报告列报的方式应能使之易于与上一年年度报告提供的信息作比较。

(5)根据国际会计准则(IAS)和国际财务报告准则(IFRS)制作合并财务报表的股票发行人,应对年度和半年度报告中的关联交易适用与第2004/109/EC号指令相同的定义。不制作合并财务报表且无义务采用国际会计准则和国际财务报告准则的股票发行人应在按照第2004/109/EC号指令披露的半年度报告中适用《欧洲经济共同体理事会在〈条约〉第54条第3款第g项的基础上关于某些类型公司的年度财务报表的第78/660/EEC号指令》[1](1978年7月25日)的关联交易定义。

(6)仅为清算和结算之目的购买的股票,可豁免第2004/109/EC号指令的大额持股通知规定,因此,"短结算周期"的最长时长应尽可能短。

(7)鉴于做市商可以免除大额持股通知义务,为使相关主管部门能够对此进行监控,寻求获得该项免除待遇的做市商应公布其针对何等股票或金融工具正在或有意以做市商身份行事。

(8)充分透明地开展做市活动至关重要。因此,做市商应能根据相关主管部门的要求,辨认与所涉发行人有关的活动,特别是辨认为做市活动之目的所持有的股票或

1 1978年8月14日《欧盟公报》L222,第11页。该指令由欧洲议会与欧盟理事会第2006/46/EC号指令(2006年8月16日《欧盟公报》L224,第1页)作出最新修正。

competent authority of identifying the activities conducted in relation to the issuer in question, and in particular the shares or financial instruments held for market making activities purposes.

(9) As regards the calendar of trading days, it is appropriate, for the sake of ease of operation, that time limits be calculated by reference to the trading days in the Member State of the issuer. However, in order to enhance transparency, provision should be made for each competent authority to inform investors and market participants of the calendar of trading days applicable for the various regulated markets situated or operating on its territory.

(10) As regards the circumstances in which notification of major holdings is to be made, it is appropriate to determine when that obligation is triggered either individually or collectively, and how that obligation is to be complied with in the case of proxies.

(11) It is reasonable to assume that natural persons or legal entities exercise a high duty of care when acquiring or disposing of major holdings. It follows that such persons or entities will very quickly become aware of such acquisitions or disposals, or of the possibility to exercise voting rights, and it is therefore appropriate to specify only a very short period following the relevant transaction as the period after which they are deemed to have knowledge.

(12) The exemption from the obligation to aggregate major holdings should be available only to parent undertakings that can demonstrate that their subsidiary management companies or investment firms fulfill adequate conditions of independence. To ensure full transparency, a statement to that effect should be notified ex ante to the relevant competent authority. In this regard, it is important that the notification mentions the competent authority supervising the management companies' activities under the conditions laid down pursuant to Council Directive 85/611/EEC of 20 December 1985 on the coordination of laws, regulations and administrative provisions relating to undertakings for collective investment in transferable securities (UCITS) [1], irrespective of whether or not they are authorized under that Directive, provided in the latter case that they are supervised under national legislation.

(13) For the purposes of Directive 2004/109/EC, financial instruments should be taken into account in the context of notifying major holdings, to the extent that such instruments give the holder an unconditional right to acquire the underlying shares or discretion as to whether to acquire the underlying shares or cash on maturity. Consequently, financial instruments should not be considered to include instruments

1 OJ L 375, 31.12.1985, p. 3, Directive as last amended by Directive 2005/1/EC of the European Parliament and of the Council (OJ L 79, 24.3.2005, p. 9).

金融工具。

(9)就交易日日历而言,为方便操作,应参照发行人所在成员国的交易日来计算各种时限。然而,为了提高透明度,应规定每一主管部门均有义务通知投资者和市场参与者位于其境内或在其境内运营的不同受监管市场各自适用的交易日日历。

(10)对于在何等情形下应对大额持股进行通知,宜确定该项义务(不论是个体或集体的义务)何时被触发以及涉及代理委托的情形下应如何履行该项义务。

(11)基于合理的假设,自然人或法人实体购买或处置大额股份时会履行高度的注意义务。该等假设意味着,一旦出现购买或处置或行使表决权的可能性,自然人或法人实体很快即会获知,因此,就相关交易发生多长时间后自然人或法人实体可视为知悉该等信息而言,应设定一个非常短的时期。

(12)母公司能够证明其下属的管理子公司或投资子公司完全符合独立性条件的,始得豁免大额持股合并计算义务。为确保充分的透明度,应提前就此向相关主管部门发送一份说明书通知。该通知有必要注明负责监管管理公司活动[指根据《欧洲经济共同体理事会协调关于可转让证券集合投资计划(UCITS)的法律、法规和规章的第85/611/EEC号指令》[1](1985年12月20日)制定之条件开展的活动]的主管部门,不论子公司是否是依据该指令获得核准的,但是未根据该指令获得核准的子公司应受国内立法监管。

(13)就第2004/109/EC号指令而言,对于赋予持有人无条件购买标的股票权利的金融工具,或对于持有人有权在金融工具到期之日决定是否购买标的股票或获得现金的金融工具,应考虑其是否适用大额持股通知规定。因此,下述工具不被视为金融工具,即标的股票价格于某一特定时刻达到某一价格水平时持有人即有权获得股票的工具。允许工具发行人或第三方在到期日授予工具持有人股票或现金的工具,亦不

1 1985年12月31日《欧盟公报》L375,第3页。该指令由欧洲议会与欧盟理事会第2005/1/EC号指令(2005年3月24日L79,第9页)作出最新修正。

entitling the holder to receive shares depending on the price of the underlying share reaching a certain level at a certain moment in time. Nor should they be considered to cover those instruments that allow the instrument issuer or a third party to give shares or cash to the instrument holder on maturity.

(14) The financial instruments in Section C of Annex I of Directive 2004/39/EC of the European Parliament and of the Council [1] which are not mentioned in Article 11(1) of this Commission directive do not qualify as financial instruments within the meaning of Article 13(1) of Directive 2004/109/EC.

(15) Directive 2004/109/EC sets high-level requirements in the area of dissemination of regulated information. The mere availability of information, which means that investors must actively seek it out, is therefore not sufficient for the purposes of that Directive. Accordingly, dissemination should involve the active distribution of information from the issuers to the media, with a view to reaching investors.

(16) Minimum quality standards for the dissemination of regulated information are necessary to ensure that investors, even if situated in a Member State other than that of the issuer, have equal access to regulated information. Issuers should ensure that those minimum standards are met, whether by disseminating the regulated information themselves or by entrusting a third party to do soon their behalf. In the latter case, the third party should be capable of dissemination in adequate conditions and have adequate mechanisms in place to ensure that the regulated information it receives emanates from the relevant issuer and that there is no significant risk of data corruption or of unauthorized access to unpublished inside information. Where the third party provides other services or performs other functions, such as media, competent authorities, stock exchanges or the entity in charge of the officially appointed storage mechanism, such services or functions should be kept clearly separated from the services and functions relating to the dissemination of regulated information. When communicating information to the media, issuers or third parties should give priority to the use of electronic means and industry standard formats so as to facilitate and accelerate the processing of the information.

(17) Additionally, by way of minimum standards, regulated information should be disseminated in a way that ensures the widest possible public access, and where possible reaching the public simultaneously inside and outside the issuer's home Member State. That is without prejudice to the right of Member States to request issuers to publish parts or all regulated information through newspapers, and to the possibility for issuers to make

1 OJ L 145, 30.4.2004, p. 1. Directive as amended by Directive 2006/31/EC (OJ L 114, 27.4.2006, p. 60).

被视为金融工具。

(14)欧洲议会与欧盟理事会第2004/39/EC号指令[1]附录一第C节中的金融工具,在本欧盟委员会指令第11条第1款中未提及的,无资格作为第2004/109/EC号指令第13条第1款所定义的金融工具。

(15)第2004/109/EC号指令对受监管信息的传播设定了高标准的要求。如果发行人仅做到信息可供获得,则意味着投资者必须积极寻找方能获取,对实现本指令目标而言并不充分。为此,传播应包括信息从发行人到媒体的积极发布,以期最终传递到投资者处。

(16)适用受监管信息传播的最低质量标准对确保投资者(即使是位于发行人所在成员国以外的成员国的投资者)查阅受监管信息的权利平等必不可少。不论是自行传播还是委托第三方代为传播受监管信息,发行人均应确保达到该等最低标准。委托第三方代为传播的,第三方应能在条件充分的状态下传播信息并备有充分的机制确保其接收的受监管信息确为相关发行人发出的信息,并且不存在数据损坏或他人未经许可擅自获得未公布的内幕信息的重大风险。第三方提供其他服务或履行诸如媒体、主管部门、证券交易所或官方指定负责存储机制的实体等职能的,上述服务或职能应始终与受监管信息的传播服务和职能明确隔离。向媒体、发行人或第三方通知信息时,应优先使用电子手段和行业标准格式,以方便和加快信息处理。

(17)此外,通过最低标准的实施,受监管信息应以尽可能可公开查阅的方式传播,如有可能,还应同时传递到发行人母国境内和境外的公众处。但是,成员国仍有权要求发行人通过报纸公布部分或全部受监管信息,发行人也仍然可在其自身网站上或在投资者能够访问的其他网站上公布受监管信息。

1 2004年4月30日《欧盟公报》L145,第1页。该指令由第2006/31/EC号指令(2006年4月27日《欧盟公报》L114,第60页)作出最新修正。

regulated information available on their own or other websites accessible to investors.

(18) Equivalence should be able to be declared when general disclosure rules of third countries provide users with understandable and broadly equivalent assessment of issuers' position that enable them to make similar decisions as if they were provided with the information according to requirements under Directive 2004/109/EC, even if the requirements are not identical. However, equivalence should be limited to the substance of the relevant information and no exception as regards the time limits set by Directive 2004/109/EC should be accepted.

(19) In order to establish whether or not a third country issuer is meeting equivalent requirements to those laid down in Article 4(3) of Directive 2004/109/EC, it is important to ensure that there is consistency with Commission Regulation (EC) No 809/2004 of 29 April 2004 implementing Directive 2003/71/EC of the European Parliament and of the Council as regards information contained in prospectuses as well as the format, incorporation by reference and publication of such prospectuses and dissemination of advertisements [1], in particular the items dealing with Historical Financial Information to be included in a prospectus.

(20) As regards the equivalence of independence requirements, a parent undertaking of a management company or investment firm registered in a third country should be able to benefit from the exemption under Article 12(4) or (5) of Directive 2004/109/EC, independently of whether the authorization is required by the law of the third country for the controlled management company or investment firm to conduct management activities or portfolio management activities, provided that certain conditions of independence are respected.

(21) The measures provided for in this Directive are in accordance with the opinion of the European Securities Committee,

HAS ADOPTED THIS DIRECTIVE:

Article 1 Subject matter

This Directive lays down detailed rules for the implementation of Article 2 (1)(i)(ii), the second subparagraph of Article 5(3), the second sentence of Article 5(4), Article 9(1), (2) and (4) Article 10, Article 12(1), (2), (4), (5) and (6), Article 12(2)(a), Article 13(1), Article 21(1), Article 23(1) and (6) of Directive 2004/109/EC.

Article 2 Procedural arrangements for the choice of the home Member State (Article 2(1)(i)(ii) of Directive 2004/109/EC)

Where the issuer makes a choice of home Member State, that choice shall be

1 OJ L 149, 30.4.2004, p. 1, as corrected by OJ L 215, 16.6.2004, p. 3. Regulation as amended by Regulation (EC) No 1787/2006 (OJ L 337, 5.12.2006, p. 17).

(18)在以下情况下可宣告具有等效性:第三国的一般披露规则为用户提供的对发行人状况的评估手段,易于理解且在很大程度上具有等效性,使用户如同按照第2004/109/EC号指令的要求(即使该等要求并不完全相同)获得信息般能够作出类似决定。然而,等效性的认定仅限于相关信息的实质内容,第2004/109/EC号指令所设时限必须严格遵守,不得例外。

(19)为确定第三国发行人是否符合与第2004/109/EC号指令第4条第3款规定等效的要求,应确保该等要求与《欧盟委员会就招募说明书所含信息以及该等招募说明书的格式、引用的信息和公布以及广告传播实施欧洲议会与欧盟理事会第2003/71/EC号指令的第809/2004号(欧共体)条例》[1](2004年4月29日)具有一致性,特别是与招募说明书所应涵盖的历史财务信息的各项相关规定一致。

(20)就独立性要求的等效性而言,只要遵守了某些独立性条件,在第三国注册的管理公司或投资公司的母公司应能享受第2004/109/EC号指令第12条第4款或第5款的豁免,不论该第三国的法律是否要求受控管理公司或投资公司获得核准后方能开展管理活动或投资组合管理活动。

(21)本指令所规定的措施与欧洲证券委员会的意见相符。

兹通过本指令如下:

第1条　标的事项

本指令就第2004/109/EC号指令第2条第1款第i项第ii目、第5条第3款第2项、第5条第4款第2句、第9条第1款、第2款和第4款、第10条、第12条第1款、第2款、第4款、第5款和第6款、第12条第2款第a项、第13条第1款、第21条第1款、第23条第1款和第6款制定了详细的实施规则。

第2条　选择母国的程序性安排

(第2004/109/EC号指令第2条第1款第i项第ii目)

发行人选择母国时,应按照披露受监管信息的程序对该项选择进行披露。

1　2004年4月30日《欧盟公报》L149,第1页,经2004年6月16日《欧盟公报》L215第3页更正。该条例经第1787/2006号(欧共体)条例(2006年12月5日《欧盟公报》L337,第17页)修正。

disclosed in accordance with the same procedure as regulated information.

Article 3 Minimum content of half-yearly non-consolidated financial statements

(Article 5(3) second subparagraph, of Directive 2004/109/EC)

1. The minimum content of the condensed set of half-yearly financial statements, where that set is not prepared in accordance with international accounting standards adopted pursuant to the procedure provided for under Article 6 of Regulation (EC) No 1606/2002, shall be in accordance with paragraphs 2 and 3 of this Article.

2. The condensed balance sheet and the condensed profit and loss account shall show each of the headings and subtotals included in the most recent annual financial statements of the issuer. Additional line items shall be included if, as a result of their omission, the half-yearly financial statements would give a misleading view of the assets, liabilities, financial position and profit or loss of the issuer.

In addition, the following comparative information shall be included:

(a) balance sheet as at the end of the first six months of the current financial year and comparative balance sheet as at the end of the immediate preceding financial year;

(b) profit and loss account for the first six months of the current financial year with, from two years after the date of entry into force of this Directive, comparative information for the comparable period for the preceding financial year.

3. The explanatory notes shall include the following:

(a) sufficient information to ensure the comparability of the condensed half-yearly financial statements with the annual financial statements;

(b) sufficient information and explanations to ensure a user's proper understanding of any material changes in amounts and of any developments in the half-year period concerned, which are reflected in the balance sheet and the profit and loss account.

Article 4 Major related parties' transactions

(Article 5(4) second sentence, of Directive 2004/109/EC)

1. In the interim management reports, issuers of shares shall disclose as major related parties' transactions, as a minimum, the following:

(a) related parties' transactions that have taken place in the first six months of the current financial year and that have materially affected the financial position or the performance of the enterprise during that period;

(b) any changes in the related parties' transactions described in the last annual report that could have a material effect on the financial position or performance of the enterprise in the first six months of the current financial year.

2. Where the issuer of shares is not required to prepare consolidated accounts, it shall disclose, as a minimum, the related parties' transactions referred to in Article 43(1)

第3条　半年度非合并财务报表必不可少的内容

（第2004/109/EC号指令第5条第3款第2项）

1.简要半年度财务报表并非按照依第1606/2002号（欧共体）条例第6条程序制定的国际会计准则制作的，其涵盖的内容至少应与本条第2款和第3款相符。

2.简要资产负债表和简要损益表应列示发行人最新的年度财务报表标题和分类汇总。缺少某些项目会使半年度财务报表对发行人资产、负债、财务状况和损益形成误导的，应纳入该等额外项目。

简要资产负债表和简要损益表也应包含以下比较信息：

（a）本会计年度上半年期末的资产负债表，以及上一会计年度期末的比较资产负债表；

（b）本指令生效两年后，还应提供当本会计年度上半年的损益表以及上一会计年度可比时期的比较信息。

3.注释应包含以下内容：

（a）确保简要半年度财务报表与年度财务报表之间具有可比性所需的充分信息；

（b）确保用户正确理解资产负债表和损益表反映的所涉半年期内任何重大数额变化和任何发展的充分信息和解释。

第4条　重大关联交易

（第2004/109/EC号指令第5条第4款第2句）

1.在中期管理报告中，股票发行人至少应披露以下重大关联交易信息：

（a）在本会计年度上半年发生且对该期间企业财务状况或业绩产生重大影响的关联交易；

（b）可能对本会计年度上半年企业财务状况或业绩产生重大影响的上一年度报告所载关联交易的任何变更。

2.股票发行人不必制作合并财务报表的，至少应披露第78/660/EEC号指令第43条第1款第7b项所述的关联交易。

(7b) of Directive 78/660/EEC.

Article 5 Maximum length of the usual 'short settlement cycle'

(Article 9(4) of Directive 2004/109/EC)

The maximum length of the usual 'short settlement cycle' shall be three trading days following the transaction.

Article 6 Control mechanisms by competent authorities as regards market makers

(Article 9(5) of Directive 2004/109/EC)

1. The market maker seeking to benefit from the exemption provided for in Article 9(5) of Directive 2004/109/EC shall notify to the competent authority of the Home Member State of the issuer, at the latest within the time limit laid down in Article 12(2) of Directive 2004/109/EC, that it conducts or intends to conduct market making activities on a particular issuer.

Where the market maker ceases to conduct market making activities on the issuer concerned, it shall notify that competent authority accordingly.

2. Without prejudice to the application of Article 24 of Directive 2004/109/EC, where in case the market maker seeking to benefit from the exemption provided for in Article 9(5) of that Directive is requested by the competent authority of the issuer to identify the shares or financial instruments held for market making activity purposes, that market maker shall be allowed to make such identification by any verifiable means. Only if the market maker is not able to identify the shares or financial instruments concerned, he may be required to hold them in a separate account for the purposes of that identification.

3. Without prejudice to the application of Article 24(4)(a) of Directive 2004/109/EC, if a market-making agreement between the market maker and the stock exchange and/or the issuer is required under national law, the market maker shall upon request of the relevant competent authority provide the agreement to such authority.

Article 7 Calendar of trading days

(Article 12(2) and (6) and Article 14(1) of Directive 2004/109/EC)

1. For the purposes of Article 12(2) and (6) and Article 14(1) of Directive 2004/109/EC, the calendar of trading days of the home Member State of the issuer shall apply.

2. Each competent authority shall publish in its Internet site the calendar of trading days of the different regulated markets situated or operating on the territory within its jurisdiction.

Article 8 Shareholders and natural persons or legal entities referred to in Article 10 of the Transparency Directive required to make the notification of major holdings

第5条　通常的“短结算周期”的最长时长

（第2004/109/EC号指令第9条第4款）

通常的“短结算周期”最长应为交易之后的3个交易日。

第6条　主管部门对做市商的控制机制

（第2004/109/EC号指令第9条第5款）

1.做市商申请享受第2004/109/EC号指令第9条第5款豁免的，最晚应于第2004/109/EC号指令第12条第2款规定的时限内向发行人的母国主管部门通知其对特定发行人开展或拟开展的做市活动。

做市商终止对所涉发行人开展的做市活动的，应通知主管部门。

2.在不影响第2004/109/EC号指令第24条适用的情形下，发行人的主管部门要求，申请享受该指令第9条第5款豁免的做市商应对为开展做市活动持有的股票或金融工具进行辨认的，应允许做市商以任何可核实的方式实施该等辨认。唯有做市商无法辨认所涉股票或金融工具时，方得要求其出于辨认之目的在独立账户中持有该等股票或金融工具。

3.在不影响第2004/109/EC号指令第24条第4款第a项的适用的情形下，根据成员国国内法律须提供做市商和证券交易所及/或发行人之间的做市协议的，做市商应经相关主管部门要求向该部门提供协议。

第7条　交易日日历

（第2004/109/EC号指令第12条第2款和第6款以及第14条第1款）

1.就第2004/109/EC号指令第12条第2款和第6款以及第14条第1款而言，应适用发行人母国的交易日日历。

2.各主管部门均应在其网站上公布位于其司法辖区或在其司法辖区内运营的不同受监管市场各自的交易日日历。

第8条　须作出大额持股通知的股东以及《透明度指令》第10条所述的自然人或法人实体

(Article 12(2) of Directive 2004/109/EC)

1. For the purposes of Article 12 (2) of Directive 2004/109/EC, the notification obligation which arises as soon as the proportion of voting rights held reaches, exceeds or falls below the applicable thresholds following transactions of the type referred to in Article 10 of Directive 2004/109/EC shall be an individual obligation incumbent upon each shareholder, or each natural person or legal entity as referred to in Article 10 of that Directive, or both in case the proportion of voting rights held by each party reaches, exceeds or falls below the applicable threshold.

In the circumstances referred to in point (a) of Article 10 of the Directive 2004/109/EC, the notification obligation shall be a collective obligation shared by all parties to the agreement.

2. In the circumstances referred to in point (h) of Article 10 of Directive 2004/109/EC, if a shareholder gives the proxy in relation to one shareholder meeting, notification may be made by means of a single notification at the moment of giving the proxy provided that it is made clear in the notification what the resulting situation in terms of voting rights will be when the proxy may no longer exercise the voting rights at its discretion.

If, in the circumstances referred to in point (h) of Article 10, the proxy holder receives one or several proxies in relation to one shareholder meeting, notification may be made by means of a single notification at the moment of receiving the proxies provided that it is made clear in the notification what the resulting situation in terms of voting rights will be when the proxy may no longer exercise the voting rights at its discretion.

3. Where the duty to make a notification lies with more than one natural person or legal entity, notification may be made by means of a single common notification.

However, use of a single common notification may not be deemed to release any of the natural persons or legal entities concerned from their responsibility in relation to notification.

Article 9 Circumstances under which the notifying person should have learned of acquisition or disposal or of possibility to exercise voting rights

(Article 12(2) of Directive 2004/109/EC)

For the purposes of point (a) of Article 12(2) of Directive 2004/109/EC, the shareholder, or the natural person or legal entity referred to in Article 10 of that Directive, shall be deemed to have knowledge of the acquisition, disposal or possibility to exercise voting rights no later than two trading days following the transaction.

Article 10 Conditions of independence to be complied with by management companies and investment firms involved in individual portfolio management

(Article 12(4) first subparagraph, and Article 12(5) first subparagraph, of Directive 2004/109/EC)

（第2004/109/EC号指令第12条第2款）

1.就第2004/109/EC号指令第12条第2款而言，进行第2004/109/EC号指令第10条所述类型的交易后，持有表决权比例达到、超过或低于适用门槛的，通知义务随即触发，通知义务是每一股东或该指令第10条所述的每一自然人或法人实体各自的义务；如果发生两方持有的表决权比例都达到、超过或低于适用的门槛的情况，则双方同时各自负有通知义务。

在第2004/109/EC号指令第10条第a目所述的情形下，通知义务为协议各方共同承担的集体义务。

2.在第2004/109/EC号指令第10条第h目所述的情形下，股东委托代理人出席某次股东会议的，可在作出委托授权时以单次通知的形式发出通知，前提是通知中应明确告知当代理人不再拥有表决裁量权时表决权将处于何种状态。

在第10条第h目所述的情形下，代理持股人就某次股东会议收到一份或多份委托代理文书的，可在收到委托代理文书时以单次通知的形式发出通知，前提是通知中明确告知当代理人不再拥有表决裁量权时表决权将处于何种状态。

3.通知工作由一个以上的自然人或法人实体承担的，可以单次共同通知的形式发出通知。

然而，采用单次共同通知时，不得被视为免除任何所涉自然人或法人实体的通知责任。

第9条　发出通知的人理应知悉购买或处置或行使表决权的可能性的情况

（第2004/109/EC号指令第12条第2款）

就第2004/109/EC号指令第12条第2款第a目而言，股东或该指令第10条所述的自然人或法人实体应被视为最迟于交易后的第2个交易日知悉表决权的购买、处置或行使的可能性。

第10条　单独进行投资组合管理的管理公司和投资公司应符合的独立性条件

（第2004/109/EC号指令第12条第4款第1项和第12条第5款第1项）

1. For the purposes of the exemption to the aggregation of holdings provided for in the first subparagraphs of Article 12(4) and (5) of Directive 2004/109/EC, a parent undertaking of a management company or of an investment firm shall comply with the following conditions:

(a) it must not interfere by giving direct or indirect instructions or in any other way in the exercise of the voting rights held by that management company or investment firm;

(b) that management company or investment firm must be free to exercise, independently of the parent undertaking, the voting rights attached to the assets it manages.

2. A parent undertaking which wishes to make use of the exemption shall, without delay, notify the following to the competent authority of the home Member State of issuers whose voting rights are attached to holdings managed by the management companies or investment firms:

(a) a list of the names of those management companies and investment firms, indicating the competent authorities that supervise them or that no competent authority supervises them, but with no reference to the issuers concerned;

(b) a statement that, in the case of each such management company or investment firm, the parent undertaking complies with the conditions laid down in paragraph 1.

The parent undertaking shall update the list referred to in point (a) on an ongoing basis.

3. Where the parent undertaking intends to benefit from the exemptions only in relation to the financial instruments referred to in Article 13 of Directive 2004/109/EC, it shall notify to the competent authority of the home Member State of the issuer only the list referred to in point (a) of paragraph 2.

4. Without prejudice to the application of Article 24 of Directive 2004/109/EC, a parent undertaking of a management company or of an investment firm shall be able to demonstrate to the competent authority of the home Member State of the issuer on request that:

(a) the organizational structures of the parent undertaking and the management company or investment firm are such that the voting rights are exercised independently of the parent undertaking;

(b) the persons who decide how the voting rights are to be exercised act independently;

(c) if the parent undertaking is a client of its management company or investment firm or has holding in the assets managed by the management company or investment firm, there is a clear written mandate for an arms-length customer relationship between the parent undertaking and the management company or investment firm.

1.就第2004/109/EC号指令第12条第4款和第5款第1项规定的股份合并计算豁免而言,管理公司或投资公司的母公司应符合以下条件:

(a)不得通过下达直接或间接的指示或任何其他方式,干涉管理公司或投资公司持有的表决权的行使;

(b)管理公司或投资公司必须独立于母公司自由地行使其管理的资产所附带的表决权。

2.有意受益于该项豁免的母公司应立即向其表决权附于管理公司或投资公司所管理的股份中的发行人的母国主管部门通知以下内容:

(a)一份该等管理公司和投资公司的名单,清单中还应注明负责监管该等公司的主管部门,并无主管部门对其进行监管的,也应相应说明,但不得述及所涉发行人;

(b)一份关于就上述各个管理公司或投资公司而言母公司符合第1款所列条件的声明。

母公司应持续更新第a目所述的名单。

3.母公司拟仅就第2004/109/EC号指令第13条所述金融工具享受豁免的,应仅向发行人的母国主管部门通知第2款第a目所述名单。

4.在不影响第2004/109/EC号指令第24条的适用的情形下,经发行人的母国主管部门请求,管理公司或投资公司的母公司应能向其证明:

(a)母公司以及管理公司或投资公司的组织结构设计使表决权能够独立于母公司行使;

(b)决定表决权行使方式的人本身独立行事;

(c)如果母公司是其管理公司或投资公司的客户,或母公司持有管理公司或投资公司所管理的资产,针对母公司和管理公司或投资公司之间的公平客户关系有明确的书面要求。

The requirement in point (a) shall imply as a minimum that the parent undertaking and the management company or investment firm must established written policies and procedures reasonably designed to prevent the distribution of information between the parent undertaking and the management company or investment firm in relation to the exercise of voting rights.

5. For the purposes of point (a) of paragraph 1, 'direct instruction' means any instruction given by the parent undertaking, or another controlled undertaking of the parent undertaking, specifying how the voting rights are to be exercised by the management company or investment firm in particular cases.

'Indirect instruction' means any general or particular instruction, regardless of the form, given by the parent undertaking, or another controlled undertaking of the parent undertaking, that limits the discretion of the management company or investment firm in relation to the exercise of the voting rights in order to serve specific business interests of the parent undertaking or another controlled undertaking of the parent undertaking.

Article 11 Types of financial instruments that result in an entitlement to acquire, on the holder's own initiative alone, shares to which voting rights are attached

(Article 13(1) of Directive 2004/109/EC)

1. For the purposes of Article 13(1) of Directive 2004/109/EC, transferable securities; and options, futures, swaps, forward rate agreements and any other derivative contracts, as referred to in Section C of Annex I of Directive 2004/39/EC, shall be considered to be financial instruments, provided that they result in an entitlement to acquire, on the holder's own initiative alone, under a formal agreement, shares to which voting rights are attached, already issued, of an issuer whose shares are admitted to trading on a regulated market.

The instrument holder must enjoy, on maturity, either the unconditional right to acquire the underlying shares or the discretion as to his right to acquire such shares or not.

A formal agreement means an agreement which is binding under the applicable law.

2. For the purposes of Article 13(1) of Directive 2004/109/EC, the holder shall aggregate and notify all financial instruments within the meaning of paragraph 1 relating to the same underlying issuer.

3. The notification required under Article 13(1) of Directive 2004/109/EC shall include the following information:

(a) the resulting situation in terms of voting rights;

(b) if applicable, the chain of controlled undertakings through which financial instruments are effectively held;

第a目的要求至少意味着，母公司和管理公司或投资公司之间必须制定合理的书面政策和程序，旨在预防表决权行使信息在母公司和管理公司或投资公司之间散布。

5.就第1款第a目而言，“直接指示”指母公司或母公司的其他受控公司下达的指明在特定情况下管理公司或投资公司应如何行使表决权的指示。

“间接指示”指母公司或母公司的其他受控公司下达的各种形式的一般或特殊指示，且该等指示限制了管理公司或投资公司与表决权的行使有关的自由裁量权，以便为母公司或母公司的其他受控公司的特定商业利益服务。

第11条　使其持有人有权单独自主地决定购买附带表决权的股票的金融工具类型

（第2004/109/EC号指令第13条第1款）

1.就第2004/109/EC号指令第13条第1款而言，可转让证券和第2004/39/EC号指令附录一第C节所述的期货、期权、互换、远期利率协议及任何其他衍生品合约均应被视为金融工具，前提是该等工具使其持有人有权单独自主按正式协议购买附带表决权的股票，且发行该等股票的发行人已获准在受监管市场交易其股票。

工具持有人在到期日必须享有无条件的购买标的股票的权利，或决定是否行使其购买上述股票的权利的自由裁量权。

正式协议指根据适用法律具有约束力的协议。

2.就第2004/109/EC号指令第13条第1款而言，持有人应就同一个标的发行人所发行的符合第1款所定义的所有金融工具做合并计算及通知。

3.第2004/109/EC号指令第13条第1款所规定的通知应包含以下信息：

（a）购买股票后，表决权的状况；

（b）通过何等受控企业链来有效持有金融工具（如适用）；

(c) the date on which the threshold was reached or crossed;

(d) for instruments with an exercise period, an indication of the date or time period where shares will or can be acquired, if applicable;

(e) date of maturity or expiration of the instrument;

(f) identity of the holder;

(g) name of the underlying issuer.

For the purposes of point (a) the percentage of voting rights shall be calculated by reference to the total number of voting rights and capital as last disclosed by the issuer under Article 15 of Directive 2004/109/EC.

4. The notification period shall be the same as laid down in Article 12(2) of Directive 2004/109/EC and the related implementing provisions.

5. The notification shall be made to the issuer of the underlying share and to the competent authority of the home Member States of such issuer.

If a financial instrument relates to more than one underlying share, a separate notification shall be made to each issuer of the underlying shares.

Article 12 Minimum Standards

(Article 21(1) of Directive 2004/109/EC)

1. The dissemination of regulated information for the purposes of Article 21(1) of Directive 2004/109/EC shall be carried out in compliance with the minimum standards set out in paragraphs 2 to 5.

2. Regulated information shall be disseminated in a manner ensuring that it is capable of being disseminated to as wide a public as possible, and as close to simultaneously as possible in the home Member State, or the Member State referred to in Article 21(3) of Directive 2004/109/EC, and in the other Member States.

3. Regulated information shall be communicated to the media in unedited full text.

However, in the case of the reports and statements referred to in Articles 4, 5 and 6 of Directive 2004/109/EC, this requirement shall be deemed fulfilled if the announcement relating to the regulated information is communicated to the media and indicates on which website, in addition to the officially appointed mechanism for the central storage of regulated information referred to in Article 21 of that Directive, the relevant documents are available.

4. Regulated information shall be communicated to the media in a manner which ensures the security of the communication, minimizes the risk of data corruption and unauthorized access, and provides certainty as to the source of the regulated information.

Security of receipt shall be ensured by remedying as soon as possible any failure or disruption in the communication of regulated information.

The issuer or the person who has applied for admission to trading on a regulated

(c)达到或超过表决权门槛的日期;

(d)对于有行使期限的工具,说明股票被购买或可被购买的日期或时期(如适用);

(e)工具的到期日;

(f)持有人的身份信息;

(g)标的发行人的名称。

就第a目而言,表决权的比例应根据发行人按第2004/109/EC号指令第15条最后披露的表决权和资本总数计算。

4.通知期限应与第2004/109/EC号指令第12条第2款及相关实施规定所列期限相同。

5.通知应发给标的股份的发行人和该发行人的母国主管部门。

金融工具涉及一只以上标的股票的,应对标的股票各自的发行人分别发送通知。

第12条　最低标准

(第2004/109/EC号指令第21条第1款)

1.第2004/109/EC号指令第21条第1款所述的受监管信息的传播应按照第2款至第5款设定的最低标准执行。

2.受监管信息应以确保能够尽可能广泛并尽可能同时在母国或第2004/109/EC号指令第21条第3款所述成员国以及其他成员国传播的方式传播。

3.受监管信息应不加编辑,全文传送给媒体。

然而,就第2004/109/EC号指令第4条、第5条和第6条所述的报告和说明书而言,如果受监管信息公告已经传送给媒体,并且该等信息指出除该指令第21条所述的官方指定的受监管信息中央存储机制之外还可从哪个网站获得相关文件,则应被视为符合本项要求。

4.受监管信息传送给媒体的方式应能确保通信安全,并将数据损坏风险和他人未经许可擅自获得的风险控制在最低程度,同时确保受监管信息来源安全。

受监管信息通信故障或中断时应尽快补救,以保证接收安全。

发行人或未经发行人同意自行申请了准入受监管市场交易的人,不对接收受监

market without the issuer's consent shall not be responsible for systemic errors or shortcomings in the media to which the regulated information has been communicated.

5. Regulated information shall be communicated to the media in a way which makes clear that the information is regulated information, identifies clearly the issuer concerned, the subject matter of the regulated information and the time and date of the communication of the information by the issuer or the person who has applied for admission to trading on a regulated market without the issuer's consent.

Upon request, the issuer or the person who has applied for admission to trading on a regulated market without the issuer's consent shall be able to communicate to the competent authority, in relation to any disclosure of regulated information, the following:

(a) the name of the person who communicated the information to the media;

(b) the security validation details;

(c) the time and date on which the information was communicated to the media;

(d) the medium in which the information was communicated;

(e) if applicable, details of any embargo placed by the issuer on the regulated information.

Article 13 Requirements equivalent to Article 4(2)(b) of Directive 2004/109/EC

(Article 23(1) of Directive 2004/109/EC)

A third country shall be deemed to set requirements equivalent to those set out in Article 4(2)(b) of Directive 2004/109/EC where, under the law of that country, the annual management report is required to include at least the following information:

(a) a fair review of the development and performance of the issuer's business and of its position, together with a description of the principal risks and uncertainties that it faces, such that the review presents a balanced and comprehensive analysis of the development and performance of the issuer's business and of its position, consistent with the size and complexity of the business;

(b) an indication of any important events that have occurred since the end of the financial year;

(c) indications of the issuer's likely future development.

The analysis referred to in point (a) shall, to the extent necessary for an understanding of the issuer's development, performance or position, include both financial and, where appropriate, non-financial key performance indicators relevant to the particular business.

Article 14 Requirements equivalent to Article 5(4) of Directive 2004/109/EC

(Article 23(1) of Directive 2004/109/EC)

A third country shall be deemed to set requirements equivalent to those set out in Article 5(4) of Directive 2004/109/EC where, under the law of that country, a condensed

管信息的媒体发生的系统性失误或缺陷负责。

5.向媒体传送受监管信息时，应明确表示该信息属于受监管信息，并清楚识别所涉发行人、受监管信息的标的以及发行人或未经发行人同意自行申请了准入受监管市场交易的人传送信息的时间和日期。

发行人或未经发行人同意自行申请了准入受监管市场交易的人，经要求应能就受监管信息的任何披露向主管部门提供如下信息：

(a)向媒体传送信息的人员姓名；
(b)安全验证的细节；
(c)信息传送给媒体的时间和日期；
(d)传送信息的媒介；
(e)发行人对受监管信息施加的任何禁制细节(如有)。

第13条　与第2004/109/EC号指令第4条第2款第b项等效的要求

(第2004/109/EC号指令第23条第1款)

第三国法律规定年度管理报告至少须涵盖如下信息的，则该国应被视为制定了与第2004/109/EC号指令第4条第2款第b项的规定等效的要求：

(a)对发行人的业务发展和业绩及其所处状况的公允审评，以及对其面临的主要风险和不确定因素的说明，以便该项审评能对发行人的业务发展和业绩及其所处状况做出均衡、全面并且与业务规模和复杂程度一致的分析；

(b)对会计年度结束后发生的任何重要事件的说明；

(c)对发行人未来可能的发展的说明。

在理解发行人的发展、业绩或所处状况所需的范围内，第a目所述的分析应包括与特定业务相关的财务和(在适当时)非财务关键绩效指标。

第14条　与第2004/109/EC号指令第5条第4款等效的要求

(第2004/109/EC号指令第23条第1款)

第三国法律规定，除了中期管理报告之外还须提供简要财务报表且中期管理报告至少应包含如下信息的，则该国应被视为制定了与第2004/109/EC号指令第5条第4

set of financial statements is required in addition to the interim management report, and the interim management report is required to include at least the following information:

(a) review of the period covered;

(b) indications of the issuer's likely future development for the remaining six months of the financial year;

(c) for issuers of shares and if already not disclosed on an ongoing basis, major related parties transactions.

Article 15 Requirements equivalent to Articles 4(2) and 5(2)(c) of Directive 2004/109/EC

(Article 23(1) of Directive 2004/109/EC)

A third country shall be deemed to set requirements equivalent to those set out in Articles 4(2)(c) and 5(2)(c) of Directive 2004/109/EC where, under the law of that country, a person or persons within the issuer are responsible for the annual and half-yearly financial information, and in particular for the following:

(a) the compliance of the financial statements with the applicable reporting framework or set of accounting standards;

(b) the fairness of the management review included in the management report.

Article 16 Requirements equivalent to Article 6 of Directive 2004/109/EC

(Article 23(1) of Directive 2004/109/EC)

A third country shall be deemed to set requirements equivalent to those set out in Article 6 of Directive 2004/109/EC where, under the law of that country, an issuer is required to publish quarterly financial reports.

Article 17 Requirements equivalent to Article 4(3) of Directive 2004/109/EC

(Article 23(1) of Directive 2004/109/EC)

A third country shall be deemed to set requirements equivalent to those set out in the first subparagraph of Article 4(3) of Directive 2004/109/EC where, under the law of that country, the provision of individual accounts by the parent company is not required but the issuer whose registered office is in that third country is required, in preparing consolidated accounts, to include the following information:

(a) for issuers of shares, dividends computation and ability to pay dividends;

(b) for all issuers, where applicable, minimum capital and equity requirements and liquidity issues.

For the purposes of equivalence, the issuer must also be able to provide the competent authority of the home Member State with additional audited disclosures giving information on the individual accounts of the issuer as a standalone, relevant to the elements of information referred to under points (a) and (b). Those disclosures may be prepared under the accounting standards of the third country.

款的规定等效的要求：

(a)所覆盖报告期的审评；

(b)关于发行人在当年会计年度后半年可能出现的发展的说明；

(c)股票发行人已经不再持续披露重大关联交易的，还需提供关于重大关联交易信息。

第15条　与第2004/109/EC号指令第4条第2款及第5条第2款第c项等效的要求

(第2004/109/EC号指令第23条第1款)

第三国法律规定由发行人内部人员自行负责年度和半年度财务信息(特别是以下各项责任)的，则该国应被视为制定了与第2004/109/EC号指令第4条第2款第c项及第5条第2款第c项的规定等效的要求：

(a)财务报表符合适用的报告框架或符合一套会计准则；

(b)管理报告中的管理审评的公允性。

第16条　与第2004/109/EC号指令第6条等效的要求

(第2004/109/EC号指令第23条第1款)

第三国法律规定发行人须公布季度财务报告的，则该国应被视为制定了与第2004/109/EC号指令第6条的规定等效的要求。

第17条　与第2004/109/EC号指令第4条第3款等效的要求

(第2004/109/EC号指令第23条第1款)

第三国法律规定，母公司不必提供独立财务报表，但是在该国注册的发行人制作合并财务报表时须纳入如下信息的，则该国应被视为制定了与第2004/109/EC号指令第4条第3款第1项的规定等效的要求：

(a)对于股票发行人：股息的计算方式和支付股息的能力；

(b)对于所有发行人：最低资本和股本要求以及流动性问题(如适用)。

为等效之目的，发行人还应能够向母国主管部门披露其他经审计的信息，针对第a目和第b目所述信息要素说明发行人作为独立个体制作的独立财务报表的情况。该等披露信息可根据第三国的会计准则制作。

Article 18 Requirements equivalent to Article 4(3) second subparagraph of Directive 2004/109/EC

(Article 23(1) of Directive 2004/109/EC)

A third country shall be deemed to set requirements equivalent to those set out in the second subparagraph of Article 4(3) of Directive 2004/109/EC in relation to individual accounts where, under the law of a third country, an issuer whose registered office is in that third country is not required to prepare consolidated accounts but is required to prepare its individual accounts in accordance with international accounting standards recognized pursuant to Article 3 of Regulation (EC) No 1606/2002 of the European Parliament and of the Council [1] as applicable within the Community or with third country national accounting standards equivalent to those standards.

For the purposes of equivalence, if such financial information is not in line with those standards, it must be presented in the form of restated financial statements.

In addition, the individual accounts must be audited independently.

Article 19 Requirements equivalent to Article 12(6) of Directive 2004/109/EC

(Article 23(1) of Directive 2004/109/EC)

A third country shall be deemed to set requirements equivalent to those set out in Article 12 (6) of Directive 2004/109/EC where, under the law of that country, the time period within which an issuer whose registered office is in that third country must be notified of major holdings and within which it must disclose to the public those major holdings is in total equal to or shorter than seven trading days.

The time frames for the notification to the issuer and for the subsequent disclosure to the public by the issuer may be different from those set out in Articles 12(2) and 12(6) of Directive 2004/109/EC.

Article 20 Requirements equivalent to Article 14 of Directive 2004/109/EC

(Article 23(1) of Directive 2004/109/EC)

A third country shall be deemed to set requirements equivalent to those set out in Article 14 of Directive 2004/109/EC where, under the law of that country, an issuer whose registered office is in that third country is required to comply with the following conditions:

(a) in the case of an issuer allowed to hold up to a maximum of 5% of its own shares to which voting rights are attached, it must make a notification whenever that threshold is reached or crossed;

(b) in the case of an issuer allowed to hold up to a maximum of between 5% and

---

1 OJ L 243, 11.9.2002, p. 1.

第18条　与第2004/109/EC号指令第4条第3款第2项等效的要求

（第2004/109/EC号指令第23条第1款）

第三国法律规定，在该国注册的发行人不必制作合并财务报表，但是须根据被欧洲议会与欧盟理事会第1606/2002号（欧共体）条例[1]第3条认可适用于欧共体的国际会计准则或者与该等准则等效的第三国国内会计准则来制作其独立财务报表的，则该国应被视为在独立财务报表方面制定了与第2004/109/EC号指令第4条第3款第2项的规定等效的要求。

为等效之目的，财务信息与该等准则不相符的，须以重述财务报表的形式列报。

此外，独立财务报表还须接受独立审计。

第19条　与第2004/109/EC号指令第12条第6款等效的要求

（第2004/109/EC号指令第23条第1款）

第三国法律规定，在该国注册的发行人从相关主体处收到大额持股通知并向公众披露该等大额持股信息的期限总天数不超过（含）7个交易日的，则该国应被视为制定了与第2004/109/EC号指令第12条第6款的规定等效的要求。

相关主体向发行人发送通知以及发行人随后向公众披露的时限可不同于第2004/109/EC号指令第12条第2款和第12条第6款的规定。

第20条　与第2004/109/EC号指令第14条等效的要求

（第2004/109/EC号指令第23条第1款）

第三国法律规定在该国注册的发行人须符合以下条件的，则该国应被视为制定了与第2004/109/EC号指令第14条的规定等效的要求：

（a）允许发行人持有自身附带表决权的股票比例最高达5%的，须在达到或超过该门槛时发出通知；

（b）允许发行人持有自身附带表决权的股票比例在5%~10%之间的，须在达到或

1　2002年9月11日《欧盟公报》L243，第1页。

10% of its own shares to which voting rights are attached, it must make a notification whenever a 5% threshold or that maximum threshold is reached or crossed;

(c) in the case of an issuer allowed to hold more than 10% of its own shares to which voting rights are attached, it must make a notification whenever the 5% threshold or the 10% threshold is reached or crossed.

For the purposes of equivalence, notification above the 10% threshold need not be required.

Article 21 Requirements equivalent to Article 15 of Directive 2004/109/EC

(Article 23(1) of Directive 2004/109/EC)

A third country shall be deemed to set requirements equivalent to those set out in Article 15 of Directive 2004/109/EC where, under the law of that country, an issuer whose registered office is in that third country is required to disclose to the public the total number of voting rights and capital within 30 calendar days after an increase or decrease of such total number has occurred.

Article 22 Requirements equivalent to Articles 17(2)(a) and 18(2)(a) of Directive 2004/109/EC

(Article 23(1) of Directive 2004/109/EC)

A third country shall be deemed to set requirements equivalent to those set out in Article 17(2)(a) and 18(2)(a) of Directive 2004/109/EC, as far as the content of the information about meetings is concerned, where, under the law of that country, an issuer whose registered office is in that third country is required to provide at least information on the place, time and agenda of meetings.

Article 23 Equivalence in relation to the test of independence for parent undertakings of management companies and investment firms

(Article 23(6) of Directive 2004/109/EC)

1. A third country shall be deemed to set conditions of independence equivalent to those set out in Article 12(4) and (5) of that Directive where, under the law of that country, a management company or investment firm as referred to in Article 23(6) of Directive 2004/109/EC is required to meet the following conditions:

(a) the management company or investment firm must be free in all situations to exercise, independently of its parent undertaking, the voting rights attached to the assets it manages;

(b) the management company or investment firm must disregard the interests of the parent undertaking or of any other controlled undertaking of the parent undertaking whenever conflicts of interest arise.

2. The parent undertaking shall comply with the notification requirements laid down in Article 10(2)(a) and (3) of this Directive.

超过5%门槛或10%上限时发出通知；

(c)允许发行人持有自身附带表决权的股票比例超过10%的，须在达到或超过5%或10%门槛时作出通知。

等效性规则并不要求就门槛超过10%的情况作出通知。

第21条　与第2004/109/EC号指令第15条等效的要求

(第2004/109/EC号指令第23条第1款)

第三国法律规定在该国注册的发行人须在表决权和资本总数发生增减后的30个日历日(含)内向公众披露该等总数的，则该国应被视为制定了与第2004/109/EC号指令第15条的规定等效的要求。

第22条　与第2004/109/EC号指令第17条第2款第a项以及第18条第2款第a项等效的要求

(第2004/109/EC号指令第23条第1款)

第三国法律规定注册地位于该国的发行人须提供会议地址、时间和议程信息的，则该国就会议信息的内容而言应被视为制定了与第2004/109/EC号指令第17条第2款第a项以及第18条第2款第a项的规定等效的要求。

第23条　管理公司和投资公司的母公司独立性测试的等效性

(第2004/109/EC号指令第23条第6款)

1.第三国法律规定第2004/109/EC号指令第23条第6款所述的管理公司或投资公司须满足如下条件的，则该国应被视为制定了与该指令第12条第4款和第5款的规定等效的要求：

(a)任何情况下，管理公司或投资公司均须自由地独立于其母公司行使其所管理的资产附带的表决权；

(b)发生利益冲突时，管理公司或投资公司须忽略母公司或母公司的任何其他受控公司的利益。

2.母公司应遵守本指令第10条第2款第a项和第3款规定的通知要求。

In addition, it shall make a statement that, in the case of each management company or investment firm concerned, the parent undertaking complies with the conditions laid down in paragraph 1 of this Article.

3. Without prejudice to the application of Article 24 of Directive 2004/109/EC, the parent undertaking shall be able to demonstrate to the competent authority of the home Member State of the issuer on request that the requirements laid down in Article 10(4) of this Directive are respected.

Article 24 Transposition

1. Member States shall bring into force the laws, regulations and administrative provisions necessary to comply with this Directive by 12 months after date of adoption at the latest. They shall forthwith communicate to the Commission the text of those provisions and a correlation table between those provisions and this Directive.

When Member States adopt those provisions, they shall contain a reference to this Directive or be accompanied by such a reference on the occasion of their official publication. Member States shall determine how such reference is to be made.

2. Member States shall communicate to the Commission the text of the main provisions of national law which they adopt in the field covered by this Directive.

Article 25

This Directive shall enter into force on the 20th day following its publication in the *Official Journal of the European Union.*

Article 26

This Directive is addressed to the Member States.

Done at Brussels, 8 March 2007.

For the Commission
Charlie McCREEVY
Member of the Commission

此外,母公司应就各个所涉管理公司或投资公司发表母公司符合本条第1款规定的条件的声明。

3.在不影响第2004/109/EC号指令第24条的适用的情形下,经发行人母国主管部门要求,母公司应能向该部门证明其遵守了本指令第10条第4款所规定的要求。

第24条　转化

1.成员国最晚应于本指令通过后满12个月时实施必要的法律、法规和规章以使本指令得到遵守。成员国应立即向欧盟委员会通知该等规定的正文以及该等规定与本指令之间的关系对照表。

成员国制定该等规定时,应在其中对本指令予以援引,或在官方正式公布该等法律、法规和规章时予以援引。援引的具体方式,由成员国决定。

2.成员国应向欧盟委员会提供其在本指令覆盖领域内通过的国内法律主要条款的文本。

第25条

本指令自公布于《欧盟公报》后的第20日生效。

第26条

本指令对象为各成员国。

2007年3月8日于布鲁塞尔通过。

欧盟委员会委员

麦克里维

DIRECTIVE 2008/22/EC OF THE EUROPEAN PARLIAMENT AND OF THE COUNCIL

欧洲议会与欧盟理事会第 2008/22/EC 号指令

DIRECTIVE 2008/22/EC OF THE EUROPEAN PARLIAMENT AND OF THE COUNCIL

(of 11 March 2008 Amending Directive 2004/109/EC on the harmonization of transparency requirements in relation to information about issuers whose securities are admitted to trading on a regulated market, as regards the implementing powers conferred on the Commission)

THE EUROPEAN PARLIAMENT AND THE COUNCIL OF THE EUROPEAN UNION,

Having regard to the Treaty establishing the European Community, and in particular Articles 44 and 95 thereof,

Having regard to the proposal from the Commission,

Having regard to the opinion of the European Economic and Social Committee [1],

Having regard to the opinion of the European Central Bank [2],

Acting in accordance with the procedure laid down in Article 251 of the Treaty [3],

Whereas:

(1) Directive 2004/109/EC [4] of the European Parliament and of the Council provides that certain measures are to be adopted in accordance with Council Decision 1999/468/EC of 28 June 1999 laying down the procedures for the exercise of implementing powers conferred on the Commission [5].

(2) Decision 1999/468/EC has been amended by Decision 2006/512/EC which

1 OJ C 161, 13.7.2007, p. 45.

2 OJ C 39, 23.2.2007, p. 1.

3 Opinion of the European Parliament of 14 November 2007 (not yet published in the Official Journal) and Council Decision of 3 March 2008.

4 OJ L 390, 31.12.2004, p. 38.

5 OJ L 184, 17.7.1999, p. 23. Decision as amended by Decision 2006/512/EC (OJ L 200, 22.7.2006, p. 11).

欧洲议会与欧盟理事会 第 2008/22/EC 号指令

（本指令于 2008 年 3 月 11 日通过，修正《协调关于证券获准在受监管市场交易的发行人的信息透明度要求的第 2004/109/EC 号指令》中关于授予欧盟委员会的实施权的规定）

欧洲议会与欧盟理事会，

根据《欧洲共同体条约》（以下简称《条约》），特别是其中的第44条和第95条，

根据欧盟委员会的提议，
根据欧洲经济与社会委员会的意见，[1]
根据欧洲中央银行的意见，[2]
依照《条约》第251条规定的程序，[3]
鉴于：

（1）欧洲议会与欧盟理事会第2004/109/EC号指令[4]规定，应根据《欧盟理事会关于制定欧盟委员会行使其被授予的实施权之程序的第1999/468/EC号决定》[5]（1999年6月28日）制定某些细则。

（2）第1999/468/EC号决定经第2006/512/EC号决定修正，后者出台了制定具有一

1 2007 年 7 月 13 日《欧盟公报》C161，第 45 页。

2 2007 年 2 月 23 日《欧盟公报》C39，第 1 页。

3 2007 年 11 月 14 日欧洲议会意见（尚未在《欧盟公报》公布）和 2008 年 3 月 3 日欧盟理事会决定。

4 2004 年 12 月 31 日《欧盟公报》L390，第 38 页。

5 1999 年 7 月 17 日《欧盟公报》L184，第 23 页。该决定经第 2006/512/EC 号决定（2006 年 7 月 22 日《欧盟公报》L200，第 11 页）修正。

introduced the regulatory procedure with scrutiny for the adoption of measures of general scope and designed to amend non-essential elements of a basic instrument adopted in accordance with the procedure referred to in Article 251 of the Treaty, inter alia, by deleting some of those elements or by supplementing the instrument with new non-essential elements.

(3) In accordance with the statement by the European Parliament, the Council and the Commission [1].concerning Decision 2006/512/EC, for the regulatory procedure with scrutiny to be applicable to instruments adopted in accordance with the procedure referred to in Article 251 of the Treaty which are already in force, those instruments must be adjusted in accordance with the applicable procedures.

(4) The Commission should be empowered to adopt the measures necessary for the implementation of Directive 2004/109/EC in order to clarify the technical aspects of some of the definitions provided under that Directive, notably the maximum length of the usual short settlement cycle, the calendar of trading days, the circumstances under which a person should have learnt of the acquisition or disposal of voting rights, the conditions of independence to be respected by market makers and management companies; take account of technical developments in financial markets; clarify the nature of the auditor's review, to define the minimum content of the condensed set of solo financial statements; elaborate further the procedures for the notification and disclosure of major holdings as well as the procedures for filing regulated information with the competent authority of the issuer's home Member State; and define minimum standards for the dissemination of regulated information and for the setting up of storage mechanisms. Since those measures are of general scope and are designed to amend non-essential elements of Directive 2004/109/EC, inter alia, by supplementing it with new non-essential elements, they must be adopted in accordance with the regulatory procedure with scrutiny provided for in Article 5a of Decision 1999/468/EC.

(5) Directive 2004/109/EC provides for a time restriction concerning the implementing powers conferred on the Commission. In their statement concerning Decision 2006/512/EC, the European Parliament, the Council and the Commission stated that Decision 2006/512/EC provides a horizontal and satisfactory solution to the European Parliament's wish to scrutinize the implementation of instruments adopted under the co-decision procedure and that, accordingly, implementing powers should be conferred on the Commission without time limit. The European Parliament and the Council also declared that they would ensure that the proposals aimed at repealing the provisions in the instruments that provide for a time limit on the delegation of implementing powers to the Commission are

1 OJ C 255, 21.10.2006, p. 1.

般适用范围的细则时须经欧盟理事会与欧洲议会审查的监管程序,该等程序旨在对依照《条约》第251条所述程序制定的基础法律文件中的非基本要素进行修正,包括但不限于删除部分该等要素或在基础法律文件中补充新的非基本要素。

(3)根据《欧洲议会、欧盟理事会和欧盟委员会关于第2006/512/EC号决定的声明》,[1]在将须经欧盟理事会与欧洲议会审查的监管程序适用于依照《条约》第251条所述程序制定且已生效的法律文件时,该等法律文件必须根据适用的程序进行调整。

(4)欧盟委员会应有权制定实施第2004/109/EC号指令所必要的细则,以阐明与该指令某些定义相关的技术性事宜,主要是通常的短结算周期的最长时长、交易日日历、在何等情况下理应知悉表决权的购买或处置、做市商和管理公司所须符合的独立性条件;反映金融市场的技术发展动态;阐明审计师审查的性质,就一套简要独立财务报表必不可少的内容作出规定;进一步说明大额股份变更通知和披露程序以及向发行人母国主管部门提交受监管信息的程序;确定传播受监管信息和设立存储机制的最低标准。由于该等细则属于一般适用范围的细则,且旨在通过在第2004/109/EC号指令中补充新的非基本要素而对该指令的非基本要素进行修正,因此,制定该等细则时必须遵循第1999/468/EC号决定第5a条规定的须经欧盟理事会与欧洲议会审查的监管程序。

(5)第2004/109/EC号指令就授予欧盟委员会的实施权设定了时间限制。在其《关于第2006/512/EC号决定的声明》中,欧洲议会、欧盟理事会及欧盟委员会声明,第2006/512/EC号决定提供了一个横向和完善的解决方案,使欧洲议会能实现对依照共同决定程序制定的法律文件的实施情况进行审查的意愿,因此,不必再对授予欧盟委员会的实施权施加时间限制。欧洲议会和欧盟理事会同时宣布,它们将确保其提案尽快通过,废止相关法律文件中就向欧盟委员会授予的实施权设定时限的条款。须经欧盟理事会和欧洲议会审查的监管程序开始实施后,第2004/109/EC号指令中设定该等时限的条款应予删除。

1 2006年10月21日《欧盟公报》C255,第1页。

adopted as rapidly as possible. Following the introduction of the regulatory procedure with scrutiny, the provision establishing that time restriction in Directive 2004/109/EC should be deleted.

(6) The Commission should, at regular intervals, evaluate the functioning of the provisions concerning the implementing powers conferred on it in order to allow the European Parliament and the Council to determine whether the extent of those powers and the procedural requirements imposed on the Commission are appropriate and ensure both efficiency and democratic accountability.

(7) Directive 2004/109/EC should therefore be amended accordingly.

(8) Since the amendments made to Directive 2004/109/EC by this Directive are technical in nature and concern committee procedure only, they do not need to be transposed by the Member States. It is therefore not necessary to lay down provisions to that effect,

HAVE ADOPTED THIS DIRECTIVE:

Article 1 Amendments

Directive 2004/109/EC is hereby amended as follows:

1. Article 2(3) shall be replaced by the following:

'3.In order to take account of technical developments on financial markets and to ensure the uniform application of paragraph 1, the Commission shall, in accordance with the procedures referred to in Article 27(2) and (2a) adopt implementing measures concerning the definitions set out in paragraph 1.

The Commission shall, in particular:

(a) Establish, for the purposes of paragraph 1(i)(ii) the procedural arrangements in accordance with which an issuer may make the choice of the home Member State;

(b) adjust, where appropriate for the purposes of the choice of the home Member State referred to in paragraph 1(i)(ii) the three-year period in relation to the issuer's track record in the light of any new requirement under Community law concerning admission to trading on a regulated market; and

(c) establish, for the purposes of paragraph 1 (l) an indicative list of means which are not to be considered as electronic means, thereby taking into account Annex V to Directive 98/34/EC of the European Parliament and of the Council of 22 June 1998 laying down a procedure for the provision of information in the field of technical standards and regulations and of rules on Information Society services * in accordance with the regulatory procedure referred to in Article 27(2) .

The measures referred to in points (a) and (b) of the second subparagraph, designed to amend non-essential elements of this Directive by supplementing it, shall be adopted in accordance with the regulatory procedure with scrutiny referred to in Article

(6)欧盟委员会应定期评价授予其实施权的条款的运行情况,以便欧洲议会与欧盟理事会判定该等权力的范围及对欧盟委员会施加的程序性要求是否适当,确保效率和民主问责两者兼备。

(7)因此,第2004/109/EC号指令应作出相应修正。

(8)本指令对第2004/109/EC号指令的修正属于技术性的修正,且仅涉及欧盟委员会程序,各成员国不必对其进行转化。因此,不必就成员国的转化作出规定。

兹通过本指令如下:

第1条 修正

第2004/109/EC号指令修正如下:

1.第2条第3款替以如下内容:

"3.为反映金融市场的技术发展动态并确保第1款的统一适用,欧盟委员会应依照第27条第2款和第2a款所述程序,就第1款的定义制定相关实施细则。

欧盟委员会尤应:

(a)为第1款第i项第ii目之目的,建立发行人可据以选择母国的程序性安排;

(b)在对第1款第i项第ii目所述母国选择适当的情形下,根据关于受监管市场交易准入的欧共体法律的任何新要求,调整发行人的3年经营记录期;

(c)为第1款第l项之目的,依照第27条第2款的监管程序制定一份指导性清单,列出不得被视为电子手段之手段,由此反映《欧洲议会与欧盟理事会制定技术标准和规章以及信息社会服务规则领域的信息提供程序的第98/34/EC号指令》(1998年6月22日)*附录五的要求。

第2项第a目和第b目所述的旨在通过补充本指令而修正其非基本要素的细则,应依照第27条第2a款所述的须经欧盟理事会与欧洲议会审查的监管程序制定。

27(2a).

* OJ L 204, 21.7.1998, p. 37. Directive as last amended by Council Directive 2006/96/EC (OJ L 363, 20.12.2006, p. 81).';

2. Article 5(6) shall be amended as follows:

(a) in the first subparagraph, the words ', in accordance with the procedure referred to in Article 27(2)' shall be deleted;

(b) the third subparagraph shall be replaced by the following:

'The measures referred to in point (a) shall be adopted in accordance with the regulatory procedure referred to in Article 27(2). The measures referred to in points (b) and (c) designed to amend non-essential elements of this Directive by supplementing it, shall be adopted in accordance with the regulatory procedure with scrutiny referred to in Article 27(2a).

Where appropriate, the Commission may also adapt the five-year period referred to in paragraph 1. That measure, designed to amend non-essential elements of this Directive, shall be adopted in accordance with the regulatory procedure with scrutiny referred to in Article 27(2a).';

3. Article 9(7) shall be replaced by the following:

'7.The Commission shall adopt implementing measures in order to take account of technical developments on financial markets and to ensure the uniform application of paragraphs 2, 4 and 5. Those measures, designed to amend non-essential elements of this Directive by supplementing it, shall be adopted in accordance with the regulatory procedure with scrutiny referred to in Article 27(2a).

The Commission shall specify the maximum length of the 'short settlement cycle' referred to in paragraph 4 of this Article, as well as the appropriate control mechanisms by the competent authority of the home Member State. Those measures, designed to amend non-essential elements of this Directive by supplementing it, shall be adopted in accordance with the regulatory procedure with scrutiny referred to in Article 27(2a).

In addition, the Commission may draw up a list of the events referred to in paragraph 2 of this Article, in accordance with the regulatory procedure referred to in Article 27(2).';

4. Article 12(8) shall be amended as follows:

(a) the words ', in accordance with the procedure referred to in Article 27(2)' shall be deleted;

(b) the following subparagraph shall be added:

'Those measures, designed to amend non-essential elements of this Directive by supplementing it, shall be adopted in accordance with the regulatory procedure with scrutiny referred to in Article 27(2a).';

* 1998年7月21日《欧盟公报》L204，第37页。该指令由欧盟理事会第2006/96/EC号指令（2006年12月20日《欧盟公报》L363，第81页）作出最新修正。”

2.对第5条第6款修正如下：

（a）删除第1项中的“根据第27条第2款的程序”；

（b）第3项替以如下内容：

“第a目所述的细则，应依照第27条第2款所述的监管程序制定。第b目和第c目所述的旨在通过补充本指令而修正其非基本要素的细则，应依照第27条第2a款所述的须经欧盟理事会与欧洲议会审查的监管程序制定。

适当时，欧盟委员会还可采用第1款所述的5年期。该等旨在修正本指令的非基本要素的细则，应依照第27条第2a款所述的须经欧盟理事会与欧洲议会审查的监管程序制定。”

3.第9条第7款替以如下内容：

“7.为反映金融市场的技术发展动态并确保本条第2款、第4款和第5款的统一适用，欧盟委员会应制定相关实施细则。该等旨在通过补充本指令而修正其非基本要素的细则，应依照第27条第2款第a项所述的须经欧盟理事会与欧洲议会审查的监管程序制定。

欧盟委员会应指明本条第4款中的“短结算周期”的最长时长，以及母国主管部门的适当控制机制。该等旨在通过补充本指令而修正其非基本要素的细则，应依照第27条第2款第a项所述的须经欧盟理事会与欧洲议会审查的监管程序制定。

此外，欧盟委员会可根据第27条第2款所述的监管程序起草一份本条第2款所述事件的清单。”

4.对第12条第8款修正如下：

（a）删除“根据第27条第2款的程序”；

（b）增加如下内容：

“该等旨在通过补充本指令而修正其非基本要素的细则，应依照第27条第2a款所述的须经欧盟理事会和欧洲议会审查的监管程序制定。”

5. Article 13(2) shall be amended as follows:

(a) the words ', in accordance with the procedure referred to in Article 27(2)' shall be deleted;

(b) the following subparagraph shall be added:

'Those measures, designed to amend non-essential elements of this Directive by supplementing it, shall be adopted in accordance with the regulatory procedure with scrutiny referred to in Article 27(2a).';

6. Articles 14(2) 17(4) and 18(5) shall each be amended as follows:

(a) the words ', in accordance with the procedure referred to in Article 27(2)' shall be deleted;

(b) the following sentence shall be added:

'Those measures, designed to amend non-essential elements of this Directive by supplementing it, shall be adopted in accordance with the regulatory procedure with scrutiny referred to in Article 27(2a).';

7. Article 19(4) shall be amended as follows:

(a) in the first subparagraph, the words ', in accordance with the procedure referred to in Article 27(2)' shall be deleted;

(b) the following subparagraph shall be added:

'The measures referred to in the first and second subparagraphs, designed to amend non-essential elements of this Directive by supplementing it, shall be adopted in accordance with the regulatory procedure with scrutiny referred to in Article 27(2a).';

8. Article 21(4) shall be amended as follows:

(a) in the first subparagraph, the words 'in accordance with the procedure referred to in Article 27(2)' shall be deleted;

(b) the following subparagraph shall be added:

'The measures referred to in the first, second and third subparagraphs, designed to amend non-essential elements of this Directive by supplementing it, shall be adopted in accordance with the regulatory procedure with scrutiny referred to in Article 27(2a).';

9. Article 23 shall be amended as follows:

(a) paragraph 4 shall be amended as follows:

(i) the following subparagraph shall be inserted after the first subparagraph:

'In the context of point (ii) of the first subparagraph, the Commission shall also adopt implementing measures concerning the assessment of standards relevant to the issuers of more than one country. Those measures, designed to amend non-essential elements of this Directive by supplementing it, shall be adopted in accordance with the regulatory procedure with scrutiny referred to in Article 27(2a).';

(ii) the following subparagraph shall be added:

5.对第13条第2款修正如下：

（a）删除“根据第27条第2款的程序”；

（b）增加如下内容：

“该等旨在通过补充本指令而修正其非基本要素的细则，应依照第27条第2a款所述的须经欧盟理事会与欧洲议会审查的监管程序制定。”

6.对第14条第2款、第17条第4款和第18条第5款均作如下修正：

（a）删除“根据第27条第2款的程序”；

（b）增加如下内容：

“该等旨在通过补充本指令而修正其非基本要素的细则，应依照第27条第2a款所述的须经欧盟理事会与欧洲议会审查的监管程序制定。”

7.对第19条第4款修正如下：

（a）删除第1项中的“根据第27条第2款的程序”；

（b）增加如下内容：

“第1项和第2项所述的旨在通过补充本指令而修正其非基本要素的细则，应依照第27条第2a款所述的须经欧盟理事会与欧洲议会审查的监管程序制定。”

8.对第21条第4款修正如下：

（a）删除第1项中的“根据第27条第2款的程序”；

（b）增加如下内容：

“第1项、第2项和第3项所述的旨在通过补充本指令而修正其非基本要素的细则，应依照第27条第2a款所述的须经欧盟理事会与欧洲议会审查的监管程序制定。”

9.对第23条修正如下：

（a）对第4款修正如下：

（i）在第1项后插入下项：

“在第1项第ii目的背景下，欧盟委员会还应就涉及1个以上国家的发行人的评估标准制定相关实施细则。该等旨在通过补充本指令而修正其非基本要素的细则，应依照第27条第2a款所述的须经欧盟理事会与欧洲议会审查的监管程序制定。”

（ii）增加如下内容：

'In the context of the previous subparagraph, the Commission shall also adopt implementing measures aimed at establishing general equivalence criteria regarding accounting standards relevant to issuers of more than one country. Those measures, designed to amend non-essential elements of this Directive by supplementing it, shall be adopted in accordance with the regulatory procedure with scrutiny referred to in Article 27(2a).';

(b) paragraph 5 shall be amended as follows:

(i) the words ', in accordance with the procedure referred to in Article 27(2)' shall be deleted;

(ii) the following sentence shall be added:

'Those measures, designed to amend non-essential elements of this Directive by supplementing it, shall be adopted in accordance with the regulatory procedure with scrutiny referred to in Article 27(2a).';

(c) in paragraph 7, the following subparagraph shall be added:

'The Commission shall also adopt implementing measures aimed at establishing general equivalence criteria for the purpose of the first subparagraph. Those measures, designed to amend non-essential elements of this Directive by supplementing it, shall be adopted in accordance with the regulatory procedure with scrutiny referred to in Article 27(2a).';

10. Article 27 shall be amended as follows:

(a) the following paragraph shall be inserted:

'2a. Where reference is made to this paragraph, Article 5a(1) to (4) and Article 7 of Decision 1999/468/EC shall apply, having regard to the provisions of Article 8 thereof.';

(b) paragraphs 3 and 4 shall be replaced by the following:

'3.By 31 December 2010, and, thereafter, at least every three years, the Commission shall review the provisions concerning its implementing powers and present a report to the European Parliament and to the Council on the functioning of those powers. The report shall examine, in particular, the need for the Commission to propose amendments to this Directive in order to ensure the appropriate scope of the implementing powers conferred on the Commission. The conclusion as to whether or not amendment is necessary shall be accompanied by a detailed statement of reasons. If necessary, the report shall be accompanied by a legislative proposal to amend the provisions conferring implementing powers on the Commission'.

Article 2 Entry into force

This Directive shall enter into force on the day following its publication in the *Official Journal of the European Union.*

“在上一项的背景下，欧盟委员会还应就涉及1个以上国家的发行人的会计准则的一般等效标准的建立，制定相关实施细则。该等旨在通过补充本指令而修正其非基本要素的细则，应依照第27条第2a款所述的须经欧盟理事会与欧洲议会审查的监管程序制定。”

(b)对第5款修正如下：

(i)删除“根据第27条第2款所述的程序”；

(ii)增加下句：

“该等旨在通过补充本指令而修正其非基本要素的细则，应依照第27条第2a款所述的须经欧盟理事会与欧洲议会审查的监管程序制定。”

(c)在第7款中增加如下内容：

“欧盟委员会还应为第1项之目的制定旨在建立一般等效标准的实施细则。该等旨在通过补充本指令而修正其非基本要素的细则，应依照第27条第2a款所述的须经欧盟理事会与欧洲议会审查的监管程序制定。”

10.对第27条修正如下：

(a)插入以下条款：

“2a.根据第1999/468/EC号决定第8条规定，引用本款内容时，应适用该决定第5a条第1款至第4款和第7条。”

(b)第3款和第4款替以如下内容：

“3.在2010年12月31日前，欧盟委员会应对关于其实施权的条款进行审评，并就该等权力的运行向欧洲议会与欧盟理事会提交1份报告，此后应至少每3年进行1次审评和报告。报告应着重审查欧盟委员会是否有必要对本指令提出修正案，以确保授予欧盟委员会的实施权维持在适当的范围之内。作出是否有必要进行修正的结论时，应附上详细的理由说明。必要时，报告应附上关于修正授予欧盟委员会实施权的条款的立法提案。”

第2条　生效

本条例应于《欧盟公报》公布，公布的次日生效。

Article 3 Addressees

This Directive is addressed to the Member States.

Done at Strasbourg, 11 March 2008.

For the European Parliament
The President
H.-G. PÖTTERING

For the Council
The President
J. LENARČIČ

第3条　对象

本指令对象为各成员国。

2008年3月11日于斯特拉斯堡通过。

欧洲议会议长	欧盟理事会主席
波特林	莱纳茨

REGULATION (EC) NO 1060/2009 OF THE EUROPEAN PARLIAMENT AND OF THE COUNCIL

欧洲议会与欧盟理事会第 1060/2009 号(欧共体)条例

REGULATION (EC) NO 1060/2009 OF THE EUROPEAN PARLIAMENT AND OF THE COUNCIL

of 16 September 2009
on credit rating agencies
(Text with EEA relevance)

THE EUROPEAN PARLIAMENT AND THE COUNCIL OF THE EUROPEAN UNION,

Having regard to the Treaty establishing the European Community, and in particular Article 95 thereof,

Having regard to the proposal from the Commission,

Having regard to the opinion of the European Economic and Social Committee [1],

Having regard to the opinion of the European Central Bank [2],

Acting in accordance with the procedure laid down in Article 251 of the Treaty [3],

Whereas:

(1) Credit rating agencies play an important role in global securities and banking markets, as their credit ratings are used by investors, borrowers, issuers and governments as part of making informed investment and financing decisions. Credit institutions, investment firms, insurance undertakings, assurance undertakings, reinsurance undertakings, undertakings for collective investment in transferable securities (UCITS) and institutions for occupational retirement provision may use those credit ratings as the

1 Opinion of 13 May 2009 (not yet published in the Official Journal).

2 OJ C 115, 20.5.2009, p. 1.

3 Opinion of the European Parliament of 23 April 2009 (not yet published in the Official Journal) and Council Decision of 27 July 2009.

欧洲议会与欧盟理事会
第1060/2009号(欧共体)条例

(2009年9月16日通过,欧洲经济区适用文本,关于信用评级机构)

欧洲议会与欧盟理事会,

根据《欧洲共同体条约》(以下简称《条约》),特别是其中的第95条,

根据欧盟委员会的提议,
根据欧洲经济与社会委员会的意见,[1]
根据欧洲中央银行的意见,[2]
依照《条约》第251条规定的程序,[3]
鉴于:

(1)投资者、借款人、发行人以及各国政府作出知情的投资和融资决策时,信用评级已成为不可或缺的一项依据,信用评级机构因而在全球证券和金融市场中发挥了重要作用。信贷机构、投资公司、保险公司、担保公司、再保险公司、可转让证券集合投资计划(UCITS)和职业退休基金管理机构在计算偿付能力相关的资本要求或投资活动风险时,均可使用信用评级作为参考。可见,信用评级对市场运行、投资者与消费者对市场的信任和信心均有重大影响。因此,按照诚信、透明、负责及良好治理原则开展

1 2009年5月13日《意见》(尚未在《欧盟公报》公布)。
2 2009年5月20日《欧盟公报》C115,第1页。
3 2009年4月23日欧洲议会意见(尚未在《欧盟公报》公布)和2009年7月27日欧盟理事会决定。

reference for the calculation of their capital requirements for solvency purposes or for calculating risks in their investment activity. Consequently, credit ratings have a significant impact on the operation of the markets and on the trust and confidence of investors and consumers. It is essential, therefore, that credit rating activities are conducted in accordance with the principles of integrity, transparency, responsibility and good governance in order to ensure that resulting credit ratings used in the Community are independent, objective and of adequate quality.

(2) Currently, most credit rating agencies have their headquarters outside the Community. Most Member States do not regulate the activities of credit rating agencies or the conditions for the issuing of credit ratings. Despite their significant importance for the functioning of the financial markets, credit rating agencies are subject to Community law only in limited areas, notably under Directive 2003/6/EC of the European Parliament and of the Council of 28 January 2003 on insider dealing and market manipulation [1]. Moreover, Directive 2006/48/EC of the European Parliament and of the Council of 14 June 2006 relating to the taking up and pursuit of the business of credit institutions [2] and Directive 2006/49/EC of the European Parliament and of the Council of 14 June 2006 on the capital adequacy of investment firms and credit institutions [3] refer to credit rating agencies. It is therefore important to lay down rules ensuring that all credit ratings issued by the credit rating agencies registered in the Community are of adequate quality and issued by credit rating agencies subject to stringent requirements. The Commission will continue to work with its international partners to ensure convergence of the rules applying to credit rating agencies. It should be possible to exempt certain central banks issuing credit ratings from this Regulation provided that they fulfill the relevant applicable conditions which ensure the independence and integrity of their credit rating activities and which are as stringent as the requirements provided for in this Regulation.

(3) This Regulation should not create a general obligation for financial instruments or financial obligations to be rated under this Regulation. In particular, it should not require undertakings for collective investment in transferable securities (UCITS) as defined in Council Directive 85/611/EEC of 20 December 1985 on the coordination of laws, regulations and administrative provisions relating to undertakings for collective investment in transferable securities (UCITS) [4] or institutions for occupational retirement

1 OJ L 96, 12.4.2003, p. 16.

2 OJ L 177, 30.6.2006, p. 1.

3 OJ L 177, 30.6.2006, p. 201.

4 OJ L 375, 31.12.1985, p. 3. Directive replaced, with effect from 1 July 2011, by Directive 2009/65/EC of the European Parliament and of the Council (See page 32 of this Official Journal).

信用评级活动至关重要，可以确保欧共体使用的信用评级独立、客观且质量优良。

（2）目前，大多数信用评级机构总部均设于欧共体以外地区。多数成员国并未对信用评级机构所从事的活动或信用评级的发布条件进行监管。信用评级机构对金融市场运行意义重大，却仅在有限的领域内受欧共体法律的管辖，相关的欧共体管辖法律主要有《欧洲议会与欧盟理事会关于内幕交易和市场操纵的第2003/6/EC号指令》[1]（2003年1月28日）。此外，《欧洲议会与欧盟理事会关于开办和经营信贷机构业务的第2006/48/EC号指令》[2]（2006年6月14日）以及《欧洲议会与欧盟理事会关于投资公司和信贷机构资本充足性的第2006/49/EC号指令》[3]（2006年6月14日）也都涉及信用评级机构。因此，当今重要的是制定相关规则，以确保在欧共体注册的信用评级机构的所有信用评级均质量优良且由信用评级机构按严格的规定发布。欧盟委员会将持续与国际伙伴合作，以确保适用于信用评级机构的规则的趋同。某些发布信用评级的中央银行，只要遵守相关适用条件（其严格程度应与本条例的规定相当）并确保其信用评级活动的独立和诚信度，可豁免于本条例。

（3）本条例不对金融工具或金融债务创设一般性义务，不要求按照本条例对金融工具或金融债券进行评级。本条例尤其不应要求《欧洲经济共同体理事会协调关于可转让证券集合投资计划（UCITS）的法律、法规和规章的第85/611/ECC号指令》[4]（1985年12月20日）所定义的可转让证券集合投资计划或《欧洲议会与欧盟理事会关于职业

---

1 2003年4月12日《欧盟公报》L96，第16页。

2 2006年6月30日《欧盟公报》L177，第1页。

3 2006年6月30日《欧盟公报》L177，第201页。

4 1985年12月31日《欧盟公报》L375，第3页。该指令被欧洲议会和欧盟理事会第2009/65/EC号指令所取代，新指令自2011年7月1日起生效（参见本期《欧盟公报》第32页）。

provision as defined in Directive 2003/41/EC of the European Parliament and of the Council of 3 June 2003 on the activities and supervision of institutions for occupational retirement provision [1] to invest only in financial instruments which are rated under this Regulation.

(4) This Regulation should not create a general obligation for financial institutions or investors to invest only in securities for which a prospectus has been published in accordance with Directive 2003/71/EC of the European Parliament and of the Council of 4 November 2003 on the prospectus to be published when securities are offered to the public or admitted to trading [2] and Commission Regulation (EC) No 809/2004/EC of 29 April 2004 implementing Directive 2003/71/EC as regards information contained in prospectuses as well as the format, incorporation by reference and publication of such prospectuses and dissemination of advertisements [3] and which are rated under this Regulation. In addition, this Regulation should not require the issuers or offerors or persons asking for admission to trading on a regulated market to obtain credit ratings for securities which are subject to the requirement to publish a prospectus under Directive 2003/71/EC and Regulation (EC) No 809/2004.

(5) A prospectus published under Directive 2003/71/EC and Regulation (EC) No 809/2004 should contain clear and prominent information on whether or not the credit rating of the respective securities is issued by a credit rating agency established in the Community and registered under this Regulation. However, nothing in this Regulation should prevent persons responsible for publishing a prospectus under Directive 2003/71/EC and Regulation (EC) No 809/2004 from including any material information in the prospectus, including credit ratings issued in third countries and related information.

(6) In addition to issuing credit ratings and performing credit rating activities, credit rating agencies should also be able to perform ancillary activities on a professional basis. The performance of ancillary activities should not compromise the independence or integrity of credit rating agencies' credit rating activities.

(7) This Regulation should apply to credit ratings issued by credit rating agencies registered in the Community. The principal aim of this Regulation is to protect the stability of financial markets and investors. Credit scores, credit scoring systems and similar assessments related to obligations arising from consumer, commercial or industrial relationships should not fall within the scope of this Regulation.

(8) Credit rating agencies should, on a voluntary basis, apply the Code of Conduct

---

1 OJ L 235, 23.9.2003, p. 10.

2 OJ L 345, 31.12.2003, p. 64.

3 OJ L 149, 30.4.2004, p. 1.

退休基金管理机构的活动与监管的第2003/41/EC号指令》[1]（2003年6月3日）所定义的职业退休基金管理机构只能对根据本条例评级的金融工具进行投资。

(4)本条例不对金融机构或投资者创设一般义务，具体而言，不得规定金融机构或投资者仅能对根据《欧洲议会与欧盟理事会关于向公众发行证券或证券获准交易时所应公布的招募说明书的第2003/71/EC号指令》[2]（2003年11月4日）和《欧盟委员会关于招募说明书所含信息、格式、通过引用方式载入相关规定、公布以及广告传播实施第2003/71/EC号指令的第809/2004/EC号（欧共体）条例》[3]（2004年4月29日）公布了招募说明书并依本条例进行了评级的证券进行投资。此外，本条例不要求发行人或要约人或请求获准在受监管市场交易其证券的人为须按第2003/71/EC号指令和第809/2004号（欧共体）条例公布招募说明书的证券取得信用评级。

(5)根据第2003/71/EC号指令和第809/2004/EC号（欧共体）条例公布的招募说明书应以清楚显著的信息说明证券的信用评级是否由在欧共体设立并根据本条例注册的信用评级机构所发布。然而，本条例任何规定均不妨碍负责根据第2003/71/EC号指令及第809/2004/EC号（欧共体）条例公布招募说明书的人在招募说明书中载入任何重大信息，包括在第三国发布的信用评级及相关信息。

(6)除了发布信用评级和开展信用评级活动外，信用评级机构应当还能进行专业的辅助活动。辅助活动的开展不应影响信用评级机构的信用评级活动的独立性或诚信度。

(7)本条例应适用于在欧共体注册的信用评级机构所发布的信用评级。本条例旨在维护金融市场的稳定和保护投资者。因消费者、商业或行业关系产生的义务的信用评分、信用评分制度和类似评估，不属于本条例的适用范围。

(8)信用评级机构应在自愿的基础上遵行国际证监会组织发布的《信用评级机构

1 2003年9月23日《欧盟公报》L235，第10页。

2 2003年12月31日《欧盟公报》L345，第64页。

3 2004年4月30日《欧盟公报》L149，第1页。

Fundamentals for credit rating agencies issued by the International Organization of Securities Commissions (IOSCO Code) . In 2006, a Communication from the Commission on credit rating agencies [1] invited the Committee of European Securities Regulators (CESR) re-established by Commission Decision 2009/77/EC [2], to monitor compliance with the IOSCO Code and report back to the Commission on an annual basis.

(9) The European Council of 13 and 14 March 2008 agreed to a set of conclusions to respond to the main weaknesses identified in the financial system. One of the objectives was to improve market functioning and incentive structures, including the role of credit rating agencies.

(10) Credit rating agencies are considered to have failed, first, to reflect early enough in their credit ratings the worsening market conditions, and second, to adjust their credit ratings in time following the deepening market crisis. The most appropriate manner in which to correct those failures is by measures relating to conflicts of interest, the quality of the credit ratings, the transparency and internal governance of the credit rating agencies, and the surveillance of the activities of the credit rating agencies. The users of credit ratings should not rely blindly on credit ratings but should take utmost care to perform own analysis and conduct appropriate due diligence at all times regarding their reliance on such credit ratings.

(11) It is necessary to lay down a common framework of rules regarding the enhancement of the quality of credit ratings, in particular the quality of credit ratings to be used by financial institutions and persons regulated by harmonized rules in the Community. In the absence of such a common framework, there is a risk that Member States take diverging measures at national level having a direct negative impact on, and creating obstacles to, the good functioning of the internal market, since the credit rating agencies issuing credit ratings for the use of financial institutions in the Community would be subject to different rules in different Member States. Moreover, diverging quality requirements as regards credit ratings could lead to different levels of investor and consumer protection. Users should, furthermore, be able to compare credit ratings issued in the Community with credit ratings issued internationally.

(12) This Regulation should not affect the use made of credit ratings by persons other than those referred to in this Regulation.

(13) It is desirable to provide for the use of credit ratings issued in third countries for regulatory purposes in the Community provided that they comply with requirements which are as stringent as the requirements provided for in this Regulation. This

1 OJ C 59, 11.3.2006, p. 2.

2 OJ L 25, 29.1.2009, p. 18.

基本行为准则》(IOSCO Code)。2006年,欧盟委员会发出的关于信用评级机构的一份通报[1]要求依据欧盟委员会第2009/77/EC号决定[2]重新设立的欧洲证券监管机构委员会(CESR)负责监控《信用评级机构基本行为准则》的合规情况,并每年向欧盟委员会汇报。

(9)2008年3月13日和14日召开的欧洲理事会会议就若干结论达成了一致,据以对金融系统主要薄弱环节作出回应。其目标之一是要改善市场的运行和激励结构,包括信用评级机构的作用。

(10)信用评级机构被认为在两方面失效。首先,信用评级机构未能在其信用评级中及早反映市场状况的恶化,其次,随着市场危机的深化,信用评级机构未能及时调整其所做的信用评级。纠正该等失误最适当的方式,就是针对利益冲突、信用评级质量、信用评级机构透明度和内部治理以及对信用评级机构活动的监控采取相应的措施。信用评级的使用者不应盲目依赖信用评级,而应始终高度谨慎地对信用评级的可靠程度进行自主的分析并开展适当的尽职调查。

(11)为了改善信用评级质量,特别是受欧共体协调的规则所监管的金融机构和个人所使用的信用评级质量,有必要制定通用的规则框架。缺乏通用框架会引发以下风险:成员国若在各自国内采用不尽相同的措施,发布信用评级供欧共体境内金融机构使用的信用评级机构亦将受不同成员国各自有别的规则所管辖, 此种现象可能对内部市场的良好运行带来直接的负面冲击并构成障碍。此外,信用评级不同的质量要求彼此的差异可能导致投资者和消费者得到的保护程度不同。再者,使用者应能对欧共体境内发布的信用评级以及国际上发布的信用评级进行比较。

(12)本条例不影响未在本条例中述及的人使用信用评级。

(13)出于欧共体监管的目的,宜对在第三国发布的信用评级的使用作出规定,使用在第三国发布的信用评级的前提是,该等信用评级遵守与本条例要求同样严格的要求。本条例引入了一项认可机制,允许在欧共体境内设立并按欧共体规定注册的信

---

1 2006年3月11日《欧盟公报》C59,第2页。

2 2009年1月29日《欧盟公报》L25,第18页。

Regulation introduces an endorsement regime allowing credit rating agencies established in the Community and registered in accordance with its provisions to endorse credit ratings issued in third countries. When endorsing a credit rating issued in a third country, credit rating agencies should determine and monitor, on an ongoing basis, whether credit rating activities resulting in the issuing of such a credit rating comply with requirements for the issuing of credit ratings which are as stringent as those provided for in this Regulation, achieving the same objective and effects in practice.

(14) In order to respond to concerns that lack of establishment in the Community may be a serious impediment to effective supervision in the best interests of the financial markets in the Community, such an endorsement regime should be introduced for credit rating agencies that are affiliated or work closely with credit rating agencies established in the Community. Nevertheless, it may be necessary to adjust the requirement of physical presence in the Community in certain cases, notably as regards smaller credit rating agencies from third countries with no presence or affiliation in the Community. A specific regime of certification for such credit rating agencies should therefore be established, in so far as they are not systemically important for the financial stability or integrity of the financial markets of one or more Member States.

(15) Certification should be possible after determination by the Commission of the equivalence of the legal and supervisory framework of a third country to the requirements of this Regulation. The equivalence mechanism envisaged should not grant automatic access to the Community but should offer the possibility for qualifying credit rating agencies from a third country to be assessed on a case-by-case basis and be granted an exemption from some of the organisational requirements for credit rating agencies active in the Community, including the requirement of physical presence in the Community.

(16) This Regulation should also require a third-country credit rating agency to meet criteria which are general prerequisites for the integrity of its credit rating activities in order to prevent interference with the content of credit ratings by the competent authorities and other public authorities of that third country, and to provide for an adequate conflict of interests policy, rotation of rating analysts and periodic and ongoing disclosure.

(17) Another important prerequisite for a sound endorsement regime and an equivalence system is the existence of sound cooperation arrangements between competent authorities of home Member States and the relevant competent authorities of third-country credit rating agencies.

(18) A credit rating agency that has endorsed credit ratings issued in a third country should be fully and unconditionally responsible for such endorsed credit ratings and for the fulfilment of the relevant conditions referred to in this Regulation.

用评级机构给予在第三国发布的信用评级认可。为认可在第三国发布的信用评级,信用评级机构应对以下事项作出认定和持续监控:请求获得认可的信用评级其相关的信用评级活动遵守了与本条例要求同样严格的要求,在实践中达到了同样的目标和效果。

(14)如果不在欧共体内建立认可机制,可能会有严重阻碍实现欧共体金融市场最佳利益所需的有效监管之忧,为此,应对在欧共体境内设立的信用评级机构的关联评级机构或与其紧密合作的信用评级机构实施上述认可机制。然而,在某些情况下,特别是涉及既未在欧共体境内运营也未与任何欧共体机构有关联的第三国的小型信用评级机构,可能有必要对在欧共体内有实体运营这一要求进行调整。因此,应为该等信用评级机构建立专门的认证机制,前提是该等机构对一个或多个成员国的金融市场的金融稳定性或诚信度不具有系统重要性。

(15)第三国法律和监管框架被欧盟委员会认定与本条例要求具有等效性后,可获得认证。在拟采用的等效机制中,不应许可第三国信用评级机构自动准入欧共体,而应对第三国适格的信用评级机构进行逐一具体评估之后予以准入,并允许其豁免欧共体对欧共体自身境内信用评级机构适用的组织结构要求(包括在欧共体境内应有实体运营的要求)。

(16)本条例还应要求第三国信用评级机构达到一定的标准,该等标准是保证信用评级机构活动诚信度的一般性先决条件,以防止第三国主管部门和其他公共机构干预信用评级内容。本条例同时还应要求第三国信用评级机构对适当的利益冲突政策、评级分析师轮换以及定期持续披露作出规定。

(17)健全的认可机制和等效制度的另一重要先决条件是母国主管部门与第三国信用评级机构相关主管部门之间存在完善的合作安排。

(18)欧共体的信用评级机构认可在第三国发布的信用评级的,应对其认可的该等信用评级以及本条例所述相关条件的满足无条件地负全部责任。

(19) This Regulation should not apply to credit ratings that a credit rating agency produces pursuant to an individual order and provides exclusively to the person who ordered it and which are not intended for public disclosure or distribution by subscription.

(20) Investment research, investment recommendations and other opinions about a value or a price for a financial instrument or a financial obligation should not be considered to be credit ratings.

(21) An unsolicited credit rating, namely a credit rating not initiated at the request of the issuer or rated entity, should be clearly identified as such and should be distinguished from solicited credit ratings by appropriate means.

(22) In order to avoid potential conflicts of interest, credit rating agencies focus in their professional activity on the issuing of credit ratings. A credit rating agency should not be allowed to carry out consultancy or advisory services. In particular, a credit rating agency should not make proposals or recommendations regarding the design of a structured finance instrument. However, credit rating agencies should be able to provide ancillary services where this does not create potential conflicts of interest with the issuing of credit ratings.

(23) Credit rating agencies should use rating methodologies that are rigorous, systematic, continuous and subject to validation including by appropriate historical experience and back-testing. Such a requirement should not, however, provide grounds for interference with the content of credit ratings and methodologies by the competent authorities and the Member States. Similarly, the requirement that credit rating agencies review credit ratings at least annually should not compromise the obligation on credit rating agencies to monitor credit ratings on a continuous basis and review credit ratings as necessary. Those requirements should not be applied in such a way as to prevent new credit rating agencies from entering the market.

(24) Credit ratings should be well-founded and solidly substantiated, in order to avoid rating compromises.

(25) Credit rating agencies should disclose information to the public on the methodologies, models and key rating assumptions which they use in their credit rating activities. The level of detail concerning the disclosure of information concerning models should be such as to give adequate information to the users of credit ratings in order to perform their own due diligence when assessing whether to rely or not on those credit ratings. Disclosure of information concerning models should not, however, reveal sensitive business information or seriously impede innovation.

(26) Credit rating agencies should establish appropriate internal policies and procedures in relation to employees and other persons involved in the credit rating process in order to prevent, identify, eliminate or manage and disclose any conflicts of interest and

(19)本条例不适用于如下所述的信用评级:信用评级机构根据专门的委托做出的私人信用评级,该等评级仅提供给委托方,不公开披露,也不通过订阅方式发送。

(20)投资研究、投资建议和其他关于某金融工具价值或价格或某金融债务的意见,均不应被视为信用评级。

(21)主动作出的信用评级,即并非经证券发行人或被评级实体要求而主动作出的信用评级,应清楚标明其属于主动提供的信用评级,并采用适当方式与按照客户请求提供的信用评级区分开来。

(22)为避免潜在的利益冲突,信用评级机构应专注于信用评级发布这一专业活动。信用评级机构不得开展顾问或咨询服务,尤其不得就结构性金融工具的设计做提议或建议。然而,信用评级机构应能提供辅助服务,前提是辅助服务的提供不会引发与信用评级发布的潜在利益冲突。

(23)信用评级机构应采用严格、系统、持续的评级方法,且该等方法须经适当的历史经验和回溯测试等加以验证。然而,上述要求不应成为主管部门和成员国干预信用评级内容和方法的理由。同样,信用评级机构应至少每年对其信用评级进行一次复核的要求,也不应当对信用评级机构持续监控信用评级并在必要时对信用评级进行复核的义务造成影响。该等要求的适用不得妨碍新的信用评级机构进入市场。

(24)信用评级应有充分的理由和事实根据,以避免评级质量下降。

(25)信用评级机构应向公众披露其在信用评级活动中所使用的评级方法、模型及关键评级假设。所披露的模型信息应足够详细,以便信用评级用户能掌握充分的信息,使其在评估是否可以依赖信用评级时,能自己做尽职调查。然而,模型信息的披露不得泄露敏感商业信息或严重阻碍创新。

(26)信用评级机构应针对员工和其他参与信用评级活动的人制定适当的内部政策与程序,以防范、识别、减少或管理和披露任何利益冲突,并始终确保信用评级及复核程序的质量、诚信度和完整性。上述政策与程序尤应包括内部控制机制和合规

ensure at all times the quality, integrity and thoroughness of the credit rating and review process. Such policies and procedures should, in particular, include the internal control mechanisms and compliance function.

(27) Credit rating agencies should avoid situations of conflict of interest and manage those conflicts adequately when they are unavoidable in order to ensure their independence. Credit rating agencies should disclose conflicts of interest in a timely manner. They should also keep records of all significant threats to the independence of the credit rating agency and that of its employees and other persons involved in the credit rating process, as well as the safeguards applied to mitigate those threats.

(28) A credit rating agency or group of credit rating agencies should maintain arrangements for sound corporate governance. In determining its corporate governance arrangements, the credit rating agency or group of credit rating agencies should have regard to the need to ensure that it issues credit ratings that are independent, objective and of adequate quality.

(29) In order to ensure the independence of the credit rating process from the business interest of the credit rating agency as a company, credit rating agencies should ensure that at least one third, but no less than two, of the members of the administrative or supervisory board are independent in a manner consistent with point 13 in Section III of Commission Recommendation 2005/162/EC of 15 February 2005 on the role of non-executive or supervisory directors of listed companies and on the committees of the (supervisory) board [1]. Moreover, it is necessary that the majority of the senior management, including all independent members of the administrative or supervisory board, have sufficient expertise in appropriate areas of financial services. The compliance officer should report regularly on the carrying out of his or her duties to the senior management and the independent members of the administrative or supervisory board.

(30) In order to avoid conflicts of interest, the compensation of independent members of the administrative or supervisory board should not depend on the business performance of the credit rating agency.

(31) A credit rating agency should allocate a sufficient number of employees with appropriate knowledge and experience to its credit rating activities. In particular, the credit rating agency should ensure that adequate human and financial resources are allocated to the issuing, monitoring and updating of credit ratings.

(32) In order to take account of the specific condition of credit rating agencies that have fewer than 50 employees, the competent authorities should be able to exempt such

1 OJ L 52, 25.2.2005, p. 51.

职能。

(27)信用评级机构应避免发生利益冲突,并在无法避免冲突时对冲突进行适当管理以确保自身独立性。信用评级机构应及时披露利益冲突。对于所有影响信用评级机构及其员工和参与信用评级活动的其他人独立性的重大威胁,信用评级机构均应保存相关记录,同时还应对其所采取的缓释威胁的保障措施保存相关记录。

(28)信用评级机构或信用评级机构集团应维持良好的公司治理安排。信用评级机构或信用评级机构集团设置其公司治理安排时,应考虑其发布的信用评级要做到独立、客观且质量优良。

(29)为确保信用评级活动不受信用评级机构公司的商业利益影响,信用评级机构应确保其董事会或监事会至少1/3(但不少于2名)成员具备符合《欧盟委员会关于上市公司非执行董事或监事的作用和关于监事会下属委员会的第2005/162/EC号建议》[1](2005年2月15日)第3节第13项标准的独立性。此外,包括董事会所有独立董事或监事会所有独立监事在内的大多数高级管理人员均应在有关的金融服务领域具有充分的专业知识。合规官应定期向高级管理人员和独立董事或独立监事报告其职务履行情况。

(30)为避免利益冲突,董事会所有独立董事或监事会独立监事的薪酬不应与信用评级机构的业绩挂钩。

(31)信用评级机构应为其信用评级活动配置足够数量的具备适当知识和经验的人员。信用评级机构尤其应确保为信用评级的发布、监控及更新配置充分的人力和财力。

(32)鉴于员工少于50人的信用评级机构的特殊情况,主管部门应能豁免该等信用评级机构履行本条例中关于独立董事或独立监事的作用、合规职能及轮换机制的

1 2005年2月25日《欧盟公报》L52,第51页。

credit rating agencies from some of the obligations laid down by this Regulation as regards the role of the independent members of the board, the compliance function and the rotation mechanism, and provided that those credit rating agencies are able to demonstrate that they comply with specific conditions. The competent authorities should examine, in particular, whether the size of a credit rating agency has been determined in such a way as to avoid compliance with the requirements of this Regulation by the credit rating agency or by a group of credit rating agencies. The application of the exemption by competent authorities of Member States should be made in such a way as to avoid the risks of fragmenting the internal market and to guarantee the uniform application of Community law.

(33) Long-lasting relationships with the same rated entities or their related third parties could compromise the independence of rating analysts and persons approving credit ratings. Those analysts and persons should therefore be subject to an appropriate rotation mechanism which should provide for a gradual change in analytical teams and credit rating committees.

(34) Credit rating agencies should ensure that methodologies, models and key rating assumptions such as mathematical or correlation assumptions used for determining credit ratings are properly maintained, up-to-date and subject to a comprehensive review on a periodic basis and that their descriptions are published in a manner permitting comprehensive review. In cases where the lack of reliable data or the complexity of the structure of a new type of financial instrument, in particular structured finance instruments, raises serious questions as to whether the credit rating agency can produce a credible credit rating, the credit rating agency should not issue a credit rating or should withdraw an existing credit rating. Changes in the quality of information available for monitoring an existing credit rating should be disclosed with that review and, if appropriate, a revision of the credit rating should be made.

(35) In order to ensure the quality of credit ratings, a credit rating agency should take measures to ensure that the information it uses in assigning a credit rating is reliable. For that purpose, a credit rating agency should be able to envisage, inter alia, reliance on independently audited financial statements and public disclosures; verification by reputable third-party services; random sampling examination of the information received; or contractual provisions clearly stipulating liability for the rated entity or its related third parties, if the information provided under the contract is knowingly materially false or misleading or if the rated entity or its related third parties fail to conduct reasonable due diligence regarding the accuracy of the information as specified under the terms of the contract.

(36) This Regulation is without prejudice to the duty of credit rating agencies to

部分义务,前提是该等信用评级机构应能证明其满足特定条件。考虑到信用评级机构或信用评级机构集团所应遵守的本条例规定,主管部门尤应核查信用评级机构是否刻意将其规模设定在可以规避该等规定的水平。成员国主管部门执行豁免规则时,应当避免引发内部市场分散的风险,并应保证欧共体法律得到统一适用。

(33)分析师和信用评级批准人员如果和相同的被评级实体或其相关第三方形成长期关系,可能会削弱评级分析师和信用评级批准人员的独立性。因此,分析师和批准人员应实行适当的轮换机制,根据该机制逐步替换分析团队成员和信用评级委员会成员。

(34)信用评级机构应确保用于确定信用评级的方法、模型以及关键评级假设(如数学或关联假设)得到妥善的维持和更新,并定期全面复核,同时,该等方法、模型及假设的说明应以方便全面复核进行的方式公布。如果由于缺乏可靠的数据,或由于某种新型金融工具(特别是结构性金融工具)结构的复杂程度较高,令人严重质疑信用评级机构是否有能力提供可信的信用评级,则信用评级机构不得发布所涉信用评级,或者其应撤销现有的信用评级。用于监控现有信用评级的相关信息一旦出现质量变化,应与该项复核一并披露,适当时还应对信用评级进行修改。

(35)为确保信用评级的质量,信用评级机构应采取相关措施以确保作为其信用评级依据的信息是可靠的信息。为此,信用评级机构应当能做到包括但不限于下列各项:以经独立审计的财务报表和公开披露的信息作为评级依据;通过声誉良好的第三方服务进行信息的核实;对所收到信息进行随机抽样检查;或设置相应的合同条款明确规定:明知信息有重大错误或具误导性但仍根据合同提供信息的,或者被评级实体或其相关第三方未就合同条款所指明的信息的准确性进行合理的尽职调查的,被评级实体或其相关第三方应承担何等法律责任。

(36)本条例不影响信用评级机构在根据《欧洲议会与欧盟理事会关于处理个人

protect the right to privacy of natural persons with respect to the processing of personal data in accordance with Directive 95/46/EC of the European Parliament and of the Council of 24 October 1995 on the protection of individuals with regard to the processing of personal data and on the free movement of such data [1].

(37) It is necessary for credit rating agencies to establish proper procedures for the regular review of methodologies, models and key rating assumptions used by the credit rating agency in order to be able to properly reflect the changing conditions in the underlying asset markets. With a view to ensuring transparency, disclosure of any material modification to the methodologies and practices, procedures and processes of credit rating agencies should be made prior to their coming into effect, unless extreme market conditions require an immediate change in the credit rating.

(38) A credit rating agency should indicate any appropriate risk warning, including a sensitivity analysis of the relevant assumptions. That analysis should explain how various market developments that move the parameters built into the model may influence the credit rating changes (for example volatility) . The credit rating agency should ensure that the information on historical default rates of its rating categories is verifiable and quantifiable and provides a sufficient basis for interested parties to understand the historical performance of each rating category and if and how rating categories have changed. If the nature of the credit rating or other circumstances makes a historical default rate inappropriate, statistically invalid, or otherwise likely to mislead the users of the credit rating, the credit rating agency should provide appropriate clarification. That information should, to the extent possible, be comparable with any existing industry patterns in order to assist investors in drawing performance comparisons between different credit rating agencies.

(39) In order to reinforce transparency of credit ratings and contribute to the protection of investors, CESR should maintain a central repository where information on the past performances of credit rating agencies and information about credit ratings issued in the past should be kept. Credit rating agencies should provide information to that repository in standardised form. CESR should make that information available to the public and should, annually, publish summary information on the main developments observed.

(40) Under certain circumstances structured finance instruments may have effects which are different from traditional corporate debt instruments. It could be misleading for investors to apply the same rating categories to both types of instruments without further explanation. Credit rating agencies should play an important role in raising awareness of

1 OJ L 281, 23.11.1995, p. 31.

资料时对个人的保护以及该等资料的自由流动的第95/46/EC号指令》[1](1995年10月24日)处理个人资料时负有保护自然人隐私权的义务。

(37)信用评级机构有必要对自身所使用的方法、模型及关键评级假设建立妥善的定期复核程序,以便能恰当地反映标的资产市场状况的变化。为确保透明度,如信用评级机构的评级方法和惯例、流程和程序出现任何重大更改,应当于该等更改生效前完成其披露,但是,极端市场状况导致必须立即变更信用评级的情况除外。

(38)信用评级机构应提出适当的风险警示,包括相关假设的敏感性分析。该项分析应解释,改变模型内置参数的各种市场变化可能会如何影响信用评级的变更(如波动性)。信用评级机构应确保其不同类别评级的历史违约率信息可以核实和量化,还应确保其提供了充分的依据,使利益相关方能了解各类别评级的历史业绩、评级类别是否出现过变更以及相应的变更方式。如果由于信用评级的性质或其他情况,导致出现不当历史违约率、在统计上无效或可能误导信用评级用户的情形,则信用评级机构应作出适当的澄清。该等信息应尽可能与信用评级业内现有的信息模式相当,以方便投资者对不同信用评级机构的业绩进行比较。

(39)为加强信用评级的透明度并保护投资者,欧洲证券监管机构委员会(CESR)应维持一个中央数据存管机构,保存关于信用评级机构的历史业绩以及与过去所发布的信用评级相关的信息。信用评级机构应以标准格式向数据存管机构提供信息。欧洲证券监管机构委员会应向公众公开该等信息,每年公布关于其所观察到的主要变化的摘要信息。

(40)在某些情形下,结构性金融工具造成的影响可能有别于传统的公司债务工具。投资者如果不作进一步解读即将相同的评级类别运用到两种不同类型的金融工具上,可能会被误导。信用评级机构应就此发挥重要的作用,提醒信用评级用户结构性金融产品与传统产品之间的具体差别。因此,信用评级机构应在评级类别上标注适

1 1995年11月23日《欧盟公报》L281,第31页。

the users of credit ratings about the specificities of the structured finance products in relation to traditional ones. Credit rating agencies should therefore clearly differentiate between rating categories used for rating structured finance instruments on the one hand, and rating categories used for other financial instruments or financial obligations on the other, by adding an appropriate symbol to the rating category.

(41) Credit rating agencies should take measures to avoid situations where issuers request the preliminary rating assessment of the structured finance instrument concerned from a number of credit rating agencies in order to identify the one offering the best credit rating for the proposed structure. Issuers should also avoid applying such practices.

(42) A credit rating agency should keep records of the methodology for credit ratings and regularly update changes thereto and also keep a record of the substantial elements of the dialogue between the rating analyst and the rated entity or its related third parties.

(43) In order to ensure a high level of investor and consumer confidence in the internal market, credit rating agencies which issue credit ratings in the Community should be subject to registration. Such a registration is the principal prerequisite for credit rating agencies to issue credit ratings intended to be used for regulatory purposes in the Community. It is therefore necessary to lay down the harmonised conditions and the procedure for the granting, suspension and withdrawal of such registration.

(44) This Regulation should not replace the established process of recognising External Credit Assessment Institutions (ECAIs) in accordance with Directive 2006/48/EC. The ECAIs already recognised in the Community should apply for registration in accordance with this Regulation.

(45) A credit rating agency registered by the competent authority of the relevant Member State should be allowed to issue credit ratings throughout the Community. It is therefore necessary to establish a single registration procedure for each credit rating agency which is effective throughout the Community. The registration of a credit rating agency should become effective once the registration decision issued by the competent authority of the home Member State has taken effect under relevant national law.

(46) It is necessary to establish a single point of entry for the submission of applications for registration. CESR should receive applications for registration and effectively inform the competent authorities in all the Member States. CESR should also provide advice in respect of the completeness of the application to the competent authority of the home Member State. The examination of applications for registration should be carried out at national level by the relevant competent authority. In order to deal efficiently with credit rating agencies, competent authorities should set up operational networks (colleges) supported by an efficient information technology infrastructure. CESR should establish a subcommittee specialised in the field of credit ratings of each of the

当记号,明确区分用于结构性金融工具的评级类别以及用于其他金融工具或金融债务的评级类别。

(41)信用评级机构应采取相关措施以避免以下情形:发行人同时请多家信用评级机构对结构性金融工具进行初步评级评估,然后从中挑选对所涉金融工具结构给予最好信用评级的信用评级机构。

(42)信用评级机构应保存信用评级方法的记录、定期更新评级方法的变更,并对评级分析师和被评级实体或其相关第三方之间交流的实质内容保持记录。

(43)为确保投资者及消费者对内部市场的高度信心,在欧共体境内发布信用评级的信用评级机构均应进行注册。作为欧共体监管的手段,该等注册是信用评级机构发布信用评级主要的先决条件。因此,有必要为上述注册的核准、暂停及撤销制定协调一致的条件和程序。

(44)本条例不应取代根据第2006/48/EC号指令认可外部信用评估机构(ECAI)的既有程序。已经在欧共体获得认可的外部信用评估机构应依照本条例申请注册。

(45)在相关成员国主管部门注册的信用评级机构应获准在全欧共体境内发布信用评级。因此,有必要为信用评级机构建立在全欧共体境内有效的单一注册程序。母国主管部门发布的注册决定根据相关的国内法律生效之时,信用评级机构的注册开始有效。

(46)有必要确定统一的注册申请材料递交窗口。欧洲证券监管机构委员会应当负责接收注册申请,并且有效地通知所有成员国的主管部门。欧洲证券监管机构委员会还应向母国主管部门提供关于申请材料完整性的建议。注册申请的审核应由成员国相关主管部门完成。为高效管理与信用评级机构的日常往来,主管部门应在高效率的信息技术基础设施的支持下建立负责具体运营事务的网络(即运营团)。欧洲证券监管机构委员会应针对信用评级机构所评的每一资产类别的信用评级分别建立专门的小组委员会。

asset classes rated by credit rating agencies.

(47) Some credit rating agencies are composed of several legal entities which, together, form a group of credit rating agencies. When registering each of the credit rating agencies being part of such a group, the competent authorities of the Member States concerned should coordinate the examination of the applications submitted by credit rating agencies belonging to the same group and the decision-making concerning the granting of registration. It should be possible, however, to refuse registration to a credit rating agency within a group of credit rating agencies when such a credit rating agency does not meet the requirements for registration while other members of such a group comply with all of the requirements for registration under this Regulation. As the college should not be entrusted with power to issue legally binding decisions, the competent authorities of home Member States of the members of the group of credit rating agencies should each issue an individual decision in respect of the credit rating agency established on the territory of the Member State concerned.

(48) The college should represent the effective platform for an exchange of supervisory information among competent authorities, coordination of their activities and supervisory measures necessary for the effective supervision of credit rating agencies. In particular, the college should facilitate the monitoring of the fulfilment of conditions for the endorsement of credit ratings issued in third countries, certification, outsourcing arrangements, and exemptions provided for in this Regulation. The activities of the college should contribute to the harmonised application of rules under this Regulation and to the convergence of supervisory practices.

(49) In order to enhance the practical coordination of activities of the college, its members should select among themselves a facilitator. The facilitator should chair the meetings of the college, establish its written coordination arrangements and coordinate its actions. During the registration process, the facilitator should assess the need to extend the period for examination of applications, coordinate such examination, and liaise with CESR.

(50) In November 2008, the Commission set up a high level group with the task of examining the future European supervisory architecture in the field of financial services, including the role of CESR.

(51) The current supervisory architecture should not be considered as the long-term solution for the oversight of credit rating agencies. Colleges of competent authorities, which are expected to streamline supervisory cooperation and convergence in this area in the Community, are a considerable step forward, but may not substitute all the advantages of more consolidated supervision of the credit rating industry. The crisis in international financial markets has clearly demonstrated that it is appropriate to examine further the

(47)某些信用评级机构由多名法人实体组成，该等法人实体共同形成了一个信用评级机构集团。作为集团一部分的各个信用评级机构注册时，所涉母国主管部门应协调其对同一集团下属不同信用评级机构递交的申请材料的审核工作，并协调注册核准的决策程序。然而，信用评级机构集团下属的某个信用评级机构达不到注册要求的，即使集团其他成员符合本条例所有注册要求，主管部门也可以拒绝对未达到要求的信用评级机构进行注册。主管部门不得授予运营团作出具有法律约束力的决定的权力，因此，信用评级机构集团下属成员的不同母国的主管部门，应针对设立于其境内的信用评级机构各自作出决定。

(48)运营团是主管部门之间有效交换监管信息的平台，各主管部门的活动以及有效监管信用评级机构所必不可少的监管措施均通过运营团得到协调。运营团尤应促进下列各项的监控：在第三国发布的信用评级获得认可的条件的满足情况、认证、外包安排及本条例规定的豁免。运营团在其活动中应致力于协调依本条例制定的规则的适用以及监管惯例的趋同。

(49)为加强运营团活动的实际协调，其成员应从彼此当中遴选一名督导员。督导员应主持运营团会议、建立运营团的书面协调安排并协调运营团的行动。注册过程中，督导员应评估申请审核期限延长的需要、协调审核工作并负责与欧洲证券监管机构委员会联络。

(50)2008年11月，欧盟委员会成立了一个高级工作组，负责审议未来欧洲金融服务领域的监管架构，包括欧洲证券监管机构委员会的作用。

(51)目前的监管架构不应视为信用评级机构监控工作的长期解决方案。通过设立主管部门的运营团，欧共体在信用评级机构领域中的监管合作和趋同预期会变得更为顺畅，从而迈出重要的一步，但欧共体仍然需要更高度整合信用评级行业监管，发挥运营团所不具备的作用。国际金融市场的危机已清楚证明，应当进一步审视大范围改革欧共体金融业规制与监管模式的必要性。为在欧共体达到必要程度的监管趋同及合作，巩固金融系统的稳定，亟须进一步扩大欧共体金融业规制与监管模式的改

need for wide-ranging reforms of the regulatory and supervisory model of the Community financial sector. In order to achieve the necessary level of Community supervisory convergence and cooperation and to underpin the stability of the financial system, further wide-ranging reforms of the regulatory and supervisory model of the Community financial sector are highly needed and should be put forward swiftly by the Commission with due consideration to the conclusions presented by the group of experts chaired by Jacques de Larosière on 25 February 2009. The Commission should, as soon as possible, and in any event by 1 July 2010, report to the European Parliament, the Council and other institutions concerned any findings in this respect and should put forward any legislative proposal needed to tackle the shortcomings identified as regards supervisory coordination and cooperation arrangements.

(52) Significant changes in the endorsement regime, outsourcing arrangements as well as the opening and closing of branches should, inter alia, be considered as material changes to the conditions for initial registration of a credit rating agency.

(53) The supervision of a credit rating agency should be carried out by the competent authority of the home Member State in cooperation with the competent authorities of the other Member States concerned, using the relevant college and keeping CESR appropriately involved.

(54) The ability of the competent authority of the home Member State and other members of the relevant college to assess and monitor compliance of a credit rating agency with the obligations provided for under this Regulation should not be limited by any outsourcing arrangements entered into by the credit rating agency. The credit rating agency should remain responsible for any of its obligations under this Regulation in the event of the use of outsourcing arrangements.

(55) In order to maintain a high level of investor and consumer confidence and enable the ongoing supervision of credit ratings issued in the Community, credit rating agencies whose headquarters are located outside the Community should be required to set up a subsidiary in the Community in order to allow for the efficient supervision of their activities in the Community and the effective use of the endorsement regime. The emergence of new actors on the credit rating agency market should also be encouraged.

(56) The competent authorities should be able to use powers defined in this Regulation in relation to credit rating agencies, persons involved in credit rating activities, rated entities and related third parties, third parties to whom the credit rating agencies have outsourced certain functions or activities, and other persons otherwise related or connected to credit rating agencies or credit rating activities. Such persons should include shareholders or members of the supervisory or administrative boards of the credit rating agencies and rated entities.

革范畴,欧盟委员会充分考虑雅克·德·拉罗西埃领导的专家小组于2009年2月25日做出的结论后,应迅速推进改革。欧盟委员会应尽快且最晚于2010年7月1日前,向欧洲议会、欧盟理事会以及其他所涉机构报告相关研究结果,并提出必要的立法提案,以解决监管协调和合作安排中出现的缺失。

(52)涉及认可机制、外包安排和分支机构的开设和关闭等的重大变更,应被视为信用评级机构首次注册条件的实质变更。

(53)母国主管部门应当与其他所涉成员国的主管部门合作,通过相关的运营团共同对信用评级机构进行监管,并保持欧洲证券监管机构委员会适当地参与监管。

(54)母国主管部门与相关运营团的其他成员评估和监控信用评级机构是否遵守本条例中的信用评级机构义务的能力,不应受该信用评级机构订立的任何外包安排的限制。信用评级机构使用外包安排时,仍应对其在本条例中的义务负责。

(55)为维持投资者与消费者的高度信心,并实现对欧共体境内发布的信用评级的持续监管,应要求总部位于欧共体境外的信用评级机构在欧共体境内设立子公司,以期高效率地监管其在欧共体境内的活动并有效地运用认可机制。此外也应鼓励新的市场主体加入信用评级机构市场。

(56)主管部门应能运用本条例就以下主体所界定的权力:信用评级机构、参与信用评级活动的人员、被评级实体及其相关第三方、承接信用评级机构外包的某些职能或活动的第三方以及与信用评级机构或信用评级活动相关或关联的其他人员。上述主体应包括信用评级机构和被评级实体的股东或其监事会或董事会的成员。

(57) The provisions of this Regulation regarding supervisory fees should be without prejudice to relevant provisions of national law governing supervisory or similar fees.

(58) It is appropriate to create a mechanism to ensure the effective enforcement of this Regulation. The competent authorities of the Member States should have at their disposal the necessary means to ensure that ratings issued in the Community are issued in compliance with this Regulation. The use of these supervisory measures should always be coordinated within the relevant college. Measures such as the withdrawal of registration or the suspension of the use for regulatory purposes of credit ratings should be imposed when they are considered to be proportionate to the significance of the breach of the obligations arising from this Regulation. In exercising their supervisory powers, competent authorities should have due regard to the interests of investors and market stability. Since the independence of a credit rating agency in the process of issuing its credit ratings should be preserved, neither the competent authorities nor the Member States should interfere in relation to the substance of credit ratings and the methodologies by which a credit rating agency determines credit ratings in order to avoid credit ratings to be compromised. In the event that a credit rating agency is subjected to pressure, it should notify the Commission and CESR. The Commission should examine on a case-by-case basis whether further action is to be taken against the Member State concerned for failure to comply with its obligations under this Regulation.

(59) It is desirable to ensure that decision-making referred to in this Regulation be based on close cooperation between the Member States' competent authorities, and the adoption of the registration decisions should therefore take place on the basis of an agreement. This is a necessary prerequisite for the efficient process of registration and performance of supervision. The decision-making should be effective, expeditious and consensual.

(60) For the efficiency of supervision and in order to avoid duplication of tasks, the competent authorities of the Member States should cooperate.

(61) It is also important to provide for exchange of information between competent authorities responsible for supervision of credit rating agencies under this Regulation and competent authorities supervising financial institutions, in particular those responsible for prudential supervision or financial stability in the Member States.

(62) The competent authorities of Member States other than the competent authority of the home Member State should be able to intervene and take appropriate supervisory measures, after informing CESR and the competent authority of the home Member State and after consulting the relevant college in the event that they have established that a registered credit rating agency whose ratings are used within their territory breaches the obligations arising from this Regulation.

(57)本条例关于监管费的规定不应影响成员国国内法律对监管费或类似费用作出的相关规定。

(58)应建立一项机制以确保本条例的有效执行。成员国主管部门应拥有必要的手段来确保信用评级在欧共体境内按照本条例的规定发布。该等监管措施的使用应当始终在相关的运营团内得到协调。诸如撤销注册或因监管原因暂停信用评级的使用等措施,在主管部门认为与违规者对本条例义务违反的严重程度成比例时,方得采用。主管部门在行使其监管权力时,应充分考虑投资者利益及市场稳定性。鉴于信用评级机构在发布信用评级过程中应保持其独立性,主管部门或成员国均不应干预信用评级的实质内容以及信用评级机构确定信用评级的方法,以免信用评级受到影响。信用评级机构遭受压力时,应通知欧盟委员会和欧洲证券监管机构委员会。欧盟委员会应视具体情形审议是否应对未遵守本条例义务的成员国采取进一步行动。

(59)宜确保本条例述及的决策以成员国主管部门之间的紧密合作为基础,因此,注册决定也应根据成员国主管部门之间的一致意见通过。这是实现高效率的注册程序和监管所必要的先决条件。决策应当有效、迅速且基于各方的共识。

(60)为了实现高效率的监管和避免职责的重复,成员国主管部门应相互合作。

(61)同时,对负责按照本条例监管信用评级机构的主管部门以及监管金融机构的主管部门(特别是成员国负责审慎监管或金融稳定的主管部门)彼此之间的信息交换作出规定,也相当重要。

(62)非母国主管部门的其他成员国主管部门如确认,其评级在该国境内使用的某注册信用评级机构违反了本条例的义务,则应能在通知欧洲证券监管机构委员会与母国主管部门并咨询相关运营团后进行干预并采取适当的监管措施。

(63) Unless this Regulation provides for a specific procedure as regards registration, certification or withdrawal thereof, the adoption of supervisory measures or the performance of supervisory powers, the national law governing such procedures including linguistic regimes, professional secrecy and legal professional privilege , should apply and the rights of the credit rating agencies and other persons under that law should not be affected.

(64) It is necessary to enhance convergence of the powers at the disposal of the competent authorities in order to achieve an equivalent intensity of enforcement across the internal market.

(65) CESR should ensure coherence in the application of this Regulation. It should enhance and facilitate the cooperation and coordination of competent authorities in supervisory activities and issue guidance where appropriate. CESR should therefore establish a mediation mechanism and peer review in order to facilitate a coherent approach by the competent authorities.

(66) Member States should lay down rules on penalties applicable to infringements of the provisions of this Regulation and ensure that they are implemented. Those penalties should be effective, proportionate and dissuasive and should at least cover cases of gross professional misconduct and lack of due diligence. It should be possible for Member States to provide for administrative or criminal penalties. CESR should establish guidelines on the convergence of practices relating to such penalties.

(67) Any exchange or transmission of information between competent authorities, other authorities, bodies or persons should be in accordance with the rules on transfer of personal data as laid down in Directive 95/46/EC.

(68) This Regulation should also provide for rules relating to exchange of information with competent authorities in third countries, particularly with those responsible for the supervision of the credit rating agencies involved in endorsement and certification.

(69) Without prejudice to the application of Community law, any claim against credit rating agencies in relation to any infringement of the provisions of this Regulation should be made in accordance with the applicable national law on civil liability.

(70) The measures necessary for the implementation of this Regulation should be adopted in accordance with Council Decision 1999/468/EC of 28 June 1999 laying down the procedures for the exercise of implementing powers conferred on the Commission [1].

(71) In particular, the Commission should be empowered, while taking account of international developments, to amend Annexes I and II, which lay down the specific

1 OJ L 184, 17.7.1999, p. 23.

（63）除非本条例就注册、认证或注册撤销、认证撤销或监管措施的制定或监管权的履行规定了特殊程序，否则应适用成员国规范上述程序的法律，包括语言规则、职业保密及法律职业保密权，并且信用评级机构及其他人在该等法律中的权利不应受到影响。

（64）有必要加强主管部门权力的趋同，在内部市场达到同等水平的执法力度。

（65）欧洲证券监管机构委员会应当确保本条例适用的趋同。欧洲证券监管机构委员会应当加强和促进主管部门在监管活动方面的合作与协调，发布适当的指引。因此，欧洲证券监管机构委员会应建立调解机制和同行审评制度，推动主管部门采取一致的监管模式。

（66）成员国应针对违反本条例规定的行为制定罚则并确保其得以实施。该等罚则应当有效、成比例且具有威慑作用，适用范围至少应涵盖重大失职行为和未履行尽职调查的情形。成员国应当能作出行政或刑事处罚的相关规定。欧洲证券监管机构委员会应就处罚惯例的趋同制定指引。

（67）主管部门、其他部门、机构或个人之间任何信息的交换或传送均应遵守第95/46/EC号指令所规定的关于个人数据转移的规则。

（68）本条例还应为成员国主管部门与第三国主管部门（特别是负责监管作出认可和认证的信用评级机构的主管部门）之间的信息交换制定规则。

（69）在不影响欧共体法律适用的情形下，就信用评级机构违反本条例规定的行为提出的任何权利主张，均应依照各成员国适用的民事责任法提出。

（70）本条例的适用所需的实施细则，应依照《欧盟理事会关于制定欧盟委员会行使其被授予的实施权之程序的第1999/468/EC号决定》[1]（1999年6月28日）制定。

（71）考虑到国际变化，欧盟委员会尤应被授予修正附录一和附录二（该等附录列出了信用评级机构对以下各项的合规的评估标准：内部组织、运营安排、员工规则、信

1 1999 年 7 月 17 日《欧盟公报》L184，第 23 页。

criteria for assessing the compliance of a credit rating agency with its duties in terms of internal organisation, operational arrangements, rules on employees, presentation of credit ratings and disclosure, and to specify or amend the criteria for determining the equivalence of the regulatory and supervisory legal framework of third countries with the provisions of this Regulation. Since those measures are of general scope and are designed to amend non-essential elements of this Regulation, inter alia, by supplementing it with new non-essential elements, they must be adopted in accordance with the regulatory procedure with scrutiny provided for in Article 5a of Decision 1999/468/EC.

(72) With a view to taking into account further developments in the financial markets, the Commission should submit a report to the European Parliament and the Council assessing the application of this Regulation, in particular the regulatory reliance on credit ratings as well as the appropriateness of the remuneration of the credit rating agency by the rated entity. In the light of that assessment, the Commission should put forward appropriate legislative proposals.

(73) The Commission should also submit a report to the European Parliament and the Council assessing incentives for issuers to use credit rating agencies established in the Community for a proportion of their ratings, possible alternatives to the 'issuer-pays' model including the creation of a public Community credit rating agency, and convergence of national rules concerning infringements of the provisions of this Regulation. In the light of that assessment, the Commission should put forward appropriate legislative proposals.

(74) The Commission should also submit a report to the European Parliament and the Council assessing developments in the regulatory and supervisory framework for credit rating agencies in third countries and the effects of those developments and of transitional provisions referred to in this Regulation on the stability of the financial markets in the Community.

(75) Since the objective of this Regulation, namely to ensure a high level of consumer and investor protection by laying down a common framework with regard to the quality of credit ratings to be issued in the internal market, cannot be sufficiently achieved by the Member States, given the current scarcity of national legislation in this field and the fact that the majority of existing credit rating agencies are established outside the Community, and can therefore be better achieved at Community level, the Community may adopt measures, in accordance with the principle of subsidiarity as set out in Article 5 of the Treaty. In accordance with the principle of proportionality, as set out in that Article, this Regulation does not go beyond what is necessary in order to achieve that objective,

HAVE ADOPTED THIS REGULATION:

用评级的列报方式和披露）的权力，规定或修正认定第三国的规制和监管法律框架是否与本条例规定等效的标准。由于该等细则属于具有一般适用范围的细则，且旨在通过补充本条例等方式而修正其中的非基本要素，因此其制定必须遵循第1999/468/EC号决定第5a条所规定的须经欧盟理事会和欧洲议会审查的监管程序。

（72）为反映金融市场的新变化，欧盟委员会应向欧洲议会与欧盟理事会呈报一份报告，评价本条例的适用情况，尤其是评价将信用评级用于监管的可靠性以及被评级实体向信用评级机构支付报酬的适当性。欧盟委员会应根据该项评价提出适当的立法提案。

（73）欧盟委员会还应向欧洲议会与欧盟理事会呈报一份报告，评估发行人大量使用在欧共体内设立的信用评级机构的动机、“发行人付费”可能的替代模式（包括设立欧共体公众信用评级机构）以及成员国对违反本条例的行为各自处理规则的趋同。欧盟委员会应当根据该项评估提出适当的立法提案。

（74）欧盟委员会还应向欧洲议会与欧盟理事会呈报一份报告，评价第三国信用评级机构的规制和监管框架的发展，以及该等发展和本条例所述的过渡规定对欧共体金融市场稳定性的影响。

（75）本条例的目标是要为内部市场发布的信用评级质量制定通用的框架，从而确保对消费者和投资者的高标准保护，而鉴于成员国目前在此领域缺乏相应的立法，况且大部分现有的信用评级机构均设立于欧共体境外，依靠成员国各自本身的力量不足以实现本条例的目标，而在欧共体这一层级上则更容易实现，因此，欧共体可依照《条约》第5条规定的辅助性原则制定相关细则。依据《条约》第5条规定的比例原则，本条例作出实现上述目标的必要规定。

兹通过本条例如下：

TITLE I SUBJECT MATTER, SCOPE AND DEFINITIONS

Article 1 Subject matter

This Regulation introduces a common regulatory approach in order to enhance the integrity, transparency, responsibility, good governance and reliability of credit rating activities, contributing to the quality of credit ratings issued in the Community, thereby contributing to the smooth functioning of the internal market while achieving a high level of consumer and investor protection. It lays down conditions for the issuing of credit ratings and rules on the organisation and conduct of credit rating agencies to promote their independence and the avoidance of conflicts of interest.

Article 2 Scope

1. This Regulation applies to credit ratings issued by credit rating agencies registered in the Community and which are disclosed publicly or distributed by subscription.

2. This Regulation does not apply to:

(a) private credit ratings produced pursuant to an individual order and provided exclusively to the person who placed the order and which are not intended for public disclosure or distribution by subscription;

(b) credit scores, credit scoring systems or similar assessments related to obligations arising from consumer, commercial or industrial relationships;

(c) credit ratings produced by export credit agencies in accordance with point 1.3 of Part 1 of Annex VI to Directive 2006/48/EC; or

(d) credit ratings produced by the central banks and which:

(i) are not paid for by the rated entity;

(ii) are not disclosed to the public;

(iii) are issued in accordance with the principles, standards and procedures which ensure the adequate integrity and independence of credit rating activities as provided for by this Regulation; and

(iv) do not relate to financial instruments issued by the respective central banks' Member States.

3. A credit rating agency shall apply for registration under this Regulation as a condition for being recognised as an External Credit Assessment Institution (ECAI) in accordance with Part 2 of Annex VI to Directive 2006/48/EC, unless it only issues the credit ratings referred to in paragraph 2.

第一编　标的事项、范围和定义

第1条　标的事项

本条例出台了一项通用的监管模式，以加强信用评级活动的诚信度、透明度、责任、良好治理和可靠性，改善欧共体境内发布的信用评级的质量，进而促进内部市场的平稳运行，同时实现对消费者和投资者的高标准保护。本条例规定了信用评级发布的条件以及信用评级机构的组织和行为规则，以提高信用评级机构的独立性并避免利益冲突。

第2条　范围

1.本条例适用于欧共体境内注册的信用评级机构发布的且已公开披露或通过订阅方式发送的信用评级。

2.本条例不适用于下列情形：

(a)根据专门的委托作出的私人信用评级，该等评级仅提供给委托方，不公开披露、不通过订阅方式发送；

(b)因消费者、商业或行业关系产生的义务的信用评分、信用评分制度或类似评估；

(c)根据第2006/48/EC号指令附录六第一部分第1.3项由出口信贷机构作出的信用评级；或

(d)由中央银行做出的符合下列情形的信用评级：

(i)并非由被评级实体付费；

(ii)未公开披露；

(iii)其发布遵循一定的原则、标准和程序，确保信用评级活动具有本条例规定的充分诚信度和独立性；且

(iv)与该等中央银行所属成员国发行的金融工具无关。

3.信用评级机构应根据本条例申请注册，获得注册是其按第2006/48/EC号指令附录六第二部分的规定被认定为外部信用评估机构(ECAI)的条件，但是，仅发布第2款所述信用评级的信用评级机构除外。

4. In order to ensure the uniform application of paragraph 2(d) the Commission may, upon submission of a request by a Member State, in accordance with the regulatory procedure referred to in Article 38(3) and in accordance with paragraph 2(d) of this Article, adopt a decision stating that a central bank falls within the scope of that point and that its credit ratings are therefore exempt from the application of this Regulation.

The Commission shall publish on its website the list of central banks falling within the scope of paragraph 2(d) of this Article.

Article 3 Definitions

1. For the purpose of this Regulation, the following definitions shall apply:

(a) 'credit rating' means an opinion regarding the creditworthiness of an entity, a debt or financial obligation, debt security, preferred share or other financial instrument, or of an issuer of such a debt or financial obligation, debt security, preferred share or other financial instrument, issued using an established and defined ranking system of rating categories;

(b) 'credit rating agency' means a legal person whose occupation includes the issuing of credit ratings on a professional basis;

(c) 'home Member State' means the Member State in which the credit rating agency has its registered office;

(d) 'rating analyst' means a person who performs analytical functions that are necessary for the issuing of a credit rating;

(e) 'lead rating analyst' means a person with primary responsibility for elaborating a credit rating or for communicating with the issuer with respect to a particular credit rating or, generally, with respect to the credit rating of a financial instrument issued by that issuer and, where relevant, for preparing recommendations to the rating committee in relation to such rating;

(f) 'rated entity' means a legal person whose creditworthiness is explicitly or implicitly rated in the credit rating, whether or not it has solicited that credit rating and whether or not it has provided information for that credit rating;

(g) 'regulatory purposes' means the use of credit ratings for the specific purpose of complying with Community law, as implemented by the national legislation of the Member States;

(h) 'rating category' means a rating symbol, such as a letter or numerical symbol which might be accompanied by appending identifying characters, used in a credit rating to provide a relative measure of risk to distinguish the different risk characteristics of the types of rated entities, issuers and financial instruments or other assets;

(i) 'related third party' means the originator, arranger, sponsor, servicer or any other party that interacts with a credit rating agency on behalf of a rated entity, including

4.为确保第2款第d项的统一适用,成员国递交请求后,欧盟委员会可依据第38条第3款所述的监管程序和本条第2款第d项的规定通过相关决定,说明该成员国中央银行属于第2款第d项规定的管辖范围,因此其信用评级豁免适用本条例。

欧盟委员会应在其网站上公布属于本条第2款第d项规定范围内的成员国中央银行清单。

第3条　定义

1.本条例应适用下列定义:

(a)“信用评级”指对某一实体、债务或金融债务、债务证券、优先股或其他金融工具的资信情况的意见,或对上述债务或金融债务、债务证券、优先股或其他金融工具发行人的资信情况的意见,按照既有的明确界定的评级类别系统发布;

(b)“信用评级机构”指其经营范围包括发布专业信用评级的法人;

(c)“母国”指信用评级机构注册地所在的成员国;

(d)“评级分析师”指履行发布信用评级所需分析职能的人;

(e)“首席评级分析师”指主要负责以下工作的人:编制某项信用评级;与发行人就某项特定信用评级或(总体而言)就发行人所发行的金融工具的信用评级进行沟通;在适当时就上述评级向评级委员会提供建议;

(f)“被评级实体” 指其资信情况在信用评级中以明示或默示的方式被评级的法人,不论其是否主动要求过进行该项信用评级,也不论其是否为该项信用评级提供过信息;

(g)“监管目的”指在成员国国内立法实施过程中,专门为遵守欧共体法律的目的而使用信用评级;

(h)“评级类别”指信用评级中使用的评级符号(如字母或数字符号,可能还附带识别字符),旨在计量相对风险以区分各类被评级实体、发行人和金融工具或其他资产的不同风险特征;

(i)“相关第三方”指发起人、安排方、保荐人、服务商或代表被评级实体与信用评级机构互动的第三方,包括通过控制与被评级实体直接或间接关联的人;

any person directly or indirectly linked to that rated entity by control;

(j) 'control' means the relationship between a parent undertaking and a subsidiary, as described in Article 1 of Council Directive 83/349/EEC of 13 June 1983 on consolidated accounts [1], or a close link between any natural or legal person and an undertaking;

(k) 'financial instrument' means any of the instruments listed in Section C of Annex I to Directive 2004/39/EC of the European Parliament and of the Council of 21 April 2004 on markets in financial instruments [2];

(l) 'structured finance instrument' means a financial instrument or other assets resulting from a securitisation transaction or scheme referred to in Article 4(36) of Directive 2006/48/EC;

(m) 'group of credit rating agencies' means a group of undertakings established in the Community consisting of a parent undertaking and its subsidiaries within the meaning of Articles 1 and 2 of Directive 83/349/EEC as well as undertakings linked to each other by a relationship within the meaning of Article 12(1) of Directive 83/349/EEC and whose occupation includes the issuing of credit ratings. For the purposes of Article 4(3)(a) a group of credit rating agencies shall also include credit rating agencies established in third countries;

(n) 'senior management' means the person or persons who effectively direct the business of the credit rating agency and the member or members of its administrative or supervisory board;

(o) 'credit rating activities' means data and information analysis and the evaluation, approval, issuing and review of credit ratings.

2. For the purposes of paragraph 1(a) the following shall not be considered to be credit ratings:

(a) recommendations within the meaning of Article 1(3) of Commission Directive 2003/125/EC [3];

(b) investment research as defined in Article 24(1) of Directive 2006/73/EC [4] and other forms of general recommendation, such as 'buy', 'sell' or 'hold', relating to transactions in financial instruments or to financial obligations; or

1 OJ L 193, 18.7.1983, p. 1.

2 OJ L 145, 30.4.2004, p. 1.

3 OJ L 339, 24.12.2003, p. 73.

4 Commission Directive 2006/73/EC of 10 August 2006 implementing Directive 2004/39/EC of the European Parliament and of the Council as regards organisational requirements and operating conditions for investment firms and defined terms for the purposes of that Directive (OJ L 241, 2.9.2006, p. 26).

(j)“控制”指《欧洲经济共同体理事会关于合并财务报表的第83/349/EEC号指令》[1](1983年6月13日)第1条所述的母公司与子公司之间的关系，或自然人或法人与某个企业之间的密切关联；

(k)“金融工具”指《欧洲议会与欧盟理事会关于金融工具市场的第2004/39/EC号指令》[2](2004年4月21日)附录一第C节所列的任何工具；

(l)“结构性金融工具”指第2006/48/EC号指令第4条第36款所述的证券化交易或计划中的金融工具或其他资产；

(m)“信用评级机构集团”指在欧共体境内设立的企业集团，其组成包括符合第83/349/EEC号指令第1条及第2条所定义的母公司及其子公司，以及第83/349/EEC号指令第12条第1款所定义的以某种关系相互关联且其经营范围包括发布信用评级的企业。就第4条第3款第a项而言，信用评级机构集团还应包括在第三国设立的信用评级机构；

(n)“高级管理人员”指实际领导信用评级机构业务的一人或多人，以及信用评级机构董事会或监事会的一名或多名成员；

(o)“信用评级活动”指数据和信息分析以及对信用评级的评估、批准、发布及复核；

2.就第1款第a项而言，下列事项不得被视为信用评级：

(a)符合欧盟委员会第2003/125/EC号指令[3]第1条第3款所定义的建议；

(b)第2006/73/EC号指令[4]第24条第1款所定义的投资研究以及其他形式的一般建议，如“买入”、“卖出”或“持有”等与金融工具交易或金融债务有关的建议；或

1 1983年7月18日《欧盟公报》L193，第1页。

2 2004年4月30日《欧盟公报》L145，第1页。

3 2003年12月24日《欧盟公报》L339，第73页。

4 欧盟委员会第2006/73/EC号指令(2006年8月10日)，就投资公司的组织结构要求和运作条件实施欧洲议会与欧盟理事会第2004/39/EC号指令，并对该指令中的术语进行界定(2006年9月2日《欧盟公报》L241，第26页)。

(c) opinions about the value of a financial instrument or a financial obligation.

Article 4 Use of credit ratings

1. Credit institutions as defined in Directive 2006/48/EC, investments firms as defined in Directive 2004/39/EC, insurance undertakings subject to the First Council Directive 73/239/EEC of 24 July 1973 on the coordination of laws, regulations and administrative provisions relating to the taking-up and pursuit of the business of direct insurance other than life assurance [1], assurance undertakings as defined in Directive 2002/83/EC of the European Parliament and of the Council of 5 November 2002 concerning life assurance [2], reinsurance undertakings as defined in Directive 2005/68/EC of the European Parliament and the Council of 16 November 2005 on reinsurance [3], undertakings for collective investment in transferable securities (UCITS) as defined in Directive 85/611/EEC and institutions for occupational retirement provision as defined in Directive 2003/41/EC may use credit ratings for regulatory purposes only if they are issued by credit rating agencies established in the Community and registered in accordance with this Regulation.

Where a prospectus published under Directive 2003/71/EC and Regulation (EC) No 809/2004 contains a reference to a credit rating or credit ratings, the issuer, offeror, or person asking for admission to trading on a regulated market shall ensure that the prospectus also includes clear and prominent information stating whether or not such credit ratings are issued by a credit rating agency established in the Community and registered under this Regulation.

2 .A credit rating agency established in the Community and registered in accordance with this Regulation shall be deemed to have issued a credit rating when the credit rating has been published on the credit rating agency's website or by other means or distributed by subscription and presented and disclosed in accordance with the obligations of Article 10, clearly identifying that the credit rating is endorsed in accordance with paragraph 3 of this Article.

3. A credit rating agency established in the Community and registered in accordance with this Regulation may endorse a credit rating issued in a third country only when credit rating activities resulting in the issuing of such a credit rating comply with the following conditions:

(a) the credit rating activities resulting in the issuing of the credit rating to be endorsed are undertaken in whole or in part by the endorsing credit rating agency or by credit rating agencies belonging to the same group;

1 OJ L 228, 16.8.1973, p. 3.

2 OJ L 345, 19.12.2002, p. 1.

3 OJ L 323, 9.12.2005, p. 1.

(c)对金融工具或金融债务价值的意见。

第4条 信用评级的使用

1.第2006/48/EC号指令所定义的信贷机构、第2004/39/EC号指令所定义的投资公司、受《欧洲经济共同体理事会协调关于直接保险(寿险除外)业务开办和经营的法律、法规和规章的第73/239/EEC号第一指令》[1](1973年7月24日)管辖的保险公司、《欧洲议会和欧盟理事会关于寿险的第2002/83/EC号指令》[2](2002年11月5日)所定义的担保公司、《欧洲议会与欧盟理事会关于再保险的第2005/68/EC号指令》[3](2005年11月16日)所定义的再保险公司、第85/611/EEC号指令所定义的可转让证券集合投资计划(UCITS)以及第2003/41/EC号指令所定义的职业退休基金管理机构,为监管目的使用信用评级的,仅可采用在欧共体境内设立并依照本条例注册的信用评级机构所发布的信用评级。

根据第2003/71/EC号指令和第809/2004号(欧共体)条例公布的招募说明书引用一项或多项信用评级的,发行人、要约人或请求获准在受监管市场交易其证券的人,应确保招募说明书中也应清楚显著地注明信用评级是否由在欧共体境内设立并根据本条例注册的信用评级机构所发布。

2.在下列情形下,在欧共体境内设立并根据本条例注册的信用评级机构应被视为发布了信用评级:信用评级已在信用评级机构的网站上或通过其他途径公布,或通过订阅方式发送且根据第10条规定的义务进行列报和披露,同时清楚指明该信用评级根据本条第3款得到认可。

3.在欧共体境内设立并根据本条例注册的信用评级机构可以认可在第三国境内发布的信用评级,前提是发布上述信用评级的信用评级活动符合下列条件:

(a)请求获得认可的信用评级其相关的信用评级工作全部或部分由作为认可方的信用评级机构所承担,或由隶属同一集团的信用评级机构所承担;

1 1973年8月16日《欧盟公报》L228,第3页。
2 2002年12月19日《欧盟公报》L345,第1页。
3 2005年12月9日《欧盟公报》L323,第1页。

(b) the credit rating agency has verified and is able to demonstrate on an ongoing basis to the competent authority of the home Member State that the conduct of credit rating activities by the third-country credit rating agency resulting in the issuing of the credit rating to be endorsed fulfils requirements which are at least as stringent as the requirements set out in Articles 6 to 12;

(c) the ability of the competent authority of the home Member State of the endorsing credit rating agency or the college of competent authorities referred to in Article 29 (college) to assess and monitor the compliance of the credit rating agency established in the third country with the requirements referred to in point (b) is not limited;

(d) the credit rating agency makes available on request to the competent authority of the home Member State all the information necessary to enable that competent authority to supervise on an ongoing basis the compliance with the requirements of this Regulation;

(e) there is an objective reason for the credit rating to be elaborated in a third country;

(f) the credit rating agency established in the third country is authorised or registered, and is subject to supervision, in that third country;

(g) the regulatory regime in that third country prevents interference by the competent authorities and other public authorities of that third country with the content of credit ratings and methodologies; and

(h) there is an appropriate cooperation arrangement between the competent authority of the home Member State of the endorsing credit rating agency and the relevant competent authority of the credit rating agency established in a third country. The competent authority of the home Member State shall ensure that such cooperation arrangements shall specify at least:

(i) the mechanism for the exchange of information between the competent authorities concerned; and

(ii) the procedures concerning the coordination of supervisory activities in order to enable the competent authority of the home Member State of the endorsing credit rating agency to monitor credit rating activities resulting in the issuing of the endorsed credit rating on an ongoing basis.

4. A credit rating endorsed in accordance with paragraph 3 shall be considered to be a credit rating issued by a credit rating agency established in the Community and registered in accordance with this Regulation.

A credit rating agency established in the Community and registered in accordance with this Regulation shall not use such endorsement with the intention of avoiding the requirements of this Regulation.

5. The credit rating agency that has endorsed a credit rating issued in a third country

(b)该信用评级机构已核实且能持续向母国主管部门证明,第三国信用评级机构发布的请求获得认可的信用评级,其相关的信用评级活动达到了与第6条至第12条的要求同样严格的要求;

(c)作为认可方的信用评级机构的母国主管部门或第29条所述主管部门的运营团(以下简称运营团),其评估和监控在第三国设立的信用评级机构是否遵守第b项所述要求的能力,不受限制;

(d)经要求,信用评级机构可向母国主管部门提供所有必要的信息,使该主管部门能持续监管本条例规定的合规情形;

(e)存在客观的理由,使得必须在第三国制定该信用评级;

(f)设立于第三国的信用评级机构在该第三国得到核准或注册,并受该第三国监管;

(g)第三国的监管体制不允许主管部门和第三国其他公共机构干预信用评级的内容和方法;

(h)作为认可方的信用评级机构的母国主管部门,以及在第三国设立的信用评级机构的相关主管部门,二者之间有适当的合作安排。母国主管部门应确保上述合作安排至少对下列内容作出规定:

(i)所涉主管部门之间的信息交换机制;及

(ii)监管活动的协调程序,该程序旨在使作为认可方的信用评级机构的母国主管部门有能力持续监控产生被认可的信用评级活动。

4.根据第3款得到认可的信用评级应被视为由设立于欧共体境内并根据本条例注册的信用评级机构所发布的信用评级。

在欧共体境内设立并根据本条例注册的信用评级机构,不应利用上述认可来规避本条例的规定。

5.信用评级机构根据第3款规定认可在第三国发布的信用评级的,仍应对其所认

in accordance with paragraph 3 shall remain fully responsible for such a credit rating and for the fulfilment of conditions set out therein.

6. Where the Commission has recognised, in accordance with Article 5(6) the legal and supervisory framework of a third country as equivalent to the requirements of this Regulation and the cooperation arrangements referred to in Article 5(7) are operational, the credit rating agency endorsing credit ratings issued in that third country shall no longer be required to verify or demonstrate that the condition laid down in paragraph 3(g) of this Article is fulfilled.

Article 5 Equivalence and certification based on equivalence

1. The credit ratings that are related to entities established or financial instruments issued in third countries and that are issued by a credit rating agency established in a third country may be used in the Community under Article 4(1) without being endorsed in accordance with Article 4(3) provided that:

(a) the credit rating agency is authorised or registered in and is subject to supervision in that third country;

(b) the Commission has adopted an equivalence decision in accordance with paragraph 6 of this Article, recognising the legal and supervisory framework of that third country as equivalent to the requirements of this Regulation;

(c) the cooperation arrangements referred to in paragraph 7 of this Article are operational;

(d) the credit ratings issued by the credit rating agency and its credit rating activities are not of systemic importance to the financial stability or integrity of the financial markets of one or more Member States; and

(e) the credit rating agency is certified in accordance with paragraph 2 of this Article.

2. The credit rating agency referred to in paragraph 1 may apply for certification. The application shall be submitted to the Committee of European Securities Regulators (CESR) in accordance with the relevant provisions of Article 15. Within five working days of receipt of the application for certification, CESR shall send the application to the competent authorities of all Member States, inviting them to consider becoming a member of the relevant college in accordance with Article 29(3)(b). The competent authorities that have decided to become members of the college shall notify CESR accordingly within 10 working days of receipt of CESR's invitation. The competent authorities that notify CESR in accordance with this paragraph shall be members of the college. Within twenty working days of receipt of the application for certification, CESR shall draw up and publish on its website a list of the competent authorities that are members of the college. Within 10 working days of the publication, the members of the college shall select a

可的信用评级以及其中设定的条件是否得到满足负全部责任。

6.欧盟委员会按照第5条第6款认定第三国法律和监管框架与本条例要求等效，且第5条第7款所述合作安排具有可操作性的，对该第三国发布的信用评级进行认可的信用评级机构不再负有核实或证明本条例第3款第g项所列条件是否得到满足的义务。

第5条　等效性和基于等效性的认证

1.与在第三国设立的实体或在第三国发行的金融工具相关的信用评级，以及在第三国设立的信用评级机构所发布的信用评级，在符合以下条件的情形下，可依照第4条第1款在欧共体境内使用，不必依照第4条第3款取得认可：

(a)该信用评级机构在该第三国获得核准或注册并受该第三国监管；

(b)欧盟委员会已根据本条第6款通过等效性决定，认定该第三国的法律和监管框架与本条例的要求等效；

(c)本条第7款所述的合作安排具有可操作性；

(d) 信用评级机构所发布的信用评级及其信用评级活动对一个或多个成员国金融市场的金融稳定性或诚信度不具有系统重要性；且

(e)信用评级机构依照本条第2款得到认证。

2.第1款所述的信用评级机构可申请认证。申请应根据第15条的相关规定向欧洲证券监管机构委员会(CESR)递交。收到认证申请的5个工作日内，欧洲证券监管机构委员会应将申请发送至所有成员国的主管部门，邀请其根据第29条第3款第b项加入相关运营团。决定成为运营团成员的主管部门，应于收到欧洲证券监管机构委员会邀请后10个工作日内通知欧洲证券监管机构委员会。根据本款规定通知了欧洲证券监管机构委员会的主管部门应成为该运营团的成员。收到认证申请的20个工作日内，欧洲证券监管机构委员会应编制一份组成运营团的主管部门名单，并在其网站上公布。名单公布后10个工作日内，运营团成员应根据第29条第5款的标准遴选一名督导员。运营团成立后，其构成和运行应当受第29条管辖。

facilitator in accordance with criteria in Article 29(5) . Following the establishment of the college, its composition and functioning shall be governed by Article 29.

3. The application for certification shall be examined in accordance with the procedure set out in Article 16. The certification decision shall be based on the criteria set out in points (a) to (d) of paragraph 1 of this Article.

The certification decision shall be notified and published in accordance with Article 18.

4. The credit rating agency may also separately apply to be exempted:

(a) on a case-by-case basis from complying with some or all of the requirements set out in Section A of Annex I and Article 7(4) if the credit rating agency is able to demonstrate that the requirements are not proportionate in view of the nature, scale and complexity of its business and the nature and range of its issuing of credit ratings;

(b) from the requirement of physical presence in the Community where such a requirement would be too burdensome and disproportionate in view of the nature, scale and complexity of its business and the nature and range of its issuing of credit ratings.

When assessing that application, the competent authorities shall take into consideration the size of the applicant credit rating agency, having regard to the nature, scale and complexity of its business and the nature and range of its issuing of credit ratings, as well as the impact of the credit ratings issued by the credit rating agency on the financial stability and integrity of the financial markets of one or more Member States. On the basis of those considerations, the competent authority may grant such exemption to the credit rating agency.

5. The decisions on the exemptions under paragraph 4 of this Article shall be subject to the relevant provisions and procedures set out in Article 16 with the exception of the second subparagraph of paragraph 7 of that Article. In the event of continued absence of agreement among the members of the relevant college on whether to grant an exemption to the credit rating agency, the facilitator shall adopt a fully reasoned decision.

For the purposes of certification, including the granting of exemptions, and supervision, the facilitator shall perform the tasks of the competent authority of the home Member State where relevant.

6. The Commission may adopt an equivalence decision in accordance with the regulatory procedure referred to in Article 38(3) stating that the legal and supervisory framework of a third country ensures that credit rating agencies authorised or registered in that third country comply with legally binding requirements which are equivalent to the requirements resulting from this Regulation and which are subject to effective supervision and enforcement in that third country.

A third-country legal and supervisory framework may be considered equivalent to

3.应依照第16条规定的程序审核认证申请。认证决定应以本条第1款第a项至第d项规定的标准为依据。

应依照第18条通知和公布认证决定。

4.信用评级机构也可单独分项申请获得下列豁免：

(a)信用评级机构能证明附录一第A节及第7条第4款所规定的要求与其业务的性质、规模和复杂程度以及其发布信用评级的性质和范围并不成比例的，可以个案方式申请豁免部分或全部该等要求；

(b)在欧共体境内开展实体运营的要求如对信用评级机构造成过重负担，且与其业务的性质、规模和复杂程度及其发布信用评级的性质和范围不成比例，则可申请豁免该等要求。

主管部门评估该项申请时，应考虑提出申请的信用评级机构的规模，根据其业务的性质、规模和复杂程度及其信用评级发布的性质和范围，以及该信用评级机构所发布的信用评级对一个或多个成员国金融市场的金融稳定性和诚信度的影响作出评估。基于该等考虑，主管部门可核准信用评级机构豁免上述要求。

5.本条第4款中的豁免决定应以遵守第16条所列相关规定及程序为前提，但不包括该条第7款第2项。相关运营团的成员一直无法就是否核准信用评级机构的豁免达成一致的，督导员应作出充分合理的决定。

进行认证（包括核准豁免）和进行监管时，督导员应在适当时履行母国主管部门的职责。

6.欧盟委员会可依据第38条第3款所述的监管程序通过等效性决定，在该等决定中说明第三国的法律和监管框架能确保在第三国获得核准或注册的信用评级机构符合与本条例规定等效的具有法律约束力的规定，且该等规定在该第三国得到有效监管与执行。

第三国的法律和监管框架如果至少符合下列条件，可被视为与本条例等效：

this Regulation if that framework fulfils at least the following conditions:

(a) credit rating agencies in that third country are subject to authorisation or registration and are subject to effective supervision and enforcement on an ongoing basis;

(b) credit rating agencies in that third country are subject to legally binding rules which are equivalent to those set out in Articles 6 to 12 and Annex I; and

(c) the regulatory regime in that third country prevents interference by the supervisory authorities and other public authorities of that third country with the content of credit ratings and methodologies.

The Commission shall specify further or amend the criteria set out in points (a) to (c) of the second subparagraph in order to take account of developments on financial markets. Those measures, designed to amend non-essential elements of this Regulation, shall be adopted in accordance with the regulatory procedure with scrutiny referred to in Article 38(2).

7. The facilitator shall establish cooperation agreements with the relevant competent authorities of third countries whose legal and supervisory frameworks have been considered equivalent to this Regulation in accordance with paragraph 6. Such arrangements shall specify at least:

(a) the mechanism for the exchange of information between the competent authorities concerned; and

(b) the procedures concerning the coordination of supervisory activities.

CESR shall coordinate the development of cooperation agreements between the competent authorities of Member States and the relevant competent authorities of third countries whose legal and supervisory frameworks have been considered equivalent to this Regulation in accordance with paragraph 6.

8. Articles 20, 24 and 25 shall apply *mutatis mutandis* to certified credit rating agencies and to credit ratings issued by them.

TITLE II ISSUING OF CREDIT RATINGS

Article 6 Independence and avoidance of conflicts of interest

1. A credit rating agency shall take all necessary steps to ensure that the issuing of a credit rating is not affected by any existing or potential conflict of interest or business relationship involving the credit rating agency issuing the credit rating, its managers, rating analysts, employees, any other natural person whose services are placed at the disposal or under the control of the credit rating agency, or any person directly or

(a)该第三国的信用评级机构须经核准或注册,并持续受到有效的监管与执法;

(b)该第三国的信用评级机构受到与第6条至第12条及附录一所列规则等效的具有法律约束力的规则管辖;且

(c)该第三国的监管体制不允许该第三国监管机构与其他公共机构干预信用评级内容和方法。

为反映金融市场的发展动态,欧盟委员会应进一步阐明或修正第2项第a目至第c目所列标准。应依照第38条第2款所述的须经欧盟理事会和欧洲议会审查的监管程序制定旨在修正本条例非基本要素的该等细则。

7.第三国法律和监管框架已根据第6款被视为与本条例等效的,督导员应与该国相关主管部门建立合作协议,该等协议至少应对下列事项作出安排:

(a)所涉主管部门之间的信息交换机制;和

(b)监管活动的协调程序。

欧洲证券监管机构委员会应协调以下主管部门之间的合作协议进展:成员国主管部门,以及其法律和监管框架已根据第6款被视为与本条例等效的第三国相关主管部门。

8.第20条、第24条及第25条规定应经适当修正后适用于获认证的信用评级机构及其发布的信用评级。

第二编　信用评级的发布

第6条　独立性和利益冲突的避免

1.信用评级机构应采取所有必要措施,以确保信用评级的发布不受下列主体的现有或潜在利益冲突或业务关系影响:发布所涉信用评级的信用评级机构本身;其经理人、评级分析师、职员;所提供的服务被该信用评级机构所使用或被该信用评级机构所控制的其他自然人;或者通过控制与该信用评级机构直接或间接关联的人。

indirectly linked to it by control.

2. In order to ensure compliance with paragraph 1, a credit rating agency shall comply with the requirements set out in Sections A and B of Annex I.

3. At the request of a credit rating agency, the competent authority of the home Member State may exempt a credit rating agency from complying with the requirements of points 2, 5 and 6 of Section A of Annex I and Article 7(4) if the credit rating agency is able to demonstrate that those requirements are not proportionate in view of the nature, scale and complexity of its business and the nature and range of issue of credit ratings and that:

(a) the credit rating agency has fewer than 50 employees;

(b) the credit rating agency has implemented measures and procedures, in particular internal control mechanisms, reporting arrangements and measures ensuring independence of rating analysts and persons approving credit ratings, which ensure the effective compliance with the objectives of this Regulation; and

(c) the size of the credit rating agency is not determined in such a way as to avoid compliance with the requirements of this Regulation by a credit rating agency or a group of credit rating agencies.

In the case of a group of credit rating agencies, competent authorities shall ensure that at least one of the credit rating agencies in the group is not exempted from complying with the requirements of points 2, 5 and 6 of Section A of Annex I and Article 7(4).

Article 7 Rating analysts, employees and other persons involved in the issuing of credit ratings

1. A credit rating agency shall ensure that rating analysts, its employees and any other natural person whose services are placed at its disposal or under its control and who are directly involved in credit rating activities have appropriate knowledge and experience for the duties assigned.

2. A credit rating agency shall ensure that persons referred to in paragraph 1 shall not be allowed to initiate or participate in negotiations regarding fees or payments with any rated entity, related third party or any person directly or indirectly linked to the rated entity by control.

3. A credit rating agency shall ensure that persons referred to in paragraph 1 meet the requirements set out in Section C of Annex I.

4. A credit rating agency shall establish an appropriate gradual rotation mechanism with regard to the rating analysts and persons approving credit ratings as defined in Section C of Annex I. That rotation mechanism shall be undertaken in phases on the basis of individuals rather than of a complete team.

5. Compensation and performance evaluation of rating analysts and persons approving

2.为确保第1款得到遵守，信用评级机构应遵守附录一第A节和第B节所列的要求。

3.经信用评级机构请求，母国主管部门可豁免信用评级机构遵守附录一第A节第2项、第5项和第6项以及第7条第4款的规定，前提是信用评级机构能够证明该等要求与其业务的性质、规模和复杂程度以及信用评级发布的性质和范围不成比例，而且：

(a)信用评级机构的员工人数少于50人；

(b)该信用评级机构已实施足以确保本条例目标得到有效遵守的措施和程序，特别是内部控制机制、报告安排以及确保评级分析师及信用评级批准人员独立性的措施；且

(c)信用评级机构并未刻意将其规模设定在可以规避信用评级机构或信用评级机构集团所应遵守的本条例的规定的水平。

主管部门应确保信用评级机构集团中至少有一家信用评级机构不享受豁免附录一第A节第2项、第5项和第6项以及第7条第4款的规定。

第7条　评级分析师、职员及其他参与信用评级发布的人

1.信用评级机构应确保，评级分析师、信用评级机构职员以及所提供的服务为该信用评级机构所用或为该信用评级机构所控制且直接参与信用评级活动的其他自然人，具有履行受托职责所需的适当知识和经验。

2.信用评级机构应确保第1款所述之人不得被允许发起或参与和被评级实体、相关第三方或通过控制而与被评级实体直接或间接关联的人关于手续费或支付费用的谈判。

3.信用评级机构应确保第1款所述之人符合附录一第C节所列的要求。

4.信用评级机构应针对评级分析师和附录一第C节所定义的信用评级批准人员建立适当的分批轮换机制。在该机制下，应分批以人为单位进行轮换，而非对整个团队作出替换。

5.评级分析师及信用评级批准人员的薪酬和绩效评价，不应取决于信用评级机构

the credit ratings shall not be contingent on the amount of revenue that the credit rating agency derives from the rated entities or related third parties.

Article 8 Methodologies, models and key rating assumptions

1. A credit rating agency shall disclose to the public the methodologies, models and key rating assumptions it uses in its credit rating activities as defined in point 5 of Part I of Section E of Annex I.

2. A credit rating agency shall adopt, implement and enforce adequate measures to ensure that the credit ratings it issues are based on a thorough analysis of all the information that is available to it and that is relevant to its analysis according to its rating methodologies.

It shall adopt all necessary measures so that the information it uses in assigning a credit rating is of sufficient quality and from reliable sources.

3. A credit rating agency shall use rating methodologies that are rigorous, systematic, continuous and subject to validation based on historical experience, including back-testing.

4. Where a credit rating agency is using an existing credit rating prepared by another credit rating agency with respect to underlying assets or structured finance instruments, it shall not refuse to issue a credit rating of an entity or a financial instrument because a portion of the entity or the financial instrument had been previously rated by another credit rating agency.

A credit rating agency shall record all instances where in its credit rating process it departs from existing credit ratings prepared by another credit rating agency with respect to underlying assets or structured finance instruments providing a justification for the differing assessment.

5. A credit rating agency shall monitor credit ratings and review its credit ratings and methodologies on an ongoing basis and at least annually, in particular where material changes occur that could have an impact on a credit rating. A credit rating agency shall establish internal arrangements to monitor the impact of changes in macroeconomic or financial market conditions on credit ratings.

6. When methodologies, models or key rating assumptions used in credit rating activities are changed, a credit rating agency shall:

(a) immediately, using the same means of communication as used for the distribution of the affected credit ratings, disclose the likely scope of credit ratings to be affected;

(b) review the affected credit ratings as soon as possible and no later than six months after the change, in the meantime placing those ratings under observation; and

(c) re-rate all credit ratings that have been based on those methodologies, models or key rating assumptions if, following the review, the overall combined effect of the changes

从被评级实体或相关第三方处取得的收入金额。

第8条 方法、模型及关键评级假设

1.信用评级机构应向公众披露其在附录一第E节第一部分第5项所定义的信用评级活动中使用的方法、模型及关键评级假设。

2.信用评级机构应制定、实施并执行适当的措施，以确保对所获得的信息进行全面分析后才发布信用评级，并确保所使用的信息根据其评级方法判断对其分析是适用的。

信用评级机构应制定所有必要措施，确保用于信用评级的信息质量过硬且来源可靠。

3.信用评级机构应使用严格、系统、持续的评级方法，该等评级方法须根据历史经验(包括回溯测试)加以验证。

4.信用评级机构在其评级中使用其他信用评级机构就标的资产或结构性金融工具所做的既有评级的，其不得以某实体或某金融工具事先已被另一信用评级机构评过级为由，拒绝对该实体或该金融工具发布信用评级。

信用评级机构在其评级中，如与其他信用评级机构对标的资产或结构性金融工具所做的既有信用评级存在差异，应对该等差异进行记录，说明其评估结果不同的理由。

5.信用评级机构应持续并至少每年一次对信用评级进行监控，并对其信用评级和方法进行复核，尤其是在发生可能会对信用评级造成影响的实质变化的情形下。信用评级机构应建立内部安排，以监控宏观经济或金融市场状况变化对信用评级的影响。

6.当信用评级活动使用的方法、模型或关键评级假设发生变更时，信用评级机构应：

(a)立即披露信用评级可能受到影响的范围，披露所采用的通信手段应与发送受影响的信用评级所用的通信手段相同；

(b)尽快并最迟于变更发生后半年(含)内复核受影响的信用评级，同时将该等评级列入观察；且

(c)复核后发现，变化产生的整体综合效应影响了信用评级的，所有基于该等方法、模型或关键评级假设得出的信用评级均应重新进行评级。

affects those credit ratings.

Article 9 Outsourcing

Outsourcing of important operational functions shall not be undertaken in such a way as to impair materially the quality of the credit rating agency's internal control and the ability of the competent authorities to supervise the credit rating agency's compliance with obligations under this Regulation.

Article 10 Disclosure and presentation of credit ratings

1. A credit rating agency shall disclose any credit rating, as well as any decision to discontinue a credit rating, on a non-selective basis and in a timely manner. In the event of a decision to discontinue a credit rating, the information disclosed shall include full reasons for the decision.

The first subparagraph shall also apply to credit ratings that are distributed by subscription.

2. Credit rating agencies shall ensure that credit ratings are presented and processed in accordance with the requirements set out in Section D of Annex I.

3. When a credit rating agency issues credit ratings for structured finance instruments, it shall ensure that rating categories that are attributed to structured finance instruments are clearly differentiated using an additional symbol which distinguishes them from rating categories used for any other entities, financial instruments or financial obligations.

4. A credit rating agency shall disclose its policies and procedures regarding unsolicited credit ratings.

5. When a credit rating agency issues an unsolicited credit rating, it shall state prominently in the credit rating whether or not the rated entity or related third party participated in the credit rating process and whether the credit rating agency had access to the accounts and other relevant internal documents of the rated entity or a related third party.

Unsolicited credit ratings shall be identified as such.

6. A credit rating agency shall not use the name of any competent authority in such a way that would indicate or suggest endorsement or approval by that authority of the credit ratings or any credit rating activities of the credit rating agency.

Article 11 General and periodic disclosures

1. A credit rating agency shall fully disclose to the public and update immediately information relating to the matters set out in Part I of Section E of Annex I.

2. A credit rating agency shall make available in a central repository established by CESR information on its historical performance data including the ratings transition frequency and information about credit ratings issued in the past and on their changes. A

第9条　外包

重要运营职能的外包不应对信用评级机构的内部控制质量以及主管部门监管信用评级机构遵守本条例义务的能力带来实质的影响。

第10条　信用评级的披露和列报

1.信用评级机构应不带选择性地及时披露所有信用评级以及终止某项信用评级的任何决定。决定终止信用评级时，披露的信息应包括作出该等决定的完整理由。

本款第1项不适用于通过订阅方式发送的信用评级。

2.信用评级机构应确保，信用评级的列报和处理均符合附录一第D节所列的要求。

3.信用评级机构发布结构性金融工具信用评级时，应在评级前添加特殊符号，将结构性金融工具的评级类别与用于其他实体、金融工具或金融债务的评级类别明确区分开来。

4.信用评级机构应披露其主动作出的信用评级的政策与程序。

5.信用评级机构发布主动做出的信用评级时，应在信用评级中以显著的方式说明被评级实体或相关第三方是否参与了信用评级工作，以及信用评级机构是否可以查阅被评级实体或相关第三方的财务报表或其他相关的内部文件。

信用评级如为主动作出的，应有相应的标示。

6.信用评级机构不应使用任何主管部门的名称以明示或暗示该部门认可或批准了该信用评级机构的信用评级或任何信用评级活动。

第11条　一般性披露和定期披露

1.信用评级机构应向公众全面披露与附录一第E节第一部分所述事项有关的信息，并在信息发生变更时立即更新。

2.信用评级机构应通过欧洲证券监管机构委员会设立的中央数据存管机构提供关于其历史业绩数据的信息，包括评级变动频率以及关于过去发布过的信用评级及其变更的信息。信用评级机构应以欧洲证券监管机构委员会所制定的标准格式向数

credit rating agency shall provide information to that repository on a standard form as provided for by CESR. CESR shall make that information accessible to the public and shall publish summary information on the main developments observed on an annual basis.

3. A credit rating agency shall provide annually to the competent authority of its home Member State and to CESR information relating to matters set out in point 2 of Part II of Section E Annex I. The competent authority of the home Member State shall disclose that information to the members of the relevant college.

Article 12 Transparency report

A credit rating agency shall publish annually a transparency report which includes information on matters set out in Part III of Section E of Annex I. The credit rating agency shall publish its transparency report at the latest three months after the end of each financial year and shall ensure that it remains available on the website of the agency for at least five years.

Article 13 Public disclosure fees

A credit rating agency shall not charge a fee for the information provided in accordance with Articles 8 to 12.

TITLE III SURVEILLANCE OF CREDIT RATING ACTIVITIES

CHAPTER I Registration procedure

Article 14 Requirement for registration

1. A credit rating agency shall apply for registration for the purposes of Article 2(1) provided that it is a legal person established in the Community.

2. The registration shall be effective for the entire territory of the Community once the registration decision issued by the competent authority of the home Member State as referred to in Article 16(7) or Article 17(7) has taken effect under the relevant national law.

3. A registered credit rating agency shall comply at all times with the conditions for initial registration.

A credit rating agency shall, without undue delay, notify CESR, the competent authority of its home Member State and the facilitator of any material changes to the conditions for initial registration, including any opening or closing of a branch within the

据存管机构提供信息。欧洲证券监管机构委员会应向公众公开该等信息,并应对其所观察到的主要变化每年公布摘要信息。

3.信用评级机构应每年向其母国主管部门及欧洲证券监管机构委员会提供与附录一第E节第二部分第2项所述事项有关的信息。母国主管部门应向相关运营团成员披露该等信息。

第12条 透明度报告

信用评级机构应每年公布一份透明度报告,报告应包含关于附录一第E节第三部分所述事项的信息。信用评级机构应至少在各会计年度结束后3个月内公布其透明度报告,并应确保报告至少在5年内仍可在该机构网站上获得。

第13条 公开披露手续费

信用评级机构不应为根据第8条至第12条提供的信息收取手续费。

第三编 信用评级活动的监督

第一章 注册程序

第14条 注册要求

1.信用评级机构只要是在欧共体设立的法人,即应依照第2条第1款申请注册。

2.第16条第7款或第17条第7款所述母国主管部门颁布的注册决定一旦依相关成员国的国内法律生效,该注册即于欧共体全境内有效。

3.注册信用评级机构应始终符合其获得初始注册时所满足的条件。

初始注册条件发生任何重大变更(包括在欧共体境内开设或关闭分支机构的任何活动)的,信用评级机构均应立即通知欧洲证券监管机构委员会、其母国主管部门以及督导员,不得无故延误。

Community.

4. Without prejudice to Articles 16 or 17, the competent authority of the home Member State shall register the credit rating agency if it concludes from the examination of the application that the credit rating agency complies with the conditions for the issuing of credit ratings set out in this Regulation, taking into consideration Articles 4 and 6.

5. Competent authorities shall not impose requirements regarding registration which are not provided for in this Regulation.

Article 15 Application for registration

1. The credit rating agency shall submit an application for registration to CESR. The application shall contain information on the matters set out in Annex II.

2. Where a group of credit rating agencies applies for registration, the members of the group shall mandate one of their number to submit all the applications to CESR on behalf of the group. The mandated credit rating agency shall provide the information on the matters set out in Annex II for each member of the group.

3. A credit rating agency shall submit its application in the language which is required under the law of its home Member State and also in a language customary in the sphere of international finance.

An application for registration sent by CESR to the competent authority of the home Member State shall be considered to be an application submitted by the credit rating agency concerned.

4. Within five working days of receipt of the application, CESR shall transmit copies of the application to the competent authorities of all Member States.

Within 10 working days of receipt of the application, CESR shall provide advice to the competent authority of the home Member State on the completeness of the application.

5. Within 25 working days of receipt of the application, the competent authority of the home Member State and the members of the relevant college shall assess whether the application is complete, taking into account the advice of CESR referred to in paragraph 4. If the application is not complete, the competent authority of the home Member State shall set a deadline by which the credit rating agency is to provide additional information to it and to CESR and shall notify the members of the college and CESR accordingly.

After assessing an application as complete, the competent authority of the home Member State shall notify the credit rating agency, the members of the college and CESR accordingly.

6. Within five working days of receipt of the additional information referred to in paragraph 5, CESR shall transmit the additional information to the competent authorities of all other Member States.

Article 16 Examination of the application for registration of a credit rating

4.在不影响第16条或第17条的情形下，母国主管部门对信用评级机构的申请进行审核后得出结论认为，该信用评级机构符合本条例所规定的信用评级发布条件的，母国主管部门应在考虑到第4条和第6条的情形下准予该信用评级机构注册。

5.主管部门不应施加本条例并未规定的注册要求。

第15条　注册申请

1.信用评级机构应向欧洲证券监管机构委员会递交注册申请。申请应包含关于附录二所述事项的信息。

2.信用评级机构集团申请注册时，集团成员应授权其中一名成员代表集团向欧洲证券监管机构委员会递交所有申请材料。被授权的信用评级机构应代表每一集团成员提供关于附录二所述事项的信息。

3.信用评级机构应同时以其母国法律规定的语言以及国际金融行业惯用的语言递交申请。

由欧洲证券监管机构委员会向母国主管部门发送的注册申请，应视为由所涉信用评级机构递交的申请。

4.收到申请后的5个工作日内，欧洲证券监管机构委员会应将申请材料复件发送至所有成员国的主管部门。

收到申请后的10个工作日内，欧洲证券监管机构委员会应针对申请材料的完整性向母国主管部门提供建议。

5.收到申请后25个工作日内，母国主管部门与相关运营团的成员应在考虑第4款所述的欧洲证券监管机构委员会建议的情况下评估申请材料是否完整。申请材料不完整的，母国主管部门应设定信用评级机构向母国主管部门和欧洲证券监管机构委员会提供补充信息的时限，并向运营团成员和欧洲证券监管机构委员会发出相应通知。

如果评估显示申请是完整的，则母国主管部门应向信用评级机构、运营团的成员及欧洲证券监管机构委员会发出相应通知。

6.收到第5款所述补充信息后的5个工作日内，欧洲证券监管机构委员会应将补充信息发送至所有成员国的主管部门。

第16条　主管部门对信用评级机构注册申请的审核

agency by the competent authorities

1. The competent authority of the home Member State and the competent authorities which are members of the relevant college shall, within 60 working days of the notification referred to in the second subparagraph of Article 15(5):

(a) jointly examine the application for registration; and

(b) do everything reasonable within their power to reach an agreement on whether to grant or refuse registration of the credit rating agency based on the compliance of the credit rating agency with the conditions set out in this Regulation.

2. The facilitator may extend the period of examination by 30 working days, in particular if the credit rating agency:

(a) envisages endorsing credit ratings as referred to in Article 4(3);

(b) envisages using outsourcing; or

(c) requests exemption from compliance in accordance with Article 6(3).

3. The facilitator shall coordinate the examination of the application submitted by the credit rating agency and shall ensure that all information necessary to carry out the examination of the application is shared among the members of the relevant college.

4. The competent authority of the home Member State shall prepare a fully reasoned draft decision following the agreement referred to in paragraph 1(b) and shall submit it to the facilitator.

In the absence of agreement among the members of the relevant college, the competent authority of the home Member State shall prepare a fully reasoned draft refusal decision based on the written opinions of the members of the college who oppose registration and shall submit it to the facilitator. The members of the college who are in favour of registration shall prepare and submit a detailed explanation of their opinions to the facilitator.

5. Within 60 working days of the notification referred to in the second subparagraph of Article 15(5) and in any event within 90 working days thereof in the event that paragraph 2 applies, the facilitator shall communicate to CESR a fully reasoned draft registration or refusal decision accompanied by the detailed explanations referred to in the second subparagraph of paragraph 4.

6. Within 20 working days of receipt of the communication referred to in paragraph 5, CESR shall provide its advice on the compliance of the credit rating agency with the requirements for the registration to the members of the relevant college. Following receipt of CESR's advice, the members of the college shall re-examine the draft decision.

7. The competent authority of the home Member State shall adopt a fully reasoned registration or refusal decision within 15 working days of receipt of CESR's advice. If the competent authority of the home Member State departs from CESR's advice, it shall

1.母国主管部门与作为相关运营团成员的主管部门应于第15条第5款第2项所述的通知发出后60个工作日内：

(a)联合审核注册申请;并

(b)在其权力范围内采取一切合理行动,根据信用评级机构对本条例所述条件的合规情况,就核准或不核准信用评级机构注册达成一致意见。

2.督导员可将审核期延长30个工作日,特别是在信用评级机构存在下列情形时：

(a)信用评级机构拟获得第4条第3款所述信用评级认可；

(b)拟使用外包服务;或

(c)请求依据第6条第3款获得豁免。

3.督导员应协调信用评级机构递交的申请的审核工作,并确保审核所需的全部信息均在相关运营团成员之间得到共享。

4.在达成第1款第b项所述一致意见后,母国主管部门应起草一份经充分论证的决定草案并呈报督导员。

相关运营团成员无法达成一致意见的,母国主管部门应根据反对核准注册的运营团成员的书面意见,起草一份经充分论证的不核准决定草案并呈报督导员。赞成核准注册的运营团成员应就其意见准备一份详细的解释并呈报督导员。

5.在第15条第5款第2项所述通知发出后60个工作日内,如第2款适用,则在通知发出后90个工作日内,督导员应向欧洲证券监管机构委员会通知经充分论证的核准注册决定草案或附有第4款第2项所述详细解释的不核准决定草案。

6.收到第5款所述通知后20个工作日内,欧洲证券监管机构委员会应就信用评级机构是否符合注册要求向相关运营团的成员提供建议。收到欧洲证券监管机构委员会的建议后,运营团成员应重新审核决定草案。

7.母国主管部门应于收到欧洲证券监管机构委员会建议后15个工作日内,通过经充分论证的核准或不核准注册的决定。母国主管部门不同意欧洲证券监管机构委员会的建议的,应提供充分的理由。欧洲证券监管机构委员会未提供建议的,母国主管

provide full reasons. If CESR has provided no advice, the competent authority of the home Member State shall adopt its decision within 30 working days of the communication to CESR of the draft decision in accordance with paragraph 5.

In the event of a continued absence of agreement among the members of the relevant college, the competent authority of the home Member State shall adopt a fully reasoned refusal decision, which shall identify the dissenting competent authorities and shall include a description of their opinions.

Article 17 Examination of the applications for registration of a group of credit rating agencies by the competent authorities

1. The facilitator and the competent authorities who are members of the relevant college shall, within 60 working days of the notification referred to in the second subparagraph of Article 15(5):

(a) jointly examine the applications for registration; and

(b) do everything reasonable within their power to reach an agreement on whether to grant or refuse registration of the members of the group of credit rating agencies based on the compliance of those credit rating agencies with the conditions set out in this Regulation.

2. The facilitator may extend the period of examination by 30 working days, in particular if any of credit rating agencies in the group:

(a) envisages endorsing credit ratings as referred to in Article 4(3);

(b) envisages using outsourcing; or

(c) requests exemption from compliance in accordance with Article 6(3).

3. The facilitator shall coordinate the examination of the applications submitted by the group of credit rating agencies and shall ensure that all information necessary to carry out the examination of the applications is shared among the members of the relevant college.

4. The competent authorities of the home Member States shall prepare individual fully reasoned draft decisions for each credit rating agency of the group following the agreement referred to in paragraph 1(b) and shall submit it to the facilitator.

In the absence of agreement among the members of the relevant college, the competent authorities of the home Member States shall prepare fully reasoned draft refusal decisions based on the written opinions of the members of the college who oppose registration and shall submit them to the facilitator. The members of the college who are in favour of registration shall prepare and submit a detailed explanation of their opinions to the facilitator.

5. Within 60 working days of the notification as referred to in the second subparagraph of Article 15(5) and in any event within 90 working days thereof in the

部门应在通知欧洲证券监管机构委员会第5款所述的决定草案后30个工作日内通过其决定。

相关运营团成员之间一直无法达成一致意见的,母国主管部门应通过经充分论证的不核准决定,在该决定中注明持反对意见的主管部门并陈述其意见。

第17条　主管部门对信用评级机构集团注册申请的审核

1.督导员和作为相关运营团成员的主管部门应于第15条第5款第2项所述通知后60个工作日内:

(a)联合审核注册申请;并

(b)在其权力范围内采取一切合理的行动,根据信用评级机构集团对本条例所述条件的合规情况,就核准或不核准信用评级机构集团成员注册达成一致意见。

2.督导员可将审核期延长30个工作日,特别是信用评级机构集团存在下列情形时:

(a)集团中的任何信用评级机构拟按第4条第3款所述获得信用评级认可;

(b)拟使用外包服务;或

(c)请求依据第6条第3款获得豁免。

3.督导员应协调信用评级机构集团递交的申请的审核工作,并确保审核所需的全部信息均在相关运营团成员之间得到共享。

4.在达成第1款第b项所述一致意见后,母国主管部门应就集团的每一信用评级机构分别起草一份经充分论证的决定草案并呈报督导员。

相关运营团成员无法达成一致意见的,母国主管部门应根据反对核准注册的运营团成员的书面意见,起草一份经充分论证的不核准决定草案并呈报督导员。赞成核准注册的运营团成员应就其意见准备一份详细的解释并呈报督导员。

5.在第15条第5款第2项所述通知发出后60个工作日内,如果第2款适用,则在通知发出后90个工作日内,督导员应向欧洲证券监管机构委员会通知经充分论证的每一

event that paragraph 2 applies, the facilitator shall communicate to CESR fully reasoned individual draft registration or refusal decisions accompanied by the detailed explanations referred to in the second subparagraph of paragraph 4.

6. Within 20 working days of receipt of the communication referred to in paragraph 5, CESR shall provide its advice on the compliance of the credit rating agencies of the group with the requirements for the registration to the members of the relevant college. Following receipt of CESR's advice, the members of the college shall re-examine the draft decisions.

7. The competent authorities of the home Member States shall adopt fully reasoned registration or refusal decisions within 15 working days of receipt of the advice of CESR. If the competent authorities of the home Member States depart from CESR's advice, they shall provide full reasons. If CESR has provided no advice, the competent authorities of the home Member States shall adopt their decisions within 30 working days of the communication to CESR of the draft decisions in accordance with paragraph 5.

In the event of continued absence of agreement among the members of the relevant college on whether to register any of the credit rating agencies of the group, the competent authority of the home Member State of such credit rating agency shall adopt a fully reasoned refusal decision, which shall identify the dissenting competent authorities and shall include a description of their opinions.

Article 18 Notification of the decision on the registration, refusal of registration or the withdrawal of registration of a credit rating agency

1. Within five working days of the adoption of a decision under Articles 16 or 17 the competent authority of the home Member State shall notify the credit rating agency concerned whether or not it has been registered. Where the competent authority of the home Member State refuses to register the credit rating agency, it shall provide full reasons in its decision.

2. The competent authority of the home Member State shall notify the Commission, CESR and the other competent authorities of any decision under Article 16, 17 or 20.

3. The Commission shall publish in the *Official Journal of the European Union* and on its website a list of credit rating agencies registered in accordance with this Regulation. That list shall be updated within 30 days of the notification referred to in paragraph 2.

Article 19 Registration and supervisory fees

The competent authority of the home Member State may charge registration and/or supervisory fees to the credit rating agency. The registration and/or supervisory fees shall be proportionate to the cost incurred by the competent authority of the home Member State.

Article 20 Withdrawal of registration

1. The competent authority of the home Member State shall withdraw the registration

信用评级机构各自的核准注册决定草案或附有第4款第2项所述详细解释的不核准决定草案。

6.收到第5款所述通知后20个工作日内，欧洲证券监管机构委员会应就集团内的信用评级机构是否符合注册要求向相关运营团的成员提供建议。收到欧洲证券监管机构委员会的建议后，运营团成员应重新审核决定草案。

7.母国主管部门应于收到欧洲证券监管机构委员会建议后15个工作日内，通过经充分论证的核准或不核准注册的决定。母国主管部门不同意欧洲证券监管机构委员会的建议的，应提供充分的理由。欧洲证券监管机构委员会未提供建议的，母国主管部门应在通知欧洲证券监管机构委员会第5款所述的决定草案后30个工作日内通过其决定。

相关运营团成员之间一直无法就集团内任一信用评级机构的注册达成一致意见的，信用评级机构各自的母国主管部门应通过经充分论证的不核准决定，在该决定中注明持反对意见的主管部门并陈述其意见。

第18条　核准、不核准或撤销信用评级机构注册决定的通知

1.根据第16条或第17条通过决定后的5个工作日内，母国主管部门应通知所涉信用评级机构其是否已获准注册。母国主管部门不核准信用评级机构的注册的，应在其决定中提供充分理由。

2.母国主管部门应向欧盟委员会、欧洲证券监管机构委员会及其他主管部门通知根据第16条、第17条或第20条作出的任何决定。

3.欧盟委员会应在《欧盟公报》及其网站公布根据本条例注册的信用评级机构名单。该名单应于第2款所述的通知发出后30天内更新。

第19条　注册费和监管费

母国主管部门可向信用评级机构收取注册费和/或监管费。注册费和/或监管费应与母国主管部门发生的成本成比例。

第20条　撤销注册

1.信用评级机构出现以下情形的，母国主管部门应撤销其注册：

of a credit rating agency where the credit rating agency:

(a) expressly renounces the registration or has provided no credit ratings for the preceding six months;

(b) has obtained the registration by making false statements or by any other irregular means;

(c) no longer meets the conditions under which it was registered; or

(d) has seriously or repeatedly infringed the provisions of this Regulation governing the operating conditions for credit rating agencies.

2. Where the competent authority of the home Member State considers that one of the conditions referred to in paragraph 1 has been met, it shall notify the facilitator and closely cooperate with members of the relevant college in order to decide whether or not to withdraw the registration of the credit rating agency.

The members of the college shall carry out a joint assessment and do everything reasonable within their power to reach an agreement on the necessity to withdraw the registration to the credit rating agency.

In the absence of agreement, the competent authority of the home Member State shall, at the request of any of the other members of the college or on its own initiative, request advice from CESR. CESR shall provide its advice within 15 working days of receipt of such request.

The competent authority of each home Member State shall adopt an individual withdrawal decision on the basis of the agreement reached within the college.

In the absence of an agreement between the members of the college within 30 working days of notification to the facilitator as referred to in the first subparagraph, the competent authority of the home Member State may adopt an individual withdrawal decision. Any deviation of its decision from the opinions expressed by the other members of the college and, where appropriate, the advice provided by CESR shall be fully reasoned.

3. The competent authority of a Member State in which credit ratings issued by the credit rating agency concerned are used and which considers that one of the conditions referred to in paragraph 1 has been met may request the relevant college to examine whether the conditions for withdrawal of registration are met. If the competent authority of the home Member State decides not to withdraw the registration of the credit rating agency concerned, it shall provide full reasons.

4. The decision on the withdrawal of registration shall take immediate effect throughout the Community, subject to the transitional period for the use of credit ratings referred to in Article 24(2) .

(a)明确放弃注册，或在注册后的前6个月期间未提供任何信用评级；

(b)通过虚假陈述或其他非法方式获得注册；

(c)不再符合获得注册时所满足的条件；或
(d)严重或反复违反本条例关于信用评级机构运营条件的规定。

2.母国主管部门认为第1款所述的任何一项条件得到满足的，应通知督导员并与相关运营团的成员紧密合作，以决定是否撤销信用评级机构的注册。

运营团成员应开展联合评估，并在其权力范围内采取一切合理的行动，就是否有必要撤销信用评级机构注册达成一致意见。

无法达成一致意见的，母国主管部门经运营团任何其他成员请求或出于主动，应请求欧洲证券监管机构委员会提供建议。欧洲证券监管机构委员会应于收到上述请求后15个工作日内提供建议。

各母国主管部门应根据运营团内达成的一致意见通过仅针对所涉信用评级机构的撤销决定。

运营团成员无法如第一项所述在向督导员发出通知后30个工作日内达成一致意见的，母国主管部门可通过仅针对所涉信用评级机构的撤销决定。其决定与运营团其他成员的意见及欧洲证券监管机构委员会的建议(如有)之间的任何偏离均应经过充分的论证。

3.成员国主管部门认为，发布在其境内使用的信用评级的信用评级机构存在第1款所述的其中一项情况的，可请求相关运营团就是否符合撤销登记的条件进行审核。母国主管部门决定不撤销所涉信用评级机构的注册的，应提供充分理由。

4.撤销注册的决定应立即在全欧共体境内生效，并适用第24条第2款所述的信用评级使用过渡期。

CHAPTER II CESR and competent authorities

Article 21 Committee of European Securities Regulators

1. CESR shall provide advice to the competent authorities in the cases provided for in this Regulation. The competent authorities shall consider that advice before taking any final decision under this Regulation.

2. By 7 June 2010, CESR shall issue guidance on:

(a) the registration process and coordination arrangements between competent authorities and with CESR, including on the information set out in Annex II, and language regime for applications submitted to CESR;

(b) the operational functioning of the colleges, including on the modalities for determining the membership to the colleges, the application of the criteria for the selection of the facilitator referred to in Article 29(5)(a) to (d) the written arrangements for the operation of colleges and the coordination arrangements between colleges;

(c) the application of the endorsement regime under Article 4(3) by competent authorities; and

(d) common standards on the presentation of the information, including structure, format, method and period of reporting, that credit rating agencies shall disclose in accordance with Article 11(2) and point 1 of Part II of Section E of Annex I.

3. By 7 September 2010, CESR shall issue guidance on:

(a) enforcement practices and activities to be conducted by competent authorities under this Regulation;

(b) common standards for assessment of compliance of credit rating methodologies with the requirements set out in Article 8(3) ;

(c) types of measures referred to in Article 24(1)(d) to ensure that credit rating agencies continue to comply with legal requirements; and

(d) information that the credit rating agency must provide for the application for certification and for the assessment of its systemic importance to the financial stability or integrity of financial markets referred to in Article 5.

4. CESR shall publish, annually and for the first time by 7 December 2010, a report on the application of this Regulation.

5. CESR shall cooperate with the Committee of European Banking Supervisors established by Commission Decision 2009/78/EC [1] and the Committee of European

1 OJ L 25, 29.1.2009, p. 23.

第二章　欧洲证券监管机构委员会和主管部门

第21条　欧洲证券监管机构委员会

1.欧洲证券监管机构委员会应在本条例规定的情形下向主管部门提供建议。各主管部门应在根据本条例作出任何最终决定前考虑该建议。

2.2010年6月7日前,欧洲证券监管机构委员会应针对下列事项发布指引:

(a)主管部门和欧洲证券监管机构委员会之间的注册流程及协调安排,包括附录二要求提供的信息,以及递交给欧洲证券监管机构委员会的申请材料的语言规则;

(b)运营团的具体运作方式,包括确定运营团成员资格的方式、遴选第29条第5款第a项至第d项所述督导员的标准的运用、运营团运作的书面安排以及不同运营团之间的协调安排;

(c)主管部门对第4条第3款的认可机制的适用;及

(d)信用评级机构根据第11条第2款及附录一第E节第二部分第1项披露信息的列报方式的通用标准,包括结构、格式、方法及报告期。

3.2010年9月7日前,欧洲证券监管机构委员会应针对下列事项发布指引:

(a)主管部门根据本条例开展的执法实践及活动;

(b)评估信用评级方法是否符合第8条第3款规定所应采用的通用标准;

(c)第24条第1款第d项所述的为确保信用评级机构持续遵守法律规定可以采取的措施类型;及

(d)如第5条所述为了申请认证以及评估信用评级机构对金融市场的金融稳定性或诚信度的系统重要性时,信用评级机构须提供的信息。

4.欧洲证券监管机构委员会应每年就本条例的适用公布一份报告,并于2010年12月7日前作出首次公布。该报告应主要包括对根据本条例注册的信用评级机构实施附录一的情况的评估。

5.欧洲证券监管机构委员会应与欧盟委员会第2009/78/EC号决定[1]所设立的欧洲

1　2009 年 1 月 29 日《欧盟公报》L25,第 23 页。

Insurance and Occupational Pensions Supervisors established by Commission Decision 2009/79/EC [1] and shall consult those Committees before publishing guidance referred to in paragraphs 2 and 3.

Article 22 Competent authorities

1. By 7 June 2010, each Member State shall designate a competent authority for the purpose of this Regulation.

2. Competent authorities shall be adequately staffed, with regard to capacity and expertise, in order to be able to apply this Regulation.

Article 23 Powers of competent authorities

1. In carrying out their duties under this Regulation, neither the competent authorities nor any other public authorities of a Member State shall interfere with the content of credit ratings or methodologies.

2. In order to carry out their duties under this Regulation, the competent authorities shall, in conformity with national law, have all the supervisory and investigatory powers that are necessary for the exercise of their functions. They shall exercise their powers:

(a) directly;

(b) in collaboration with other authorities; or

(c) by application to the competent judicial authorities.

3. In order to carry out their duties under this Regulation, the competent authorities shall, in conformity with national law, have the power in their supervisory capacity to:

(a) access any document in any form and to receive or take a copy thereof;

(b) demand information from any person and if necessary to summon and question a person with a view to obtaining information;

(c) carry out on-site inspections with or without announcement; and

(d) require records of telephone and data traffic.

The competent authorities may use the powers referred to in the first subparagraph only in relation to credit rating agencies, persons involved in credit rating activities, rated entities and related third parties, third parties to whom the credit rating agencies have outsourced certain functions or activities, and persons otherwise related or connected to credit rating agencies or credit rating activities.

Article 24 Supervisory measures by the competent authorities of the home Member State

1. Where the competent authority of the home Member State has established that a registered credit rating agency breaches the obligations arising from this Regulation, it

1 OJ L 25, 29.1.2009, p. 28.

银行业监管机构委员会以及欧盟委员会第2009/79/EC号决定[1]所设立的欧洲保险与职业养老金监管机构委员会合作，并在公布第2款和第3款所述指引前咨询该等委员会的意见。

第22条 主管部门

1.2010年6月7日前，各成员国应指定与本条例相关的主管部门。

2.各主管部门应在能力和专长方面有充分的人员配置，以具备适用本条例的能力。

第23条 主管部门的权力

1.履行其在本条例中的职责时，主管部门或成员国任何其他公共机构均不得干预信用评级内容或方法。

2.为履行其在本条例中的职责，主管部门应依照成员国国内法律拥有一切行使其职能所需的监管和调查权力。主管部门应以下列方式行使其权力：

(a)直接行使；
(b)与其他部门合作行使；或
(c)诉诸有管辖权的司法部门。

3.为履行本条例中的职责，主管部门应依照成员国国内法律拥有以下监管权力：

(a)查阅任何形式的任何文件并接收其复件或对其进行复制；
(b)要求任何人提供信息并在必要时传唤任何人员并向其提问；
(c)开展现场检查(不论是否提前作出检查公告)；及
(d)要求提供电话记录和数据通信记录。

主管部门仅可对下列主体行使第一项所述权力：信用评级机构、参与信用评级活动的人、被评级实体和相关第三方、承接信用评级机构外包的某些职能或活动的第三方，以及与信用评级机构或信用评级活动相关或有关联的其他人。

第24条 母国主管部门的监管措施

1.母国主管部门确定注册信用评级机构违反了本条例产生的义务的，可以采取下列措施：

1 2009年1月29日《欧盟公报》L25，第28页。

may take the following measures:

(a) withdraw the registration of that credit rating agency in accordance with Article 20;

(b) temporarily prohibit that credit rating agency from issuing credit ratings with effect throughout the Community;

(c) suspend the use, for regulatory purposes, of the credit ratings issued by that credit rating agency with effect throughout the Community;

(d) take appropriate measures to ensure that credit rating agencies continue to comply with legal requirements;

(e) issue public notices;

(f) refer matters for criminal prosecution to its relevant national authorities.

2. Credit ratings may continue to be used for regulatory purposes following the adoption of measures in points (a) and (c) of paragraph 1 during a period not exceeding:

(a) ten working days if there are credit ratings of the same financial instrument or entity issued by other credit rating agencies registered under this Regulation; or

(b) three months if there are no credit ratings of the same financial instrument or entity issued by other credit rating agencies registered under this Regulation.

A competent authority may extend the period referred to in point (b) of the first subparagraph by three months in exceptional circumstances relating to the potential for market disruption or financial instability.

3. Before taking any measures referred to in paragraph 1, the competent authority of the home Member State shall notify the facilitator and shall consult the members of the relevant college. The members of the college shall do everything reasonable within their power to reach an agreement on the necessity to take any measures referred to in paragraph 1.

In the absence of agreement between the members of the college, the competent authority of the home Member State shall, at the request of any member of the college or on its own initiative, request advice from CESR. CESR shall provide its advice within 10 working days of receipt of such request.

In the absence of agreement between the members of the college on whether to take any measures referred to in paragraph 1 within 15 working days after the matter was notified to the facilitator as referred to in the first subparagraph, the competent authority of the home Member State may adopt a decision. Any deviation of that decision from the opinions expressed by the other members of the college and, where appropriate, the advice provided by CESR shall be fully reasoned. The competent authority of the home Member State shall notify its decision, without undue delay, to the facilitator and CESR.

(a)根据第20条撤销信用评级机构的注册；

(b)暂时禁止信用评级机构在欧共体全境发布信用评级；

(c)为监管目的暂停该信用评级机构发布的信用评级在欧共体全境的使用；

(d)采取适当措施以确保该信用评级机构持续遵守法律规定；

(e)发布公告；

(f)将相关事宜移送相关国家级监管机构进行刑事追诉。

2.第1款第a目与第c目的措施通过后，信用评级可继续在一定期限内用于监管目的，该等期限：

(a)如有其他依本条例注册的信用评级机构对相同金融工具或实体发布信用评级，不得超过10个工作日；或

(b)若无任何其他依本条例注册的信用评级机构对相同金融工具或实体发布信用评级，不得超过3个月。

在可能造成市场扰乱或金融不稳定的特殊情形下，主管部门可将第一项第b目所述期限延长3个月。

3.在采取第1款所述任何措施之前，母国主管部门应通知督导员，并征求相关运营团的成员的意见。运营团的成员应在其权力范围内采取一切合理的行动，以就是否有必要采取第1款所述的措施达成一致意见。

相关运营团成员无法达成一致意见的，母国主管部门经运营团任何成员请求或出于主动，应请求欧洲证券监管机构委员会提供建议。欧洲证券监管机构委员会应于收到上述请求后10个工作日内提供建议。

按第1项通知督导员相关事宜后15个工作日内，运营团成员无法就是否采取第1款所述的任何措施达成一致意见的，母国主管部门可自行通过决定。其决定与运营团其他成员的意见及欧洲证券监管机构委员会的建议（如有）之间的任何偏离均应经过充分的论证。母国主管部门应通知督导员及欧洲证券监管机构委员会其决定，不得无故延误。

This paragraph shall apply without prejudice to Article 20.

Article 25 Supervisory measures by competent authorities other than the competent authority of the home Member State

1. Where the competent authority of a Member State has established that a registered credit rating agency whose ratings are used within its territory breaches the obligations arising from this Regulation, it may take the following measures:

(a) adopt the supervisory measures referred to in Article 24(1)(e) and (f);

(b) adopt measures referred to in Article 24(1)(d) within its jurisdiction and, where so doing, duly consider the measures already taken or envisaged by the competent authority of the home Member State;

(c) impose the suspension of the use of credit ratings of that credit rating agency for regulatory purposes by institutions referred to in Article 4(1) whose registered office is located within its jurisdiction, subject to the transitional period referred to in Article 24 (2);

(d) request the relevant college to examine whether the measures referred to in points (b)(c) or (d) of Article 24(1) are needed.

2. Before the adoption of measures referred to in points (a)(b) or (c) of paragraph 1, the competent authority shall notify the facilitator and consult the members of the relevant college. The members of the college shall do everything reasonable within their power to reach an agreement on the necessity to take any measures referred to in points (a) and (b) of paragraph 1. In the event of disagreement, the facilitator shall, at the request of any of the members of the college or on its own initiative, request advice from CESR. CESR shall provide its advice within 10 working days of receipt of such request.

3. In the absence of an agreement between the members of the relevant college within 15 working days of the matter being notified to the facilitator in accordance with paragraph 2, the competent authority of the Member State concerned may adopt a decision. Any deviation of its decision from the opinions expressed by the other members of the college and, where appropriate, the advice provided by CESR shall be fully reasoned. The competent authority of the Member State concerned shall notify its decision, without undue delay, to the facilitator and CESR.

4. This Article shall apply without prejudice to Article 20.

CHAPTER III Cooperation between competent authorities

Article 26 Obligation to cooperate

1.The competent authorities shall cooperate where it is necessary for the purposes of this Regulation, including in cases where the conduct under investigation does not constitute an infringement of any legislative or regulatory provision in force in the Member

本款的适用不应对第20条造成影响。

第25条　非母国主管部门的主管部门的监管措施

1.某一成员国主管部门确定，发布在其境内使用的信用评级的信用评级机构违反了本条例所产生的义务的，可采取如下措施：

(a)采取第24条第1款第e目和第f目所述的监管措施；

(b)在其司法管辖区内采取第24条第1款第d目所述的措施，同时还要充分考虑母国主管部门已经采取或计划采取的措施；

(c)暂停第4条第1款所述的在其司法管辖区内注册的机构为监管目的使用该信用评级机构的信用评级，除非处于第24条第2款所述的过渡期；

(d)要求相关运营团审核是否需要采取第24条第1款第b目、第c目或第d目所述措施。

2.采取第1款第a目、第b目或第c目所述措施前，主管部门应通知督导员，并征求相关运营团的成员的意见。运营团的成员应在其权力范围内采取一切合理行动，就采取第1款第a目和第b目所述措施的必要性达成一致意见。成员意见不一致的，督导员经运营团任何成员请求或出于主动，应请求欧洲证券监管机构委员会提供建议。欧洲证券监管机构委员会应于收到上述请求后10个工作日内提供其建议。

3.根据第2款通知督导员相关事宜后15个工作日内，相关运营团的成员之间无法达成一致意见的，所涉成员国的主管部门可通过决定。其决定与运营团其他成员的意见及欧洲证券监管机构委员会的建议(如有)之间的任何偏离均应经过充分的论证。所涉成员国主管部门应通知督导员及欧洲证券监管机构委员会其决定，不得无故延误。

4.本条规定的适用不应对第20条产生影响。

第三章　主管部门之间的合作

第26条　合作义务

1.主管部门应在就本条例而言必要的情形下进行合作，包括在被调查的行为并不违反所涉成员国的任何现行立法或监管规定的情形下。

State concerned.

2. The competent authorities shall also cooperate closely with the competent authorities responsible for supervision of the undertakings referred to in Article 4(1) .

Article 27 Exchange of information

1. The competent authorities shall, without undue delay, supply each other with the information required for the purposes of carrying out their duties under this Regulation.

2. The competent authorities may transmit to the competent authorities responsible for supervising the undertakings referred to in Article 4(1) central banks, the European System of Central Banks and the European Central Bank, in their capacity as monetary authorities, and, where appropriate, to other public authorities responsible for overseeing payment and settlement systems, confidential information intended for the performance of their tasks. Similarly, such authorities or bodies shall not be prevented from communicating to the competent authorities information that the competent authorities may need in order to carry out their duties under this Regulation.

Article 28 Cooperation in case of a request with regard to on-site inspections or investigations

1. The competent authority of one Member State may request the assistance of the competent authority of another Member State with regard to on-site inspections or investigations.

The competent authority making such request shall inform CESR of any request referred to in the first subparagraph. In the event of an investigation or inspection with cross-border effect, the competent authorities may request CESR to assume coordination of the investigation or inspection.

2. Where a competent authority receives a request from a competent authority of another Member State to carry out an on-site inspection or an investigation, it shall:

(a) carry out the on-site inspection or investigation itself;

(b) allow the competent authority which submitted the request to participate in an on-site inspection or investigation;

(c) allow the competent authority which submitted the request to carry out the on-site inspection or investigation itself;

(d) appoint auditors or experts to carry out the on-site inspection or investigation; or

(e) share specific tasks related to supervisory activities with the other competent authorities.

Article 29 Colleges of competent authorities

1. Within 10 working days of receipt of an application for registration under Article 15, the competent authority of the home Member State, or, in the case of a group of credit rating agencies, the competent authority of the home Member State of the credit rating

2.主管部门应与负责监管第4条第1款所述企业的主管部门紧密合作。

第27条 信息交换

1.主管部门应互相提供履行本条例职责所必要的信息,不得无故延误。

2.主管部门可向负责监管第4条第1款所述企业的主管部门、各成员国中央银行、欧洲中央银行体系和欧洲中央银行等货币管理当局,以及负责监控支付系统和结算系统的其他公共机构(如有)传送履行其职责所必要的保密信息。同样,上述部门或机构通知主管部门该主管部门履行其本条例项下职责可能需要的信息时不应受到阻碍。

第28条 请求开展现场检查或调查时的合作

1.成员国主管部门可要求另一成员国的主管部门就现场检查或调查提供协助。

提出上述请求的主管部门应就第一项所述的任何请求通知欧洲证券监管机构委员会。对于跨境调查或检查,主管部门可请求欧洲证券监管机构委员会协调调查或检查。

2.主管部门收到另一成员国主管部门开展现场检查或调查的请求后,应:

(a)亲自开展现场检查或调查;
(b)允许提出请求的主管部门参与现场检查或调查;

(c)允许提出请求的主管部门自行开展现场检查或调查;

(d)委托审计师或专家完成现场检查或调查;或
(e)与其他主管部门分担监管活动的具体职责。

第29条 主管部门运营团

1.收到根据第15条提出的注册申请后10个工作日内,母国主管部门或(如果涉及信用评级机构集团)根据第15条第2款获得授权的信用评级机构所在的母国主管部门应成立一个主管部门运营团,以期履行第4条、第5条、第6条、第16条、第17条、第20条、

agency mandated under Article 15(2) shall establish a college of competent authorities in order to facilitate the exercise of the tasks referred to in Articles 4, 5, 6, 16, 17, 20, 24, 25 and 28.

2. The college shall comprise the competent authority of the home Member State and the competent authorities referred to in paragraph 3 in the case of a single agency, or the competent authorities of the home Member States and the competent authorities referred to in paragraph 3 in the case of a group of rating agencies.

3. A competent authority other than the competent authority of the home Member State may at any time decide to become a member of the college provided that:

(a) a branch which is a part of the credit rating agency or of one of the undertakings in the group of credit rating agencies is established within its jurisdiction; or

(b) the use for regulatory purposes of credit ratings issued by the credit rating agency or the group of credit rating agencies concerned is widespread or has or is likely to have a significant impact within its jurisdiction.

4. The competent authorities other than the members of the college as referred to in paragraph 3 in the jurisdictions of which the credit ratings issued by the credit rating agency or by the group of credit rating agencies concerned are used may participate in a meeting or in an activity of the college.

5. Within 15 working days of the establishment of the college, its members shall select a facilitator, consulting CESR in the absence of agreement. For that purpose, at least the following criteria shall be taken into account:

(a) the relationship between the competent authority and the credit rating agency or the group of credit rating agencies;

(b) the extent to which credit ratings will be used for regulatory purposes in a particular territory or territories;

(c) the place in the Community where the credit rating agency or group of credit rating agencies pursues or is planning to pursue the most important part of its credit rating activities; and

(d) administrative convenience, burden optimisation, and an appropriate distribution of the workload.

Members of the college shall review the selection of the facilitator at least every five years to ensure the selected facilitator remains the most appropriate following the criteria referred to in the first subparagraph.

6. The facilitator shall chair the meetings of the college, coordinate the actions of the college and ensure efficient exchange of information among members of the college.

7. In order to ensure close cooperation between competent authorities within the college, the facilitator shall, within 10 working days of his or her selection, establish

第24条、第25条和第28条所述的职责。

2.涉及单一信用评级机构的，运营团应由母国主管部门和第3款所述的主管部门组成，涉及评级机构集团的，运营团应由集团下属各评级机构的母国主管部门和第3款所述的主管部门组成。

3.非母国主管部门的主管部门，可于下列情形下随时决定成为运营团的成员：

（a）作为信用评级机构组成部分的分支机构，或作为信用评级机构集团其中一个企业组成部分的分支机构，在其司法管辖区内设立；或

（b）所涉信用评级机构或信用评级机构集团所发布的信用评级，在其司法管辖区内被广泛用于监管目的，或其使用实际上或可能在其司法管辖区内造成重大的影响。

4.对于并非第3款所述运营团成员的主管部门，所涉信用评级机构或信用评级机构集团所发布的信用评级在其司法管辖区内使用的，该等主管部门可参加运营团的会议或活动。

5.运营团设立后15个工作日内，其成员应遴选出一名督导员，无法就督导员人选达成一致意见的，可征求欧洲证券监管机构委员会的意见。为此，至少应考虑以下遴选标准：

（a）主管部门和信用评级机构或信用评级机构集团之间的关系；

（b）在特定的一个或多个辖区内，信用评级在多大程度上被用于监管目的；

（c）信用评级机构或信用评级机构集团在欧共体境内何等地点从事或计划从事其最重要的信用评级活动；及

（d）行政上的方便、职责负担的优化及工作量的适当分配。

运营团的成员应至少每5年审评一次督导员人选，以确保选出的督导员是符合第1项所述标准最适当的人选。

6.督导员应主持运营团会议、协调运营团行动并确保运营团的成员之间高效率的信息交换。

7.为确保运营团内主管部门之间的紧密合作，督导员应于当选后10个工作日内，就下列事项在运营团框架内建立书面协调安排：

written coordination arrangements within the framework of the college regarding the following matters:

(a) information to be exchanged between competent authorities;

(b) the decision -making process between the competent authorities, without prejudice to Articles 16, 17, and 20;

(c) cases in which the competent authorities must consult each other;

(d) cases in which the competent authorities must apply the mediation mechanism referred to in Article 31; and

(e) cases in which the competent authorities may delegate supervisory tasks in accordance with Article 30.

8. In the absence of agreement concerning the written coordination arrangements under paragraph 7, any member of the college may refer the matter to CESR. The facilitator shall give due consideration to any advice provided by CESR concerning the written coordination arrangements before agreeing their final text. The written coordination arrangements shall be set out in a single document containing full reasons for any significant deviation from the advice of CESR. The facilitator shall transmit the written coordination arrangements to the members of the college and to CESR.

Article 30 Delegation of tasks between competent authorities

The competent authority of the home Member State may delegate any of its tasks to the competent authority of another Member State subject to the agreement of that authority. Delegation of tasks shall not affect the responsibility of the delegating competent authority.

Article 31 Mediation

1. CESR shall establish a mediation mechanism to assist in finding a common view among the competent authorities concerned.

2. on the event of disagreement between competent authorities concerning an examination or action under this Regulation, they shall refer the matter to CESR for mediation. The competent authorities concerned shall give due consideration to the advice of CESR and shall provide full reasons for any deviation from that advice.

Article 32 Professional secrecy

1. The obligation of professional secrecy shall apply to all persons who work or who have worked for CESR, for the competent authority or for any authority or person to whom the competent authority has delegated tasks, including auditors and experts contracted by the competent authority. Information covered by professional secrecy shall not be disclosed to another person or authority except where such disclosure is necessary for legal proceedings.

2. All the information exchanged between CESR and the competent authorities and

(a)主管部门之间将交换的信息；

(b)主管部门之间的决策程序(不影响第16条、第17条及第20条)；

(c)主管部门应互相征求意见的情形；

(d)主管部门应适用第31条所述调解机制的情形；及

(e)主管部门可根据第30条将监管职责委托给其他实体的情形。

8.无法就第7款中的书面协调安排达成一致意见的，运营团的任何成员均可将事项移交给欧洲证券监管机构委员会处理。在同意书面协调安排的最终文本前，督导员应充分考虑欧洲证券监管机构委员会所提出的任何建议。书面协调安排应载于一份单一文件中，与欧洲证券监管机构委员会建议出现重大偏离的，该文件应提供充分理由。督导员应将书面协调安排发送给运营团的成员及欧洲证券监管机构委员会。

第30条　主管部门之间的职责委托

经另一成员国主管部门同意，母国主管部门可将其任何职责委托给该主管部门。职责委托不应对作为委托方的主管部门的责任造成任何影响。

第31条　调解

1.欧洲证券监管机构委员会应建立一项调解机制，以协助所涉主管部门达成共识。

2.主管部门在依本条例进行的审核或行动上意见不一的，应将该事宜移交欧洲证券监管机构委员会调解。所涉主管部门应充分考虑欧洲证券监管机构委员会的建议，与该建议出现偏离的，应提供充分理由。

第32条　职业保密

1.职业保密义务适用于欧洲证券监管机构委员会、主管部门或接受主管部门职责委托的任何部门或个人的前任或现任工作人员，包括主管部门所聘请的审计师和专家。属于职业保密范围内的信息不得披露给其他人或部门，该项披露对法律程序确属必要的除外。

2.欧洲证券监管机构委员会和主管部门之间以及主管部门之间根据本条例交换

between competent authorities under this Regulation shall be considered confidential, except where CESR or the competent authority concerned states at the time of communication that such information may be disclosed or where such disclosure is necessary for legal proceedings.

Article 33 Disclosure of information from another Member State

The competent authority of a Member State may disclose the information received from a competent authority of another Member State only if it has obtained the express agreement of the competent authority that transmitted the information and, where applicable, the information is disclosed only for the purposes for which that competent authority gave its agreement, or where such disclosure is necessary for legal proceedings.

CHAPTER IV Cooperation with third countries

Article 34 Agreement on exchange of information

The competent authorities may conclude cooperation agreements on exchange of information with the competent authorities of third countries only if the information disclosed is subject to guarantees of professional secrecy which are at least equivalent to those set out in Article 32.

Such exchange of information shall be intended for the performance of the tasks of those competent authorities.

With regard to transfer of personal data to a third country, Member States shall apply Directive 95/46/EC.

Article 35 Disclosure of information from third countries

The competent authority of a Member State may disclose the information received from competent authorities of third countries only if it has obtained the express agreement of the competent authority that has transmitted the information and, where applicable, the information is disclosed only for the purposes for which that competent authority gave its agreement, or where such disclosure is necessary for legal proceedings.

的所有信息均应视为保密信息，除非欧洲证券监管机构委员会或所涉主管部门在发出信息通知时指明该等信息可予披露，或上述披露对法律程序确属必要。

第33条　披露来自其他成员国的信息

成员国主管部门唯有获得发送信息的另一成员国主管部门明确同意，方可披露从该主管部门接收到的信息，并且，该信息只能按该主管部门同意的目的披露（如适用）；或者，在对法律程序确属必要的情况下，成员国主管部门也可做上述披露。

第四章　与第三国合作

第34条　信息交换协议

唯有披露的信息受到至少与第32条规定的职业保密保证同等严格的保证时，主管部门方可与第三国主管部门缔结信息交换合作协议。

上述信息交换应以使该等主管部门履行职责为目的。

对于个人数据向第三国的传送，成员国应适用第95/46/EC号指令。

第35条　披露来自第三国的信息

成员国主管部门唯有获得发送信息的第三国主管部门明确同意，方可披露来自该主管部门的信息，并且，该信息只能按该主管部门同意的目的披露（如适用）；或者，在对法律程序确属必要的情况下，成员国主管部门也可做上述披露。

TITLE IV PENALTIES, COMMITTEE PROCEDURE, REPORTING AND TRANSITIONAL AND FINAL PROVISIONS

CHAPTER I Penalties, committee procedure and reporting

Article 36 Penalties

Member States shall lay down the rules on penalties applicable to infringements of the provisions of this Regulation and shall take all measures necessary to ensure that they are implemented. The penalties provided for shall be effective, proportionate and dissuasive.

Member States shall ensure that the competent authority disclose to the public every penalty that has been imposed for infringement of this Regulation, unless such disclosure would seriously jeopardise the financial markets or cause disproportionate damage to the parties involved.

By 7 December 2010 the Member States shall notify the rules referred to in the first subparagraph to the Commission. They shall notify the Commission without delay of any subsequent amendment thereto.

Article 37 Amendments to Annexes

The Commission may amend the Annexes in order to take account of developments, including international developments, on financial markets, in particular in relation to new financial instruments and with regard to convergence of supervisory practice.

Those measures, designed to amend non-essential elements of this Regulation, shall be adopted in accordance with the regulatory procedure with scrutiny referred to in Article 38(2).

Article 38 Committee procedure

1. The Commission shall be assisted by the European Securities Committee established by Commission Decision 2001/528/EC[1].

2. Where reference is made to this paragraph, Article 5a(1) to (4) and Article 7 of Decision 1999/468/EC shall apply, having regard to the provisions of Article 8 thereof.

3. Where reference is made to this paragraph, Article 5 and Article 7 of Decision

1 OJ L 191, 13.7.2001, p. 45.

第四编　罚则、委员会程序、报告和过渡规定及最终条款

第一章　罚则、委员会程序和报告

第36条　罚则

成员国应针对违反本条例规定的行为制定适用的罚则，并采取一切必要的措施以确保其得以实施。规定的处罚应当有效、成比例且具有威慑作用。

成员国应确保主管部门可向公众披露对违反本条例实施的各项处罚，但上述披露会严重危害金融市场或对所涉各方造成不成比例损害的除外。

2010年12月7日前，各成员国应通知欧盟委员会第1项所述的规则。之后如有任何修正，成员国应立即通知欧盟委员会。

第37条　对附录的修正

欧盟委员会可修正附录，以反映金融市场（包括国际金融市场）的发展动态，尤其是新金融工具及监管实践趋同等方面的发展动态。

应依照第38条第2款所述的须经欧盟理事会和欧洲议会审查的监管程序制定旨在修正本条例非基本要素的该等细则。

第38条　委员会程序

1.欧盟委员会应得到欧盟委员会第2001/528/EC号决定[1]所设立的欧洲证券委员会的协助。

2.根据第1999/468/EC号决定第8条规定，引用本款内容时，应适用该决定的第5a条第1款至第4款和第7条。

3.引用本款内容时，应当适用第1999/468/EC号决定的第5条和第7条（如涉及该决

1　2001年7月13日《欧盟公报》L191，第45页。

1999/468/EC shall apply, having regard to the provisions of Article 8 thereof.

The period laid down in Article 5(6) of Decision 1999/468/EC shall be set at three months.

Article 39 Reports

1. By 7 December 2012, the Commission shall make an assessment of the application of this Regulation, including an assessment of the reliance on credit ratings in the Community, the impact on the level of concentration in the credit rating market, the cost and benefit of impacts of the Regulation and of the appropriateness of the remuneration of the credit rating agency by the rated entity (issuer-pays model) and submit a report thereon to the European Parliament and the Council.

2. By 7 December 2010, the Commission shall, in the light of discussions with the competent authorities, assess the application of Title III of this Regulation, in particular of the cooperation of the competent authorities, the legal status of CESR and supervisory practices. The Commission shall present a report on those matters to the European Parliament and to the Council, accompanied, where appropriate, by proposals for a review of that Title.

That report shall include a reference to the Commission proposal of 12 November 2008 for a regulation on credit rating agencies and to the report of the Committee on Economic and Monetary Affairs of the European Parliament of 23 March 2009 relating to that proposal.

3. By 7 December 2010, the Commission shall, in the light of developments in the regulatory and supervisory framework for credit rating agencies in third countries, present a report to the European Parliament and to the Council concerning the effects of those developments and of the transitional provisions referred to in Article 40 on the stability of financial markets in the Community.

CHAPTER II Transitional and final provisions

Article 40 Transitional provision

Credit rating agencies operating in the Community before 7 June 2010 (existing credit rating agencies) which intend to apply for registration under this Regulation, shall adopt all necessary measures to comply with its provisions by 7 September 2010.

Credit rating agencies shall submit their application for registration no earlier than 7 June 2010. Existing credit rating agencies shall submit their application for registration by 7 September 2010

Existing credit rating agencies may continue issuing credit ratings which may be used for regulatory purposes by the financial institutions referred to in Article 4(1) unless registration is refused. Where registration is refused, Article 24(2) shall apply.

定第8条规定）。

第1999/468/EC号决定第5条第6款规定的期限应设定为3个月。

第39条　报告

1.2012年12月7日前，欧盟委员会应对本条例的适用情况作出评价，其中包括评价欧共体境内对信用评级的依赖程度、信用评级市场集中度受到的影响、本条例所造成影响的成本和收益以及被评级实体向信用评级机构支付报酬（即发行人付费模式）的适当性，评价结束后，欧盟委员会应向欧洲议会与欧盟理事会递交评价报告。

2.2012年12月7日前，欧盟委员会应根据与主管部门的讨论结果评价本条例第三编的适用情况，特别是主管部门之间的合作、欧洲证券监管机构委员会的法律地位及监管实践。欧盟委员会应就该等事宜向欧洲议会与欧盟理事会提交报告，并在适当时附上对该编进行审评的提案。

该报告应援引欧盟委员会2008年11月12日提出的针对信用评级机构制定条例的建议以及欧洲议会经济与货币事务委员会2009年3月23日针对上述建议的报告。

3.2010年12月7日前，欧盟委员会应根据第三国信用评级机构的规制和监管框架的进展情况向欧洲议会与欧盟理事会提交一份报告，说明该等框架的进展情况和第40条所述的过渡规定对欧共体金融市场稳定性造成的影响。

第二章　过渡规定和最终条款

第40条　过渡规定

2010年6月7日前于欧共体境内运营的信用评级机构（现有信用评级机构），如有意根据本条例申请注册，应于2010年9月7日前制定履行本条例规定所必要的所有措施。

信用评级机构最早可自2010年6月7日起开始递交注册申请。现有信用评级机构则应于2010年9月7日前递交注册申请。

现有信用评级机构可继续发布可被第4条第1款所述的金融机构用于监管目的的信用评级，但被拒绝注册的信用评级机构除外。在被拒绝注册的情形下，应适用第24条第2款的规定。

Article 41 Entry into force

This Regulation shall enter into force on the 20th day following its publication in the *Official Journal of the European Union*.

It shall apply from its date of entry into force. However:

— Article 4(1) shall apply from 7 December 2010 and

— points (f)(g) and (h) of Article 4(3) shall apply from 7 June 2011.

This Regulation shall be binding in its entirety and directly applicable in all Member States.

Done at Strasbourg, 16 September 2009.

For the European Parliament	*For the Council*
The President	*The President*
J. BUZEK	C. MALMSTRÖM

ANNEX I INDEPENDENCE AND AVOIDANCE OF CONFLICTS OF INTEREST

Section A Organisational requirements

1. The credit rating agency shall have an administrative or supervisory board. Its senior management shall ensure that:

(a) credit rating activities are independent, including from all political and economic influences or constraints;

(b) conflicts of interest are properly identified, managed and disclosed;

(c) the credit rating agency complies with the remaining requirements of this Regulation.

2. A credit rating agency shall be organised in a way that ensures that its business interest does not impair the independence or accuracy of the credit rating activities.

The senior management of a credit rating agency shall be of good repute and sufficiently skilled and experienced, and shall ensure the sound and prudent management of the credit rating agency.

At least one third, but no less than two, of the members of the administrative or supervisory board of a credit rating agency shall be independent members who are not involved in credit rating activities.

The compensation of the independent members of the administrative or supervisory board shall not be linked to the business performance of the credit rating agency and shall be arranged so as to ensure the independence of their judgement. The term of office of the independent members of the administrative or supervisory board shall be for a preagreed fixed period not exceeding five years and shall not be renewable. The dismissal of

第41条　生效

本条例自公布于《欧盟公报》后的第20日生效。

本条例自生效日起适用。然而：

第4条第1款自2010年12月7日起适用，且第4条第3款第f目、第g目、第h目自2011年6月7日起适用。

本条例所有内容对各成员国均具有约束力，并可直接适用于所有成员国。

2009年9月16日于斯特拉斯堡通过。

欧洲议会议长　　　　欧盟理事会主席

布泽克　　　　马姆斯壮

附录一　独立性和利益冲突的避免

第A节　组织结构要求

1.信用评级机构应设立董事会或监事会。其高级管理人员应确保：

(a)信用评级活动的独立性，包括独立于所有政治和经济的影响或限制；

(b)妥当识别、管理和披露利益冲突；

(c)信用评级机构遵守本条例的其他要求。

2.信用评级机的组建方式应确保其商业利益不损害信用评级活动的独立性或准确性。

信用评级机构的高级管理人员应具有良好的声誉和足够的技能和经验，并应确保对信用评级机构稳健而审慎的管理。

信用评级机构董事会或监事会的成员中，应至少有1/3且不得少于两名是不参与信用评级活动的独立董事或独立监事。

独立董事或独立监事的薪酬，不得与信用评级机构的业绩挂钩，其薪酬安排也应确保其做判断时的独立性。独立董事或独立监事的任期应为事先约定的固定任期，不超过5年，亦不得展延。独立董事或独立监事只有在发生不当行为或专业表现不佳时才能予以免职。

independent members of the administrative or supervisory board shall take place only in case of misconduct or professional underperformance.

The majority of members of the administrative or supervisory board, including its independent members, shall have sufficient expertise in financial services. Provided that the credit rating agency issues credit ratings of structured finance instruments, at least one independent member and one other member of the board shall have in-depth knowledge and experience at a senior level of the markets in structured finance instruments.

In addition to the overall responsibility of the board, the independent members of the administrative or supervisory board shall have the specific task of monitoring:

(a) the development of the credit rating policy and of the methodologies used by the credit rating agency in its credit rating activities;

(b) the effectiveness of the internal quality control system of the credit rating agency in relation to credit rating activities;

(c) the effectiveness of measures and procedures instituted to ensure that any conflicts of interest are identified, eliminated or managed and disclosed; and

(d) the compliance and governance processes, including the efficiency of the review function referred to in point 9 of this Section.

Opinions of the independent members of administrative or supervisory board issued on the matters referred to in points (a) to (d) shall be presented to the board periodically and shall be made available to the competent authority on request.

3. A credit rating agency shall establish adequate policies and procedures to ensure compliance with its obligations under this Regulation.

4. A credit rating agency shall have sound administrative and accounting procedures, internal control mechanisms, effective procedures for risk assessment, and effective control and safeguard arrangements for information processing systems.

Those internal control mechanisms shall be designed to secure compliance with decisions and procedures at all levels of the credit rating agency.

A credit rating agency shall implement and maintain decision-making procedures and organisational structures which clearly and in a documented manner specify reporting lines and allocate functions and responsibilities.

5. A credit rating agency shall establish and maintain a permanent and effective compliance function department (compliance function) which operates independently. The compliance function shall monitor and report on compliance of the credit rating agency and its employees with the credit rating agency's obligations under this Regulation. The compliance function shall:

(a) monitor and, on a regular basis, assess the adequacy and effectiveness of the measures and procedures put in place in accordance with point 3, and the actions taken

董事会或监事会应有大部分成员（包括其独立董事或独立监事）在金融服务方面具备足够的专长。如信用评级机构发布结构性金融工具的信用评级，则董事会或监事会中应至少有1名独立董事或独立监事和1名其他成员对结构性金融工具市场有深入了解并具备资深的相关经验。

在董事会或监事会的所有责任之外，独立董事或独立监事还应承担监控以下事项的特定职责：

(a)信用评级工作准则的制定和信用评级机构在信用评级活动中所使用的方法的制定；

(b)信用评级机构针对信用评级活动的内部质量控制系统的有效性；

(c)用以确保利益冲突得到识别、消除或管理和披露的措施和程序的有效性；及

(d)合规和治理程序，包括本节第9款所述复核职能部门的效率。

独立董事或独立监事应定期向董事会或监事会提出就第a项至第d项所述事项发布的意见，并经主管部门要求向其提供上述意见。

3.信用评级机构应制定充分的政策与程序，以确保本条例中的义务得到遵守。

4.信用评级机构应有健全的行政和会计程序、内部控制机制、有效的风险评估程序以及对信息处理系统的有效控制和保障安排。

该等内部控制机制应旨在确保信用评级机构各个层级的决定和程序均得到遵守。

信用评级机构应实施并维持决策程序和组织结构，以书面方式清楚地规定不同的汇报层级关系并对职能与责任作出分配。

5.信用评级机构应建立并维持一个常设、有效且独立运行的合规职能部门（以下简称合规职能部门）。合规职能部门应监控并报告信用评级机构及其职员工遵守本条例的信用评级机构义务的情况。合规职能部门应：

(a)针对根据第3款所制定的措施与程序，并针对信用评级机构为解决其义务履行的薄弱环节所采取的行动是否充分和有效，作出监控和定期评估；

to address any deficiencies in the credit rating agency's compliance with its obligations;

(b) advise and assist the managers, rating analysts, employees as well as any other natural person whose services are placed at the disposal or under the control of the credit rating agency or any person directly or indirectly linked to it by control who is responsible for carrying out credit rating activities, to comply with the credit rating agency's obligations under this Regulation.

6. In order to enable the compliance function to discharge its responsibilities properly and independently, a credit rating agency shall ensure that the following conditions are satisfied:

(a) the compliance function has the necessary authority, resources, expertise and access to all relevant information;

(b) a compliance officer is appointed and is responsible for the compliance function and for any reporting with regard to compliance required by point 3;

(c) the managers, rating analysts, employees and any other natural person whose services are placed at the disposal or under the control of the credit rating agency or any person directly or indirectly linked to it by control who is involved in the compliance function is not involved in the performance of credit rating activities they monitor;

(d) the compensation of the compliance officer is not linked to the business performance of the credit rating agency and is arranged so as to ensure the independence of his or her judgement.

The compliance officer shall ensure that any conflicts of interest relating to the persons placed at the disposal of the compliance function are properly identified and eliminated.

The compliance officer shall report regularly on the carrying out of his or her duties to senior management and the independent members of the administrative or supervisory board.

7. A credit rating agency shall establish appropriate and effective organisational and administrative arrangements to prevent, identify, eliminate or manage and disclose any conflicts of interest referred to in point 1 of Section B. It shall arrange for records to be kept of all significant threats to the independence of the credit rating activities, including those to the rules on rating analysts referred to in Section C, as well as the safeguards applied to mitigate those threats.

8. A credit rating agency shall employ appropriate systems, resources and procedures to ensure continuity and regularity in the performance of its credit rating activities.

9. A credit rating agency shall establish a review function responsible for periodically reviewing its methodologies, models and key rating assumptions, such as mathematical or correlation assumptions, and any significant changes or modifications thereto as well as

(b)在遵守信用评级机构在本条例中的义务方面,向下列人等提供建议和协助:经理人;评级分析师;职员;所提供的服务为信用评级机构所用或为信用评级机构所控制的其他自然人;通过控制与信用评级机构直接或间接关联并负责开展信用评级活动的人。

6.为使合规职能部门能恰当、独立地履行其责任,信用评级机构应确保下列各项条件得到满足:

(a)合规职能部门拥有必要的权限、资源、专长并可查阅所有相关的信息;

(b)任命1名合规官负责合规职能并对第3款规定的合规情况进行报告;

(c)经理人、评级分析师、职员以及所提供服务为信用评级机构所用或为信用评级机构所控制的其他自然人,或是通过控制与信用评级机构直接或间接关联并参与履行合规职责的人,均不得参与该等人自身负责监控的信用评级活动。

(d)合规官的薪酬不与信用评级机构的业绩挂钩,其薪酬安排也应确保合规官做判断时的独立性。

合规官应确保能够正确识别并消除合规职能部门人员本身的任何利益冲突。

合规官应定期向高级管理人员和独立董事或独立监事报告其职责的履行情况。

7.信用评级机构应制定适当和有效的组织和行政安排,以防范、识别、消除或管理和披露第B节第1款所述的任何利益冲突。信用评级机构应安排保存以下各项内容的记录:影响信用评级活动独立性的所有重大威胁,包括第C节所述的关于评级分析师的规则的重大威胁,以及用以缓释该等威胁的保障。

8.信用评级机构应采用适当的制度、资源及程序,以确保其信用评级活动持续、规律地进行。

9.信用评级机构应设立复核职能部门,负责定期复核其方法、模型及关键评级假设(如数学或关联假设)及其任何重大变更或修改以及用于或拟用于评估新金融工具的该等方法、模型及关键评级假设的适当性。

the appropriateness of those methodologies, models and key rating assumptions where they are used or intended to be used for the assessment of new financial instruments.

That review function shall be independent of the business lines which are responsible for credit rating activities and report to the members of the administrative or supervisory board referred to in point 2 of this Section.

10. A credit rating agency shall monitor and evaluate the adequacy and effectiveness of its systems, internal control mechanisms and arrangements established in accordance with this Regulation and take appropriate measures to address any deficiencies.

Section B Operational requirements

1. A credit rating agency shall identify, eliminate or manage and disclose, clearly and prominently, any actual or potential conflicts of interest that may influence the analyses and judgments of its rating analysts, employees, or any other natural person whose services are placed at the disposal or under the control of the credit rating agency and who are directly involved in the issuing of credit rating and persons approving credit ratings.

2. A credit rating agency shall disclose to the public the names of the rated entities or related third parties from which it receives more than 5 % of its annual revenue.

3. A credit rating agency shall not issue a credit rating in any of the following circumstances, or shall, in the case of an existing credit rating, immediately disclose where the credit rating is potentially affected by the following:

(a) the credit rating agency or persons referred to in point 1, directly or indirectly owns financial instruments of the rated entity or a related third party or has any other direct or indirect ownership interest in that entity or party, other than holdings in diversified collective investment schemes, including managed funds such as pension funds or life insurance;

(b) the credit rating is issued with respect to the rated entity or a related third party directly or indirectly linked to the credit rating agency by control;

(c) a person referred to in point 1 is a member of the administrative or supervisory board of the rated entity or a related third party; or

(d) a rating analyst who participated in determining a credit rating, or a person who approved a credit rating, has had a relationship with the rated entity or a related third party which may cause a conflict of interests.

A credit rating agency shall also immediately assess whether there are grounds for re-rating or withdrawing the existing credit rating.

4. A credit rating agency shall not provide consultancy or advisory services to the rated entity or a related third party regarding the corporate or legal structure, assets, liabilities or activities of that rated entity or related third party.

该复核职能部门应独立于具体负责信用评级活动的业务部门，并向本节第2款所述的董事会或监事会成员报告。

10.信用评级机构应监控和评价其各项制度、内部控制机制以及根据本条例所建立的安排的适当性和有效性，并针对任何薄弱环节采取适当措施。

第B节　运营要求

1.信用评级机构应识别、消除或管理并清楚且显著地披露任何可能影响下列人等的分析判断的实际或潜在利益冲突：其评级分析师；职员；或所提供的服务为信用评级机构所用或为信用评级机构所控制并直接参与信用评级发布的其他自然人；以及负责批准信用评级的其他人。

2.信用评级机构如有超过5%的年收入来自被评级实体或相关第三方，则应向公众披露该等被评级实体或相关第三方的名称。

3.在下列任何情形下，信用评级机构均不得发布信用评级。信用评级已经发布了的，则须立即披露下列情形可能对信用评级产生的影响：

(a)信用评级机构或第1款所述之人直接或间接拥有被评级实体或相关第三方的金融工具，或直接或间接拥有该实体或第三方的所有者权益，但在分散型集合投资计划(包括养老金或寿险等管理基金)中持有单位的例外；

(b)针对通过控制与信用评级机构直接或间接关联的被评级实体或相关第三方发布信用评级；

(c)第1款所述之人为被评级实体或相关第三方董事会或监事会的成员；或

(d)参与确定信用评级的评级分析师或信用评级批准人员与被评级实体或相关第三方的关系，可能造成利益冲突的。

信用评级机构也应立即评估是否有理由重新评级或撤销现有信用评级。

4.信用评级机构不得向被评级实体或相关第三方就该被评级实体或相关第三方的公司结构或法律结构、资产、负债或活动提供咨询或顾问服务。

A credit rating agency may provide services other than issue of credit ratings (ancillary services). Ancillary services are not part of credit rating activities; they comprise market forecasts, estimates of economic trends, pricing analysis and other general data analysis as well as related distribution services.

A credit rating agency shall ensure that the provision of ancillary services does not present conflicts of interest with its credit rating activities and shall disclose in the final ratings reports any ancillary services provided for the rated entity or any related third party.

5. A credit rating agency shall ensure that rating analysts or persons who approve ratings do not make proposals or recommendations, either formally or informally, regarding the design of structured finance instruments on which the credit rating agency is expected to issue a credit rating.

6. A credit rating agency shall design its reporting and communication channels so as to ensure the independence of the persons referred to in point 1 from the other activities of the credit rating agency carried out on a commercial basis.

7. A credit rating agency shall arrange for adequate records and, where appropriate, audit trails of its credit rating activities to be kept. Those records shall include:

(a) for each credit rating decision, the identity of the rating analysts participating in the determination of the credit rating, the identity of the persons who have approved the credit rating, information as to whether the credit rating was solicited or unsolicited, and the date on which the credit rating action was taken;

(b) the account records relating to fees received from any rated entity or related third party or any user of ratings;

(c) the account records for each subscriber to the credit ratings or related services;

(d) the records documenting the established procedures and methodologies used by the credit rating agency to determine credit ratings;

(e) the internal records and files, including non-public information and work papers, used to form the basis of any credit rating decision taken;

(f) credit analysis reports, credit assessment reports and private credit rating reports and internal records, including non-public information and work papers, used to form the basis of the opinions expressed in such reports;

(g) records of the procedures and measures implemented by the credit rating agency to comply with this Regulation; and

(h) copies of internal and external communications, including electronic communications, received and sent by the credit rating agency and its employees, that relate to credit rating activities.

8. Records and audit trails referred to in point 7 shall be kept at the premises of the

信用评级机构可提供信用评级发布以外的服务(以下简称辅助服务)。辅助服务并非信用评级活动的一部分;该等服务包括市场预测、经济趋势的预估、定价分析以及其他一般数据分析及相关分销服务。

信用评级机构应确保辅助服务的提供不会与信用评级活动发生利益冲突,并应在最终评级报告中披露向被评级实体或任何相关第三方提供的任何辅助服务。

5.信用评级机构应确保,对于其预期将发布信用评级的结构性金融工具,评级分析师或信用评级批准人员不会就其设计作出正式或非正式的提议或建议。

6.信用评级机构的汇报层级关系和信息沟通渠道的设计应确保第1款所述之人独立于信用评级机构为商业目的开展的其他活动。

7.信用评级机构应安排保存信用评级活动和审计留痕(如有)的充分记录。该等充分记录应包括:

(a)对于每项信用评级决定:参与确定信用评级工作的评级分析师的身份信息、信用评级批准人员的身份信息、是经客户要求做出的还是主动做出的信用评级、采取信用评级行动的日期;

(b)从任何被评级实体或相关第三方或任何评级用户收到的手续费的相关账目记录;

(c)各项信用评级或相关服务的每一订阅人的账目记录;

(d)信用评级机构用以确定信用评级的既有程序和方法的记录;

(e)作为信用评级决定依据的内部记录及档案,包括非公开信息和工作文件;

(f)信用分析报告、信用评估报告以及作为上述报告中所表达的意见依据的私人信用评级报告和内部记录(包括非公开信息和工作文件);

(g)信用评级机构为遵守本条例而实施的程序和措施的记录;及

(h)由信用评级机构及其员工收到和发出的、与信用评级活动有关的内部和外部通信(包括电子通信)的复件;

8.第7款所述的记录和审计留痕应在注册信用评级机构办公场所保存至少5年,并

registered credit rating agency for at least five years and be made available upon request to the competent authorities of the Member States concerned.

Where the registration of a credit rating agency is withdrawn, the records shall be kept for an additional term of at least three years.

9. Records which set out the respective rights and obligations of the credit rating agency and the rated entity or its related third parties under an agreement to provide credit rating services shall be retained for at least the duration of the relationship with that rated entity or its related third parties.

Section C Rules on rating analysts and other persons directly involved in credit rating activities

1. Rating analysts, employees of the credit rating agency as well as any other natural person whose services are placed at the disposal or under the control of the credit rating agency and who is directly involved in credit rating activities, and persons closely associated with them within the meaning of Article 1(2) of Directive 2004/72/EC [1], shall not buy or sell or engage in any transaction in any financial instrument issued, guaranteed, or otherwise supported by any rated entity within their area of primary analytical responsibility other than holdings in diversified collective investment schemes, including managed funds such as pension funds or life insurance.

2. No person referred to in point 1 shall participate in or otherwise influence the determination of a credit rating of any particular rated entity if that person:

(a) owns financial instruments of the rated entity, other than holdings in diversified collective investment schemes;

(b) owns financial instruments of any entity related to a rated entity, the ownership of which may cause or may be generally perceived as causing a conflict of interest, other than holdings in diversified collective investment schemes;

(c) has had a recent employment, business or other relationship with the rated entity that may cause or may be generally perceived as causing a conflict of interest.

3. Credit rating agencies shall ensure that persons referred to in point 1:

(a) take all reasonable measures to protect property and records in possession of the credit rating agency from fraud, theft or misuse, taking into account the nature, scale and complexity of their business and the nature and range of their credit rating activities;

(b) do not disclose any information about credit ratings or possible future credit

1 Commission Directive 2004/72/EC of 29 April 2004 implementing Directive 2003/6/EC of the European Parliament and of the Council as regards accepted market practices, the definition of inside information in relation to derivatives on commodities, the drawing up of lists of insiders, the notification of managers' transactions and the notification of suspicious transactions (OJ L 162, 30.4.2004, p. 70).

且经所涉成员国主管部门要求即应向其提供。

信用评级机构注册被撤销的，记录应继续保存至少3年。

9.列明信用评级机构和被评级实体或其相关第三方各自在信用评级协议中的权利义务的记录，至少应在与被评级实体或其相关第三方之间关系存续期间留存。

第C节　关于评级分析师和直接参与信用评级活动的其他人的规则

1.评级分析师、信用评级机构职员、所提供服务为该信用评级机构所用或为该信用评级机构所控制的且直接参与信用评级活动的其他自然人，以及第2004/72/EC号指令[1]第1条第2款所定义的与上述人员密切相关的人，在其主要分析责任范围内不得买卖任何被评级实体所发布、担保或以其他方式支持的任何金融工具或从事该等金融工具的交易，但在分散型集合投资计划（包括养老基金或寿险等管理基金）中持有单位的除外。

2.第1款所述的任何人有下列情形的，不得参与或影响任何特定被评级实体的信用评级的确定：

（a）拥有该被评级实体的金融工具（但在分散型集合投资计划中持有单位的除外）；

（b）拥有与被评级实体相关的任何实体的金融工具（但在分散型集合投资计划中持有的单位例外），且该所有权可能会形成利益冲突或一般可能被视为形成利益冲突；

（c）近期与被评级实体之间有雇佣关系、商业关系或其他可能形成利益冲突或一般可能被视为形成利益冲突的关系；

3.信用评级机构应确保第1款所述之人：

（a）在考虑到其业务性质、规模和复杂程度及其信用评级活动的性质和范围的情形下，采取所有合理的措施以保护信用评级机构拥有的财产和记录不被诈骗、偷窃或滥用；

（b）除了被评级机构或其相关第三方外，不向他人披露任何关于信用评级机构现

1 《欧盟委员会就公认市场惯例、对商品衍生品内幕消息的定义、内幕人士名单的编制、管理人交易的通知以及可疑交易的通知实施欧洲议会与欧盟理事会第 2003/6/EC 号指令的第 2004/72/EC 号指令》（该指令于 2004 年 4 月 29 日通过）（2004 年 4 月 30 日《欧盟公报》L162，第 70 页）。

ratings of the credit rating agency, except to the rated entity or its related third party;

(c) do not share confidential information entrusted to the credit rating agency with rating analysts and employees of any person directly or indirectly linked to it by control, as well as with any other natural person whose services are placed at the disposal or under the control of any person directly or indirectly linked to it by control, and who is directly involved in the credit rating activities; and

(d) do not use or share confidential information for the purpose of trading financial instruments, or for any other purpose except the conduct of the credit rating activities.

4. Persons referred to in point 1 shall not solicit or accept money, gifts or favours from anyone with whom the credit rating agency does business.

5. If a person referred to in point 1 considers that any other such person has engaged in conduct that he or she considers to be illegal, he or she shall report such information immediately to the compliance officer without negative consequences to him or herself.

6. Where a rating analyst terminates his or her employment and joins a rated entity, which he or she has been involved in rating, or a financial firm, with which he or she has had dealings as part of his or her duties at the credit rating agency, the credit rating agency shall review the relevant work of the rating analyst over two years preceding his or her departure.

7. A person referred to in point 1 shall not take up a key management position with the rated entity or its related third party within six months of the credit rating.

8. For the purpose of Article 7(4) credit rating agencies shall ensure that:

(a) the lead rating analysts shall not be involved in credit rating activities related to the same rated entity or its related third parties for a period exceeding four years;

(b) the rating analysts shall not be involved in credit rating activities related to the same rated entity or its related third parties for a period exceeding five years;

(c) the persons approving credit ratings shall not be involved in credit rating activities related to the same rated entity or its related third parties for a period exceeding seven years.

The persons referred to in points (a)(b) and (c) of the first subparagraph shall not be involved in credit rating activities related to the rated entity or related third parties referred to in those points within two years of end of the periods set out in those points.

Section D Rules on the presentation of credit ratings

I. General obligations

1. A credit rating agency shall ensure that any credit rating states clearly and prominently the name and job title of the lead rating analyst in a given credit rating

有或未来可能发布的信用评级的信息；

(c)不与下列人等共享第三方委托给信用评级机构的保密信息：评级分析师；通过控制与信用评级机构直接或间接关联的任何人的员工；以及所提供的服务为通过控制与该信用评级机构直接或间接有关的任何人所用或为其所控制且直接参与信用评级活动的其他自然人；及

(d)除了开展信用评级活动之外，不得以金融工具交易为目的或为其他目的使用或共享保密信息。

4.第1款所述之人不得向与信用评级机构有业务往来的任何人索取金钱、礼物或好处，也不得接受该等人的金钱、礼物或好处。

5.第1款所述的任何人认为第1款所述的其他人从事了其认为属于非法的行为的，应立即向合规官报告，报告人不得因该等报告行为受到负面影响。

6.评级分析师终止其与信用评级机构之间的雇佣关系后，如加入的被评级实体是其参与过评级工作的被评级实体，或者加入的金融公司是其在信用评级机构原有的职责范围内有过业务往来的金融公司，则信用评级机构应对该评级分析师离职前两年内的相关工作进行审查。

7.在信用评级发布后6个月内，第1款所述之人不得担任相关被评级实体或其相关第三方的重要管理职位。

8.就第7条第4款而言，信用评级机构应确保：

(a)首席评级分析师参与同一被评级实体或其相关第三方的信用评级活动时间最长不得超过4年；

(b)评级分析师参与同一被评级实体或其相关第三方的信用评级活动时间最长不得超过5年；

(c)信用评级批准人员参与同一被评级实体或其相关第三方的信用评级活动时间最长不得超过7年。

第一项第a目、第b目及第c目所述之人在相应各项规定期限结束后两年内不得参与和以上各项所述被评级实体或其相关第三方有关的信用评级活动。

第D节　信用评级的列报规则

I.一般性义务

1.信用评级机构应确保，任何信用评级均清楚且显著地注明在特定信用评级活动中的首席评级分析师姓名和职称，以及主要负责批准信用评级的人的姓名和职位。

activity and the name and position of the person primarily responsible for approving the credit rating.

2. A credit rating agency shall ensure that at least:

(a) all substantially material sources, including the rated entity or, where appropriate, a related third party, which were used to prepare the credit rating are indicated together with an indication as to whether the credit rating has been disclosed to that rated entity or its related third party and amended following that disclosure before being issued;

(b) the principal methodology or version of methodology that was used in determining the rating is clearly indicated, with a reference to its comprehensive description; where the credit rating is based on more than one methodology, or where reference only to the principal methodology might cause investors to overlook other important aspects of the credit rating, including any significant adjustments and deviations, the credit rating agency shall explain this fact in the credit rating and indicate how the different methodologies or these other aspects are taken into account in the credit rating;

(c) the meaning of each rating category, the definition of default or recovery and any appropriate risk warning, including a sensitivity analysis of the relevant key rating assumptions, such as mathematical or correlation assumptions, accompanied by worst-case scenario credit ratings as well as best-case scenario credit ratings are explained;

(d) the date at which the credit rating was first released for distribution and when it was last updated is indicated clearly and prominently; and

(e) information is given as to whether the credit rating concerns a newly issued financial instrument and whether the credit rating agency is rating the financial instrument for the first time.

3. The credit rating agency shall inform the rated entity at least 12 hours before publication of the credit rating and of the principal grounds on which the rating is based in order to give the entity an opportunity to draw attention of the credit rating agency to any factual errors.

4. A credit rating agency shall state clearly and prominently when disclosing credit ratings any attributes and limitations of the credit rating. In particular, a credit rating agency shall prominently state when disclosing any credit rating whether it considers satisfactory the quality of information available on the rated entity and to what extent it has verified information provided to it by the rated entity or its related third party. If a credit rating involves a type of entity or financial instrument for which historical data is limited, the credit rating agency shall make clear, in a prominent place, such limitations of the credit rating.

2.信用评级机构应至少：

(a)注明准备信用评级时用过的所有具有实质重要性的资料来源[包括被评级实体或相关第三方(如有)],并注明信用评级是否已向该被评级实体或其相关第三方披露,是否于披露之后发布之前做过修正；

(b)清楚注明用于确定评级的主要评级方法或方法版本,应引用一份对该等方法或版本作出全面说明的文献;如果信用评级依据一种以上方法作出,或如果仅引用一种主要方法可能导致投资者忽略信用评级的其他重要方面(包括任何重大调整和偏离),则信用评级机构应在信用评级中说明该等事实,并说明其在信用评级中如何兼顾不同方法或上述其他重要方面；

(c)解释各评级类别的含义、违约或赔偿的定义以及任何适当的风险警示(包括相关关键评级假设的敏感性分析,如数学或关联假设)连同最差情景下的信用评级以及最佳情景下的信用评级；

(d)清楚且显著地注明信用评级的首次发布和最后更新的日期;并且

(e)说明信用评级是否涉及新发行的金融工具以及信用评级机构是否首次为该金融工具进行评级。

3.信用评级机构应在公布信用评级前至少提前12小时通知被评级实体信用评级结果以及评级的主要依据,以便被评级实体有机会提醒信用评级机构注意任何事实错误。

4.信用评级机构应于披露信用评级时清楚且显著地说明信用评级的属性和限制。披露信用评级时,信用评级机构尤应以显著的方式说明,其认为所获得的关于被评级实体的信息质量是否令人满意,以及其在多大程度上核实了被评级实体或其相关第三方提供的信息。信用评级所涉实体或金融工具类别只存在有限的历史数据的,信用评级机构应在显著的位置标明信用评级所受到的限制。

In a case where the lack of reliable data or the complexity of the structure of a new type of financial instrument or the quality of information available is not satisfactory or raises serious questions as to whether a credit rating agency can provide a credible credit rating, the credit rating agency shall refrain from issuing a credit rating or withdraw an existing rating.

5. When announcing a credit rating, a credit rating agency shall explain in its press releases or reports the key elements underlying the credit rating.

Where the information laid down in points 1, 2 and 4 would be disproportionate in relation to the length of the report distributed, it shall suffice to make clear and prominent reference in the report itself to the place where such disclosures can be directly and easily accessed, including a direct web link to the disclosure on an appropriate website of the credit rating agency.

II. Additional obligations in relation to credit ratings of structured finance instruments

1. Where a credit rating agency rates a structured finance instrument, it shall provide in the credit rating all information about loss and cash–flow analysis it has performed or is relying upon and an indication of any expected change in the credit rating.

2. A credit rating agency shall state what level of assessment it has performed concerning the due diligence processes carried out at the level of underlying financial instruments or other assets of structured finance instruments. The credit rating agency shall disclose whether it has undertaken any assessment of such due diligence processes or whether it has relied on a third–party assessment, indicating how the outcome of such assessment impacts on the credit rating.

3. Where a credit rating agency issues credit ratings of structured finance instruments, it shall accompany the disclosure of methodologies, models and key rating assumptions with guidance which explains assumptions, parameters, limits and uncertainties surrounding the models and rating methodologies used in such credit ratings, including simulations of stress scenarios undertaken by the agencies when establishing the ratings. Such guidance shall be clear and easily comprehensible.

4. A credit rating agency shall disclose, on an ongoing basis, information about all structured finance products submitted to it for their initial review or for preliminary rating. Such disclosure shall be made whether or not issuers contract with the credit rating agency for a final rating.

Section E Disclosures

I. General disclosures

A credit rating agency shall generally disclose the fact that it is registered in accordance with this Regulation and the following information:

如果缺乏可靠的数据，或新型金融工具结构的复杂程度或获得的信息的质量令人不满意或令人严重质疑信用评级机构是否能够提供可信的信用评级，则信用评级机构不得发布信用评级或应撤销现有评级。

5.宣布信用评级时，信用评级机构应于新闻稿或报告中说明信用评级的关键要素。

第1款、第2款和第4款所列信息与所发布的报告长度不成比例时，只需在报告中清楚且显著地指出上述披露信息可于何处简便直接地查阅，包括提供披露该等信息的信用评级机构网站的直接链接。

II.结构性金融工具信用评级的附加义务

1.信用评级机构对结构性金融工具进行评级时，应在信用评级中提供所有关于其已开展或赖以评级的损失和现金流分析的信息，并注明信用评级任何预期的变更。

2.信用评级机构应说明其在多大程度上评估了对结构性金融工具的标的金融工具或其他资产开展的尽职调查过程。信用评级机构应披露对上述尽职调查过程的任何评估是否由其自身作出，抑或依赖第三方的评估作出，并说明该等评估的结果对信用评级的影响。

3.信用评级机构发布结构性金融工具信用评级时，应附上对方法、模型及关键评级假设的披露，并附上对该等信用评级中所使用的模型和评级方法的相关假设、参数、限制及不确定性的说明性指引，包括信用评级机构在确定评级结果时所进行的压力情境模拟。上述指引应当清楚且易于理解。

4.信用评级机构应持续披露递交给其进行初审或初步评级的关于所有结构性金融产品的信息。不论发行人是否委托该信用评级机构做最终评级，信用评级机构均应完成上述披露。

第E节　披露

I.一般性披露

信用评级机构应对其已根据本条例进行注册的事实以及下列信息作一般性披露：

1. any actual and potential conflicts of interest referred to in point 1 of Section B;

2. a list of its ancillary services;

3. the policy of the credit rating agency concerning the publication of credit ratings and other related communications;

4. the general nature of its compensation arrangements;

5. the methodologies, and descriptions of models and key rating assumptions such as mathematical or correlation assumptions used in its credit rating activities as well as their material changes;

6. any material modification to its systems, resources or procedures; and

7. where relevant, its code of conduct.

II. Periodic disclosures

A credit rating agency shall periodically disclose the following information:

1. every six months, data about the historical default rates of its rating categories, distinguishing between the main geographical areas of the issuers and whether the default rates of these categories have changed over time;

2. annually, the following information:

(a) a list of the largest 20 clients of the credit rating agency by revenue generated from them; and

(b) a list of those clients of the credit rating agency whose contribution to the growth rate in the generation of revenue of the credit rating agency in the previous financial year exceeded the growth rate in the total revenues of the credit rating agency in that year by a factor of more than 1, 5 times. Any such client shall be included on the list only where, in that year, it accounted for more than 0.25 % of the worldwide total revenues of the credit rating agency at global level.

For the purposes of this point, 'client' means an entity, its subsidiaries, and associated entities in which the entity has holdings of more than 20%, as well as any other entities in respect of which it has negotiated the structuring of a debt issue on behalf of a client and where a fee was paid, directly or indirectly, to the credit rating agency for the rating of that debt issue.

III. Transparency report

A credit rating agency shall make available annually the following information:

1. detailed information on legal structure and ownership of the credit rating agency, including information on holdings within the meaning of Articles 9 and 10 of Directive

1.第B节第1款所述的任何实际或潜在利益冲突；

2.辅助服务的清单；

3.信用评级机构关于信用评级公布及其他相关通信的政策；

4.其薪酬安排的一般性质；

5.评级方法以及对信用评级活动中使用的模型和关键评级假设（如数学或关联假设）及其实质变更的说明；

6.其系统、资源或程序的任何实质改动；及

7.其行为准则（如有）。

II.定期披露信用

评级机构应定期披露下列信息：

1.每半年披露一次其评级类别的历史违约率数据（各类别的相关数据又按发行人所在各大地理区域细分），以及各个类别评级的违约率是否随时间变动；

2.每年披露一次下列信息：

（a）为信用评级机构带来最多收入的前20名客户名单；及

（b）在上一会计年度为信用评级机构带来的收入增长率大于信用评级机构于该年度总收入增长率1.5倍的客户名单。上述客户只有在该年带给信用评级机构的收入达到信用评级机构全球总收入0.25%以上的，方须纳入该等名单中。

就本款而言，"客户"指某个实体、其子公司以及该实体在其中拥有超过20%股权的关联实体，以及其他有下列情形的主体——即某个实体代表某客户就某债券发行的结构设计为该等主体进行谈判，而费用已直接或间接支付给对该债权发行进行评级的信用评级机构。

III.透明度报告

信用评级机关应每年公布一次下列信息：

1.关于信用评级机构的法律结构和所有权的详细信息，包括《欧洲议会与欧盟理事会协调关于证券获准在受监管市场交易的发行人的信息透明度要求的第

2004/109/EC of the European Parliament and of the Council of 15 December 2004 on the harmonization of transparency requirements in relation to information about issuers whose securities are admitted to trading on a regulated market [1];

2. a description of the internal control mechanisms ensuring quality of its credit rating activities;

3. statistics on the allocation of its staff to new credit ratings, credit rating reviews, methodology or model appraisal and senior management;

4. a description of its record-keeping policy;

5. the outcome of the annual internal review of its independent compliance function;

6. a description of its management and rating analyst rotation policy;

7. financial information on the revenue of the credit rating agency divided into fees from credit rating and non-credit rating activities with a comprehensive description of each; and

8. a governance statement within the meaning of Article 46a(1) of Council Directive 78/660/EEC of 25 July 1978 on the annual accounts of certain types of companies [2]. For the purposes of that statement, the information referred to in Article 46a(1)(d) of that Directive shall be provided by the credit rating agency irrespective of whether it is subject to Directive 2004/25/EC of the European Parliament and of the Council of 21 April 2004 on takeover bids [3].

ANNEX II INFORMATION TO BE PROVIDED IN THE APPLICATION FOR REGISTRATION

1. Full name of the credit rating agency, address of the registered office within the Community

2. Name and contact details of a contact person and of the compliance officer

3. Legal status

4. Class of credit ratings for which the credit rating agency is applying to be registered

5. Ownership structure

6. Organisational structure and corporate governance

7. Financial resources to perform credit rating activities

8. Staffing of credit rating agency and its expertise

9. Information regarding subsidiaries of credit rating agency

10. Description of the procedures and methodologies used to issue and review credit

1 OJ L 390, 31.12.2004, p. 38.

2 OJ L 222, 14.8.1978, p. 11.

3 OJ L 142, 30.4.2004, p. 12.

2004/109/EC号指令》[1]（2004年12月15日）第9条和第10条所定义的持股信息；

2.对确保信用评级活动质量的内部控制机制的说明；

3.新信用评级、信用评级复核、评级方法或模型评价以及高级管理人员的岗位编制统计数据；

4.记录保存政策的说明；

5.其独立合规职能部门的年度内部审查结果；

6.对其管理层和评级分析师轮换政策的说明；

7.信用评级机构分别来自信用评级和非信用评级活动的收入的财务信息，并提供其各自的全面说明；及

8.《欧洲经济共同体理事会关于某些类型公司的年度财报的第78/660/EEC指令》[2]（1978年7月25日）第46a条第1款所定义的治理说明书。就该说明书而言，该指令第46a条第1款第d项所述的信息应由信用评级机构提供，不论其是否受《欧洲议会与欧盟理事会关于收购竞标的第2004/25/EC号指令》[3]（2004年4月21日）所管辖。

附录二　注册申请材料中需提供的信息

1.信用评级机构全名、在欧共体境内的注册地址

2.联系人和合规官姓名和详细的联络信息

3.法律地位

4.信用评级机构申请注册的信用评级类别

5.所有权结构

6.组织结构和公司治理

7.开展信用评级活动的资金来源

8.信用评级机构的人员配置及其专长

9.信用评级机构子公司的信息

10.发布和复核信用评级的程序和方法说明

1　2004年12月31日《欧盟公报》L390，第38页。

2　1978年8月14日《欧盟公报》L222，第11页。

3　2004年4月30日《欧盟公报》L142，第12页。

ratings

11. Policies and procedures to identify, manage and disclose any conflicts of interests

12. Information regarding rating analysts

13. Compensation and performance evaluation arrangements

14. Services other than credit rating activities, which the credit rating agency intends to provide

15. Programme of operations, including indications of where the main business activities are expected to be carried out, branches to be established, and setting out the type of business envisaged

16. Documents and detailed information related to the expected use of endorsement

17. Documents and detailed information related to the expected outsourcing arrangements including information on entities assuming outsourcing functions.

11.识别、管理和披露利益冲突的政策与程序

12.评级分析师的信息

13.薪酬和绩效评价安排

14.信用评级机构拟提供的非信用评级活动的服务

15.运营计划，包括对预期开展主要业务活动的地点、拟设立的分支机构以及预期业务类型的说明

16.关于预期使用的认可的文件和详细信息

17.预期的外包安排的相关文件和详细信息，包括关于承担外包职能的实体的信息。

Corrigendum to Regulation (EC) No 1060/2009 of the European Parliament and of the Council

欧洲议会与欧盟理事会关于信用评级机构的第 1060/2009 号(欧共体)条例勘误

Corrigendum to Regulation (EC) No 1060/2009 of the European Parliament and of the Council of 16

September 2009 on credit rating agencies
(Official Journal of the European Union L 302 of 17 November 2009)

On page 27, Annex I, Section C, point 3(c):

for:

'c)(...) and who is directly involved in the credit rating activities; and',

read:

'c)(...) and who is not directly involved in the credit rating activities; and'.

欧洲议会与欧盟理事会
关于信用评级机构的
第1060/2009号(欧共体)条例勘误

2009年9月16日通过
(于2009年11月17日《欧盟公报》L 302上公布)

附录一第C节第3款第c项:
原文:
“c)(……),和直接参与信用评级活动的其他自然人;及”
改为:
“c)(……),和不直接参与信用评级活动的其他自然人;及”

Glossary 词汇表

Action Plan for ' Modernising Company Law and Enhancing Corporate Governance in the European Union'	《欧盟公司法现代化和加强欧盟公司治理之行动计划》
Age of the financial statements	账龄
Arranger	安排方
Audit trails	审计留痕
Back-testing	回溯测试
Base prospectus	基本招募说明书
Benefits in kind	实物福利
Best-case scenario	最佳情景
Buy-back programmes	回购计划
Cash settlement	现金结算
Chain of controlled undertakings	受控企业链
Charter of Fundamental Rights of the European Union	《欧盟基本权利宪章》
Chinese walls	隔离墙
Code of Conduct Fundamentals for credit rating agencies	《信用评级机构基本行为准则》
Collective investment undertaking other than the closed- end type'	非封闭式集合投资计划
College	运营团
Commission Recommendation 2005/162/EC of 15 February 2005 on the role of non-executive or supervisory directors of listed companies and on the committees of the (supervisory) board	《欧盟委员会关于上市公司非执行董事或监事的作用和关于监事会下属委员会的第 2005/162/EC 号建议》(2005 年 2 月 15 日)
Commission Regulation (EC) No 809/2004 of 29 April 2004 implementing Directive 2003/71/EC of the European Parliament and of the Council as regards information contained in prospectuses as well as the format, incorporation by reference and publication of such prospectuses and dissemination of advertisements	《欧盟委员会就招募说明书所含信息以及该等招募说明书的格式、引用的信息和公布以及广告传播实施欧洲议会与欧盟理事会第 2003/71/EC 号指令的第 809/2004 号(欧共体)条例》(2004 年 4 月 29 日)
Committee of European Securities Regulators (CESR)	欧洲证券监管机构委员会
Committee of Wise Men on the regulation of European securities markets	欧洲证券市场监督专家委员会

续表

Commodity dealers	商品交易商
Company Law Directives	《公司法指令》
Compliance officers	合规官
Condensed balance sheet	简要资产负债表
Condensed profit and loss account	简要损益表
Consultative committee	咨询委员会
Controlled undertaking	受控企业
Convertible notes	可转换票据
Consolidated accounts	合并财务报表
Council Decision 1999/468/EC of 28 June 1999 laying down the procedures for the exercise of implementing powers conferred on the Commission	《欧盟理事会关于制定欧盟委员会行使其被授予的实施权之程序的第 1999/468/EC 号决定》(1999 年 6 月 28 日)
Council Directive 78/660/EEC of 25 July 1978 based on Article 54(3)(g) of the Treaty on the annual accounts of certain types of companies	《欧洲经济共同体理事会在〈条约〉第 54 条第 3 款第 g 项的基础上关于某些类型公司的年度财务报表的第 78/660/EEC 号指令》(1978 年 7 月 25 日)
Council Directive 80/390/EEC of 17 March 1980 coordinating the requirements for the drawing up, scrutiny and distribution of the listing particulars to be published for the admission of securities to official stock exchange listing	《欧洲经济共同体理事会协调关于获准在官方证券交易所上市的证券所应公布的上市具体信息之编制、审查与发布要求的第 80/390/EEC 号指令》(1980 年 3 月 17 日)
Council Directive 85/611/EEC of 20 December 1985 on the coordination of laws, regulations and administrative provisions relating to undertakings for collective investment in transferable securities (UCITS)	《欧洲经济共同体理事会协调关于可转让证券集合投资计划(UCITS)的法律、法规和规章的第 85/611/EEC 号指令》(1985 年 12 月 20 日)
Council Directive 89/298/EEC of 17 April 1989 coordinating the requirements for the drawing up, scrutiny and distribution of the prospectus to be published when transferable securities are offered to the public	《欧洲经济共同体理事会协调关于向公众发行可转让证券所公布的招募说明书的编制、审查与发布要求的第 89/298/EEC 号指令》(1989 年 4 月 17 日)
Council Directive 89/592/EEC of 13 November 1989 coordinating regulations on insider dealing	《欧洲经济共同体理事会协调关于内幕交易监管的法规的第 89/592/EEC 号指令》(1989 年 11 月 13 日)
Council Directive 93/22/EEC of 10 May 1993 on investment services in the securities field	《欧洲经济共同体理事会关于证券领域投资服务的第 93/22/EEC 号指令》(1993 年 5 月 10 日)
Council Directive 93/6/EEC of 15 March 1993 on the capital adequacy of investment firms and credit institutions	《欧洲经济共同体理事会关于投资公司和信贷机构的资本充足性的第 93/6/EEC 号指令》(1993 年 3 月 15 日)

续表

Coupon payment	息票支付
Covered warrants	备兑权证
Credit institution	信贷机构
Credit rating agency	信用评级机构
Credit scores	信用评分
Custodians	托管人
Data corruption	数据损坏
Debt securities	债务证券
Deferred compensation	递延薪酬
Depositary receipts	存托凭证
Derivatives on commodities	商品衍生品
Directive 2000/12/EC of the European Parliament and of the Council of 20 March 2000 relating to the taking up and pursuit of the business of credit institutions	《欧洲议会与欧盟理事会关于开办和经营信贷机构业务的第 2000/12/EC 号指令》(2000 年 3 月 20 日)
Directive 2003/6/EC of the European Parliament and of the Council of 28 January 2003 on insider dealing and market manipulation (market abuse)	《欧洲议会与欧盟理事会关于内幕交易和市场操纵(市场滥用)的第 2003/6/EC 号指令》(2003 年 1 月 28 日)
Directive 2004/109/EC of the European Parliament and of the Council of 15 December 2004 on the harmonization of transparency requirements in relation to information about issuers whose securities are admitted to trading on a regulated market and amending Directive 2001/34/EC	《欧洲议会与欧盟理事会协调关于证券获准在受监管市场交易的发行人的信息透明度要求并修正〈第 2001/34/EC 号指令〉的第 2004/109/EC 号指令》(2004 年 12 月 15 日)
Directive 2004/25/EC of the European Parliament and of the Council of 21 April 2004 on takeover bids	《欧洲议会与欧盟理事会关于收购竞标的第 2004/25/EC 号指令》(2004 年 4 月 21 日)
Directive 98/34/EC of the European Parliament and of the Council of 22 June 1998 laying down a procedure for the provision of information in the field of technical standards and regulations	《欧洲议会与欧盟理事会制定技术标准和规章领域的信息提供程序的第 98/34/EC 号指令》(1998 年 6 月 22 日)
Diversified collective investment schemes	分散型集合投资计划
Documents on Display	备查文件
ECAI	外部信用评估机构
End users	终端用户
European Convention on Human Rights	《欧盟人权公约》
European Securities Committee	欧洲证券委员会

续表

Existing shares with voting rights	附带表决权的现有股票
Facilitator	督导员
Fast-track procedures	快速通道程序
First Council Directive 68/151/EEC of 9 March 1968 on coordination of safeguards which, for the protection of the interests of members and others, are required by Member States of companies within the meaning of the second paragraph of Article 481 of the Treaty, with a view to making such safeguards equivalent throughout the Community	《欧洲经济共同体理事会协调关于〈欧洲共同体条约〉第 48 条 1 第 2 款所定义的公司所在的成员国为保护成员和其他人利益所规定的保障措施以实现在全欧共体内提供等效保障的第 68/151/EEC 号第一指令》(1968 年 3 月 9 日)
Fourth Council Directive 78/660/EEC of 25 July 1978 on the annual accounts of certain types of companies	《欧洲经济共同体理事会关于某些类型公司的年度财务报表的第 78/660/EEC 号第四指令》(1978 年 7 月 25 日)
Front running	抢跑交易
Grey lists	灰名单
Historical default rates	历史违约率
Home Member State	母国
Host Member State	东道国
Indices	指数
Informed assessment	知情评估
Interim management statement	中期管理说明书
International Accounting Standards; IAS	国际会计准则
International Financial Reporting Standards; IFRS	国际财务报告准则
Issuer	发行人
Lead rating analyst	首席评级分析师
Legal professional privilege	法律职业保密权
Management companies	管理公司
Market makers	做市商
Material contracts	重大合同
Measures	指标
Memorandum and articles of association	公司章程大纲和细则
Money market instruments	货币市场工具
Mortgage bonds	抵押债券
Multiple trading	交叉上市交易

续表

Non-profit-making	非营利性
Offer of securities to the public	向公众发行证券
Offering programme	发行方案
Offerors	要约人
Ongoing obligations	持续义务
Originator	发起人
Overseas European territories	海外欧洲领地
Paying agents	代理付款人
Placing	配售
Plan for distribution	分销计划
Plan for distribution of the securities	证券分销计划
Principle of risk-spreading	风险分散原则
Proportional	成比例
Prospectus	招募说明书
Proxy	代理
Public trading	公开交易
Qualified investors	合格投资者
Rated entities	被评级实体
Rating analysts	评级分析师
Rating category	评级类别
Regulated market	受监管市场
Related party transaction	关联交易
Reorganisation and winding up	重组和停业清理
Resale	转售
Restated financial statements	重述财务报表
Right of judicial review	司法审查权
Risk capital action plan	《风险资本行动计划》
Securities issued in a continuous or repeated manner	持续或重复发行的证券
Securities note	证券说明
Securities regulators	证券监管机构
Selling shareholders	售股股东

续表

Senior management	高级管理人员
Seniority	清偿优先权
Sensitivity analysis	敏感性分析
Servicer	服务商
Seventh Council Directive 83/349/ EEC of 13 June 1983 on consolidated accounts	《欧洲经济共同体理事会关于合并财务报表的第 83/349/EEC 号第七指令》(1983 年 6 月 13 日)
Short settlement cycle	短结算周期
Single passport	单一护照
Sponsor	保荐人
Statement by the European Parliament, the Council and the Commission concerning Decision 2006/512/EC	《欧洲议会、欧盟理事会和欧盟委员会关于第 2006/512/EC 号决定的声明》
Statute of the European System of Central Banks and of the European Central Bank	《欧洲中央银行体系及欧洲中央银行章程》
Storage mechanism	存储机制
Structured finance instrument	结构性金融工具
Supranational institutions	超国家机构
TARGET	《欧洲中央银行关于货币政策工具和程序以及欧洲间实时全额自动结算系统(TARGET)的指引》
Transferable securitised debts	可转让证券化债务
Transitional and final provisions	过渡规定和最终条款
Trading venues	交易场所
Type	类型
Units of a collective investment undertaking	集合投资计划份额
Warning	警示
Warrants	权证
Window trading	窗口交易
Worst-case scenario	最差情景
Yields	收益率

Postscript

China's capital market was established and has developed on the basis of the experience of major foreign capital markets. As a result China constantly is faced with issues for which it needs to acquire knowledge of, learn from and refer to examples set by foreign capital market systems. However, the current Chinese translations of foreign securities- and futures-related legislations are not sufficiently systematic, professional, authoritative and are often inaccurate. The acquisition of a comprehensive and precise knowledge of the operating systems and regulatory rules of major foreign capital markets is essential for China to benefit from the experience developed and lessons drawn by these markets and thus is objectively necessary for China to further improve the Chinese capital market system construction, promote a stable development of said system and enhance the participation of Chinese market entities in international competition. For the aforementioned purposes, the China Securities Regulatory Commission (CSRC) initiated the project to translate the most important foreign capital market legislations published as the Digest of Legislation Related to Foreign Capital Markets (hereinafter referred to as the "Digest"). The Shenzhen Stock Exchange (SZSE) has taken charge of the translation project of laws and regulations governing the capital markets in the European Union.

To facilitate the implementation of the project, at the SZSE we have established a mechanism in accordance with the general standards required by the CSRC, which consisted of entrusting the translation to a translation team through a selection process and the translation review to relevant experts to ensure the quality of the translation. One the one hand, the translation team was selected based on its competences in legal translation and the quality of its trial translation. On the other hand, the translation draft was reviewed and validated by individuals from relevant units and departments of the CSRC and prestigious universities deemed to be experts in the concerned foreign languages and the Chinese language, well versed in Chinese and relevant foreign laws and having an in-depth knowledge of both Chinese and foreign capital markets. Those experts whose work experience and educational background are the most relevant to the subject matters dealt with in specific sections of the translation draft were designated to revise the same. The translation draft underwent multiple rounds of revision and random quality check and was finalized after adequate communications with the translators.

后　记

中国资本市场是在学习、借鉴境外主要资本市场经验的基础上建立并发展起来的。在此过程中，仍不断遇到需要了解、借鉴、参考境外市场制度的问题。但是，现有的境外证券期货法律中文译本，存在系统性、专业性、权威性、准确性不足等问题。全面、准确掌握境外主要资本市场运行制度、监管规则，是科学借鉴成熟市场经验教训的必要基础，是进一步完善市场制度建设、推进市场稳定发展、推动市场主体参与国际竞争的客观要求。为此，中国证监会启动了打造介绍境外市场法律制度权威平台的项目，即组织翻译主要资本市场重要法律规则，并将翻译成果编辑成《境外资本市场重要法律文献译丛》（以下简称《译丛》）公开出版发行。在本次项目上，深圳证券交易所承担了欧盟证券市场重要法律文献翻译出版的有关工作。

为了做好此项工作，我们根据中国证监会的统一要求，建立了“择优确定翻译人员、专家评审保证翻译质量”的工作机制。一方面，以法律文献翻译实力和试译稿质量为标准，择优选定翻译单位；另一方面，从证监会系统相关单位、部门和知名高校院所等推荐的“三通”专家（即精通中外语言、精通中外法律、精通中外资本市场）中，抽选工作学习经历与具体项目最相关的专家对翻译稿进行多轮审校以及质量抽检，并在与翻译人员进行充分沟通的基础上定稿。

As the *Laws Governing the Securities Exchange within the European Union*, as part of the Digest, is about to come to the press, as the undertaker for the translation and publication of the book, we would like to express our earnest and profound gratitude to the many organizations and individuals as follows. First of all, we would like to thank the CSRC's Department of Legal Affairs and the staff members involved in this project for their great contribution to the wide-ranging and sophisticated overall planning and guidance for the translation and publication of this book. The very first volume of the Digest, *The Markets in Financial Instruments Directive of the European Union* (MiFID) translated and published under their direction, has been an excellent model for us to follow. Secondly, our thanks are due to the translation team from Ubica Translation Center Beijing led by Ms. Chu Naiming and the panel of review composed of experts, including Professor Guo Li, Associate Professor Hong Yanrong and Associate Professor Xi Chao; together they completed the translation and the review work conscientiously and rigorously. In particular, our thanks go to Professor Shen Sibao from the School of Law, University of International Business and Economics who, amid his heavy schedule, took up the overall and final review of the work and contributed a preface for this book. Thirdly, we owe our gratitude to relevant departments and units of the CSRC and the SZSE for the valuable support they gave to our endeavor. Finally, we thank the staff members at Law Press · China, especially Ms. Shen Xiaoying and Ms. Hu Yifang, who contributed enormously to the editing and publication of the book. Again, the SZSE addresses its most sincere thanks to all those who are mentioned above!

Due to time constraints pertaining to the translation and editing work, errors and inaccuracies in the book will be inevitable. Your comments, criticism and corrections will be welcome.

Shenzhen Stock Exchange

July 2013

在《译丛》之《欧盟证券监管法规汇编》即将付梓之际，作为本书翻译出版的承办单位，我们有许多发自肺腑的感谢之辞：首先，感谢中国证监会法律部及其相关工作人员，作为《译丛》的组织者，他们为本书的翻译和出版做了全面且细致的统筹和指导，其组织完成的《译丛》之《欧盟金融工具市场指令》为本书树立了榜样；其次，感谢瞿乃明女士带领的北京优笔客翻译中心的翻译团队，郭雳教授、洪艳蓉副教授、习超副教授等评审专家，他们以认真负责的态度和严谨务实的作风，完成了翻译和审校工作，其中特别要感谢对外经济贸易大学法学院沈四宝教授在百忙之中拨冗亲自承担总译校，并为本书作序；再次，感谢中国证监会其他相关会内部门及其工作人员，深圳证券交易所相关部门及其工作人员，对我们工作的支持；最后，感谢法律出版社及其相关工作人员，尤其是沈小英女士、胡艺芳女士，为本书的编辑、出版做了大量工作。我们在此一并致以诚挚的谢意！

由于编译时间有限，书中难免有疏漏、不足之处，欢迎读者批评指正。

深圳证券交易所

2013年7月

图书在版编目(CIP)数据

欧盟证券监管法规汇编 / 中国证券监督管理委员会组织编译.—北京:法律出版社,2013.7
(境外资本市场重要法律文献译丛)
ISBN 978-7-5118-5106-2

Ⅰ.①欧… Ⅱ.①中… Ⅲ.①欧洲国家联盟—证券法—汇编 Ⅳ.①D950.228

中国版本图书馆 CIP 数据核字(2013)第 148944 号

责任编辑/胡艺芳　　**装帧设计**/贾丹丹

出版/法律出版社　　**编辑统筹**/财税出版分社
总发行/中国法律图书有限公司　　**经销**/新华书店
印刷/北京中科印刷有限公司　　**责任印制**/吕亚莉

开本/787 毫米×1092 毫米 1/16　　**印张**/26.5　**字数**/604 千
版本/2013 年 10 月第 1 版　　**印次**/2013 年 10 月第 1 次印刷

法律出版社/北京市丰台区莲花池西里 7 号(100073)
电子邮件/info@lawpress.com.cn　　**销售热线**/010-63939792/9779
网址/www.lawpress.com.cn　　**咨询电话**/010-63939796

中国法律图书有限公司/北京市丰台区莲花池西里 7 号(100073)
全国各地中法图分、子公司电话:
第一法律书店/010-63939781/9782　**西安分公司**/029-85388843　**重庆公司**/023-65382816/2908
上海公司/021-62071010/1636　**北京分公司**/010-62534456　**深圳公司**/0755-83072995

书号:ISBN 978-7-5118-5106-2　　**定价**:143.00 元

(如有缺页或倒装,中国法律图书有限公司负责退换)